"This book is a winner. Robert Utley's *Lone Star Justice* and *Lone Star Lawmen* are the best books ever written about the Texas Rangers. His brilliant account makes the story of the Rangers central to an understanding of Texas history, and his talent for vivid storytelling enthralls us to the very end."   —Howard R. Lamar, author of *The New Encyclopedia of the American West*,
Sterling Professor Emeritus of History at Yale University

"Exploring both the darkness and the sunshine, his well-rounded book is certain to create controversy among both supporters and detractors of the Rangers."   —Elmer Kelton, author of the Sons of Texas trilogy

"No one has done more to illuminate the real American Western experience and separate it from fictionalizing and folklore than Robert Utley. *Lone Star Lawmen* completes his landmark history of the Texas Rangers, from the last days of the outlaws to the modern challenges of patrolling an international border. Throughout, Utley is cogent, authoritative, and unfailingly interesting, a Lone Star Historian at his best."
—William C. Davis, author of *Three Roads to the Alamo*

"Most historians and enthusiasts have naively viewed 'motorized Rangers' as less interesting or proficient than 'horseback Rangers.' Utley shatters this myth by reconstructing the turbulent evolution of the Rangers from frontier lawmen into an internationally respected investigative force. Perseverance, adaptability, and dedication to timeless core values have sustained the Rangers through periods of political instability and questionable leadership. This is why there are, and will always be, Texas Rangers."
—Byron A. Johnson, Director, Texas Ranger Hall of Fame and Museum

"This sequel gathers steam . . . A valuable addition to the library of Texana."
—*Kirkus Reviews*

continued . . .

"An action-packed assessment of an American institution."
—*The Virginian-Pilot*

"An intense look at the colorful history of the Rangers ... As always, [Utley's] research is impeccable. ... His fame borders on mythic. The Texas Ranger evokes heroic images of the Old West, the sentinel planted steadfastly between law-abiding citizens and the outlaws and mountebanks who preyed on them. ... Robert Utley, former chief historian of the National Park Service, who's written a long list of books dealing with conflict, armed and cultural, in the early West, takes an intense look at the colorful history of the Rangers and traces their evolution from a loose-knit group of citizen soldiers on the 1830s frontier to a small but highly effective group of lawmen at the turn of the twentieth century."
—*The Denver Post*

"A splendid, indeed brilliant new work by an outstanding historian of the American West. Using official records and sources never before consulted, Robert Utley has given us an original, balanced, and beautifully written narrative that traces the evolution of those legendary citizen-soldiers into lawmen—some outstanding, some flawed."
—Howard R. Lamar,
Sterling Professor Emeritus of History at Yale University

"A rip-snortin', six-guns-blazin' saga of good guys and bad guys who were sometimes one and the same."
—*Kirkus Reviews*

"Well-written and exciting."
—*Library Journal*

"Extensively researched and well-written, this new and exciting history of the Texas Rangers is certain to replace Walter P. Webb's classic, but dated, account. ... In a politicized age often critical of the Rangers, Utley is, above all, fair-minded and never stampeded by folklore or myth."
—William H. Goetzmann, author of *Exploration and Empire:
The Explorer and the Scientist in the Winning of the American West*

"*Lone Star Justice* swings across a hundred years of men 'living up to the legend' with tremendous narrative force. ... Utley does not paint these men in a flattering light, but as who they were—trained soldiers and scouts who had little love for anyone opposing the supremacy of Texas in territories its government declared its own."
—*Corpus Christi Caller-Times*

"Utley's careful portrayal of the Texas Rangers' evolution from citizen soldiers to Old West lawmen ... offers a clear-eyed view of the Rangers themselves. [A] finc book."
—*Publishers Weekly*

Books by the Author

The Last Days of the Sioux Nation
1963

Frontiersmen in Blue: The United States Army and the Indian,
1846–1865
1967

Frontier Regulars: The United States Army and the Indian, 1865–1890
1974

The Indian Frontier of the American West
1984; 2003

High Noon in Lincoln: Violence on the Western Frontier
1987

Cavalier in Buckskin: George Armstrong Custer and the
Western Military Frontier
1988; 2001

Billy the Kid: A Short and Violent Life
1989

The Lance and the Shield: The Life and Times of Sitting Bull
1993

A Life Wild and Perilous: Mountain Men and the Paths to the Pacific
1997; 2004 (as *After Lewis and Clark*)

Lone Star Justice: The First Century of the Texas Rangers
2002

Custer and Me: A Historian's Memoir
2004

Lone Star Lawmen

THE SECOND CENTURY OF THE TEXAS RANGERS

Robert M. Utley

BERKLEY BOOKS, NEW YORK

THE BERKLEY PUBLISHING GROUP
Published by the Penguin Group
Penguin Group (USA) Inc.
375 Hudson Street, New York, New York 10014, USA
Penguin Group (Canada), 90 Eglinton Avenue East, Suite 700, Toronto, Ontario M4P 2Y3, Canada
(a division of Pearson Penguin Canada Inc.)
Penguin Books Ltd., 80 Strand, London WC2R 0RL, England
Penguin Group Ireland, 25 St. Stephen's Green, Dublin 2, Ireland (a division of Penguin Books Ltd.)
Penguin Group (Australia), 250 Camberwell Road, Camberwell, Victoria 3124, Australia
(a division of Pearson Australia Group Pty. Ltd.)
Penguin Books India Pvt. Ltd., 11 Community Centre, Panchsheel Park, New Delhi—110 017, India
Penguin Group (NZ), 67 Apollo Drive, Rosedale, North Shore 0745, Auckland, New Zealand
(a division of Pearson New Zealand Ltd.)
Penguin Books (South Africa) (Pty.) Ltd., 24 Sturdee Avenue, Rosebank, Johannesburg 2196,
South Africa

Penguin Books Ltd., Registered Offices: 80 Strand, London WC2R 0RL, England

The publisher does not have any control over and does not assume any responsibility for author or third-party websites or their content.

LONE STAR LAWMEN

BERKLEY® is a registered trademark of Penguin Group (USA) Inc.
The "B" design is a trademark belonging to Penguin Group (USA) Inc.

PRINTING HISTORY
Oxford University Press hardcover edition / 2007
Berkley trade paperback edition / March 2008

ISBN: 978-0-425-21938-6

PRINTED IN THE UNITED STATES OF AMERICA

10 9 8 7 6 5 4 3 2 1

For Bobby Nieman, a Rangers' historian . . .

and

Glenn Elliott, a Ranger's Ranger

CONTENTS

CONTENTS

MAPS

Illustrations follow pages 112 and 240

PREFACE

SOME YEARS AGO a friend contracted with a New York publisher to write a history of the Texas Rangers. He had in mind a complete history of the Rangers, but his editor instructed him to end the story as soon as they climbed down from their horses, and so he did. Most general readers associate the Texas Rangers with men on horseback who took on Mexicans, Indians, and outlaws to tame Texas in the nineteenth century. When they dismounted, they no longer fit the stereotype and presumably lost their appeal to readers.

I too had in mind a complete history of the Rangers. By the time they dismounted and took to automobiles, however, I had a full book. Fortunately my editor, at considerable inconvenience, agreed to let me finish the story in a second volume. This volume includes horses too, of course, because Texas contains large areas of difficult topography, but the new century largely motorized the Rangers.

To me the story of this second century is as compelling as the story of the first. No work as comprehensive as my first volume, *Lone Star Justice*, has ever been written about the twentieth-century Rangers. The historiography is mainly anecdotal, confined to books and articles about segments of the history but featuring none that ties all the segments into a single institutional history. I intend *Lone Star Lawmen* to be that history.

I embarked on this history with a bias that I expected would dominate the work. General and scholarly reading, together with the periodic effusions of critics in the media, had fostered a negative view of the Texas Rangers in the twentieth century. I did not think they would fare well in my treatment. Except for the decade of the Mexican Revolution, however, I found little to support this recurrent stereotype. Readers of my book should not expect to find the attitudes that fueled the atrocities of 1910–20 to apply to the Rangers who followed. I have not hesitated to criticize where I felt it warranted. But I have found little to fault in the decades since 1920. As this book reflects, I have ended the twentieth century with a healthy respect for the efficiency and effectiveness of the Texas Rangers.

For the first thirty-five years of the twentieth century, the Rangers remained part of the Adjutant General's Department and thus in theory a military unit. They retained much of their character as Old West lawmen while many other states moved forward in police method and organization. After 1935, the Rangers combined with the highway patrol in the newly created Department of Public Safety. In this setting they evolved into professional crime fighters, focusing primarily on criminal investigation.

Thus the twentieth century featured two breeds of Texas Rangers, the old and the new. But the new kept the name of the old and clung to the history, the traditions, and even the legendry that had gained pride and renown for the old. Like other states, Texas has a criminal investigative arm of state government. In deference to the past, it is made up of officers called Texas Rangers, a term and probably an organization destined to endure for the foreseeable future.

Lone Star Justice drew in part on voluminous official records of the Adjutant General's Department preserved in the Texas State Library and Archives. The years until 1920 are also preserved in the records of the Adjutant General. When the Rangers moved to the Department of

Public Safety, they took with them their records for 1920 to 1935. These records, together with official Ranger records for 1935 to the early 1970s, have disappeared. As late as the 1960s, doctoral students used these records in the basement of the Department of Public Safety headquarters in Austin. They are no longer there, nor in the state archives, and all attempts to learn what happened to them have met with failure. No one at the department knows, or professes to know. Anecdotal revelations suggest deliberate destruction or a history of sporadic purloining.

In the early 1990s the department turned over a body of records to the state archives. They begin in the early 1970s and end in the mid-1990s. They contain much valuable material, although the records of many significant events are missing.

Fortunately, the state archives preserves the papers of the successive governors for part of my period, from 1911 to 1957. Some collections contain significant documents relating to the Rangers.

I recite this sad story not only to fault a major state agency for ignoring state laws for the preservation of official records—an agency, moreover, that takes great pride in its history. I am also explaining why some of my documentation must rest on doctoral dissertations or master's theses that benefited from these records before they disappeared. As my endnotes reveal, I have relied on these works where they cite records now missing.

As a partial substitute for this vital base of original sources, I commend the Texas Ranger Hall of Fame and Museum in Waco, which houses archives rich in Ranger history. Throughout the twentieth century, some Rangers kept copies of many of the documents they sent or received, as well as newspaper scrapbooks and pictorial material, and in retirement donated them to the Hall of Fame. This body of sources has helped immeasurably in filling some of the documentary vacuum created by the Department of Public Safety or its constituent Ranger division.

BOTH ACTIVE AND RETIRED RANGERS are notoriously reticent in providing information they fear may reflect unfavorably on the force or on other

Rangers. Nevertheless, I am grateful to the following for helping in both direct and indirect ways: Captain Barry Caver, retired captain Jack Dean, and retired Rangers Glenn Elliott and Ralph Wadsworth.

I cannot express enough gratitude to Robert Nieman. "Bobby," a successful businessman who is a splendid "grass-roots" historian, is the repository of more Ranger information and lore than any other person I know. He has interviewed dozens of Rangers, both active and retired, and edits the *Texas Ranger Dispatch Magazine*, the online publication of the Texas Ranger Hall of Fame and Museum. He is also a member of the Hall of Fame's board of directors. Bobby has freely made available to me his interviews, photographs, and personal conclusions and judgments. He has reviewed every chapter, shown me where I have gone astray, and counseled me on paths I have missed but should follow. But for his contributions, constantly offered through e-mail and personal visits, this book would have fallen far short of my expectations.

Thus I feel personally indebted to some Rangers who communicated with me through Nieman's oral history program. I thank them here rather than merely noting them in the bibliography: former Ranger and DPS chief of criminal law enforcement Jim Ray (deceased), retired captain David Brynes, retired captain Bob Prince, and Ranger Ed Gooding (deceased).

At the Texas State Library and Archives, I single out Donaly Brice and John Anderson for guiding me through the complexities of documentary and photographic holdings. Their personal interest in my project is exceeded only by their assistance in my research. The other members of the archival staff deserve warm acknowledgment.

At the Texas Ranger Hall of Fame and Museum in Waco, I am indebted to archivist Christina Stopka and librarian Judy Shofner for their interest and aid as well as their willingness to seek material yet to be catalogued. Director Byron Johnson has shown continuing interest in this work.

As always, the efficient staff at the Center for American History at the University of Texas at Austin provided valuable aid when I repeatedly set up my laptop in their domain. Lisa Anderson at the library of

Southwestern University in Georgetown operates the most efficient interlibrary loan system I have ever used.

Others meriting thanks are J'Nell Pate, Sharon Spinks, Rick Miller, Jody Ginn, Joe White, Mary Williams, Jerry Thompson, George Díaz, and Harold Weiss.

As always, I appreciate the hard work and counsel of Peter Ginna, my editor at Oxford University Press, and Carl D. Brandt, my literary agent of seventeen years.

I am also grateful to Peter Dana, who generated the computerized maps for this book as well as earlier books.

As with all my books, my wife, Melody Webb, read and critiqued the entire manuscript, sometimes bluntly but never without superior judgment. My gratitude, deepening with each book over a period of twenty-five years, is as heartfelt as ever.

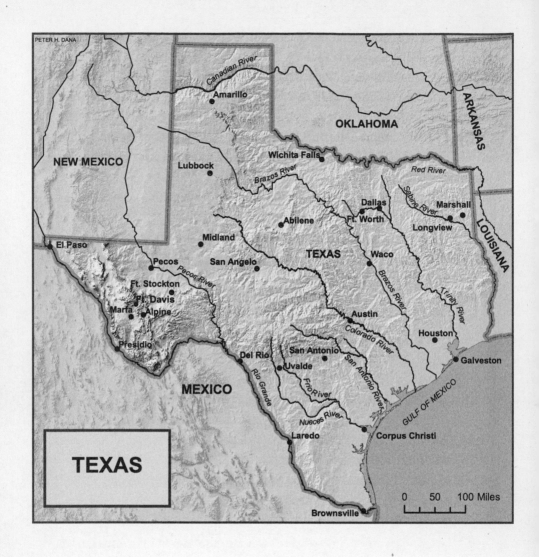

PETER H. DANA

NEW MEXICO

OKLAHOMA

ARKANSAS

Canadian River

Amarillo

Wichita Falls

Red River

Lubbock

Brazos River

Dallas

Sabine River

Marshall

Abilene

Ft. Worth

Longview

LOUISIANA

El Paso

Midland

TEXAS

Waco

Pecos

San Angelo

Brazos River

Ft. Stockton

Pecos River

Trinity River

Ft. Davis

Marfa

Alpine

Austin

Houston

Presidio

Colorado River

Del Rio

San Antonio

Galveston

Uvalde

San Antonio River

MEXICO

Rio Grande

Frio River

GULF OF MEXICO

Nueces River

Laredo

Corpus Christi

TEXAS

0   50   100 Miles

Brownsville

Prologue

"ONE RIOT, ONE RANGER." A single Ranger could quell an incipient riot. Rangers and Texans alike reveled in the image of the stalwart, fearless lawman facing down an angry mob. On occasion it came close enough to happening to provide at least an inspiration for the slogan.

"No man in the wrong can stand up against a fellow that's in the right and keeps on a comin'." Captain Bill McDonald made certain his men embraced his motto, and it embedded itself in the Ranger tradition. Rangers, of course, routinely bowled over men in the wrong, although how many may not have been in the wrong was rarely questioned.

As the nineteenth century gave way to the twentieth, the Texas Rangers had become the substance of history as well as a flowering legend. They also served as the model for state law agencies in other states and territories, and for the state police movement that spread across the nation in the coming decades.

A century later, of constabularies around the world, only the Royal Canadian Mounted Police could compete with the Texas Rangers in nearly universal name recognition. The Mounties began in 1873 as a frontier force designated the North-West Mounted Police and evolved into a national institution admired for their scarlet tunics, precision drill, and efficient policing.

By contrast, the Texas Rangers began in the 1830s as a tradition rather than an institution. Officially they bore the Ranger designation only sporadically for decades. Not until after half a century fighting Indians did they evolve from some-time citizen soldiers into full-time lawmen. In both incarnations, they disdained uniforms and all other military attributes.[1]

Aside from these differences, the two institutions displayed another significant contrast. The Mounties projected a consistently favorable image, prompting widespread admiration. The Rangers displayed varied images, but the most conspicuous were polar opposites almost from the beginning. These images formed the bright side and the dark side of the history of the Texas Rangers. Unlike the Canadian Mounted Police, the Texas Rangers were either idolized or abominated.

MODERN TEXAS RANGERS like to trace their origins to 1823, when impresario Stephen F. Austin coined the term but never could make it a reality. The contemporary record better supports 1835, the eve of the Texas Revolution against Mexico. The "rangers" of Austin's concept were not lawmen but citizen soldiers charged with "ranging" the frontier against marauding Indians. During the decade of the Texas Republic, 1836–45, such companies began to take shape—volunteers called out for three or six months to contend with Indians or with Mexicans who had yet to acknowledge Texan independence. They provided their own horses and arms, and rode under a variety of designations. Only gradually did the term "ranger" come into popular usage.

Over the decades, outstanding leaders captained some of these companies—Jack Hays, Matt Caldwell, Ben McCulloch, and Rip Ford, to name four. The model for all subsequent captains, John Coffee Hays pioneered mounted combat by adopting the first revolving pistol, the five-shot Paterson Colt. At the Battle of Walker Creek in 1844, he and fourteen Rangers took on seventy Comanche warriors and employed the revolver so effectively that only twenty Indians escaped the battlefield unhurt.

2

In the Mexican War of 1846–48 Hays commanded the federalized First Texas Mounted Volunteers, all former Rangers. General Zachary Taylor kept one of Hays's companies, Ben McCulloch's Gonzales Rangers, attached to his headquarters because of their unsurpassed reconnaissance skills. At the Battle of Monterey (the contemporary spelling), Hays's regiment proved themselves first-rate combat soldiers and arguably the critical factor in Taylor's victory. Later, under General Winfield Scott, Hays's men demonstrated their excellence in antiguerrilla operations. Armed with the new Walker Colt, the first six-shooter, they repeatedly defeated overwhelming numbers of Mexican lancers.

The Mexican War transformed the Texas Rangers from men celebrated by Texas into men celebrated by the entire nation. They emerged as national heroes not only because of their battlefield success but because of media appeal. Their unorthodox ways attracted journalists. They wore no uniforms, carried no flags, enjoyed an easy camaraderie between officers and enlisted men, and scorned military regulations. They also indulged in unmilitary ruffianly high jinks that correspondents delighted in describing.[2]

A dark stain marred the Ranger record in the Mexican War. For both Generals Taylor and Scott, the undisciplined Rangers constantly made trouble. But their worst misdeeds sprang from vivid memories of the Alamo and Goliad massacres during the Texas Revolution, perpetrated by Mexican president Santa Anna, and incidents of Mexican cruelty during the decade of the Texas Republic. The Rangers came to Mexico to exact revenge, and they gained it not only on the battlefield but in atrocities against noncombatants. In February 1847, for example, reacting to the destruction of a military supply train, Captain Mabry B. ("Mustang") Gray's Ranger company put to death the entire male population of the nearby village of Ramos, twenty-four men. And in Mexico City in December 1847, after one of Hays's Rangers was slashed to death in a district called Cutthroat, Rangers rode the streets of Cutthroat throughout an entire night, systematically shooting down anyone who appeared in the sights of their heavy Walker Colts. The next morning, wagons hauled eighty corpses to the morgue.

Little wonder that Mexicans called the Rangers *Los Diablos Tejanos*. And little wonder that General Taylor asked superiors "that no more troops may be sent to this column from the State of Texas."[3]

The 1850s brought Ranger units into repeated collisions with Comanches, both along the frontier of settlement and in their homeland north of Red River, the Indian Territory. The widely applauded captain of this period was John Salmon Ford, "Rip" Ford, who had served as Hays's adjutant in the Mexican War. In fact, the Rangers proved no more successful than the Regular Army at keeping raiding parties out of the frontier settlements. Ford's celebrated victory over Iron Jacket's Comanches at the Battle of Antelope Hills in 1858 merely intensified the raids, both in revenge and to restock the horse herds Ford had seized. Ranger fights could be easily glorified, however, and the Ranger image flourished.[4]

Although a Confederate Ranger regiment fought Indians on the northwestern frontier during the Civil War, the Ranger renown faded in the turmoil of war and Reconstruction. Not until 1874 did the state legislature bring the Rangers back to life, now as a permanent institution. Mustered to fight Indians, they discovered that the Regular Army had finally conquered the Comanches, leaving few Indians to fight. But Texas was a violent, crime-ridden place, and the Rangers transformed themselves into lawmen. Such they have been ever since.

The last of the citizen soldier outfits, however, revived memories of the Mexican War. From 1874 to 1877 Leander McNelly's Ranger company contended with Mexican stock thieves. McNelly not only crossed the Rio Grande to violate Mexican sovereignty but also used intimidation, torture, and even execution to carry out his mission. Mexicans did not forget McNelly.[5]

FOR THE LAST QUARTER of the nineteenth century, the lawmen of the Old West did battle with stock thieves; stagecoach, train, and bank robbers; fence cutters; belligerents in the political, ethnic, and family feuds that rocked many counties; and the bad men, both Mexican and Texan, who made the international border a perpetually turbulent zone extending from Brownsville to El Paso. At the turn of the century four exceptional leaders—the "Four Great Captains"—enhanced Ranger prestige. They were John A. Brooks, John H. Rogers, William J. McDonald, and John R. Hughes. Other captains also demonstrated superior abilities, but not all. The good captains led good companies in the tradition of Hays and McCulloch. The bad captains, usually politically blessed, had mediocre to bad companies. But on the whole, the Texas Rangers emerged from the nineteenth century with a well-deserved reputation as effective lawmen.[6]

For Mexicans and Mexican Americans, however, no great captain could brighten the dark side of the Rangers. Firmly planted in their collective memory were the deeds of Hays, Gray, McNelly, and others. *Rinches*, they called the Rangers, although they also applied this term to any mounted white man with a gun: sheriffs and their deputies, federal customs inspectors, and even cowboys. All dressed alike, and all could be seen as *rinches*—Rangers. They were thugs who shot Mexican prisoners "while trying to escape"—the "Ranger conviction" occasionally noted in the sources.[7]

To the Old West Rangers—extensions of the "Anglo" (that is, white-skinned) establishment that ran Texas—Mexicans were an inferior people who, whether good or bad, all looked alike. Doubtless scattered abuse toward Mexicans marred the record of 1880–1910, but rare was the intentional injustice. Most were products of mistaken identity or misread circumstances, although few Mexicans could be convinced of that.

In fact, the Old West lawmen operated within what may be labeled a "six-shooter culture." They tended to be men who knew how to use a six-shooter and boasted a record to prove it. An element of that culture was physical violence applied to an adversary who did not warrant shooting—"bending" a pistol barrel over a man's skull to subdue him. The good captains of these Old West decades kept the worst features of this culture under control, and the record yields few instances of deliberate persecution by Rangers. In the first decade of the twentieth century, the good captains began to retire. The six-shooter culture still prevailed, and no strong captains remained to control it. In interviewing prospective recruits, captains even placed disproportionately high value on six-shooter skills. The minuscule pay of the Ranger private, forty dollars a month, attracted men with few other qualities than the six-shooter mindset. Rangers of greater competence soon moved on to better-paying jobs, as county sheriffs and deputies, inspectors of stockmen's associations, and officers of the federal customs service.[8]

THE SIX-SHOOTER CULTURE prevailed even after some Rangers began to abandon the famed 1873 army Colt revolver for the new 1911 army Colt automatic pistol, which fired seven shots from a magazine in the pistol grip and an eighth if a round was chambered and the safety on. Its main advantage was a magazine that allowed rapid reloading, but it lacked the accuracy of the old favorite, which continued to be the weapon of choice.

Even more than the handgun, Rangers adopted improved shoulder weapons. The celebrated Winchester '73, "the gun that won the West," began to give way to the improved Winchester M1894 and M1895. They fired smokeless cartridges and packed greater velocity.

Still other technological advances served as harbingers of the new era. As the railroads had revolutionized Ranger operations in the 1880s, so now the increasing use of automobiles, telegraphs, and telephones gave Rangers new and more effective means of travel and communication.

All of this, providing better tools of the trade, only reinforced the six-shooter culture.

Although a pale shadow of the Ranger battalion established by the Texas Legislature in 1874, the Ranger Force of the early twentieth century reflected the military purpose for which it had been created. Organized to fight Indians, it had lost its intended mission when the U.S. Army conquered the tribes that had ravaged the Texas frontier for half a century. As lawmen, the Rangers nevertheless retained their military chain of command: from the governor as commander in chief to the adjutant general to the company captain.

The adjutant general also commanded the state militia, not a burdensome responsibility in the early years. By the twentieth century, however, the Texas National Guard increasingly preoccupied that officer, leaving him little time or inclination to act as a police chief.

The captains thus took on more power even as their quality declined. The caliber of the men they commanded also declined. Critics accused them of bullying citizens, of clinging to the towns rather than trailing bad men in desert or brush, of reluctance to yield the comforts of Pullman cars to the discomforts of the saddle, of frequenting saloons and gambling joints and swaggering drunkenly in the streets, of abusing their authority—in general, of losing their effectiveness as lawmen.

Such was the condition and reputation of the Texas Rangers when the Mexican Revolution erupted in 1910. For a decade, as a squad of revolutionary leaders struggled for control, it tore Mexico apart. Chaos swept the entire nation. Countless thousands of people lost their property, their livelihood, and their lives. The United States and all other nations withheld diplomatic recognition from the succession of warlords who temporarily gained ascendance over the others.

From 1910 until 1920, the Mexican Revolution also stirred turmoil along an international boundary extending nine hundred miles from the Gulf of Mexico to El Paso and repeatedly spilled over into Texas. To counter the spillage, the United States government deployed the army and a host of customs and immigration officers and agents of the Justice Department. The state deployed the Texas Rangers—at a time of unprecedented weakness, effectiveness, and reputation. A century later that decade remains the blackest period in the history of the Texas Rangers.

[1]
The Border, 1910–1915

As the decade opened, the Texas Ranger Force consisted of only three tiny companies. Of the "four great captains" who had guided the force into the twentieth century, only John R. Hughes and John H. Rogers remained. They overshadowed the third captain, M. E. Bailey, who did little to attract public attention.

Hughes commanded a company of only five men, based in Ysleta, on the Rio Grande just below El Paso. Here and elsewhere on the river, he had gained his sobriquet of "Border Boss." He made up in influence and competence what he lacked in manpower. A Ranger for twenty-four years, a captain for eighteen, at fifty-six he had lost none of the intellect, courage, vigor, endurance, and zest for rangering that had gained him the respect of lawmen all over Texas.[1]

Rogers enjoyed a reputation nearly as compelling but less glamorous. A Ranger for twenty-seven years, a captain for almost twenty, he had served with distinction. As deeply ingrained as his Ranger qualities were a devout Presbyterianism and an abhorrence of intoxicants in any form. Admirers said he tackled every task with a rifle in one hand and a Bible in the other. Also, in a state where the battle between "drys" and "wets" dominated almost every election, he vigorously championed the cause of prohibition.

The gubernatorial election of 1910 sent Oscar B. Colquitt to the statehouse. The drys had furiously opposed him, and his victory profoundly discouraged Captain Rogers. Offered an appointment as a deputy United States marshal, on January 29, 1911, just after Colquitt's inauguration, Rogers resigned his commission.[2]

The departure of Rogers left John R. Hughes, the last of the "four great captains," to watch sadly as the Ranger Force declined in numbers, proficiency, and public respect.

AT AGE FIFTY, Oscar B. Colquitt settled into the governor's chambers early in 1911, just as the Mexican Revolution erupted. Stocky, handsome, an effective platform speaker, he had resisted the reforms of the Progressive movement spreading across the nation and entered office as a staunch advocate of limited government and low taxes. His belligerent insistence on employing the sovereign powers of the state against Mexican revolutionaries in Texas kept him at odds with the federal government but earned him the applause of many citizens.[3]

Colquitt's adjutant general, Henry Hutchings, came to his office with a military record. Born in England and brought to America as an infant, he had risen in the Texas National Guard while editing an Austin newspaper. Forty-six in 1911, slender, dark complexioned, his gaunt face adorned with a brushy mustache, he brought military ability to his office but devoted himself almost exclusively to the Guard.[4]

In the past, governors had left most appointments of Ranger captains to the adjutant general, although a few slipped in by the political route. Colquitt selected the captains himself, a practice that his successors continued. Sometimes even sergeants and privates, normally picked by the captains, owed their commissions to the governor's backing. The Colquitt regime began the steady politicization of the Texas Rangers.

Colquitt left the veteran Hughes in place as captain of Company A, but hardly had his term begun when he appointed John J. Sanders of Lockhart captain of Company B, bumping Captain M. E. Bailey to sergeant. Former sheriff of Caldwell County, Sanders was almost fifty-seven but still a tough, rugged giant at six feet, two inches. Practitioner of direct and forceful methods, a product of the six-shooter culture, Sanders commanded the respect of most South Texas sheriffs, who shared his approach to law enforcement. One did not trifle with J. J. Sanders without risk to life and limb.[5]

A strange development allowed Colquitt to name two more captains. In a meeting in Hutchinson, Kansas, in September 1911, President William Howard Taft turned to Governor Colquitt for aid in dealing with border ferment. He would increase the Ranger Force, Colquitt promised, if the United States would pay for the new men. Taft agreed. On October 1, 1911, the adjutant general expanded the force from two to three companies, each with a captain, a sergeant, and twelve privates, for a total of forty-two instead of twelve.[6]

Federal funding proved sufficient to allow Colquitt to add two captains. One, William Smith, worked out of Austin as a "detective." The trivial investigations assigned him suggest his level of competence and usefulness.

The second captain, named on October 5, was J. Monroe Fox. He came from Missouri to settle near Houston but later moved to Austin as a policeman. Fox was almost forty-five, smooth shaven, with light hair and complexion and a medium build. Barely literate, vain and cocksure, gravely deficient in leadership, he reveled in his captaincy and compiled a record of which only he could be proud. When jurisdictional conflicts led to the withdrawal of federal funding after only four months, the Ranger Force reverted to its earlier strength. Colquitt, however, preserved Fox's captaincy, and he would figure in Ranger annals for years to come.[7]

The Rangers provided governors another source of patronage—commissions as Special Rangers. These drew no pay from the state but could carry firearms and exercise all the powers of regular Rangers. Some special appointments were justified. Inspectors of stockmen's associations, for example, ranchmen and their cowboys riding big spreads far from a law officer, railroad conductors, former lawmen who had enemies seeking revenge—such men could usually make a strong case for a special commission, especially if backed by influential patrons. But politically powerful men in occupations devoid of danger simply enjoyed the prestige. As specials proliferated, they caused the Ranger Force more trouble than they were worth and sometimes acute embarrassment.

Together the governor and the legislature determined the fate of the Ranger Force. In 1901 the legislature had enacted a new charter for the Rangers, to be repeated verbatim in 1911 and again in 1917. It authorized a Ranger Force (the first use of the term) consisting of four companies of mounted men, each composed of a captain, a sergeant, and twenty privates. Pay was set at $100 a month for captains, $50 for sergeants, and $40 for privates. As in earlier times, Rangers had to furnish their own horses and guns. A quartermaster in Austin managed supply and logistics. Thus the authorized force numbered eighty-nine, a strength no legislature would ever pay for. Each biennium, thereforc, governor and legislature negotiated the appropriation that would determine actual Ranger strength. With low taxes and limited government the creed of almost every Texas politician, small wonder appropriations compressed the Ranger Force to as few as a dozen men.[8]

MAY 8, 1911, dramatized for all Texans the reality of the Mexican Revolution. They had observed the turmoil in Mexico with casual interest since the day six months earlier when Francisco Madero raised the flag of revolution against Porfirio Díaz, strongman ruler of Mexico for thirty-four years. But on that May 8, the revolution breached the border.

The place was El Paso, in the far western corner of Texas. Across the Rio Grande, El Paso faced Ciudad Juárez, a prize Mexican factions fought over because it afforded easy access to its sister city. El Paso provided a secure base for revolutionary plotters, a haven for refugees from the firing squad, and most vitally a gateway for the flow of arms, ammunition, provisions, recruits, and other war-making resources into Mexico. A prosperous city of nearly eighty thousand people, El Paso drcw its strategic value for Mexican revolutionists from its position as a railway crossroads. Even when the United States tried to impose its neutrality laws and close the border, the railroads brought implements of war that, one way or another, reached buyers in Mexico.

For several months, El Pasoans had anticipated a battle for Juárez with both excitement and dread. The garrison of Fort Bliss, the local militia, the county sheriff's department, and the city police force guaranteed security and order. The danger lay in stray (or deliberate) bullets that found their way across the border, as had happened on April 13 when two citizens of Douglas, Arizona, were killed and eleven wounded by fire from a clash across the border at Agua Prieta.

The Texas Rangers contributed almost nothing to the security force in El Paso. The "company" headquartered at Ysleta, fifteen miles down the valley, consisted of Captain Hughes and five men, whose responsibilities covered all West Texas.

To his credit, Governor Colquitt recognized the merit of Captain Hughes, whom he came to appreciate by reading the dispatches Hughes sent from El Paso to his superior, Adjutant General Henry Hutchings. Expecting an imminent attack on the Díaz garrison of Juárez by the Madero forces of Francisco "Pancho" Villa and Pascual Orozco, Hughes wired Hutchings, "We will have our war paint on. Wish you could be there."[9]

Hughes's enthusiasm reflected the mood of the city. Ever since the threat of battle loomed, people had anticipated less danger than spectacle—a spectator sport. With Juárez strangled by his troops, however, Madero ordered a withdrawal. Fearing another Agua Prieta, he preferred to avoid battle rather than antagonize the United States and perhaps precipitate intervention. Orozco launched the attack anyway.

Hughes and the few men left in his command mingled with the crowds in El Paso as the battle raged for two days. The Rangers joined with sheriff's deputies and soldiers in vainly trying to keep the throngs of citizens out of harm's way, but they enjoyed the show too. "We are all up here watching the fight at Juárez," he wired the adjutant general on May 9. "Wish you and all the force could be here to enjoy the Fun."[10]

As Madero had feared, bullets flew across the river, killing six and wounding fifteen. Most hit spectators lining the river bank, but some reached deep into the city and struck down people seeking safety. After bloody fighting, the rebels won. Early in the afternoon of May 10, the Díaz commander surrendered the city.[11]

The Battle of Juárez proved decisive in the overthrow of Porfirio Díaz. On May 25, 1911, he resigned the presidency and sailed into European exile. The Madero regime, however, was only the first stage of a revolutionary ordeal destined to last for a decade. The turbulence along the border confronted both the federal and state governments with repeated crises of policy and kept them constantly embroiled with each other in tension and conflict.

Governor Colquitt believed that the U.S. Army should have occupied Juárez, a conviction he reasserted each time Juárez threatened to explode again. Meantime, he directed Captain Hughes to station himself and his men in El Paso and to act as the governor's personal representative in monitoring the unfolding revolution and its impact on Texas.[12]

Although the long reign of Porfirio Díaz ended, the Mexican Revolution had hardly begun. Madero headed the central government, but his army maintained precarious control of only part of the country. For another eight years, the Rio Grande frontier poisoned relations between the United States and Mexico, between Texas and Mexico, and even between the United States and Texas. In the turmoil that wracked nine hundred miles of boundary from Brownsville to El Paso, the Texas Rangers would play an increasingly prominent part.

GOVERNOR COLQUITT CONCENTRATED his little Ranger Force on the Mexican frontier, chiefly to deal with the pandemonium generated by the Mexican Revolution. Routine duties elsewhere, however, continued to stretch the force beyond its limits.

Stock theft remained the epidemic crime. Gangs of rustlers preyed on herds of cattle, horses, sheep, and goats. Often they allied themselves with county officials and even sheriffs, deputies, or their kin. Stockmen's associations employed their own inspectors and detectives, usually also commissioned as special Rangers, but still repeatedly appealed to the governor for help from the regular Rangers.

Another constant call came from district judges presiding over volatile trials. Threats against witnesses and jurors, or one faction against another, courted violence and even gunplay. A Ranger sitting near the judge calmed a courtroom full of partisans. The danger lay also in the streets and saloons before the trial.

Black people posed a special problem. Only lightly touched by the Civil War, Texas provided a refuge for planters and their slaves from elsewhere in the South, thus greatly augmenting the black population. During Reconstruction, occupying black soldiers inflamed a largely rural population incensed over the demise of the Confederacy. Ever since, Jim Crow white supremacy had gripped Texas as tightly as anywhere in the South. The indictment or merely the arrest of a black frequently produced a mob of otherwise respectable citizens determined to take the law into their own hands. Often local authority did not even call for Rangers. Sometimes, when summoned, they reached the scene in time to quell the riot, but usually the victim had already been lynched and incinerated. Such savageries occurred repeatedly through the 1930s.

Texans had always indulged in violent politics, and Rangers had always been involved, usually to keep the peace at the polls. For Colquitt and his successors, however, Rangers increasingly intimidated citizens likely to vote for a candidate not approved by the establishment. Sometimes Mexicans voting as a controlled bloc were targeted; in other elections they favored the approved candidate and enjoyed Ranger aid.

The election of 1912, returning Colquitt to the statehouse and replacing William Howard Taft with Woodrow Wilson in the White House, was particularly bitter. Counties all over South Texas flooded the governor's desk with appeals for Rangers to prevent violence on election day. Colquitt despaired of stretching his fifteen Rangers to meet the need. "I presume we will have to abandon the border question until the election is over," he complained as he ordered men to the endangered county seats.[13]

EL PASO REMAINED a hot spot as rivals contended over Juárez. In March 1912 Madero lieutenant Pascual Orozco formally broke with his chief and by spring held Juárez. Madero's federal armies advanced north through Chihuahua under command of the fierce General Victoriano Huerta. Rumor circulated that in another battle for Juárez federals or Orozco rebels might deliberately fire into El Paso. Governor Colquitt fulminated against the Taft administration's secrecy and lack of cooperation, and he sent National Guard officers to El Paso to draw up plans for a state offensive if the regulars failed to react decisively.[14]

"Pirate Island," near Ysleta, had long caused border troubles. An area of several square miles, it lay north of the Rio Grande but south of the international boundary, which the intricacies of international law had left in a long-abandoned river channel now overgrown with chaparral. Only longtime residents knew where the boundary lay. Cattle and horse thieves used the island as a holding pen for stock stolen on the U.S. side.

On May 21, 1912, several hundred Orozco soldiers from Juárez trotted down the road on Pirate Island. As it veered toward the Texas boundary, they encountered two Rangers, Charles R. Moore and Charles H. Webster, backed by nineteen U.S. cavalrymen. The army lieutenant, fearful of violating the boundary, had his men fall back. But the Rangers knew where the boundary lay, and they stood firm as about thirty Mexicans formed a skirmish line and galloped toward them, shouting, "Muerte! Muerte!" Moore threw up his arm and shouted in Spanish, "Stop. This is Texas. The road is the line."

The rebel captain halted the charge and sent English-speaking emissaries to talk with the Rangers. "We told them," Moore reported, "that they would have to do their marching and fighting on their own side of the line, and that we would arrest any men, Federals or rebels, who came to our side." The cavalry lieutenant commended Moore and Webster to the governor of Texas as "cool, collected men of nerve and good judgment who upheld the Rangers' reputation of not making mistakes."[15]

The danger to El Paso seemed to end when, without harm to its sister city, Juárez fell to General Huerta on August 16, 1912. Rebels of one persuasion or another, however, roamed the countryside all the way down to Ojinaga. Ranchers feared for their stock, and El Pasoans could not shake the fear of another fight for Juárez.

In fact, one began to take shape in January 1913 but was over-shadowed by developments elsewhere. Early in February, another ambitious revolutionist, General Bernardo Reyes, tried to overthrow Madero. Fighting broke out in Mexico City. Reyes died in the first day's clash, but the battle for the capital raged for ten days until on February 18 General Huerta, defecting to the rebels, ended the Madero regime. Four days later he had Madero assassinated and seized the presidency for himself.

As an Orozco general tightened another armed noose around Juárez in January 1913, Rangers Moore (recently promoted to sergeant) and Webster had another adventure on the edge of Pirate Island. On January 29, with a deputy sheriff, they encountered a rebel unit on the wrong side of the boundary and exchanged fire. Moore and the deputy both took aim on a horseman bearing a flag and brought him down. Prudently the Rangers did not search the heavy brush for casualties, but Moore scooped up the flag and sent it to General Hutchings. The flag bearer was so close, Moore observed, that he undoubtedly sustained serious damage and would not soon be in shape to use a Mauser carbine like the one retrieved from the saddle of his captured horse.[16]

Throughout the decade of the Mexican Revolution, El Paso continued to be a flash point, periodically threatened with another battle for Juárez. But at the other end of the Texas frontier with Mexico, another flash point flared even more brightly. Brownsville and its satellite communities would endure the worst of the revolutionary violence. Allied with the Texas Rangers—if not actually led by them—citizens responded with the worst retaliation of which Texas was capable.

LIKE EL PASO, Brownsville lay in a distant corner of Texas, the extreme southern tip just above the mouth of the Rio Grande. Like El Paso, Brownsville enjoyed intimate relations with a sister city, Matamoros, across the river. Until early in the twentieth century, however, unlike El Paso and unlike Laredo two hundred miles up the river, Brownsville lacked a link to the Texas railway system that afforded commercial access to the nation. Economically, socially, and culturally, Brownsville and its hinterland made up a world apart from the rest of Texas.

Arid chaparral plains extended 150 miles north to the Nueces River, which reached the Gulf of Mexico at Corpus Christi. This "Nueces Strip" (the territory between the Nueces and the Rio Grande) had been cow country since Spanish times, when the Crown awarded huge land grants to favored *rancheros*. Some retained their grants and their social preeminence, but since the Mexican War they had seen most of the land pass into Anglo ownership through marriage, legal technicalities, flagrant fraud, even intimidation and violence.

As a few rancheros clung to their spreads in the last half of the nineteenth century, Anglos assembled enormous ranches. The biggest and most famous was the King Ranch, almost a million acres amassed by steamboat captain Richard King after the Mexican War. In 1885 his widow appointed Robert J. Kleberg Jr. as manager. He married into the King family, and for decades Robert and Caesar Kleberg and a handful of other Anglo cattle barons dominated the economy of the Nueces Strip and wielded powerful influence in Texas politics. From Richard King's earliest years, the Texas Rangers enjoyed an especially close relationship with the King Ranch.

Despite its remoteness and isolation, however, Brownsville caused constant problems in Austin. However few they were, Texas Rangers drew repeated Brownsville postings.[17]

THE RAILROAD TRANSFORMED the Lower Valley. On July 4, 1904, the St. Louis, Brownsville, and Mexico Railroad reached Brownsville and at once began to extend up the valley toward Hidalgo County. With 160 miles of rail tying it to the national rail system at Corpus Christi, Brownsville no longer looked with envy on Laredo.

The Lower Valley, together with the treeless flatlands sweeping to the north, promised an agricultural bonanza: subdivided ranch lands, irrigation systems based on the river or artesian wells, two or three growing seasons each year, cheap Mexican labor, and a railroad to haul agricultural products to market. Special excursion trains brought prospective immigrants by the thousands, most from the frigid Midwest, and smooth-talking promoters spun a compelling vision of prosperity and comfort in warm, healthful South Texas. In less than a decade an agricultural revolution created the "Magic Valley" and gave birth to another district to the north, the "Winter Garden," centered on Crystal City. Towns sprouted along the railroad. Cattle yielded first place to truck farming. Population soared from 43,000 in 1900 to 116,000 in 1920.[18]

The newcomers not only revolutionized the economy but intruded into the placid, comfortable world of South Texas. Minority Anglos and majority Mexicans had long since reached an accommodation, one that preserved Anglo supremacy but provided care for loyal *vaqueros* and *peónes*. The accommodation did not quiet Mexican resentment of discrimination and several generations of progressive land loss, but it ensured that Mexican workers had help when help was needed. In return, they gave fealty and obedience to the *patrón*, including voting how he decreed.

The accommodation thus promoted "boss rule" in politics. The large ranchers, including some Mexican rancheros, voted their followers as a bloc, and the bosses ensured that some of the patronage fell to men with Spanish surnames. The most powerful boss was James B. Wells of Cameron County, and he extended his influence over other counties by delegating power to other bosses. They mediated factional disputes within the Democratic Party and battled contentious Republicans, who drew strength from control of federal patronage until Woodrow Wilson's victory in 1912.

Then came the farmers. In less than a decade they destroyed the old system. Mostly midwesterners, they brought stereotypical views of Mexicans as lazy, ignorant, and inferior. The reciprocal obligations that had maintained harmony between Anglo and Mexican collapsed as the newcomers treated Mexicans with contempt and as mere wage laborers, employed when needed to get in the crops, discharged when the need passed.

Although many of the farmers failed, the most painful consequences of the agricultural revolution fell on the Mexican population (whether U.S. or Mexican citizens). The old relationship to the Anglo minority had indeed kept them inferior but rarely if ever in want and always with a patrón (Anglo or Mexican) to turn to with legal or other problems. The farmers, however, disdained them socially and converted them into wage slaves.

The immigrants also brought with them a Progressive repugnance of boss rule, with its endemic corruption and voting fraud. When they failed to take over the regular Democratic Party, they formed the Independent Party and drew further strength from Republicans and dissident Democrats. Trumpeting reformist "good government" platforms, they plunged into city and county political conflicts that had always been bitterly, sometimes violently, contentious. They proved as viciously and fraudulently contentious as the bosses. In addition, politics now grew even more heated by racial animosity.

The Texas Rangers usually did the bidding of the Anglo establishment, which meant the big ranchers like the Klebergs and the bosses like Jim Wells. Wells sometimes influenced the appointment of Rangers and invariably served, without fee, as defense counsel for any Ranger charged with any violation of law.

BLUFF, BURLY CAPTAIN John J. Sanders established his headquarters at Del Rio, the better to keep watch on the border. Throughout much of 1912, he and parts of his small company covered their own sector of the border while also entraining repeatedly for El Paso to aid Captain Hughes.

Twice in 1912, however, Sanders was called to Brownsville to keep order on election day—the first for municipal elections in early April, the second for the local and national elections of November 1912. He discovered how easily Rangers could fall victim to South Texas politics.

Sanders and four Rangers had been in Brownsville scarcely two weeks when, on November 10, 1912, they became embroiled in an incident that dramatized the political trap. Shortly after midnight on November 10, Cameron County deputy sheriffs Pat Haley and Andrew

Uresti roused Sanders in his quarters at Fort Brown. They asked him to help arrest one Ygnacio Treviño, wanted for murder and rape, who had slipped across the river from his Matamoros refuge to attend a dance. Waking Rangers Richard C. "Red" Hawkins and Joe Jenkins, Sanders accompanied the deputies to a suburban house where they hauled Treviño out of bed, bundled him into a hack, and set off for the county jail. In the darkened streets they encountered three horsemen on two horses. They were special city policemen filling in for sick regulars, and they and their friends would later claim that they merely notified the men in the hack that a city ordinance required running lights at night. The Rangers and deputies insisted that the horsemen started shooting without warning, setting off a gun battle that knocked a policeman from his horse and lodged a bullet in Joe Jenkins's arm. The hack's horses bolted, and by the time they were reined in and turned back to the scene, the gunmen had vanished.

After locking Treviño in jail and sending Jenkins for medical attention, Sanders telephoned Sheriff C. T. Ryan and with him and the handful of Rangers and deputies set forth in search of the policeman who had been shot from his horse. Someone identified him as Toribio Rodriguez and pointed out his home. The lawmen burst into his residence, dragged the wounded, fully clothed man from his bed, and started down the street. Sanders gripped Rodriguez's right arm, Hawkins his left, and the sheriff and deputies brought up the rear. While they walked down a nearby alley, a gunshot rang out; the officers, they later claimed, scattered to identify its location but failed. The wounded Rodriguez began stumbling, and a hack had to be summoned to get him to the jail.

Rodriguez had a bullet in his arm and one in his back. Sanders and his friends argued that Rodriguez had received both wounds in the initial gunfight, but a doctor affirmed that he had examined Rodriguez before the state and county lawmen arrived and found only an arm wound. Despite the welter of charges and countercharges, one of the deputies, probably Uresti, almost certainly shot Rodriguez in the back. After dictating a florid dying declaration the following day (with how much coaching one may wonder), Rodriguez died.

Whether knowingly or not, Sanders and his Rangers had been caught in the racially charged personal and political feuding that change had brought to the Lower Valley. The Cameron County lawmen and the city police carried on a deadly political feud, rooted in the clash between the longtime bosses and the Progressive newcomers. The Rangers may not have openly sided with the county officers, but the sheriff was an ex-Ranger as were some of the deputies, and the policemen drew the obvious conclusion. Sanders averred that he had escaped a deliberately contrived ambush, one designed to liberate Ygnacio Treviño, a former policeman, and kill the Ranger captain.

The conduct of Sanders and his two Rangers in the events that led to the death of Toribio Rodriguez displayed bad judgment, unwarranted brutality, and the cover-up of a murder committed by a deputy sheriff. Although a grand jury exonerated all the state and county officers, Sanders had not heard the last of the Rodriguez affair. A melodramatically revised version would later help ruin his career.[19]

Brownsville's tempestuous politics extended up the Rio Grande Valley into Hidalgo and Starr counties. Politics were but one aspect of the momentous changes that had swept the Lower Valley in the first decade of the twentieth century. The horrors that afflicted South Texas in 1915 can only be understood as an outgrowth of these changes.

FOR MEXICANS of South Texas, the agricultural revolution, so overtly demeaning, also served as a somewhat liberating influence. No longer need they bury old antagonisms dating from the Mexican War, the loss of their landed heritage, and the constant daily reminders of social inferiority. In their minds and among themselves, they could now give vent to long-festering resentment. They could talk about the misdeeds of the despised gringo. They could even spin schemes to take revenge.

As the Mexican Revolution raged across the Rio Grande, moreover, Texas provided haven for refugees and a base from which to organize and launch new revolutionary movements. A revolutionary mood swept South Texas Mexicans, creating partisan fervor for or against contending factions across the border, stirring patriotic feelings, and fueling anti-Americanism.

Adding to the ferment was the agitation of Ricardo and Enríque Flores Magón. They had used both Texas and California as bases from which to contest the dictatorship of Porfirio Díaz. Their Mexican Revolutionary Party and their newspaper, *Regeneración*, had promoted a liberal alternative to the tyranny of Díaz. Their programs sought change in Mexico, but their targets included American entrepreneurs in Mexico and the plight of border Mexicans. The overthrow of Díaz only spurred them to further involvement in the Mexican Revolution. Although the Flores Magón brothers ran afoul U.S. neutrality laws and squandered much of their effectiveness in federal courts and prisons, the ultimate failure of the movement lay in a political party whose only purpose was to provide liberal cover for Ricardo Flores Magón's basic objective—anarchism. Although anarchism was too abstruse to appeal to many South Texas Mexicans, Flores Magón's newspaper, universally read aloud to the illiterate, constantly reminded them of gringo injustice. It also laid groundwork for the next step toward the terror of 1915—a program well within the understanding of the most ignorant Mexican laborer.[20]

This program gained renown as the *Plan de San Diego*. Its origins were murky and its goals fantasy. Two versions emerged early in 1915. Each labored under a grandiloquently constructed version of the Flores Magón ideology, but both called for a revolution against the gringos. The oppressed would rise against their oppressors, regain for Mexico or as an independent republic all the territory lost in the Mexican War, return Indian lands to the Indians, mobilize blacks to form their own republic from six additional American states, and execute all Anglo males over the age of sixteen. Although the revolt would occur across the entire American Southwest, the focus was and remained South Texas. The bearer caught with a copy of the plan, Basilio Ramos, stood in court charged with sedition. The judge thought the scheme so absurd that he declared that Ramos ought to be charged with lunacy, not conspiracy against the United States. To the vast population of angry

Mexicans, however, the Plan of San Diego tapped deeply held longings and seemed worth a try.[21]

Among the closest friends and supporters of the Flores Magón brothers were Aniceto Pizaña and Luis de la Rosa. Pizaña had founded a Mexican Revolutionary Party group in Brownsville as early as 1904. Stocky and curly headed, he managed his own ranch, Los Tulitos, near San Benito and lived a respectable family life. But the ugly discrimination increasingly imposed on Mexicans by the midwestern newcomers infuriated him, and he devoted much time and effort to spreading the ideas and commentary of Ricardo Flores Magón. So did Luis de la Rosa, Pizaña's closest friend. Slightly older but of slimmer build, and with light complexion and red hair and mustache, a flamboyant tough, de la Rosa organized Magón groups all over South Texas and promoted the party's cause with rising militance. Pizaña and de la Rosa did not author the Plan of San Diego. Pizaña, content on his ranch, rejected it. But from the first de la Rosa emerged as a vocal proponent of the plan and its field general.[22]

As BACKDROP TO the Plan of San Diego, developments during 1914 inflamed anti-American fervor still more and heightened the plan's appeal to border Mexicans.

A seemingly trivial incident opened the year. Late in February 1914 some of Huerta's soldiers stole eleven horses belonging to Clemente Vergara. They were pastured on an island in the Rio Grande near his ranch at Palafox, about forty miles up the river from Laredo, opposite the Mexican village of Hidalgo. To negotiate the recovery of his horses, Vergara boated across the river. At once he fell into the hands of Huerta soldiers, who within a few days had tortured and executed him. A furious Governor Colquitt excoriated Ranger captain John J. Sanders for not investigating and reporting the incident, and set off an exchange of bristling correspondence with William Jennings Bryan, secretary of state in the administration of the new American president, Woodrow Wilson. Colquitt wanted federal sanction to send Rangers into Mexico to find Vergara. Bryan of course refused. On March 7 Vergara's body turned up on the Texas bank of the Rio Grande. The reports of Sanders and the U.S. consul at Nuevo Laredo strongly implied that Texas Rangers had crossed into Mexico and dug up Vergara's corpse. The explosive reaction in Washington and Mexico, however, led to a hurried rewriting of the first reports and the explanation that unknown parties, not Rangers, had retrieved the body from a Mexican cemetery.[23]

The army commander in Texas drew a more critical conclusion. In mid-March 1914 he advised the chief of staff in Washington that "the Texas Rangers naturally take advantage of the present conditions to aggrandize themselves." Border tensions were so high, however, that even a single Ranger (Sanders?) "could become a source of international danger." The border was a powder magazine, he believed, and one man, Vergara, "could easily be the match that would explode it."[24]

Woodrow Wilson regarded President Huerta as a thug and withheld U.S. diplomatic recognition of his government. No other foreign government having extended recognition, in August 1914 Huerta abdicated and left Mexico. With his iron rule lifted, civil war again erupted as three "Men of the North" fought for the succession. They were Venustiano Carranza in Coahuila, Francisco "Pancho" Villa in Chihuahua, and Alvaro Obregón in Sonora. American sentiment heavily favored Villa, who assumed himself the front-runner for U.S. recognition and aid. But Wilson withheld recognition of all the revolutionists, which meant that Mexico had no entity with which Americans at any level of government could deal.

The fear of South Texas citizens surpassed the actual threat of murder and plunder. For their benefit, however, in December 1914 Governor Colquitt blustered that if Mexican bullets fell in Texas, "I will promptly send the State Rangers to give protection to our citizens, and these Rangers will shoot to kill."[25]

Oscar Colquitt could do no such thing. He had served the traditional two terms as governor, and the summer primary, ratified in one-party Texas by the November general election, had handed the governor's mansion to James E. Ferguson. Ferguson's term of office opened with the Plan of San Diego, and he would be the governor who more than carried out Colquitt's parting effusion.

IN JANUARY 1915 "Farmer Jim" Ferguson occupied his office in the big capitol building on the hill looking down Austin's Congress Avenue. In one-party Texas, conservative Democrats battled liberal Democrats, with the Democratic primary the determining election. Ferguson had won office against the conservative wing on a program that excluded the prohibition issue altogether (which earned him the support of the "wets") and focused instead on the plight of the rural poor, especially the tenant farmer.

Ferguson looked like what he was, a Temple banker. But his blunt, colorful platform oratory and his pose as a successful businessman who had never lost touch with his humble origins on a hardscrabble farm marshaled a powerful rural constituency against the urban Democratic establishment. Ferguson would wield immense, often rowdy, political power in Texas for a generation. But his first challenge coincided with his inauguration: the Plan of San Diego. A scrappy, activist politician to the core, he dealt with it decisively.[26]

Ferguson's inauguration coincided with a significant event in Ranger history. After twenty-eight years as a Ranger, twenty-two as a captain, John R. Hughes retired. He had been one of the truly great captains, and his departure left the Ranger Force with none but mediocrities or worse in positions of leadership.

[2]

The "Bandit War," 1915

ANGLOS PERSISTED in calling the conflict that raged across South Texas in 1915–16 the "bandit war." It was no such thing. Banditry, mainly stock theft, had troubled South Texas since the Mexican War. "Bandits" from both sides of the border were involved, not all of them Mexicans.

Most of the Mexicans of late 1915 whom Anglos called bandits were amateur soldiers fighting under the Plan of San Diego. How many took its objectives seriously is unknown. Many probably did. But others seized on it as a means of striking back at the oppressive gringo while also exacting revenge and gaining plunder. Some were Mexicans from south of the border, even from the army of the leading revolutionist, Venustiano Carranza. But some were U.S. citizens of Mexican extraction who lived and worked in South Texas.

The people of South Texas knew that most of the marauders were not ordinary bandits, and so did state and federal authorities. Although often called bandits, those fighting for the Plan of San Diego also came to be known as *Sediciosos* (Seditionists).

Plan of San Diego activity could be readily distinguished from the usual banditry. Instead of simple stock theft, it targeted Anglos and establishment Mexicans and the infrastructure that symbolized the transformation of the Lower Valley—irrigation systems, railroads, telegraphs, and automobiles.[1]

THE PROBLEMS OF GOVERNOR JAMES E. FERGUSON in the opening months of his administration arose as much from the consternation of the Lower Valley citizens as from a rise in traditional banditry. As early as February 12, 1915, Captain John Sanders reported stealing rampant and every town calling for Rangers. Meetings of Plan of San Diego activists caused alarm. Citizens petitioned for more Rangers, and the legislature responded with an appropriation of $10,000 to add ten Rangers to the force for five months.[2]

In the first half of 1915, the outlawry stoking citizen fears may well have been essentially local. But on July 4, 1915, a raiding party of forty Mexican irregulars crossed the Rio Grande and began operations under the Plan of San Diego. They killed two Anglos on a ranch near Lyford and rode the chaparral for two weeks, constantly eluding the posses and military units that gave chase. Three of Sanders's Rangers participated off and on in the pursuit. En route the aggressors looted a store and killed an Anglo boy, Bernard Boley, near Raymondville, but lost two of their men in an exchange of fire with pursuers. Observers readily identified the leader of the marauders by his red hair and mustache, freckled face, and big dun-colored horse—Luis de la Rosa.[3]

De la Rosa's opening raid terrorized Anglos and shook Governor Ferguson with a wave of protests and appeals. The panicked voters of South Texas had to be quieted. Ferguson chose an unorthodox man who would employ unorthodox methods.

HENRY LEE RANSOM, forty-one, with gray hair and eyes and medium stature, had a violent history and had murdered an attorney who crossed him. As Houston chief of police he had to be let go because of violent and unlawful tactics. He had been a Ranger for almost a year in 1905 and a month and a half in 1909, and also claimed experience as a prison guard. He came to Ferguson's attention on the recommendation of Jacob F. Wolters of Houston, a Democratic leader and National Guard general. Ransom had served in the Philippine Insurrection (1899–1903), a shameful chapter of American history in which soldiers tortured and executed prisoners. As a veteran of such practices and as a product of the six-shooter culture, he excelled.

Ransom had not changed his methods, recalled William W. Sterling (later adjutant general), who quoted him as declaring that "a bad disease calls for bitter medicine. The Governor sent me down here to stop this trouble, and I am going to carry out his orders. There is only one way to do it. President Díaz proved that in Mexico."[4]

Governor Ferguson chose Ransom for precisely this approach. E. A. Sterling, William's rancher father, told of a conversation in the governor's private office in which Ferguson recounted the mission he had assigned to Ransom. The governor said that "he had given Ransom instructions to go down there and clean up that nest, that thing had been going on long enough, and to clean it up if he had to kill every damned man connected with it." "I firmly told Ransom," Sterling quoted Ferguson, "that if he didn't do it—if he didn't clean that nest up down there that I would put a man down there that would." And he added meaningfully, "I have the pardoning power and we will stand by those men, and I want that bunch—that gang cleaned up."[5]

When reported in the newspapers, Ferguson's appointment so upset Sheriff W. T. Vann of Cameron County that he hastened to Austin to try to talk him out of it. The response: "Ransom will make you a good man if you will warm up to him." No, Vann replied, "I don't like his style. I have heard a good deal about Captain Ransom, and I don't want him down there." The governor refused to relent.[6]

On July 20, 1915, Ferguson swore in Henry L. Ransom as captain of newly constituted Company D and dispatched him to Houston to begin recruiting—many, according to Bill Sterling, "convict guards who were trained to shoot fleeing convicts with buckshot." At the same time, over Sheriff Vann's vigorous protest, Ferguson arranged for Captain Sanders to withdraw his men from the South Texas trouble zone and for Ransom to take full charge. Captain J. Monroe Fox and his company had already been sent west to the Big Bend country, with headquarters at Marfa. The new captain established his headquarters at Harlingen and covered a district embracing ten counties, including Vann's own Cameron County. Ransom's Rangers thus operated in the huge area targeted by the Sedeciosos.[7]

AUGUST 1915 fixed the pattern of the Plan of San Diego uprising for three months: Sediciosos springing from the chaparral to kill Anglos and unsupportive Mexicans, burn railroad bridges, cut telegraph and telephone lines, loot stores, and clash with military patrols and civilian posses; posses composed of Rangers and vengeful deputies and civilians expanding the "bandit war" to subject all Mexicans deemed "suspicious" to Captain Ransom's methods.[8]

Dawn of August 3 brought a fateful clash at the ranch of Aniceto Pizaña, Los Tulitos, about twenty-five miles north of Brownsville. Pizaña, who had managed the ranch for more than a decade, had incurred the enmity of his neighbor, Jeff Scribner, who informed a cavalry lieutenant that Pizaña and his hands were "notorious cattle and horse thieves," also suspected of complicity in the recent burning of a railroad trestle. With Scribner and five civilians far in the lead, a cavalry contingent of twenty troopers bore down on the ranch. In an exchange of gunfire between the civilians in advance and men at the ranch, an off-duty soldier fell dead and three civilians were wounded. The cavalry made its way through the chaparral, surrounded the house, and burst in. They found Pizaña's brother, his aged mother, and his twelve-year-old son, who had been shot through the leg.

Participant accounts differ on what happened at Los Tulitos. The most likely scenario is that Scribner and the others in advance exchanged fire with Pizaña's ranch hands, who then fled into the chaparral. Only after this shootout did the cavalry arrive on the scene. Later on August 3, a civilian posse from San Benito and another cavalry unit showed up. Sheriff Vann and Ransom and three Rangers almost certainly were with this bunch, who found two men hiding in the house. Several civilians appealed to the senior army officer to take these captives in charge rather than entrust them to the civil officers, who might kill them "while attempting to escape." A search of the house turned up great quantities of Mexican Revolutionary Party literature and copies of *Regeneración*. These seemed convincing evidence of Pizaña's complicity in the Plan of San Diego.

Ricardo Flores Magón's movement helped inspire the Plan of San Diego, but in 1915 the two were entirely separate strategies. Pizaña had promoted the Magón agenda but had not joined the Sediciosos. Crossing the Rio Grande, he pondered his next move. News of more atrocities reached him, together with word that his son's leg had been amputated. Overtures from Luis de la Rosa would ultimately resolve the issue, transforming Aniceto Pizaña into a dedicated Sedicioso.[9]

In the next few days violence escalated. Reports indicated that raiders might be ranging as far north as Kingsville, with the King Ranch the objective. On August 4 Caesar Kleberg, manager of the Norias division of the ranch, joined with Cameron County political boss Jim Wells to urge Adjutant General Hutchings (reappointed by Ferguson) to come down at once. Hutchings declined, but the next day he changed his mind. Summoning Captain Fox and his company from Marfa, Hutchings boarded an overnight train to Brownsville. He arrived on August 6 and Fox, with seven men, on August 7.[10]

On the very day Hutchings reached Brownsville, August 6, Luis de la Rosa and fourteen Sediciosos swept down on Sebastian, thirty miles north of Brownsville, robbed a store, and executed A. L. Austin—well and unfavorably known to Mexicans as president of the Sebastian Law and Order League—and his son. Hutchings himself organized the pursuit, piling Sheriff Vann and Captain Ransom with four Rangers in automobiles and racing north. Believing the marauders would turn back toward Mexico by a favored crossing of Arroyo Colorado, Paso Real, the posse headed there to cut them off, apparently increasing to as many as twenty by the time they reached their destination, well after nightfall. As Vann and Hutchings sat in an auto keeping watch on the crossing, Ransom and the rest of the posse "rounded up" a nearby ranch house. Sounds of great commotion brought Vann running to the house. Amid much shouting, cursing, and confusion, someone began firing, and a father and one of his two sons dropped dead in their backyard. The second son crawled bleeding into the house. The next morning the posse searched the house. Beneath a bed they discovered the wounded man, who fired a pistol at Ranger Joe Anders, slightly wounding him in the eye. Stripping off the mattress, the Rangers riddled the man. What set off the nighttime melee was mere suspicion the three men had been involved in the murder of the Austins. The two victims killed outside the house were not armed.[11]

TWO DAYS LATER, on the hot afternoon of August 8, Customs Inspector D. Portus Gay lazed on his front porch near the Brownsville depot. Noting a special train steaming out of the station, he walked over to learn why. The ticket agent replied that the coach bore Adjutant General Hutchings, Captain George Head of the local militia company, Captains Ransom and Fox with their Rangers (number uncertain, but probably a dozen), and several local law officers. They were headed for Norias, headquarters of the Norias division of the King Ranch, seventy miles up the railroad. Sensing action, Gay retrieved his rifle and boarded the regular northbound train at 3:30 PM. At San Benito he picked up a fellow customs officer, Joe Taylor, and at Harlingen still another, Marcus Hines ("Baby Elephant"), together with Cameron County deputy sheriff Gordon Hill (son of prominent developer Lon C. Hill).[12]

Undoubtedly more than mere rumors, which were indeed rife, summoned so formidable an expedition to Norias. Hutchings was in Brownsville because pressed by Caesar Kleberg and Jim Wells. Kleberg had also requested protection from the army, and that very day a corporal and seven regular soldiers had taken station at Norias. Probably the Ranger expedition set forth in response to a telegram from Kleberg.

The regular train paused at Norias at 5:30 PM, leaving Gay and his companions. The station stop consisted of a large two-story house serving as Norias division headquarters of the King Ranch, a railroad section house, and a structure for railroad tools. General Hutchings and his contingent were not there; with most of the Norias ranch hands, they had taken to the brush in search of raiders supposed to be menacing the Sauz division of the King Ranch. The Norias headquarters housed eight soldiers and two cowboys, Frank Martin (a former Ranger) and Lauro Cavazos, ranch carpenter George Forbes and his wife, and the cook and her husband. In the section house were both Anglo and Mexican railroad employees.

At 6:00 PM some of the men sauntered outside and spotted an approaching body of horsemen. Marcus Hines speculated that they were the Hutchings party returning. Then Gay made out their headgear—sombreros. "Look at those big hats," he said, "they are damned bandits!"[13]

Actually, they were not "bandits." They were Sediciosos, about sixty men led by Luis de la Rosa. Portus Gay said most were from Mexico, joined by a few "greaser outlaws" from the U.S. side. In fact, twenty-five from Mexico were Constitutionalist (Carranza) soldiers, under a major and a captain, and those from Texas included a group loyal to Aniceto Pizaña. At this point he himself had not yet decided to join the Sedeciosos, but his nephew, Ricardo Gómez Pizaña, played a prominent part in the fight. Before attacking, the major unfurled a paper and had his first sergeant read it to all. It stated the object of the expedition in terms of the Plan of San Diego, although another apparently was to secure railroad tools with which to wreck a train.[14]

Without any reconnaissance or much of a plan, the Sediciosos charged, most from the east. The civilians lay behind the railroad grade and opened fire. Some of the assailants slipped to the west and took positions in the toolhouse and behind a stack of railroad ties. Frank Martin and George Forbes (who had been hit in the elbow) raced to the fence around the ranch house and took on this threat. At once they discovered still another bunch of Sediciosos charging from the west. But the soldiers opened a deadly fire with their army Springfields that stopped this movement, killed the leader's horse, and drove the remnant to the tool and section houses. At the same time, the men behind the railroad grade forced their opponents to shift to these railroad structures.

Some broke windows in the section house, entered, and fired from there. Railroad employees in this house caused the ranch defenders to lessen their fire. One of the Sedicioso leaders, Antonio Rocha, approached an old Mexican woman and asked how many gringos they faced, "Why don't you go over there and see," she replied in Spanish, "you cowardly bastard of a white burra?" Rocha rammed a pistol in her mouth and pulled the trigger.[15]

Shortly before 8:30 PM the rebels burst from their positions and charged, "shooting and yelling like Indians," according to Gay. Although running low on ammunition, the defenders laid down a heavy, unaimed fusillade. A bullet caught one of the rebel leaders, and the rest turned and fled. The battle was over.

Neither side suffered severe casualties. In the ranch house, Martin and Forbes lay wounded along with two soldiers. In the section house the Mexican woman sprawled on the floor, her brains blown out. The attackers counted four dead left on the battlefield, three wounded (one so badly that a Carranza captain "finished him off"), and three missing, marked on the rolls as deserters.[16]

With bullets no longer flying, the defenders telephoned to Brownsville and Kingsville for help. Late at night trains arrived from both directions, bringing reinforcements, including Sheriff Vann from Brownsville and Sheriff A. Y. Baker from Edinburg. Meantime, immediately after the attackers withdrew, the Hutchings party had returned and begun to lecture the weary veterans on how the battle ought to have been conducted.

Captain Ransom pompously explained what he would have done. Joe Taylor cut him off. "Listen, WE were here—we did not get a man killed—we were here when they came, we were here when they left, and we are still here, and I don't know what you all would have done if you had been here, but I do know that there WAS NOT A GOD DAMNED SON OF A BITCH OF YOU HERE!" It was a fact that not all the Rangers, especially Captain Fox, would remember as the passing years wrapped the Norias battle in legend.[17]

The next morning the Rangers seized an opportunity to spread their message and their self-image throughout Mexico and the United States. The northbound train brought Brownsville photographer Robert Runyon and his tripod and cumbersome glass-plate Kodak. He photographed

Captain Fox, Special Ranger Tom Tate, and an unidentified third man astride their horses with lariats bound around the legs of two dead rebels and the neck of a third. A fourth body lay next to the three. Back in Brownsville Runyon converted the image into a picture postcard and added it to the hundreds of chiefly revolutionary scenes that he marketed widely. Captions made clear that the picture showed Rangers and the corpses of "bandits" killed at Norias. The images circulated widely and were printed in many newspapers, rousing fury among Mexicans everywhere, strengthening the Plan of San Diego movement, and tarnishing the reputation of the Texas Rangers among thinking people.

Later criticism elicited the explanation that Runyon merely took a snapshot of Rangers dragging the bodies away for burial, that Norias had no "hearse." Left unexplained was why a wagon could not be found at the headquarters of a working ranch, or the corpses slung over the rumps of horses, or ranch hands assigned the task, or why the horsemen chose to maneuver their horses backward to drag the bodies, or indeed why the Rangers uncharacteristically bothered to bury the dead at all. That the picture was staged is demonstrated by the fact that Runyon exposed at least six views, all with slightly different shadows and positions of the subjects, and for some, a different camera angle. Moreover, he took still other photographs of the bodies in association with other Rangers. So the picture that so damaged the Ranger image was no mere snapshot. Whether to imply a victory in which they took no part, or project their power to rebellious Mexicans, or reassure Anglos they were winning the "bandit war," the Rangers readily cooperated as Runyon arranged multiple compositions of the same scene. It achieved all three purposes.

The night before, young Gordon Hill had upbraided the Rangers by asking, "If you are such hell-roaring fighters, why don't you go after them?" They were still well within range of pursuit, but the officers decided to wait for daylight. Then, of course, they delayed still longer as Runyon exposed his series of glass plates. By the time they did get the pursuit under way, it was too late. The Sediciosos easily escaped across the Rio Grande.[18]

RANGER MISDEEDS during the uprising far surpassed posturing in front of a camera. As Sedicioso aggressions mounted through August and September, so did indiscriminate retaliation against any Mexican suspected of taking part in the depredations, aiding raiders, or even sympathizing with their cause. Rangers set the example, but local lawmen and vigilantes followed the example. A "blacklist" circulated, and the name of any "suspicious" Mexican could be entered on it by anyone for any reason. By the dozens and then by the scores, such "suspects" were "evaporated." The hangman's noose evaporated some, but bullets evaporated most "while attempting to escape."[19]

Captain Fox eagerly embraced Ransom's methods. Betraying the mindset of his proud pose with dead Mexicans at Norias, on August 14 he informed a newsman that "We got another Mexican—but he's dead." A week later he reported seizing Tomás Aguilar, who "admitted" participating in various depredations and was thought to have been involved in the Austin murders. "Of course he tried to make his escape but we killed him."[20]

Fox's involvement in the "bandit war" ended on August 28, when Hutchings ordered him back to the Big Bend. Nothing the indiscreet captain said or did prompted the transfer. Rather the ranches of state senator Claude Hudspeth, a staunch Ranger supporter whose word was fiat to Hutchings, had been targeted by stock thieves. He wanted Fox sent back to his assigned station. At the same time, Governor Ferguson defined Ransom's district as the southern counties of Cameron, Hidalgo, Starr, Zapata, Jim Hogg, and Brooks. In response to the Norias fight, Hutchings had summoned Sanders and his company from Del Rio, and now the governor assigned him the northern counties of Willacy, Kleberg, Nueces, Jim Wells, Duval, and Webb. Headquartered at Norias at first, he moved in late September to Alice.[21]

DURING THE SUMMER of 1915, panic swept through both Anglo and Mexican populations. The Plan of San Diego uprising gave genuine cause for panic. On August 26, in Monterrey, Luis de la Rosa and Aniceto Pizaña issued a manifesto calling "all good Mexicans" to arms. Printed in newspapers all over Mexico and Texas, the manifesto was a declaration of war.[22]

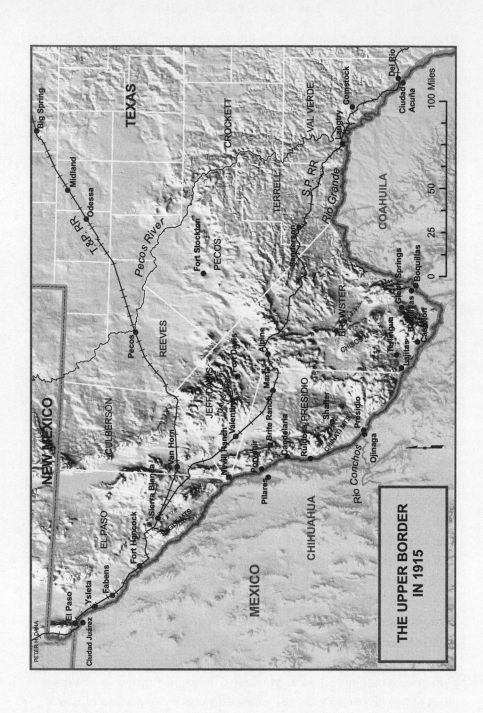

THE UPPER BORDER
IN 1915

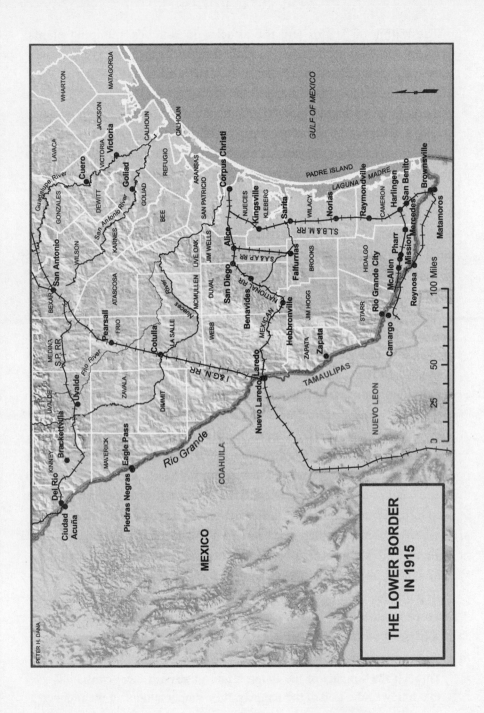

THE LOWER BORDER
IN 1915

The killing of Anglos and the attacks on ranches, pumping plants, irrigation canals, and railroad trestles reverberated through the Lower Valley, setting off a stampede to get out of harm's way. "They brought their women and children into town," recalled Lon C. Hill, "and a great many just got on the train, left their chickens and hogs and cows, and everything else, and just went to Corpus and San Antonio, and went from there to Canada—just scattered all over the country; there were some places there just absolutely depopulated—wasn't anybody there."[23]

A like stampede swept the Mexican population. If they refused or even hesitated to aid the rebels, the rebels killed them. If they did as commanded, or even aroused suspicion of aid or sympathy, they went on the blacklist and invited evaporation by Rangers or their cohorts. So the Mexicans emulated the Anglos: they fled across the border to Mexico. Military officers at river checkpoints reported as many as fifty families a day crossing with their household possessions. Some told that they had been given several days' notice to vacate their homes. Others saw their houses burned to the ground. In places Rangers burst into the homes of Mexicans and confiscated all the firearms, which left them defenseless against rebels and evaporators.[24]

Ransom's evaporations are harder to particularize than Fox's. But after Fox departed in late August, Ransom and his men were the only Rangers in the Lower Valley. Testimony in the legislative investigation of the Ranger Force in 1919 and the Fall congressional hearings of 1920 leaves no doubt of Ranger executions, although usually expressed in such terms as hearing "talk" on the streets the next day. Estimates of the number of victims, killed not only by Rangers but local lawmen and vigilantes, generally range between one hundred and three hundred, although an improbable five thousand also crept into the record.[25]

Republican political leader Rentfro B. Creager thought the number between one hundred and two hundred, and, in contrast to the generalities of most who bore witness, he spoke explicitly:

> Through the conduct of the Rangers and ill advised local constabulary that followed the lead of the Rangers, they simply multiplied the number

of bandits with whom we had to contend. They would go out and hang them to trees until practically dead, or would shoot and leave dead on the ground some Mexican, who was as innocent as you. . . . The result of that was you would make that man's brothers and relatives for two or three generations bandits or potential bandits.[26]

Army scout John Peavy told of an incident in late September near Ebenezer, in Hidalgo County. Driving up the river road, he and his commander came on about ten Mexicans hanging from limbs beside the road. Judge Wells, passing several weeks later, counted eleven badly decomposed bodies that had been dragged into the brush. He recalled that each had been shot in the forehead. Peavy dates this deed September 28, 1915. Two days earlier Ransom and a detachment of Rangers had "scouted" from Harlingen to Pharr up the road past Ebenezer.[27]

That such executions were not uncommon was confirmed by former Ranger Virgil Lott. Twenty years later, he wrote, "gruesome skeletons" could still be found in the brush, lying in neatly arranged rows, side by side, each with a trim, round hole in the forehead squarely between the empty eye sockets. He called these holes "brands of the Texas rangers . . . the never-failing 45-colts." Betraying his own sentiments, he added his thanks to God "for their heroic efforts."[28]

Actually, Ransom's Rangers did little fighting. They "scouted" all over their sector, reporting their daily whereabouts each month but recording not a hint of their atrocities. At times Rangers joined pursuing posses led by Sheriffs W. T. Vann and A. Y. Baker but rarely got close enough to raiders to exchange fire.

Rather than Ransom's Rangers, the U.S. Army did most of the serious fighting and sustained the heaviest casualties. Major General Frederick Funston had commanded the Southern Department at Fort Sam Houston in San Antonio since February 1915. At first he minimized the rebellion as ordinary outlawry. As the Sediciosos inflicted more and more casualties on his border force of 1,100, however, he changed his mind. At the end of August 1915 he called for reinforcements.[29]

JAMES B. MCALLEN managed one of the largest, oldest, and most promi-nent ranches in the Lower Valley, with headquarters some thirty-two miles northwest of Edinburg, in Hidalgo County. It had been a Spanish land grant but had come into Anglo possession through intermarriage. McAllen maintained a home for his family in Brownsville but, assisted by a Mexican woman, spent the summer and fall months at the ranch. On September 24, 1915, a Mexican raiding party approached the ranch headquarters. The leader dismounted, knocked on the latticed door, and demanded of the Mexican woman to see McAllen. She woke him from a nap and told him he had some unwanted visitors. He grabbed a twelve-gauge shotgun, went to the door, and sent both barrels of buck-shot crashing through the lattice into the waiting man.

The fourteen rebels, fresh from another ranch raid, took positions in outlying buildings and began firing. McAllen dodged from one window to another firing back, the Mexican woman keeping him armed with freshly loaded Winchesters. For an hour the battle raged. McAllen killed another attacker and wounded three, two mortally. Unwilling to take more casualties, they withdrew.

Meantime, the word had spread by telephone. A cavalry unit raced toward the McAllen ranch, while Captain Ransom loaded two of his Rangers into Bill Sterling's new Dodge automobile and raced for the scene. The reinforcements were too late, of course. McAllen had already won the battle. More Rangers arrived, and they rode to the nearby Young ranch and from there set forth to run down the raiders. Before dawn the next morning the Rangers found a house where the fugitives had forced the residents to give aid before continuing to the Rio Grande.

Near noon the same day, as the Rangers napped on the front porch of the Young ranch house, two Mexicans rode up to explain to the ranchman how they had been compelled to provide food and bandages to the marauders. They then turned and rode back toward their home. As recalled by a watching cowboy, Ransom and his men "waited until they got about 300 yards from the headquarters and began to follow them. These two Mexicans pulled over to the side of the road to let them pass, and when they did, the Rangers just shot them off their horses, turned around and went back to the ranch and went back to sleep."[30]

AFTER MIDNIGHT on October 18, 1915, the regular southbound train had just passed Olmito on its run to Brownsville. Only six miles north of the city, steaming at thirty miles an hour, the engineer spotted a rail being pulled out of position. He hit the brakes but too late. The locomotive, tender, and baggage car rolled over, crushing the engineer and scalding the fireman. The two passenger coaches derailed but remained upright and tilting to one side.

A passenger coach carried District Attorney John I. Kleiber, state quarantine officer Dr. Edgar S. McCain, stockman and former Ranger Harry Wallis, three off-duty soldiers, two in uniform, and several other passengers. Thrown to the floor between the seats, they distinctly heard repeated shouts of "Viva Carranza," "Viva Luis de la Rosa," and "Viva Aniceto Pizaña." A fusillade of bullets riddled the coach from both sides.

Four gunmen entered and ranged up and down the aisle shouting, cursing, and firing their rifles. A Mexican boy took refuge in the toilet. Dr. McCain quickly followed. Wallis hurried to join him, but a man at the end of the car fired twice, hitting him in the shoulder and carrying away a finger. Wallis crowded into the toilet and bolted the door. Rebels pounded on the door and pried it partly open. The boy slipped out and shouted that two gringos remained inside. Bullets shredded the door. One hit Dr. McCain, standing on the toilet, in the abdomen.

Kleiber hugged the floor between two seats. Opposite him a cavalryman looked into the aisle. Kleiber saw a rifle thrust into the soldier's face and fired. Streams of blood flowed across the slanting aisle and covered the district attorney. A raider, his faced hidden by a big bandana cut with eye holes, prodded Kleiber with his rifle barrel and demanded money. Acting near death from the splotches of blood on his suit, Kleiber handed over his purse, his watch fob, and even surrendered his shoes. Meantime, a leader at the end of the coach kept cursing in Spanish and shouting, *Vengase! Vengase!* Others took up the refrain, and soon the attackers had abandoned the coach and disappeared into the night. Behind they left a dead engineer and soldier, a mortally hit Dr. McCain, the soldier whose blood had covered Kleiber but who eventually recovered, another wounded soldier, the badly hurt Wallis, and the scalded fireman. Unharmed were a Mexican family and a Jewish salesman who claimed to be German.[31]

The deed had been planned nearby for two days and carried out by sixty Sediciosos led by both Luis de la Rosa and Aniceto Pizaña. They had extracted spikes and fishplates enough to loosen the western rail and run a heavy wire from the rail to a crowbar driven into the earth. As the train bore down on the site, they hauled back the crowbar and pulled the rail enough out of alignment to wreck the train. Having looted and shot up the cars, they quickly escaped, scattering at once for the Rio Grande.[32]

By daylight Ransom and seven Rangers had shown up, together with Sheriff Vann and a deputy. They immediately began to search the area for suspects. The guilty of course had already escaped into Mexico, only four miles to the south. But Ransom came up with four suspects and Vann with two. As Vann later testified, "Captain Ransom had them [the four] and walked them over to me and says, I am going out [and] kill these fellows, are you going with me? I says no, and I don't believe you are going. He says, if you haven't got guts enough to do it, I will go myself, I says, that takes a whole lot of guts, four fellows with their hands tied behind them, it takes a whole lot of guts to do that."

Vann turned to question his two suspects. One wore military shoes thought to have been taken from a soldier on the train. He explained that he had bought them in Brownsville from a merchant who was also an undertaker. Vann drove to town and ascertained that the shoes had indeed been removed by the mortician from a soldier who had drowned in the river and that the mortician had sold them in his store. Back at the wreck site, Vann's deputy confirmed that Ransom had taken his four suspects into the woods and shot them. Now he intended to execute Vann's prisoners. "No, they are my two," replied the sheriff. "He hasn't enough Rangers here to kill my two at all." Motored to Brownsville, they were jailed and later proved innocent. The local coroner later testified that in the days following the train wreck, seventeen bodies were found. He did not see these bodies himself but always heard that Rangers had done it.[33]

MILITARY OFFICERS along the border severely disapproved of Ransom's evaporations and complained to General Funston. In September Funston had asked Governor Ferguson to stop his Rangers from firing indiscriminately across the Rio Grande. In early November, with Ransom's abuses so flagrant that they could no longer be ignored, Funston again wrote Ferguson to protest unlawful executions. The governor replied that "I fear it is in part true" and promised he was "taking up the matter vigorously." This consisted of instructing General Hutchings to handle the matter "with an iron hand." In turn Hutchings issued an explicit directive to the three Ranger captains: (a) to prevent the execution of all Mexicans except by due process of law, (b) to notify county and city officers and all citizens that any unlawful execution of Mexicans "will be at their peril," and (c) to promptly report to the adjutant general all casualties with names of witnesses.[34]

This was rank hypocrisy. The only guilty captain at this time was Ransom, and he well knew from his conversation with the governor what was expected of him. Regardless of the adjutant general's instructions, Ransom would continue his practice and ignore all three requirements of the directive to Ranger captains.

WHILE EXPRESSING genuine grievances of Mexican residents of South Texas, the Plan of San Diego rebellion gained momentum within the context of the Mexican Revolution. Venustiano Carranza exercised a shaky hold over Coahuila and Tamaulipas, and vied with Pancho Villa for international recognition. Woodrow Wilson disliked Carranza intensely, but increasingly he seemed to be the choice of the Latin American nations the president had invited to help mediate the issue. Desperately needing U.S. recognition as the legitimate head of the Mexican government, Carranza walked a diplomatic tightrope. If rebel fighters continued to find haven in Mexico, he invited a U.S. invasion.

If he moved too aggressively against the Sediciosos, he alienated thousands of their supporters in Mexico. Publicly, he claimed to be making every possible effort to suppress the rebels. In reality, his efforts only occasionally went beyond tokenism.[35]

Carranza's commander in Matamoros, General Emiliano Nafarrate, scarcely concealed his sympathy for the Plan of San Diego, and Pizaña and de la Rosa openly walked the streets of the city. Carranzista soldiers often took part in Sedicioso raids, as at Norias and in the train wreck at Olmito. At length, on October 12, Carranza transferred Nafarrate and his entire garrison south to Victoria. The new commander, Eugenio López, seemed ready to move against the rebel concentrations, but he failed to stop the raids or curtail the activities of de la Rosa and Pizaña.[36]

Bowing to Latin American consensus, on October 19, 1915, the day after the Olmito train wreck, Wilson extended de facto U.S. recognition to Carranza as "First Chief" of the Mexican Republic. Other nations promptly followed suit. Although still inhibited by strong public support of the Sediciosos, Carranza could now afford to move more aggressively against their movement, which continued to raise the specter of war despite U. S. recognition. On November 23 Carranza met with Governor Ferguson and Adjutant General Hutchings in Nuevo Laredo. The "First Chief" took the occasion to introduce his new commander in Matamoros, his nephew General Alfredo Ricaut, and pledge cooperation in ending border troubles. He reinforced the pledge by traveling to Matamoros and meeting with American civil and military officers.[37]

General Ricaut moved decisively against the Sedicioso bases south of the river. Almost at once the raiding declined dramatically. On January 12, 1916, he arrested Aniceto Pizaña in Matamoros. Accomplices were seized in Monterrey. Truly the "bandit war" seemed at an end.

It was not. That the raids had almost ceased meant only that Ricaut had disrupted the Sediciosos, not that they had ceased plotting to carry out the Plan of San Diego. The U.S. diplomats and military officers in all the border cities as well as the Mexican interior reported widespread support of the Plan among Carranza officials and active organizing efforts of local Sedicioso cells. De la Rosa remained at large, even though Carranza had ordered his arrest. General Nafarrate, still at Victoria, harbored de la Rosa and sought to revive the Sedicioso aggressions. Pizaña appeared on the streets of Matamoros, although General Ricaut gave assurances that he was kept under constant surveillance. Evidence mounted throughout the early months of 1916 that forecast another offensive. "We are sitting on dynamite as it were," warned the U.S. consul in Matamoros.[38]

THE DYNAMITE GREW even more volatile because of developments far to the west. Wilson's recognition of Carranza infuriated Pancho Villa, who had thought he would win the coveted prize. At the same time, his erratic, violent behavior had weakened his armies and diminished his stature. Taking revenge, and hoping to provoke the Americans into a war that would topple Carranza, on January 19, 1916, one of his generals stopped a train at the Santa Ysabel River, dragged eighteen American mining engineers off, and executed them. Then before dawn on March 9 Villa and four hundred fighters attacked the border town of Columbus, New Mexico. Seventeen Americans died, but the military garrison, both in street fighting and a vigorous pursuit, felled 130 of the attacking force. Six days later a punitive expedition under Brigadier General John J. Pershing crossed the border and thrust deep into Mexico in a vain effort to catch Villa.[39]

Neither Wilson nor Carranza wanted war, but the continued presence of American troops on Mexican soil outraged Mexicans and damaged Carranza's prestige. It also powered the growing revival of Sedicioso planning for another offensive against the Lower Valley.

GENERAL FUNSTON had been heavily reinforced, as he had requested at the end of August 1915. Even so, he did not believe he could head off further Sedicioso depredations so long as Mexico remained a safe haven. The only solution, he declared on May 22, 1916, was to seize positions south of the border and keep both Mexican troops and Sediciosos busy protecting themselves and their interests on their own soil. Already bogged down in an intervention that had become a diplomatic and military nightmare, the Wilson administration ignored Funston.

Funston assigned the Brownsville district to an unusually competent and bold officer, Brigadier General James Parker, who assumed command on May 18. Without committing any orders to paper, Funston let Parker know that he should pursue raiders across the border. On June 15 twenty-four Sediciosos crossed the Rio Grande nine miles west of Brownsville but were so suddenly hit by an army patrol that they scattered back toward the Rio Grande.

The next day Parker responded as he had promised. U.S. cavalry crossed the border and skirmished with General Ricault's troops. Although a minor operation, the crossing sent a powerful message to Carranzistas and Sediciosos alike: General Parker would no longer allow the Rio Grande to halt pursuit of raiders. Funston could not have the advanced bases in Mexico he wanted, but Parker's offensive moves served adequate notice. General Ricaut gave fulsome promises to Parker that no more raids would take place, and he made good his word.[40]

On the very next day, June 19, reacting to the rising crisis created by Pershing's continued operations in Mexico, President Wilson mobilized the entire National Guard of the United States, 100,000 strong, and sent it to the border. In the Brownsville district, Parker soon commanded a combined total of 31,400 regulars and guardsmen.

The "bandit war" had ended.

RANGER "EVAPORATIONS" had not. Captain Ransom's methods had settled firmly in the Ranger Force, and his men continued to execute "suspicious" Mexicans. The six-shooter culture of earlier Rangers had metastasized into brutality, torture, and unlawful execution.

Immediately at fault was Governor Ferguson's choice of Henry Ransom to clean up South Texas by whatever means necessary. He knew and approved of what Ransom was doing, indeed had instructed him to do it. In a larger context, however, other influences came to bear. The citizens of South Texas either endorsed the Ransom technique or did not want to examine it. County and city officers, joined by vigilantes, perpetrated deeds as terrible as Ransom's. Public approval is thus one explanation of Ranger conduct. It cannot, however, excuse it, especially since the Rangers set the example. As the only statewide law enforcement agency, one with a long and generally creditable history, the Texas Rangers should have taken the lead in upholding the law, not in undermining it.

A critical influence was the politicization of the Ranger Force begun by Governor Colquitt and intensified by Governor Ferguson, symbolized by the retirement in 1915 of the last of the outstanding Ranger captains, John R. Hughes. None remotely approaching his proficiency appeared during the decade of the Mexican Revolution. Their view of the law, reflecting Ransom's, led to repeated abuse of the law, and they either recruited men of like mind or steeped them in the same view.

Adjutant General Henry Hutchings bears large responsibility. Preoccupied by the National Guard, he exerted almost no control of the Ranger Force. To be sure, both Colquitt and Ferguson ruled the force more directly than any governor since Sam Houston. They used Hutchings, when they used him at all, mainly as a conduit for transmitting communications to the captains. Still, Hutchings knew what Ransom's men were doing and left no evidence that he seriously tried to influence either the governors or the captains.

The "bandit war" of 1915 tainted the Ranger image more blackly than any episode in their history. But the Mexican Revolution had not ended, and more was to come.

[3]

The Big Bend, 1913–1919

WEST TEXAS DIFFERED from East Texas as night from day. The Balcones Escarpment sharply divided cotton from cattle. Along this great curving rim, the major rivers of Texas dropped from the Edwards Plateau to the black soil of the Gulf Plain, en route scouring massive limestone ledges to create the Texas Hill Country. Below the escarpment, except in the cattle kingdom of the Nueces Strip, the Old South of cotton and rice endured even as cities, industry, and commerce encroached. Above the escarpment, the Old West of horsemen, cattle, and vast distance attracted more stockmen. Railroads, automobiles, and telegraph and telephone lines shrank the distance. Still, West Texas remained an arid land of grassy plains, sandy deserts, and craggy, barren mountains. The tree-clad Davis Mountains afforded the only relief.

No part of West Texas challenged human intrusion as formidably as the Big Bend. Trickling southeast from El Paso, the Rio Grande refreshed itself from the Conchos River, flowing out of the Sierra Madre of Mexico, then swung through plunging canyons before turning northeast. The bend cradled the lofty Chisos Mountains and foothills, buttes, and lesser mountains extending north to the Southern Pacific Railroad.

But the worst tangle overlooked the Rio Grande in the upper Big Bend. A thinly grassed plateau extended almost to the river before falling abruptly to the valley in a chaos of mountains, gorges, ridges, buttes, spring-fed arroyos, and sheer rimrocks.

About twenty Anglo cattlemen grazed the plateau and the western slopes of the mountains, although one cow required hundreds of acres for subsistence. These ranchers drew their wants from the railroad towns of Marathon, Alpine, Marfa, Valentine, and Van Horn. A few primitive roads bore automobile traffic, but horse and mule remained the chief means of transport. Motorized vehicles penetrated the wild terrain bordering the valley at their peril. Tiny Mexican trading villages dotted the valley on both sides of the river. Dominating the valley, Presidio and Ojinaga faced each other across the Rio Grande at the mouth of the Conchos River.

EQUALLY RUGGED deserts and mountains lay across the Rio Grande in Chihuahua, the resort of revolutionary armies and gangs of bandits. Both, as well as Texas outlaws, preyed on the huge ranches that overspread the area. Both bandits and revolutionary foragers ravaged the herds. While the foragers fed their armies, the bandits crossed their stock into Texas, where Big Bend ranchers paid the price, altered the brands, and ran the animals to market with their own herds. By 1915 the Chihuahuan ranches had been depleted, and the Big Bend began to attract the attention of Mexican bad men. Federal customs inspectors, called river guards, joined with cavalry units and Texas Rangers to contend with smugglers and bandits.[1]

The premier river guard in the Big Bend was Joe Sitter. Fifty-three in 1913, the intense, brawny, heavily mustached Sitter had compiled a long and distinguished record as a lawman, including three years (1893–96) as a Ranger in Captain Hughes's company at Ysleta, since 1899 as a mounted inspector of the customs service. For years, whatever his title, Big Benders had known Sitter simply as "the law."[2]

Sitter's nemesis was an equally powerful personality, the premier bandit of the Big Bend, Chico Cano. He too sported a huge mustache and curly black hair, and he ruled a bandit gang that included his brothers and other family members as well as a corps of swaggering bravos. A river guard called him a "thoroughbred outlaw." At times Villistas, at times Carranzistas, at times mere bandits, and at times all three, the Cano gang achieved near mythic status in the Big Bend.[3]

Sitter wanted Cano, and on February 10, 1913, he got him. Scouting the Rio Grande near Pilares with fellow inspector Jack Howard and stock association inspector Ad Hardwick, Sitter gave chase to a band of Mexican horsemen. Cano was one of them. His horse stumbled, and he fell captive to Sitter. Enroute to Marfa, however, the officers rode into an ambush. A bullet mortally wounded Howard, another hit Hardwick in the leg, and a third grazed Sitter's head. Chico Cano escaped, vowing "he would not be satisfied until he got Joe Sitter's scalp."[4]

Two years later, in May 1915, Cano laid a clever trap. He had a report circulated in Valentine, Sitter's headquarters, that smuggled horses had been sighted near Pilares. Sitter rose to the bait, leading a posse of four on the thirty-mile ride to Pilares. Besides another customs officer, Charles Craighead, Sitter had enlisted three of Captain Fox's Rangers based at Valentine—Harry C. Trollinger, A. P. "Sug" Cummings, and Eugene B. Hulen. Trollinger was a four-year veteran, but Cummings and Hulen had enlisted only a few weeks earlier and lacked any law enforcement experience. Hulen owed his appointment to his politically powerful brother, railroad executive John A. Hulen, who had been adjutant general in 1902–7 and would distinguish himself in the coming European war.

The group made camp on the night of May 23, 1915, at a water hole five miles from the Rio Grande near Pilares. During the night they heard horses passing and Mexicans talking. The next morning the officers picked up a trail of horses, distinctly (and deliberately) marked by trailing ropes, leading into a box canyon. Hiding their pack mules, the men followed the trail on horseback. Despite worries of a trap voiced by his subordinates, Sitter boldly led them into the canyon. With Hulen he rode to a hilltop to scan the broken terrain while sending the other three scouting up a ravine on the canyon floor.

With Cummings in the lead and Craighead and Trollinger following, the men had ridden only a short distance when they spurred their mounts to the lip of the ravine. A fusillade of rifle fire cut the air around them and tore up the ground. Hastily dismounting, they tumbled back into the ravine, then ran toward a large rock for cover. A burst of fire from behind the rock turned them back to the ravine. On a nearby hilltop they spotted Sitter and Hulen frantically waving them back down the ravine. As they raced in retreat, their comrades above provided covering fire. Now afoot, the three made their way back to the mules, unpacked them, and rode bareback in a vain attempt to unite with Sitter and Hulen. Finally they abandoned the effort and headed for the McGee ranch. They knew their companions were still mounted, they later explained, and knew from the gunfire they were still fighting and could probably free themselves from the trap.

At the McGee ranch, a Mexican vaquero bore a message to the ranch of John Pool, who drove his car to the Lucas Brite ranch and telephoned the news to Marfa. A posse of eleven customs officers and Rangers reached the Pool ranch by auto that night. The next morning's search disclosed Sitter and Hulen in their hilltop position. Sitter had at least ten bullet holes in him, and his skull had been smashed with rocks. Hulen's body was in like condition. Save for Sitter's dead horse, all the arms, equipment, and clothing had been carried away. Subsequent inquiry identified the assailants as thirty to forty bandits, including Chico, José, and Manuel Cano.[5]

Chico Cano had his revenge on Joe Sitter, but a cloud of suspicion quickly fell on the three survivors. In leaving the battleground, had they cowardly abandoned their fellow officers to a certain fate? Adjutant General Hutchings ordered Fox to make a thorough investigation. As the captain had great difficulty putting any words to paper in a coherent sequence, he probably made this report orally, as he was in Hutchings's Austin office on June 8. Their conclusion may be inferred from the discharge of Cummings and Trollinger on June 18. Thoroughly humiliated, Trollinger appealed to Governor Ferguson, who advised General

Hutchings that he thought the Ranger did not deserve such censure. On October 18, 1915, Fox reinstated Trollinger in Company B.[6]

LIKE SAN ANTONIO, El Paso hosted a nest of Mexican plotters, failed revolutionists preparing for another grab at power. Among the most prominent was Pascual Orozco, former Huertista who had taken refuge in El Paso after the collapse of the Huerta regime in August 1914. Orozco's prospects brightened in 1915 when Huerta, in Spanish exile, received offers of money and munitions from German agents hoping to distract American attention from the war in Europe. Stirred by visions of a well-financed invasion led by Huerta and Orozco, the so-called El Paso group made frantic preparations. From the moment Huerta set foot ashore in New York, federal agents kept him under constant watch. On June 27, 1915, when he and Oroszco joined at trainside in tiny Newman, New Mexico, the agents pounced. Both men wound up as guests of the U.S. Army at Fort Bliss.

Free on bail while federal and state authorities argued over what to do with the two celebrities, on July 3 Orozco shook off his watchers and vanished from El Paso. Alerted, Fox's Rangers met every train stopping at Valentine but caught no sight of the fugitive. Army patrols combed the deserts around El Paso and in the upper Big Bend. Meantime, Orozco and four of his top officers made their way south toward Mexico. On August 28 they took over Dick Love's ranch in the Eagle Mountains southwest of Van Horn. Scared off by some of Love's cowboys, the gang hurried south as a Culberson County posse formed in Van Horn and took up the pursuit of what all regarded as simply another Mexican bandit gang. At dawn of August 30 they discovered the quarry camped in a canyon of the Van Horn Mountains, only nine miles from the Rio Grande. Shouting for their surrender, the possemen charged down the slope. Surprised, the Mexicans opened a ragged fire. The attackers took positions to return the fire. For twenty minutes the two sides shot at each other, until all five of the Mexicans had fallen dead. Only then did someone observe that one of the five looked like Pascual Orozco.

Once confirmed, the report of Orozco's death made headlines in both Mexico and the United States. To Mexicans of all factions in both countries, he became an instant martyr, "assassinated" by Texas Rangers who made no effort to take him prisoner. Angry protests swept El Paso, San Antonio, the lower Rio Grande Valley, and the Big Bend. Citizens called for more soldiers and Rangers to douse the rage and prevent violence. In reality, the posse had consisted of about a dozen men: the sheriff of Culberson County, Love's cowboys, customs officers, and stockmen association inspectors. Not a single Texas Ranger participated. Yet to this day Orozco and his companions are regarded has having been "rangered."[7]

MORE THAN THE SEDICIOSOS of South Texas, the Big Bend raiders deserved the label "bandit." Captain Fox's Rangers did almost nothing to prevent their ravaging sweeps. Fifteen Rangers and a handful of river guards and sheriff's deputies lacked the numbers to anticipate and head off incursions. Individual Rangers worked closely with stockmen but accomplished little beyond day after day in the saddle. Fox himself seems to have occupied himself chiefly with riding railroad coaches hither and yon but disclosing little else. On June 19, 1916, he reported from Marfa, "Everything quite [he always got this word wrong] here a lot of excitement but nothing has happened."[8]

Only a month earlier plenty had happened, and it dramatized how thoroughly the Big Bend's defense relied on the U.S. cavalry. On May 5, 1916, a gang of eighty bandits crossed the Rio Grande at San Vicente. Most fell on Glenn Springs, the rest on Boquillas. Nestled amid southern foothills of the Chisos Mountains near the bottom of the Big Bend, Glenn Springs consisted of a candelilla wax factory, a village of fifty Mexican workers, a store, and nine soldiers quartered in tents and an adobe barracks with a sheet-iron roof covered, for coolness, with dried candelilla plants and other desert vegetation. Boquillas—one town of this name on the Texas side, the other on the Mexican side—lived off an American-owned silver mine in Mexico. An aerial tramway conveyed the ore across the river for transport on pack mules to the railroad at Marathon. Jesse Deemer operated a store that provided goods to workers on both sides of the river.

Glenn Springs had settled into a pitch darkness before midnight of May 5 when seventy-five bandits struck. Seven soldiers in the barracks fought valiantly as the other two, after trying to join their comrades, slipped quietly into the hills. The battle raged for three hours, with the bandits taking casualties. Then a blazing torch made of rags saturated in kerosene landed on the barracks roof, which exploded in flames and drove the soldiers from their defenses. Three were shot dead, but the other four, three severely burned, found refuge in the dark hills, where they joined their two comrades and two civilians. Below, seven-year-old Tommy Compton, son of the store owner, was the final casualty when struck in the forehead by a bullet. The raiders spent the night looting the store and other buildings and loading pack mules. At dawn they pulled out.

The other bandits reached Deemer's store about 10:00 AM on May 6. Deemer offered no resistance, and the raiders, soon joined by some from Glenn Springs, methodically packed and loaded the contents of the store. With Deemer and his assistant as prisoners, they crossed into Mexico, robbed the office of the silver mine, and proceeded with seven more prisoners.

Glenn Springs and Boquillas were stunning forays. As soon as he learned of the raids, General Funston ordered Major George T. Langhorne to lead two troops of cavalry from Fort Bliss in pursuit of the bandits, crossing into Mexico if necessary. At the same time he started another command from Fort Clark, east of the Big Bend. Langhorne detrained at Marathon and marched directly south to Boquillas. Captain Fox of the Rangers reached Glenn Springs on May 10, but if he continued with or even saw Langhorne he did not report it. The cavalry crossed the Rio Grande at Boquillas on May 11 and for the next sixteen days ranged as far as one hundred miles to the south in a largely fruitless search for the bandits. When he returned, however, Langhorne could boast the captives freed, the plunder recovered, several bandits killed and wounded, and the rest dispersed.[9]

Against this background, hardly two weeks later, Captain Fox reported all "quite," "nothing has happened."

ON APRIL 6, 1917, the United States declared war on the Central Powers and plunged into World War I. In Austin the state legislature sat in regular session. The war afforded political cover for Senator Claude Hudspeth, who represented most of West Texas, to respond to a delegation of constituents that assembled in his capitol office. The U.S. Army had not ended the depredations of Mexican bandits, and they wanted a law to increase the Ranger Force. Citing the threat to the border incited by German propaganda, Hudspeth introduced legislation to create a "Ranger Home Guard" of one thousand men, raise Ranger salaries, and appropriate $250,000 to carry out its provisions. Governor Ferguson warmly embraced the bill as a war measure.

Legislator José T. Canales, representing the Brownsville district, opposed the bill. Rangers had committed terrible atrocities on Mexicans during the "bandit war" of 1915, and their behavior had not improved. He wanted no more Rangers on the state payroll. Ferguson summoned Canales to his office, where they were joined by South Texas political boss Jim Wells. The governor appealed to Canales's patriotism and urged him to back the legislation. Canales replied by describing the lawless deeds the Rangers continued to inflict on Mexicans. "I will give you my word of honor," Ferguson answered, that he would remove any Ranger Canales named as not "a humane and good officer." Canales shook the governor's hand and declared that, on that appeal, "I am going over there and champion that bill." The legislature passed the Hudspeth bill on May 25, 1917, to take effect in ninety days.[10]

Either Ferguson had changed his mind about the Rangers, or he still took refuge in the dissembling that had cloaked his understanding with Captain Ransom in 1915. Whether sincere or not, Ferguson could not fulfill his promise. Only a week after the law took effect on August 18, 1917, the House voted to impeach him. In a battle over his power to fire faculty members of the University of Texas, he had lost his temper and vetoed the school's entire appropriation. In the midst of this

55

controversy, scandals both old and new had risen to haunt him with allegations of misappropriation and embezzlement of state funds. On September 24 the Senate found him guilty of impeachable offenses. Lieutenant Governor William P. Hobby moved into the governor's office.[11]

A youthful thirty-nine and a former journalist, Hobby desperately wanted to be elected governor in his own right, but his first months proved politically shaky as he strove to win the support of the drys in the prohibition controversy. Although not of high priority, the Ranger issue called on his attention. Dismissing the veteran Henry Hutchings, Hobby named James A. Harley adjutant general only four days after taking office. Thirty-four in 1917, Harley had been a Seguin lawyer before elected to the state senate in 1912. Here he cemented his relationship with the presiding officer, Lieutenant Governor Hobby. Also, Harley served briefly as a National Guard officer on the border. He brought no other military experience to his new post, even though the Texas Guard prepared to fight in Europe.[12]

For Harley, of even greater urgency was the election of William P. Hobby as governor, which meant winning the Democratic primary on July 27, 1918. Hobby gained strength when he bowed to dry demands for a special session of the legislature to consider prohibition and other measures, but he then confronted the political resurrection of James E. Ferguson. Although he had been barred by the Senate from ever holding public office in Texas, the wily politico brushed that off as a technicality and entered the race for the Democratic nomination. As always, Ferguson commanded strong support of the poor, especially tenant farmers. Despite his bright reformist façade, Hobby fought back with every tool of incumbency, including the Texas Rangers. Not even Colquitt and Ferguson had so radically politicized the Ranger Force.[13]

Harley's political operative was William M. Hanson. Fifty-two in 1918, fair haired and light complexioned, a strapping six and a half feet tall, he had served for years as a U.S. marshal on the Texas border, then launched successful oil and agricultural ventures in Mexico. After the downfall of Díaz, he dabbled in revolutionary politics until 1914, when the revolution destroyed his estate and all his property. Carranza ordered him before a firing squad as a Huertista spy, but friends got him expelled instead. Hanson returned to Texas with a seething hatred of Carranza and a resolve to do all in his power to prod the United States into a war with Mexico. He knew Mexico and the border as few others did, and he seemed an ideal addition to the adjutant general's staff. Appointed "Inspector" with the rank of captain in January 1918, he kept an office in San Antonio and, after penning a series of reports on conditions in Mexico, devoted himself largely to promoting the Hobby candidacy.[14]

For new and serving captains alike, loyalty to Hobby became the acid test. Likewise, sergeants and privates were expected to promote the Hobby candidacy. Special Rangers multiplied as Hobby appointed men of dubious need to carry a gun and arrest law-breakers, such as editors, executives, and bankers.

As BANDIT DEPREDATIONS continued to plague the Big Bend, the army moved to cover the area thoroughly. In October 1917 the entire Eighth Cavalry, headed by Colonel George T. Langhorne, took station in the troubled area. Langhorne commanded the Big Bend District from headquarters in Marfa. "We of the Eighth considered him the finest officer in the entire army," recalled one of his troopers. Langhorne placed troops at eleven valley towns from Boquillas on the east to Candelaria on the west and retained others in the railroad towns.

After taking office in September 1917, Governor Hobby used the authority of the Ranger Home Guard law to create new companies. By January 1918 he had eleven in service, which of course offered the patronage of more captains and more men. At full strength (captain, sergeant, and fourteen privates per company), the Ranger Force would have numbered about 175, double the number Harley inherited in September. Because some of the companies had only begun to recruit, however, the number actually in service fell far short of this figure.

Monroe Fox continued to oversee most of the Big Bend from Marfa. His men occasionally rode with military patrols but appear to have accomplished little—not enough, at least, to gain much recognition in either Ranger or military records. "Although they were often involved in the border conflict," recalled a cavalry trooper, "the Rangers always got back to safe inland towns in a hurry, and never did they ride the river."[15]

The lethargy of Fox and his men would soon change dramatically.

LUCAS BRITE OWNED one of the biggest cattle spreads in the Big Bend and had operated it for thirty-three years. The headquarters—ranch house, post office, store, foreman Van Neill's house, and various other structures—lay on a plateau at the foot of Capote Peak, near the edge of the Candelaria Rim, about thirty-five miles southwest of Marfa and twenty south of Valentine. As dawn broke on Christmas Day 1917, the Brites awoke in their Marfa home. But at the ranch about thirty bandits galloped up to the corrals. Neill and his wife and three children were in their home. His father, Sam Neill, and his mother had come to spend Christmas. Sam Neill, an old Ranger and customs inspector, grabbed his rifle and went to the front yard, where he confronted a horseman. "Kill all the gringos," the man shouted. "I shot," declared Neill, "and he didn't, of course, holler no more." The battle was on, and for half an hour the two sides exchanged fire, Sam and his son in the house, the bandits from cover around it. A bullet hit Sam's leg and another grazed his nose, but he and his son continued to fire from the windows.

The bandits sent in a young Mexican boy, a ranch hand who had been milking, to demand surrender. The Neills refused, so the boy went to the nearby home of the postmaster, who crouched with his rifle at a window, and obtained the keys to the store and post office. The firing ended as the bandits plundered the contents of these buildings and rounded up Brite's herd of prime horses. At this time the mail hack from Candelaria topped the rim and fell into the hands of the attackers. They killed the two Mexican passengers but escorted driver Mickey Welch and his hack to the store. After they had finished packing the loot, they took Welch inside, hanged him to a rafter, slit his throat, and gutted his torso.

James Cobb, who lived with his family a mile and a half distant, heard the firing and drove his Ford close enough to the ranch to see what was happening, then returned to get his family and speed to the Kennersley ranch twelves miles to the east. From there, about 11:00 AM, he telephoned Lucas Brite in Marfa, who in turn called Colonel Langhorne, the sheriff, the Rangers, and the customs officers.

In less than half an hour Langhorne had a procession of autos loaded with cavalrymen speeding toward the Brite ranch, preceded by a civil posse that included three of Fox's Rangers. The rescuers reached their destination just as the bandit gang began to descend the rough trail down the Candelaria Rim. They got close enough to shoot several of the quarry and make them drop much of the loot. But the autos could not get down the steep road, and because Brite's horses had been taken, Langhorne had to wait until mounted cavalry came from Valentine.

Alerting his troops at Ruidosa by Signal Corps line, Langhorne led his motley column down the rim during Christmas night. The next afternoon the troops from Ruidosa and other stations crossed the Rio Grande at Los Fresnos and engaged the fleeing bandits in a running fight. Before they scattered into the mountains, ten had been killed and more of the Brite goods recovered. The troopers recrossed the river to the American side.

Who these bandits were prompted much speculation. The one Sam Neill shot wore a Carranzista uniform jacket, but some contended, credibly, that Pancho Villa had ordered the raid and garbed some of the raiders to look like Carranzistas. Villa still controlled the Mexican side of the Big Bend, and he still fumed at American support of Carranza.[16]

Although Captain Fox apparently did not take part in the pursuit of the Brite ranch raiders, he seems to have plotted some form of retaliation. On December 29, 1917, after wishing the Ranger quartermaster in Austin a happy New Year, he asked that six Mauser rifles and a supply of rifle and pistol cartridges be sent him by express. "You should come out and see the circus show when we do get started," he quipped.[17]

FOX HIMSELF DID NOT attend the circus, but he ordered it, as he later conceded. The objective was Porvenir, a mountain-girt village of about 140 people in the Rio Grande Valley about thirty miles above Candelaria and thirty south of Valentine. The residents eked out a bare subsistence by farming and tending goats and cattle. The men often held wage jobs in the railroad towns. Only one Anglo, John Bailey, lived in Porvenir with his Mexican wife. Another Anglo, well-educated Harry Warren, lived a mile from the town and taught the school.

The ranchers above the rim, led by John Pool, regarded Porvenir as a nest of bandits who scouted for and guided the raiders from across the river. Captain Henry H. Anderson's cavalry troopers at the Evetts ranch, twelve miles upriver, knew better. They scouted the valley almost daily and bought provisions from the townspeople. Nevertheless, the ranchers convinced Captain Fox that Porvenir bore heavy responsibility for the Brite ranch raid, and Fox dispatched Bud Weaver and seven Rangers to make an example of the community.[18]

The composition of this squad gives the lie to the widespread image of the career Texas Ranger. Leadership went to Bud Weaver, forty-three, with a year and a half as a Ranger and no prior law enforcement experience. The other seven ran the gamut from nineteen to thirty-nine years of age. At the time of their enlistment, six named their occupation as cowboy, stockman, or ranchman (i.e., cowboy), one as farmer, and one as laborer (Weaver). Two had been Rangers for three years, one for two years, three for one year and four months, and two for four months. As a whole, they hardly qualified as veterans or professional lawmen. In the old days, Captain Hughes would not have entrusted any important mission to such a group. He would have gone in command himself.[19]

With John Pool and a contingent of fellow cattlemen, Weaver and his men descended on Porvenir at midnight on January 26, 1918. Turning the people out of their rude dwellings, mostly *jacales* of poles and mud, they lined up the men and unsuccessfully searched them for arms. Some scoured the homes and came up with two rifles, a shotgun, and a holstered pistol belonging to John Bailey. The Rangers arrested three men, said to be wearing shoes taken from the Brite store, and escorted them to a camp in the mountains. After two days of interrogation about the Brite raid, the three were turned loose.

The next afternoon, January 28, the Rangers, with Pool and three fellow ranchmen, turned up at Captain Anderson's camp bearing orders from Colonel Langhorne to aid them in any way possible. Weaver explained that they wanted soldiers to surround Porvenir while the Rangers searched the village for firearms and, they had reason to believe, Chico Cano. Anderson's experience convinced him of Porvenir's innocence in the Brite raid and any other wrongdoing and certainly of harboring Chico Cano. Moreover, the Rangers acted nervous and possibly somewhat affected by whiskey, which they periodically imbibed on the ride to Porvenir. Anderson telephoned Marfa to protest, but Langhorne told him to follow orders.[20]

Once again, about midnight on January 28, invaders swept into Porvenir. While the soldiers established a perimeter around the town, the Rangers and ranchmen, their faces masked with large bandanas, went from house to house turning out the men. The lawmen herded their prisoners down the road about a quarter of a mile and halted. Weaver informed Captain Anderson that he wanted to question the villagers in their own tongue and that the soldiers could return to their camp. They walked to their horses, mounted, and had ridden only a short distance when they heard gunfire at the village. After a moment of indecision, Anderson turned his troopers back to Porvenir. There they discovered fifteen men, including two teenagers, lying dead, their bodies riddled with bullets and each with a bullet in the head. Only a few old men had been spared. The Rangers had departed.[21]

The executioners told another story. Preparing to question the prisoners, they had suddenly been targeted by a volley from brush along the riverbank. The noise stampeded their horses. They fell to the ground and shot back, silencing the firing. They then "rounded up" the Porvenir dwellings, where they found abundant booty from the Brite store, together with the saddle of Ranger Trollinger, abandoned when Chico Cano killed Joe Sitter and Gene Hulen. By then they had recovered their horses, and they rode to the Fitzgerald ranch. They did not return to Porvenir because of the fear of a nighttime ambush. They did not know how many if any Mexicans had been killed until the next day, when Colonel Langhorne, having heard from Captain Anderson, notified Captain Fox. By implication, any dead Mexicans died in the exchange of fire between the lawmen and their assailants.[22]

Agitated by Harry Warren, the issue made news in the United States. To back his claims, on February 2 he induced the mayor of Ojinaga to depose seven men who had either been present or had firsthand knowledge. All agreed with Warren's telling of what had happened, and all denied that anyone from Porvenir had been at the Brite ranch or that the town contained any of the merchandise stolen from the Brite store. The Ojinaga officials passed their findings upwards, and at length the Carranza government lodged a protest in Washington. The State Department asked the army to investigate.[23]

Still, the truth surfaced with difficulty. Captain Anderson reported finding slain bodies but said nothing about the role of his troops. Colonel Langhorne adopted the Ranger interpretation until the official army investigation assembled the affidavits of eight widows and certified the validity of Warren's account. By this time, in May 1918, the adjutant general had faced up to the truth.[24]

Captain Fox failed to report Porvenir for three weeks, although on January 31 he asked the quartermaster in Austin for more Winchester cartridges, "as we might run out." His men, he said, had been using a great many lately. When swelling publicity finally forced a report on February 18, Fox recounted the usual cover-up version.[25]

The strangest "investigation," if such indeed it was, took place only seven days after the Porvenir massacre. Captain William M. Hanson, who had been Harley's "Special Investigator" for less than a week, arrived in Marfa on February 6. His report, written in San Antonio two days later, made no reference, direct or indirect, to Porvenir. It was a lengthy analysis of the relative strength of the Hobby and Ferguson campaigns in the Big Bend. It discussed the political views of Captain Fox and found him not only loyal to Hobby but active in promoting his candidacy. Hanson met with leading stockmen (including one who had been a Porvenir executioner) and declared them not only strong backers of Captain Fox but likely to advance the Hobby campaign.[26]

62

Hanson steadily maintained that he had investigated Porvenir, and he seems to have wanted this document regarded as the report. As the content makes clear, however, he went to Marfa for a familiarization visit, to take the measure of Fox's political leanings, and to stir support for Hobby. He probably heard little or nothing of Porvenir even after arriving in Marfa. Even a serious inquiry at this early day could not have turned up enough sound evidence to counter the version Fox submitted on February 18. Hanson's report addressed the true purpose of his trip.

By May 1918, however, when the army confirmed Warren's charges, General Harley had to concede their veracity. Worse, something had to be done because the publicity was harming the Hobby campaign, due to climax in the Democratic primary in late July. On May 27 Harley summoned Fox to Austin and told him his company would be disbanded and the Porvenir Rangers discharged. "I don't think I am getting a fair deal," Fox protested, and returned to Marfa. On June 4 he received the order disbanding Company B effective June 8. The order discharged the five Porvenir Rangers remaining in the company (the other three had resigned) and transferred the rest to Captain Jerry Gray's Company D, which would replace Fox's company at Marfa. On June 11 Fox wrote a blistering letter of resignation to Hobby, accusing him of purely political motives. If any wrongs were done, he said, he should have been discharged and the fate of his Rangers submitted to the grand jury of Presidio County. Harley replied on July 3 denying that politics had anything to do with the issue and that Hobby had any part in disbanding the company—both flagrant untruths. By arresting, disarming, and then killing fifteen Mexicans, Rangers had constituted themselves judge, jury, and executioners. "The laws and Constitution of this State," he declared, "must be superior to the will of any peace officer." A ringing affirmation of high principle, the letter sounded a refrain contrary to the record established by the Rangers ever since Captain Ransom went to South Texas. Harley had it published widely in Texas newspapers.[27]

The decisive move against the perpetrators of the Porvenir massacre doubtless added some weight to the Hobby candidacy, but on other and more compelling issues he went on to an overwhelming primary victory against Ferguson.

Years later, "as he hoisted a stein of beer" in an Austin saloon, Fox gave his recollection of the fight near Candelaria. He and eight Rangers and six stockmen had cornered Cano's gang in the river bottom. "We got them where they couldn't get away," Fox recounted. "We'd wait for a bandit to reveal his position and then we'd let him have it. Only a few of the gang escaped . . . for when the scrap was over we found sixteen bodies in the brush." A big scandal blew up, but an investigation justified the Rangers and the stockmen.[28]

EDWIN W. NEVILL, part of a family of oldtime Rangers, had run cattle in the Big Bend as long as Luke Brite and knew it as well. His lower ranch, a two-room cabin of cottonwood logs, stood in the Rio Grande Valley six miles above Porvenir and his more substantial upper ranch six miles farther up the river. Nevill's wife and three youngsters lived in Van Horn, where the latter could attend school. Ed and his eighteen-year-old son Glenn occupied the lower ranch while weaning calves from cows. A Mexican family lived in one of the rooms of the cabin, the man to help in ranch work, his wife to keep house and cook. They had three small children.

On March 25, 1918, hardly two months after the Porvenir massacre, Nevill was in Van Horn loading his big truck with supplies when soldiers told him they had been alerted by the valley stations to the possibility of an impending raid. He left at once, arriving at the lower ranch late in the afternoon. About 9:00 PM, during supper, he and his son heard hoofbeats outside. They grabbed rifles just as a burst of gunfire shredded the door. Seventeen Mexicans took cover at the outbuildings and opened a hot fire. Ed and Glenn returned the fire until bullets singing through the room decided them to try to escape in the outside darkness. Followed by Glenn, Ed bolted from the porch and ran toward a ditch 250 yards distant. Bullets took off his hat and three times knocked his rifle from his hand, but he made it. As he searched the brush for Glenn, the attackers ransacked his house and, shortly after midnight, rode away.

The Mexican ranch hand had escaped at the first fire and within six miles met a cavalry patrol chasing the rumors of another raid. A messenger bore the news to Captain Anderson's camp at Evetts ranch, and by 3:30 AM he and his troop had reached the Nevill ranch. Glenn lay near the front door, riddled with bullets and his head bludgeoned. He died three hours later. The Mexican woman sat propped against the wall in her room, a bullet in the head and another in the chest. A stick had been rammed up her vagina, and a severed breast lay on either side—possibly a warning to Mexicans who consorted with Anglos. The children had witnessed the barbarity but had not been otherwise harmed.

Colonel Langhorne at once dispatched Anderson with his and another cavalry troop, backed by a mule pack train, in pursuit. They crossed the Rio Grande at Pilares and followed the bandit trail for seventy miles on the Mexican side, until it doubled back to Pilares, Mexico. Here the fugitives set up an ambush, but Anderson charged into the town and fought a desperate battle with them and other Pilares residents. After killing ten and flushing the rest, Anderson's men recovered Nevill's horses and other plunder, and recrossed the Rio Grande.[29]

Although Nevill had always got along well with his Mexican neighbors, he had borne the brunt of an angry retaliation for the Porvenir massacre. Unlike Brite, he had little to steal, but his ranch offered an easily accessible target. Moreover, the army eventually tied many kin of the Porvenir victims to the Nevill raid.

While Porvenir simmered in controversy and Fox continued to mismanage Company B, the big raids on the ranches of the well-liked Brite and Nevill prompted public action. On April 12, 1918, three hundred stockmen and their families gathered in Van Horn to talk about the raids. Colonel Langhorne attended. More significantly, state senator Claude Hudspeth, now a candidate for the U.S. House of Representatives, and Richard Dudley, candidate to succeed Hudspeth in the state senate, joined the group. Colonel Langhorne admitted that his soldiers did not know the rough country and its trails well enough to guarantee security and welcomed any help he could get. The angry ranchers demanded that the state raise a new company of Rangers who did know the country and its inhabitants. Hudspeth and Dudley journeyed to Austin and urged Governor Hobby to authorize such a company at once. Facing a heated primary race with Jim Ferguson, Hobby promptly complied.

The result was Company N, Ranger Force, also called the "Hudspeth Rangers" and the "Cow-boy Border Patrol." The organizers of this measure had no trouble signing up sixteen recruits, mainly their own cowboys, because the governor had promised to pay them $110 per month, $70 more than a regular Ranger received. One of the organizers, moreover, Dick Love, was indicted for buying oats known to have been stolen from the army and accused, with his brother, of stirring up sympathy for Ed Nevill as a cover for big salaries for an unneeded force.

Despite the clearly political drive behind the Hudspeth Rangers, however, they performed well. Not only did they know the country and the Mexicans, they served under an exceptionally competent captain, D. G. Knight. He had been one of Hughes's Rangers in 1912–14 and before that sheriff of Presidio County for fourteen years. Nearing sixty, he retained his rugged outdoor build and led in the Hughes tradition. Posting his men at strategic points between Candelaria and Fort Hancock, he kept in touch with them and with Colonel Langhorne by telephone each day. The combination of Hudspeth Rangers and the army kept the Big Bend quiet all summer. By August, however, citing a tight budget, Harley notified Knight that Company N would be disbanded at the end of the month. Less than a month earlier, of course, Hobby had won the Democratic primary.[30]

MEXICAN BANDITRY, especially in the Big Bend region, would continue into the 1920s. The United States would continue to experience stormy relations with Mexico. But the Mexican revolutionary decade ended in 1920. On May 21 Venustiano Carranza fell to an assassin's bullet. On July 29 Pancho Villa laid down his arms, submitted to President-elect Alvaro Obregón, and went into a retirement destined also to end in assassination.

For the Texas Rangers, one era had closed as another opened.

[4]

Austin, 1918–1919

JOSÉ TOMÁS CANALES represented the Brownsville district in the lower house of the Texas legislature. He enjoyed close ties to political boss James B. Wells but harbored a streak of independence that sometimes overrode his loyalty to Wells. Born in 1877 into the landed Spanish aristocracy of South Texas, "J. T." had risen in life through a variety of experiences, both Mexican and Anglo. At sixteen he had abandoned his Catholic upbringing for a lifelong devotion to Presbyterianism. When he followed the railroad to Brownsville in 1903, he held a law degree from the University of Michigan. Later he married an Anglo and adopted her Anglo niece. Honest, idealistic, moral, emotional, intensely patriotic as both American and Texan, well educated in American schools, active in the predominately Anglo political world of Jim Wells, he still cherished his ethnic heritage, his extended Mexican American family, and his paternalistic relations with the oppressed majority of South Texas. His law partnership often defended humble Tejanos who had tangled with the law.

Canales also prized the Texas Rangers. As a youth he worked with them on the family's sprawling ranch southwest of Corpus Christi. He knew and admired Captains John R. Hughes and John H. Rogers and Sergeant Will Wright. The Rangers helped protect the family cattle herds and those of the neighboring King Ranch, whose managers and vaqueros J. T. knew as friends. He regarded the Ranger Force as essential to law enforcement in South Texas.[1]

Canales lamented the occasional brutality of these early Rangers toward Mexicans. The Ranger misconduct of the Ferguson regime, however, outraged him. The wholesale "evaporation" of Mexicans by Captain Henry L. Ransom's company during the "bandit war" of 1915 drew J. T.'s attention to the declining character of the force and its leadership, and led him in early 1917 to gain Governor Ferguson's "word of honor" to clean house. Ferguson's impeachment intervened, although he probably would not have made good on his promise anyway. Canales respected Governor William P. Hobby, elevated from lieutenant governor after Ferguson's downfall, as a fellow progressive and advocate of clean government, and vigorously supported his campaign for election in his own right. To Hobby Canales turned for assurances of reform in the Ranger Force.

Early in March 1918, on the eve of the special legislative session Hobby called at the behest of the drys, Canales met in the governor's office with Hobby, Adjutant General James A. Harley, Captain William M. Hanson, and Francisco A. Chapa, the perennial gubernatorial advisor on behalf of the Tejano voters. For the first time, J. T. learned that Hanson had been named "Special Investigator" and placed in charge of all Ranger operations. The Brownsville representative then launched into a severe critique of the quality and performance of the Ranger Force, setting forth instances of cruel and unlawful treatment of Mexicans, including the executions that began with Captain Ransom in 1915.

Hobby had already explained his Ranger policy in a January letter to Chapa, pledging that "the type of an old time ranger known as the 'gun man' will be eliminated under my administration, and only men who are peaceful and law abiding, and yet who are firm, will be employed in the service." Against this background Harley and Hanson patiently heard

Canales out. Hanson replied that he would correct the evils. After the meeting, he took Canales aside and asked him to bring whatever complaints he had directly to him, and they would be taken care of.

Canales had heard almost the same words from Governor Ferguson a year earlier and had believed them. Trusting that the forthright Hobby would live up to his word, J. T. hit the campaign trail in his behalf.[2]

DESPITE THE GOVERNOR'S fine words, the Ranger Force contained many of the type of man he vowed to get rid of. The adjutant general inaugurated what Captain Hanson broadcast widely as the new "Harley policy." It seems not to have been committed to paper until the legislative investigation of 1919, presumably the undated "Rules Governing Texas Rangers" that he inserted into the record. They described an ideal lawman, a gentleman well versed in the law and always acting strictly according to law, treating all persons with courtesy and respect, careful to bring no reproach on himself or the force, neatly and inconspicuously attired, promoting good fellowship among comrades, and abstaining from swearing, drinking, and gambling. Few of any rank met that standard or even tried.[3]

On March 28, 1918, Captain Hanson met with civic leaders in Brownsville to explain the Harley policy. They warmly embraced it but expressed their emphatic opposition to Captain Ransom, who in any event had been reassigned to Sweetwater. They promised to drop all opposition to the Ranger Force and cooperate with the new captain, Charles F. Stevens. "I feel I have healed the breach perfectly," Hanson boasted. "All we have to do now is to make good."[4]

Making good with Captain Stevens proved difficult.

A HOBBY APPOINTEE lacking Ranger experience but who described his occupation as "peace officer," Stevens was forty-seven, with black hair and medium build, when named a captain in November 1917. Rigid, righteous, full of certitude and self-esteem, he lacked any quality to equip him as peacemaker. He promoted the Hobby campaign more vigorously than the Harley policy, to which he gave only lip service. He worked his Rangers hard but paid no attention to how they treated Mexicans. This set off conflict with Sheriff W. T. Vann. Angrily, the captain withheld cooperation with Vann's department, then cut off all communication, refusing to answer letters or speak to him, even on the telephone.[5]

The conflict escalated when Stevens's Rangers burst into the homes of Mexican suspects and seized firearms. This pattern reverberated in Austin and brought Hanson back to Brownsville. He sought to set up a meeting between the principals in Jim Wells's home, but Stevens refused to sit in the same room with Vann. So Hanson dropped Vann and met with Wells and Stevens. Wells asked Stevens by what authority he disarmed Mexicans, to which Stevens replied that he did not pretend to have any authority, he just did it. Wells declared that "when you want to come to search my house, I will shoot you between the eyes." "We got pretty warm, and that ended it," according to Wells.[6]

By August, responding to warnings of J. T. Canales that Stevens had set off a Mexican exodus across the Rio Grande that would continue if he were not withdrawn, and with the primary election over, Harley transferred Stevens and his company to Marathon. His replacement was Captain W. W. Taylor. A forty-eight-year-old rancher with ten years service as sheriff of Kimble County, Taylor was named captain on August 16, 1918, just as Stevens transferred. Although doubtless a political appointee, Taylor handled Brownsville with a finesse alien to Stevens.[7]

Stevens was not the only flawed captain. Carroll Bates, K. F. Cunningham, and Jerry Gray, recent Hobby appointees from civil life, had their faults. Captains Fox and Ransom, appointees respectively of Colquitt and Ferguson, also fouled the reputation of the force. But Fox departed in June 1918 in the scandal over Porvenir; and Ransom, spending the night of April 2, 1918, in a Sweetwater hotel, heard a burst of gunfire outside his door, walked into the hallway to investigate, and died in the crossfire of a personal feud.[8]

Incensed at continued Ranger misbehavior, J. T. Canales stepped up his criticism, especially of Hanson. The two had forged a pragmatic political alliance to advance the Hobby campaign in South Texas, where the governor's progressive allies challenged the entrenched bosses, who usually counted on the Mexican vote. For Canales, the shaky cooperation had rested in part on Hobby's promise to reform the Rangers and in part on a genuine affinity for the man and his program.

The Hanson-Canales partnership fell apart even before the election. On October 14, 1918, on a northbound train from Brownsville, Canales and Hanson argued over Ranger conduct. Although they talked of several instances in which Canales believed Hanson had either ignored or whitewashed a Ranger offense, the dispute grew heated when they came to a recent action of the tough but well-regarded Ranger John J. Edds.

Before daybreak on October 6, Edds and two other Rangers "rounded up" the house of Jesús Sánchez on the Saenz ranch near Rio Grande City. They sought his son Alonso as an army deserter, but he was actually only a "slacker" who had avoided the draft by settling in Matamoros. Posting his comrades on guard, Edds entered the fenced backyard and discerned two cots bearing sleeping figures. Carefully examining them, he thought one of the men resembled the descriptions of Alonso Sánchez. Awakened, the man sleepily asked what was wanted. Edds replied that he wanted to talk. According to Edds, the man suddenly sprang at him and seized the barrel of his Winchester. The two wrestled around the yard as Edds almost lost his grip on the rifle. At that moment, he pulled the trigger and sent a bullet into his opponent's groin. As he lay bleeding to death, the other man got up. He identified himself as Zaragoza Sánchez and the dying man as his cousin, Lisandro Muñoz. Alonso Sánchez had crossed from Matamoros for a *baile* but had returned before midnight. Edds had killed the wrong man.[9]

To Edds and Hanson, the Ranger had acted in self-defense. To Canales, he had committed murder or at least manslaughter. The wording of Edds's affidavits alone convicted him, Canales believed, and he challenged Hanson to get the opinion of a judge on the Court of Criminal Appeals. Hanson refused. Leaving a furious Hanson on the coach, a furious Canales got off the train at Kingsville. With the election approaching, Hanson had stalled the investigation of the Muñoz killing to avoid alienating Mexican voters. Only after the powerful Guerra family of Hidalgo County pushed the issue did Hanson begin a tentative probe.[10]

On December 12, 1918, an incident on the streets of Brownsville brought the anger of J. T. Canales to high pitch. Captain Taylor's sergeant, Frank Hamer, stopped Canales. Hamer was a big, muscular man, sometime Ranger and sometime gunman with a reputation for toughness and a record of lethal gun fighting. Hamer attempted to question Canales about an incident involving a Canales kinsman recently apprehended and abused by Rangers. Canales refused to answer. Hamer glared at Canales and spat out, "You are hot-footing it here, between here and Austin and complaining to the governor and the adjutant general about the Rangers, and I am going to tell you if you don't stop that you are going to get hurt." Incredulous, Canales asked Hamer to repeat what he said, which he did. Canales then summoned mechanic Jesse Dennett from his nearby auto garage, repeated Hamer's words, and asked him, with Dennett as witness, whether he had said that. "Yes," answered Hamer and stalked away.[11]

Angry and frightened, Canales dashed off a long and emotional letter to Governor Hobby protesting Hamer's action. Canales blamed "this corrupt Republican intriguer, Hanson," for putting Hamer up to the deed and characterized the force in Brownsville as a "gang of ruffians, who are called State Rangers." Hobby wired in reply that he would investigate and see that justice was done. The task of course fell to Harley, who apologized to Canales and ordered Hamer, whom Hanson had just labeled "the best Ranger in Texas," to leave Canales alone.[12]

After the Hamer affair, Canales began to ponder how to reform the Ranger Force without abolishing it. He wanted Rangers, just not the kind that had prevailed under the Hobby and two previous administrations. The state legislature would convene in January 1919, and Canales would again represent the Brownsville district in the lower house.

TEXANS WERE READY to plunge into the European war even before the U.S. declaration of April 6, 1917. Once war came, they exuded an intense patriotism and demanded unanimous and enthusiastic public support for the soldiers in France and for sacrifice at home. Nearly a million men registered for the draft, and nearly 200,000 served in the armed forces. Two infantry divisions composed largely of the Texas National Guard fought valiantly in France. The large German population of Texas—45,000 immigrants and 172,000 of German descent—felt the sting of suspicion and discrimination. The Ranger Home Guard Act of May 1917 aimed in part at German subversion, propaganda, espionage, and even armed incursions from Mexico.

A year later Governor Hobby, running hard in the Democratic primary, seized on the public mood to promote a bill in the legislature that emerged in late May 1918 as the "Hobby Loyalty Act." The wording was lengthy and elaborate, but essentially it prohibited anyone from speaking or acting disloyally against U.S. participation in the war. The penalty was confinement in the penitentiary for two to twenty-five years. In early June, Adjutant General Harley established the Loyalty Secret Service Department and placed it under Captain Hanson's command. In each of Texas's 252 counties, three "Loyalty Rangers" would be appointed to carry out the provisions of the Hobby Loyalty Act. The Ranger Home Guard Act of May 1917, with its provision for a thousand Rangers, provided the authority.[13]

The Hobby Loyalty Act was not a Texan anomaly. States all over the nation enacted such legislation, as indeed did the federal government. In Texas, however, Hanson quickly recognized the political potential of the Loyalty Rangers and moved to exploit it.

With nearly two months remaining until the primary, he brought pressure to bear on local campaign chairmen to ensure that loyalty and special appointments went only to Hobby backers and that they distributed campaign literature and otherwise worked in behalf of their candidate. After Hobby's victory, such Loyalty Rangers as were recruited either did nothing or worked to root out what they perceived as suspect loyalty.[14]

The loyalty issue burst with a vengeance on Abilene and surrounding counties shortly after the war broke out. A branch of the national Farmers' and Laborers' Protective Association (FLPA), largely German farmers, surfaced in this area and frightened patriotic citizens with its pacifism and "socialistic" goal of forming cooperatives as a defense against capitalist exploitation. Judges and sheriffs flooded first Governor Ferguson and then Governor Hobby with appeals to commission whole squads of local men as special Rangers, and to dispatch extra regular Rangers. Federal agents of the justice department worked with Ranger sergeant Sam McKenzie to gather evidence against the culprits. They were "not only adventurers," declared Judge Joe Burkett, "but are made up of, in most cases, ex-criminals and convicts. Indeed, hard citizens, with damnable designs."[15]

They were no such thing. Fifty were rounded up and hauled into a Fort Worth federal courtroom charged with seditious conspiracy to prevent conscription. Almost all the defendants turned out to be honest, upright citizens guilty of no more than striving to establish marketing and purchasing cooperatives and indulging in intemperate antiwar talk. The jury found all but one innocent, but the public and the Rangers concentrated in Abilene and Sweetwater still looked on them as disloyal, socialistic troublemakers.[16]

A more serious problem associated with the war erupted on the border, as Mexicans fled to Mexico in numbers rivaling the deluge of 1915. Critics of Captain Stevens attributed the exodus to the persecution by his Rangers, especially the unlawful search of homes and seizure of firearms. Others ascribed it to young men of draft age escaping conscription into the U.S. Army.

It was both. Tejano "slackers," averse to fighting for a nation that oppressed them, slipped across the Rio Grande. To make matters worse, German propaganda swept the border communities warning of the government's intent to conscript women as cooks and nurses and even old men as soldiers. As Harley observed, "The Mexican laboring people . . . are very credulous and easily deceived." That disarmament by Rangers furnished another motive became clear when Harley withdrew the feared Captain Stevens and, in September 1918, deployed Francisco Chapa and Captain Hanson to stage a series of speeches assuring the remaining Mexicans that Captain Taylor's men would not mistreat them. Even J. T. Canales shared the speakers' platform. He still clung to Hobby's pledge to clean up the force.[17]

JOSÉ T. CANALES and his wife, Anne, drove their auto into Austin on Sunday night, January 12, 1919. The city vibrated with animated throngs from all over Texas converging on the capital for the regular session of the state legislature, for the inauguration of William P. Hobby as governor in his own right, and for rejoicing over the end of the Great War and the return of the boys from France.

Canales had come several days early to try to persuade General Harley to undertake a genuine reform of the Ranger Force and so avoid a legislative battle that could only harm the Hobby administration. On Monday evening, while he talked with another legislator in the lobby of the Driskill Hotel, in strolled Ranger sergeant Frank Hamer, who had threatened him in Brownsville several weeks earlier. Their eyes locked, and Hamer passed on. Here also Canales encountered General Harley, who asked him to come to his office. They went to the capitol and with Francisco Chapa present discussed Canales's charges against the Rangers. Receiving not even the usual soothing promises of reform, J. T. served notice that he would introduce a reform bill on Wednesday, when the legislature convened. From the capitol, Canales went to the Avenue Hotel. As he talked with other legislators, he again spotted Hamer conspicuously displaying himself. "I took his action as a challenge that I would be intimidated if I would make any charges against these rangers or introduce any law attempting to regulate them," J. T. declared.[18]

The next morning, angry over three years of stonewalling, the continued thuggery of the Rangers, what he viewed as the bad faith of Harley, Hanson, and Chapa, and especially the menace he read into Hamer's apparent stalking, Canales composed what became House Bill 5 when introduced on Wednesday the fifteenth, the first day of the legislative session. It was a modest measure, limiting Ranger strength to the actual number on the eve of the "bandit war" (twenty-four officers and men); setting a higher pay scale; requiring a bond to ensure proper performance of duty; fixing qualifications of age (twenty-five), experience (two years as a peace officer), and character (moral); and requiring certification by a county commissioners court as a "peaceful and law-abiding citizen." To guard against abuse of authority, Rangers must not use violence unless a prisoner resisted, must allow bail, and must promptly relinquish a prisoner to the nearest local officer rather than taking him to the county where the offense occurred—all on penalty of discharge from the force and liability for civil damages under the bail.[19]

The parliamentary maneuvering over the bill sparked passionate debate. Explaining the bill, Canales heatedly charged the Rangers with repeated murders, violent abuse, and unlawful treatment of prisoners. He cited several incidents to back his allegations. Representative Barry Miller seized the initiative as the administration's point man. "No finer page of Texas history has ever been written," he orated, "than the one written by the Rangers of Texas." The Canales bill would cripple them. Opponents wallowed in such rhetoric of Texas chauvinism and summoned the Alamo and San Jacinto to rank with the Texas Rangers. Canales shouted emotional responses full of biblical metaphors.

Then General Harley counterattacked. He called for a full legislative investigation into the conduct of the force, so that the legislature could know whether to "legislate *for* or *against* its existence." For Canales, of course, the issue was never whether to abolish the force, only to abolish unlawful behavior. Also, Harley wanted the inquiry to focus on the "motives that actuate men to make complaint"–i.e., Canales.

Thus the investigation of the Ranger Force stemmed from the request of the adjutant general, not the legislator from Brownsville. Harley also framed the focus of the investigation: to maintain a force or not, and to inquire into the purposes of the unnamed Representative Canales. The joint resolution authorizing the investigation reflected Harley's concept, explicitly the probe of critics, implicitly the retention or elimination of the Ranger Force.[20]

The investigation opened on January 30 in a hearing room on the second floor of the capitol. Representative William Bledsoe of Lubbock presided over a joint committee of three senators and three representatives. The administration had enlisted two powerful men to help defend Harley and the Rangers: Robert E. Lee Knight, a Hobby stalwart and former legislator, and Dayton Moses, attorney for the Southwest Cattle Raisers Association. Over the next two weeks, in twelve days of testimony, the committee heard eighty witnesses. Canales sought to document instances of unlawful and violent Ranger conduct. Knight and Moses, defending Harley and Hanson, fought for preserving the force (a false issue) and tried to convict Canales of opposition to any force as well as to suggest that his attack was grounded in delusion, obsession, and mental unbalance (not only a false issue, but an unseemly personal attack on a respected state legislator).[21]

The daily proceedings revealed the entire cast of characters as inept. All parties blundered clumsily through and beyond the forms of an official inquiry. The chairman, the committee members, and the two "defense attorneys" seemed to have only a foggy notion of their purpose and how to go about it. Their vaguely phrased questions elicited vaguely phrased answers from all but a few witnesses. All witnesses strongly supported the Ranger Force, many defended its conduct, and critics took refuge in circumlocutions designed to avoid direct censure. No one, including Knight, Moses, or Canales, spoke clearly and articulately. Substantive issues drowned in extended debate over the admissibility of contested paths of inquiry or even of clearly relevant issues. A reader ponders fruitlessly the meaning of page after page of halting, cumbersome verbiage. The seventeen hundred pages of transcript provided legislators with little guidance in deciding whether to abolish or reform the Ranger Force, and if to reform, how.

As a basis for proceeding, on January 30 Canales filed six charges designed to demonstrate the validity of his call for reform and reserved the right to submit more at a later date. Ultimately the charges numbered nineteen. He had thrown them together hastily and clearly had not given much thought to whether they could be proved in a legislative forum. By this time no one could argue that Captain Fox's Rangers had not executed fifteen Mexicans at Porvenir on January 28, 1918—certainly the most heinous offense. No charge, however, mentioned the atrocities committed by Captain Ransom and his men during the "bandit war"of 1915. Those details came out in the testimony of Sheriff Vann and others, thus adding weight to the image of Rangers acting as judge, jury, and executioner. Captain Sanders's involvement in the killing of Brownsville policeman Toribio Rodriguez in 1912 was also recalled in pejorative terms.

Had Canales rested his case on the deeds of Fox and Ransom alone, he would have shown that the Ranger Force had spun out of control. But he threw in other charges worded so generally that, although possibly true, could not be unequivocally demonstrated. How could legislators of limited intellect frame questions to bring out whether the Ranger Force contained desperate men whose only qualification was skilled gun fighting? Or that the adjutant general protected Rangers who committed unlawful acts and failed to conduct investigations that would have eliminated notoriously bad men? Or that he used the Rangers to show special favors to political friends of the administration? Or that Captain Hanson pursued all investigations with the aim of whitewashing the Rangers?

Most of the nineteen charges dealt with particular incidents. Canales heaped special venom on four Rangers of Captain Stevens's company in South Texas: John J. Edds, A. P. Locke, John D. Sittre, and George W. Saddler. Edds in particular drew heavy fire. A pugnacious, veteran lawman, protégé of the highly respected Captain William L. Wright, Sergeant Edds drew praise from nearly everyone questioned and compiled a solid record of accomplishment. Whether he was brutal and unlawful as well could be alleged but not proved.

Canales made much of Edds's mistaken killing of Lisandro Muñoz on October 6, 1918, the act that precipitated his break with Hanson. Edds had to admit entering the Sánchez property without a warrant—"I never heard of a warrant for a deserter"—but the evidence of a scuffle over the Ranger's rifle persuaded Captain Wright, local authorities, and a grand jury that Edds, on the verge of being overpowered by the larger man, had pulled the trigger in self-defense. Even so, Canales judged Edds guilty of murder. Understandably, the legislators remained skeptical.[22]

Additional charges spelled out in detail crimes committed by Edds and other Rangers. In any court of law, the evidence Canales presented would have raised enough "reasonable doubt" to clear the accused Rangers. It leaves today's historian to conclude that these offenses may or may not have happened; we cannot know.[23]

A charge that occupied the legislators off and on throughout the hearings centered on the disappearance of Florencio García on April 4, 1918. Captain Stevens had been investigating the repeated theft of stock from the Piper plantation south of Brownsville. Suggestive evidence implicated García, a Piper hand, as the ring leader. Stevens sent Rangers A. P. Locke and George W. Saddler to pursue the investigation. They arrested García, and instead of taking him back to Brownsville escorted him twenty miles northeast to Point Isabel. They claimed they wanted to enlist Ranger John D. Sittre in the interrogation. He was there and spoke fluent Spanish. Questioning, however, elicited no satisfactory answers, and García was lodged for the night in the town jail. The next morning they mounted García on his mule and astride their horses set forth on the road directly to the west. An auto bearing two soldiers and a young civilian followed. In five miles the road forked. The car turned south toward Brownsville while the horsemen continued on the road to San Benito. Within about five hundred yards, at the entrance to the Wait ranch, they halted and resumed the interrogation. García yielded no more than a promise to seek the answers to their questions. They let him go and never saw him again.

More than a month later, in late May 1918, someone discovered human bones in the Wait pasture next to the road where the Rangers said they had freed García. The bones were only part of a body, widely scattered, and bleached white. Members of García's family identified items of clothing at the site as belonging to him. Stevens defended his men but had them arrested for murder in Brownsville and released on bail. One experienced stockman insisted that he had never seen cow bones turn white in a mere few weeks. Speculation centered on a car loaded with Mexicans seen near the Wait ranch at the time of García's supposed release. Perhaps García had been murdered by fellow stock thieves. Perhaps he had simply disappeared into Mexico. Perhaps the pieces of clothing did not belong to the bones. Or perhaps Saddler, Locke, and Sittre had simply "evaporated" Florencio García. If so, two grand juries refused to indict them.[24]

Most of Canales's formal charges ended as inconclusively, although some proved to be pure fabrication or the work of local officers. A few disclosed flagrant Ranger misconduct, especially one in which a Ranger had already been convicted of murder and sent to the penitentiary, another in which Captain Sanders had tried to pistol-whip an attorney at his seat in a Falfurrias courtroom. And whether inconclusive or not, the inquiry into the nineteen charges and others that surfaced incidentally, such as the Ransom executions, traced a continuing theme that validated Canales's basic indictment: the Ranger Force had committed terrible wrongs that could be remedied only by a thorough overhaul.

As if to reinforce the theme, on February 9, at the height of the hearings, four Rangers made sensational headlines. The day before, rookie captain K. F. Cunningham (a Hobby political appointee), in Austin from his headquarters at Eagle Pass, joined with Ranger B. C. Veale, Ranger quartermaster captain Harry Johnston (a Hobby appointee who rarely even showed up at the office), and Tom Mayberry, a special Ranger who guarded Camp Mabry. Imbibing liberally from a quart of whiskey, they drove out to Barton Springs for some pistol practice, then into the hills south of Austin for more shooting and drinking. Somewhere they picked up two women. At the second stop, Cunningham and Veale got into a violent argument and began shooting at each other. A bullet hit Cunningham in the neck, and he sent another into Veale's back, killing him. Harley instantly discharged Cunningham, Johnston, and Mayberry, and an embarrassed committee agreed that the matter need not be pursued further.[25]

The hearings ended on February 13, and five days later the committee submitted its report. The legislators cleared General Harley of all charges and declared him "entitled to the commendation of the Senate and House for the able, efficient, impartial, and fearless manner in which he has discharged the duties placed upon him as the head of the

Ranger Force." Likewise, they acquitted Captain Hanson of all charges and heaped similar praise on him. The Ranger Force should be maintained, they declared, although they conceded the "gross violation of both civil and criminal laws" by some of its members.

In particular, the committee singled out the case of Florencio García, "killed while in custody of three rangers under circumstances that show it to have been murder." The explanation of Saddler, Sittre, and Locke "was wholly unsatisfactory."

As for the killing of Lisandro Muñoz, Sergeant Edds had acted negligently but with no criminal intent. Captain Stevens also came under reproach for unlawful search of homes and confiscation of firearms. In all expressions of censure, however, the committee named no names. More generally, it conceded that "many of the men of the ranger force pride themselves in their reputation of being quick with their guns, and desiring to have the reputation of bad men rather than faithful and efficient officers of the law."

As for reform, the committeemen thought a smaller force, higher pay, and a more centralized organization would yield men of character, responsibility, and integrity, "conservators of the peace and diligent in the enforcement of the laws." They rejected Canales's bid for a bonding measure.

Heaping praise on Harley, Hanson, Knight, and Moses, the committee closed by finding that "Hon. J. T. Canales has been prompted by no improper motives." The *Dallas News* editorialist thought that something of a putdown. "The salient fact is that he proved the existence of a shocking and intolerable condition that demands correction."

A jubilant Harley ignored such sniping. "Committee report all we could ask for," he telegraphed Knight and Moses. "Vindication complete thanks to you." Omitting the second sentence, he sent telegrams to a handful of supporters in South Texas, including Sergeants J. J. Edds and Frank Hamer.[26]

The committee report set off another rancorous debate in the House. Canales brought his original HB 5 out of committee, and the hearing chairman, William Bledsoe, introduced a substitute version representing

Harley's views. Contention over these two bills grew so passionate and personal that it brought Bledsoe and Canales face to face in a near fistfight. In the end the Bledsoe substitute for the original Canales bill won overwhelmingly in both the House and the Senate. Except for raising Ranger pay and setting a limit of seventy-five Rangers, the measure drew largely on existing law and added a few features of mainly cosmetic value. "I do not recognize my child," Canales sadly admitted on the house floor.[27]

EVEN AS THE LEGISLATURE debated the new law during March 1919, Harley moved to improve the image of the Ranger Force. On March 10, declaring the wartime emergency ended, he disbanded three companies, discharging some men (including two captains), and moving some to other companies. He also fired Captain Sanders for the attempted pistol-whipping of an attorney and pressured Captain Stevens to resign, which he refused to do. Captains Cunningham and Johnston, involved in the Austin shooting of February 8, also received discharges. Sergeant Edds had been suspended during the hearings but won reinstatement in March. Sittre had been discharged a week after the hearings, and both Locke and Saddler had resigned before the hearings.[28]

On May 19, 1919, Governor Hobby appointed captains under the new law. Hanson got the newly authorized Headquarters Company in Austin. Of the rest, only Will Wright of Company K and Roy Aldrich (promoted from sergeant) as quartermaster had the competence and character to be good captains. W. M. Ryan, Jerry Gray, J. L. Anders, and Charles Stevens were mediocrities or worse. The list infuriated Claude Hudspeth, now a U.S. congressman. Addressing "Dear Sunny Jim," Hudspeth declared: "I went to Austin and untangled the fangs of Venustiano Canales from around your neck and yet you fired all your best captains, which included my friends." Harley lamely explained that the governor had named the captains, but some of Hudspeth's friends found themselves captains again.[29]

In the wake of the new law, the legislature dealt generously with the Ranger Force. The autumn of 1919 brought not only adequate funding for the coming two years but an end of the Harley-Hanson leadership. Harley stepped down to run unsuccessfully for Congress, then briefly sample the oil and gas boom before settling into a San Antonio law practice. Hanson turned up as chief investigator for the congressional subcommittee of Senator Albert B. Fall, seeking to amass enough evidence against Mexican iniquities to justify the U.S. intervention Hanson had promoted ever since his expulsion from Mexico.

Under the leadership of W. D. Cope, an adjutant general more sensitive to the mission and reputation of the Texas Rangers, the force put the contentious years of the Mexican Revolution behind and entered the 1920s. The legislative hearings and the new law did little to transform the Rangers in the mode sought by J. T. Canales. The exposure of a "shocking and intolerable condition," as the *Dallas News* labeled it, led to greater care in selecting recruits and greater awareness of public opinion. But this remained the chief legacy of the determined and principled drive for meaningful reform launched by Canales.

[5]

Pat Neff's "Battles of Peace," 1921–1925

PAT MORRIS NEFF swore the oath of office as governor of Texas on January 18, 1921. A Waco attorney and former legislator, fifty years of age, his ruggedly handsome looks, energy, and platform oratory gave promise of a successful tenure. He embodied the austere morality of a staunch Baptist, vigorously championed the prohibition of liquor recently embedded in both state and national constitutions, and worked tirelessly for strong law enforcement. His agenda consisted of a long list of progressive reforms he wanted made into law. Hardly any found favor in the legislature, with which he warred throughout his two terms. After he stepped down in 1925, he wrote a book about his governorship. It recounted not only his legislative conflicts but his struggle against crime and vice in the oil boomtowns, against bootleggers and moonshiners, and against labor unions that disrupted commerce and transportation. He titled it *The Battles of Peace*.[1]

For his battles against lawbreakers, Neff turned to the Ranger Force, shaken somewhat by the Canales legislative hearings of 1919 but better for the departure of Adjutant General James Harley and Captain William Hanson. The law enacted on March 31, 1919, after the hearings, authorized four field companies and a headquarters company, for a total of seventy-five officers and men. A salary boost made the force more attractive—captains to $150 a month, sergeants to $100, and privates to $90.[2]

To be adjutant general, Governor Neff named Thomas D. Barton, a short, slim man with a smooth, youthful face who looked out of place among a squad of burly Rangers. He was an Amarillo druggist, a combat veteran of World War I, and a man who thought he might like to be governor some day. He kept a tight leash on the Rangers and often led their raids. A month after his inauguration, Neff appointed the captains. Held over from the Hobby administration were William L. Wright, Quartermaster Roy W. Aldrich, and Jerry Gray, the first two highly able, the last deficient in leadership and judgment. Of the three new appointees, Roy Nichols and Tom Hickman proved capable, A. W. Cunningham mediocre.[3]

Canales had not destroyed the six-shooter culture. Rangers met violence with violence and shot to kill when circumstances seemed to warrant. But the captains, mindful of the embarrassing excesses disclosed by the Canales hearings, kept the worst features of the culture under control. Occasionally a Ranger strayed across the line into unlawful behavior, usually forfeiting his commission as a result, but the atrocities of 1915–18 had been put largely in the past.

Ironically, the politics that had darkened the Ranger image now made possible its recovery. Politics created the climate in which the governor, adjutant general, and most of the captains provided leadership that elevated the effectiveness and reputation of the Rangers. Whatever their shortcomings, Governor Neff valued them, as he made clear at the end of his administration:

> Whether on the open range, in the piney woods, amid the chaparrals, or in the thronging marts of trade, this hero on horseback is the bravest of the brave, and the nerviest of the nervy.... Their work and worth to a Governor in behalf of law enforcement, when he is honestly trying to enforce the law, can scarcely be overestimated. Long live the Texas Rangers![4]

LIKE MOST GOVERNORS, Pat Neff believed in the primacy of local law enforcement. County sheriffs and city police should take the lead in upholding the law. But Neff also understood the limitations under which they labored: politics, corruption, and intimidation of prosecutors and juries by criminals. Where he thought necessary, even over the protest of local authorities, he did not hesitate to send in the Rangers and even the National Guard.

One major influence limited Neff's total dedication to law enforcement: the Ku Klux Klan. The new Klan, not the Klan of Reconstruction times, dated from 1915, but not until after World War I did it tap into national discontent and become a force to be reckoned with. Although ideologically nativist and racist, its main appeal drew on local conditions rather than alien abominations. Industrialization and urbanization underlay a wave of postwar crime and violence and a decline in traditional morality.

The new Klan stood for the rigid law enforcement proclaimed by Governor Neff. It also stood for the restoration of the moral values of Victorian America and, while working in behalf of Neff's own morality, enforced its code with a criminal brutality that contradicted his dedication to law and order.

Coincident with the beginning of Neff's first term, Klan membership spread swiftly through all social classes, not just in Texas but throughout much of the nation. In large numbers, poor farmers and laborers, the middle classes, political and business leaders, and the clergy either joined the hooded order or approved its agenda. Most of the sheriffs, deputies, and policemen in Texas may have held membership or applauded the crusade against malefactors.

In the first months of Neff's tenure the Klan launched a reign of terror destined to last three years. Victims were people who offended the Klan code of morality, from adulterers to bootleggers and moonshiners to attorneys with black or criminal clients. Hooded gangs whipped, tarred, and feathered the culprits, leaving them as examples for public viewing. Peace officers looked the other way or even, under the hood, took part in the savagery.

How warmly the Texas Rangers embraced Klan doctrine and tactics can only be guessed. With the Klan trumpeting its dedication to law enforcement and the governor making it a prime objective of his administration, the movement held appeal. Moreover, Neff never uttered a critical word against the Klan or employed Rangers in cases of Klan violence. Twice, during his absence from the state, Lieutenant Governor T. W. Davidson dispatched Rangers to ferret out hooded floggers. Some Rangers left written evidence of qualified approval, and there are hints that some held membership. As Adjutant General Barton's vigorous role in promoting law enforcement grew more visible and his designs on the governor's office more apparent, the Klan openly backed his candidacy, and some Rangers even campaigned in his behalf.[5]

Whatever the attitudes of individual Rangers, the Klan agenda appealed to so many Texans that it provided a powerful social, economic, and political context for all that happened in Texas during Pat Neff's administration. Although no Klansman himself, when questioned about the Klan Neff took refuge in generalities about the need for tough law enforcement. By his refusal to criticize the Klan and use Rangers against Klan offenses, therefore, he tolerated the torture of people whose morality did not correspond with his own.

The governor's stance may have infected the Ranger Force. Rangers quietly approved of much of the Klan agenda but abhorred its criminal acts. A few held membership. Personally conflicted, they probably felt relief that Governor Neff chose not to employ them against the Klan.

THE BATTLES OF greatest importance to Pat Neff all came together in the oil boomtowns, a challenge he inherited from his predecessor. Here prohibition of intoxicants, now contained in both the U.S. and the Texas constitutions, combined with state laws against gambling to collide with the appetites of oil workers. Neff would cooperate with honest county authority or circumvent dishonest county authority in contending with the manufacture and import of liquor, gambling, prostitution, rampant crime, government corruption, and social disorder. Rangers moved from

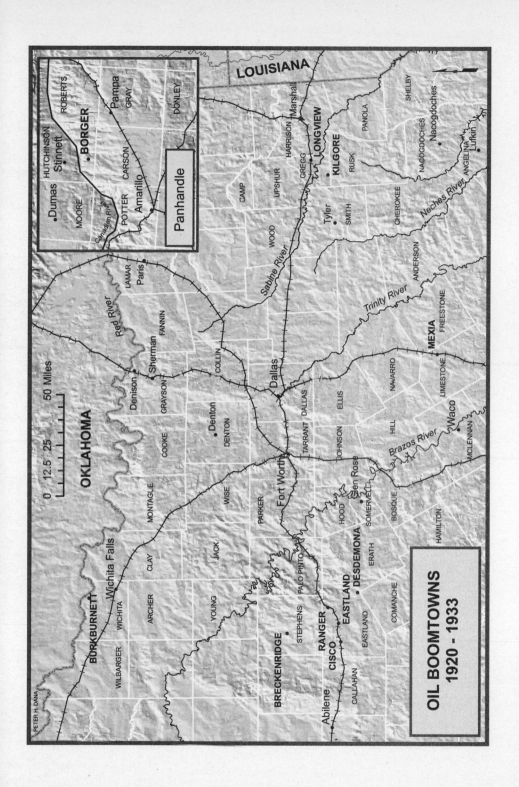

OIL BOOMTOWNS
1920 - 1933

LOUISIANA

Panhandle

OKLAHOMA

50 Miles

0   12.5   25

PETER H. DANA

merely keeping order to enforcement of state laws, their efforts overlapping with those of federal prohibition agents.

On January 10, 1901, Spindletop blew Texas into the oil age. Other gushers in the Gulf plain around Houston and Beaumont created the phenomenon of the oil boomtown and focused exploration efforts in southeastern Texas. Because cowmen had long cursed oil in their water wells, North Texas attracted some interest and even blew its own gusher in 1911, at Electra, thirty miles west of Wichita Falls. In the following years, however, as exploration spread south and west as far as Abilene, huge discoveries in Oklahoma stifled interest in North Texas—until October 25, 1917. On that day, just outside the little town of Ranger, in Eastland County, the Texas and Pacific Coal Company set off a towering spout. As wells burgeoned all around Ranger, big companies like Texas, Humble, Gulf, and Magnolia joined with individual wildcatters in rushing to promising locations all over North Texas.[6]

Ranger was but one of a host of oil boomtowns, large and small, enduring and transitory, that erupted all over North Texas after 1918. All suffered more or less the same trauma. Swarms of wildcatters, company men, and laborers overwhelmed a small ranching or railroad town. Hotels, boarding houses, restaurants, grocery stores, and mercantile houses served a few, but the rest crowded into tents, barns, and even pigsties, and did without common necessities. Tradesmen of uncertain probity hastily set up shop on the streets, dispensing at scandalous prices a scattering of food and other goods. Bootleggers, prostitutes, gamblers, and criminals of every specialty preyed on the workers. Among them were crooks masquerading as lawmen who sold their services to local officers and practiced their real profession behind the badge. The true "laws"—the oilmen term for peace officers, crooked or not—stood helplessly aside, accepted bribes to look the other way, or bought into criminal enterprises themselves. So did other town and county officials. Chaos reigned day and night, made worse by the end of several years of drought that brought constant deluges and converted dusty roads, streets, and workplaces into quagmires of glutinous mud.

No county or town could afford enough deputies or policemen to control the boomtowns. Only the state had the resources. Substantial citizens, honest judges, clergymen, and oil company executives plagued with equipment hijacking appealed for state help. Governors Hobby and Neff both recognized the state's obligation. Beginning under Hobby and building under Neff, the boomtowns provided the primary employment of the Texas Rangers.

ROY W. ALDRICH had served as quartermaster of the Ranger Force since 1918. Fifty-one in 1920, tall, slender, gregarious, friendly, he played a role at headquarters far larger than routine logistics and finances. On the one hand, he encouraged, advised, and passed on gossip to buck Rangers in the field; and they in turn divulged information to him that their captains did not officially report. On the other hand, he served Hobby's adjutant general W. D. Cope and then Neff's Thomas D. Barton almost as a line deputy for Ranger operations, often acting for and speaking on their behalf as well as leading raids in the field. His background fully equipped him for service beyond quartermaster: veteran of the Philippine Insurrection and Boer War, Oklahoma sheriff for four years, and Ranger sergeant under the infamous Captain Henry Ransom in the "bandit war" of 1915.

Aldrich gained much boomtown experience in the wave of crime and vice that swept North Texas in the final year of the Hobby administration. Burkburnett, Ranger, Desdemona, Breckenridge, and smaller towns suffered all the afflictions of the typical boomtown, including local officials on the take. Working out of Wichita Falls and Fort Worth, Rangers went undercover, gathered evidence, then launched swift raids that shut down illegal dives and brought both managers and patrons into court. Aldrich led many such raids. So did Tom Hickman, rising to prominence as a competent captain overseeing North Texas from Fort Worth. Aldrich worked closely with two of Hickman's Rangers in Wichita Falls, Manuel T. Gonzaullas and James W. McCormick. Both, as well as Hickman and Aldrich, were destined for long and distinguished careers in the Rangers.[7]

The raids of 1920 were successful, but almost no one suffered any penalty in court, and in January 1921 newly inaugurated Pat Neff found his desk piled with complaints about wide-open oil towns in North Texas. Eastland and Stephens counties seemed the worst, and Ranger the worst of the worst. Early in February, Adjutant General Barton went to Ranger to see for himself. He found the town indeed a cesspool of iniquity, with the Commercial Hotel the centerpiece. On February 11 he dispatched Captain Aldrich to organize a raid. With three Rangers brought down from Breckenridge, Aldrich and the county attorney appeared at the Commercial Hotel about 10:00 PM on Saturday night the twelfth. While two Rangers went up the fire escape in the rear to the third floor, the reported gambling hall, Aldrich and the third Ranger raced up the front stairs and burst into a large room packed with gamblers and gambling equipment. Fifteen men scrambled to safety, but the two Rangers arrested ninety. Sending for Justice of the Peace J. N. McFatter, Aldrich turned all the prisoners and gambling paraphernalia over to him. The proprietors, Alfred "Kid" Jordan and Cleve Barnes, promised to ensure the appearance of their customers in court and pay their fines, so McFatter released them.

They did as promised, paid fines amounting to $1,800 for their patrons, and stood charged with multiple violations of the law. A jury tried Cleve Barnes, heard fifty witnesses, and after thirty minutes' deliberation found him not guilty. That set the precedent, and both he and Jordan went free of further prosecution. As Aldrich had remarked, the gambling emporium at the Commercial Hotel "was conducted with about as much secrecy as a grocery store," and it could not possibly have operated without the knowledge of local officers. Both Neff and Barton saw no point in tying up Rangers in a town whose peace officers would not cooperate, and on April 1 they pulled all Rangers out of all the North Texas boomtowns except Wichita Falls. As the governor remarked of Ranger, "We had no trouble getting the evidence, but much trouble in finding anyone to use it. It was like being all dressed up with nowhere to go."[8]

WITHOUT RANGERS, oil towns across North Texas continued to boom, but by the end of 1921 Neff had little choice but to dress up and go elsewhere—this time Mexia. In August 1921 soaring gushers marked

Mexia as lying atop another rich oil pool. A quiet cotton town fifty miles northeast of Waco, Mexia blew up almost overnight as the usual throngs of workers and parasites swarmed in. By the end of the year the population had exploded from 2,500 to 55,000. Crime, violence, gambling, prostitution, and drinking flourished. Local officials brought in crooked "laws" from other oil towns and shared in the largess. In December 1921 Adjutant General Barton sent an undercover Ranger to investigate the complaints pouring in on the governor. The report so startled Barton that he sent him back, this time with a federal prohibition officer. The pair returned with a report even worse than the first. The governor turned once again to the Rangers.

The Rangers had been severely cut back. Eastland County's state senator, Joe Burkett, had defended the men arrested in the raid on Ranger and bore special enmity for the Ranger Force. In August 1921 he spurred the legislature to reduce the force from seventy-five to fifty and slash appropriations for other expenses.

Nevertheless, on January 7, 1922, Governor Neff mounted a formidable assault on Mexia. Autos drove out of Austin bearing Barton himself, Assistant Attorney General Clifford Stone, six federal prohibition officers, and ten Rangers from Headquarters Company. At the same time two cars drove south from Wichita Falls with ten Rangers. Captain Frank Hamer led the Austin contingent, Captain Tom Hickman the Company B oilfield veterans now based in Wichita Falls. Captain Roy Aldrich also included himself in the expedition.[9]

Now thirty-four, Frank Hamer was a tough muscular giant weighing 230 pounds and standing an impressive six feet three. He had an intermittent history as a regular and special Ranger dating from 1906 as well as a violent history as a hired gunman for San Saba feudists that in 1917 cost him his special commission. In January 1919 Adjutant General Harley had taken him on as a sergeant attached to the legislative committee investigating the Rangers, and in this capacity he had menaced Representative José Canales in both Brownsville and Austin. In and out again both as private and sergeant, he had just taken over as captain of Headquarters Company when Governor Neff mounted the expedition against Mexia. Hamer excelled as a marksman with every type of firearm, hand and shoulder. His trademark was a powerful swing of the right arm that smashed the flat of his hand against an opponent's ear. "Captain Hamer's open palm always took the fight out of the hardiest ruffian," observed a colleague, who also marveled at his mastery of foot fighting; "few antagonists could stand up under his mule-like kicks." Stolid, given less to words than action, he would emerge in coming years as a skilled criminal investigator, a fiercely effective lawman, and while hardly peaceful, the most widely admired peace officer in Texas.[10]

A Gainesville stockman familiar with all North Texas, at thirty-six Thomas R. Hickman had been a Ranger for only three years but a captain for more than a year, testimony to political connections if not experience. Despite no previous record as a lawman, he had bombarded the governor and adjutant general with applications ever since the Ferguson administration and quickly made himself into an efficient, courageous, and honest peace officer. Tall, slim, and wiry, he dressed immaculately, often in western garb, and figured prominently in Ranger affairs for the next decade. In contrast to Hamer, with whom he frequently worked, Hickman projected an outgoing personality, although a close friend described him as alternating between depression and elation. An accomplished horseman, he delighted in rodeos, for which he served as a judge in both the United States and Europe. "Tom truly loved publicity," recalled his friend; "he was his own press agent, and a good one."[11]

Mexia lay in Limestone County next to the boundary with Freestone County. The town supported plenty of illegal dives, but the undercover agents had identified as prime targets two spacious emporiums across the line in Freestone County—the Winter Garden and the Chicken Farm. Both accommodated large numbers of patrons, who gambled, drank, and danced under the watchful eyes of armed guards. The two establishments were well marked and operated so openly that the authorities could hardly be ignorant of their existence.

Brandishing shotguns and machine guns, at 11:00 PM Hamer and his squad fell on the Winter Garden while Hickman and his men barged into the Chicken Farm. Both had been temporarily shut down by a court injunction, but the Rangers arrested twenty-two owners and staff, and confiscated the gambling equipment and liquor. The next day Assistant Attorney General Stone called a meeting at the Winter Garden of the district judge, district attorney, and the county judges, attorneys, and sheriffs of both Freestone and Limestone counties. "All of these officials," according to Barton, "claimed ignorance of any such resorts and seemed amazed that such could have been running."[12]

Headquartered at the Winter Garden, Hamer and Hickman began rounding up lawbreakers in both counties. At once they discovered this a pointless exercise. Judges, prosecutors, and lawmen withheld cooperation; witnesses feared to testify; no jail could hold so many prisoners; nor did the captains have enough Rangers to guard them. On January 11, four days after the first raids, Governor Neff proclaimed martial law in the precincts on both sides of the county line. Brigadier General Jacob F. Wolters, a Houston attorney, moved in with a troop of forty-two national guardsmen and a handful of staff officers. Hamer and Hickman remained with thirteen Rangers, as did the federal prohibition officers.

General Wolters established his headquarters in the Mexia city hall and housed his troops in the Winter Garden, which also afforded a large room that could be used as a jail. Suddenly local authorities grew co-operative and suspended all police and deputies named by the general. Hundreds of "vagabonds" fled at once, while soldiers dragged others before Wolters to receive "sundown orders"—be gone by sundown. The Rangers arrested scores of malefactors, sat them in front of a military judge advocate, and extracted confessions and depositions. Trucked to the makeshift jail, they awaited transfer to the appropriate federal, state, or local authorities.

Investigation by airplane confirmed reports that the Trinity River bottoms near Young, on the eastern edge of Freestone County, contained thriving whiskey stills. With aerial photographs, undercover Rangers mapped the locations of the roads and stills, and learned that a ring of local officers operated them. On February 2, therefore, Governor Neff placed all of Freestone County under martial law. Barton led a caravan of autos bearing Rangers and federal officers in a nighttime drive to

Young. The next day, with the airplane overhead signaling targets, they seized seven stills, destroyed three hundred gallons of whiskey, and rounded up eighty-five suspects.

By the end of February 1922 General Wolters could declare Mexia and vicinity and Freestone County truly cleaned up. Governor Neff lifted martial law. For soldiers and lawmen alike, the winter had been hard—cold, rainy, and muddy—and the mission demanding. But the final tally testified to their success: 602 arrests, 27 stills captured, 2,270 gallons of liquor and 215 barrels of corn mash destroyed, 13 autos used for liquor transport turned over to federal authorities, 53 stolen autos returned to their owners, $4,000 worth of narcotics seized, $5,000 worth of gambling equipment confiscated.

More important, Mexia stayed clean. A new police chief, former Ranger Alfred Mace, and an entire new police department kept the city under firm control, and other city and county offices fell to capable, honest men.

Rangers and soldiers had worked together effectively and harmoniously. General Wolters paid the Rangers high tribute: "Courageous and impersonal in the performance of duty, they exemplified on every occasion the highest ideals and best traditions of the Ranger Force." As for Captains Hamer and Hickman, no state boasted more efficient officers, "possessing the combination of intelligence, physical strength, power of endurance, and energy."[13]

Other boomtown cleanups proved less enduring. When the Rangers arrived, the dives closed and the criminals left town. When the Rangers left, the criminals returned and the dives reopened. But at Mexia, thanks to Wolters, Hamer, Hickman, and Chief Mace, Pat Neff had won his most conspicuous battle of peace.

ALONG THE RIO GRANDE FRONTIER, prohibition and smuggling united to place such heavy demand on the border Rangers as to exclude almost every other crime, including the perennial struggle against stock thieves. Rangers and federal customs officers had contended with smuggling for decades, but national prohibition in the United States transformed it into a huge operation dealing almost exclusively in liquor. "Horsebackers," the multiplying bands of Mexican smugglers were called. Chasing them down in the South Texas chaparral and the Big Bend was hard, dangerous work, more often than not ending in a shootout. Lacking the publicity of the boomtown raiders, the border Rangers scored repeated successes and seized enough whiskey and tequila to warm the heart of a fervid dry like Governor Neff.

The star of this offensive never gained (nor wanted) the accolades showered on Hamer and Hickman. Fifty-three in 1921, bespectacled and physically unimposing, William L. Wright embodied probity, ideals, and professionalism acquired as a young Ranger under Captain John H. Rogers at the turn of the century. Afterward, he had served for fifteen years as the respected sheriff of Wilson County when Governor Hobby brought him back to the Rangers in 1918 as a captain. Not only in character did Will Wright personify the old-time Rangers, before governors Colquitt, Ferguson, and Hobby politicized them. Wright's sector, from the Nueces to the Rio Grande, kept him constantly in the saddle, rarely in an automobile. Will Wright would serve long, successfully, and honorably, but without the dash and glamour of his fellow captains.[14]

Typically, with half a dozen Rangers and one or two federal customs officers, Wright scouted back and forth in the South Texas chaparral looking for horsebacker trails. They could be identified because the smugglers used small horses and mules shod all around. When the Rangers found a trail, a chase ensued in which they usually overtook the quarry, either moving or in camp. Sometimes the Mexicans threw up their hands and surrendered, but as often they shot it out before surrendering or escaping into the brush. Major encounters occurred in February and September 1921, but the climax came in November. In three fights in five days, Wright and his men captured six smugglers, killed or wounded at least twenty, and confiscated sixty-three horses and four thousand quarts of whiskey. The captain apologized for letting horsebackers escape in the bush, "but they will have something to remember from the Rangers."[15]

The Big Bend raised different but equally formidable obstacles to apprehending horsebackers and rustlers: the tangled mountains, rims, and canyons that had bedeviled Rangers since the 1870s. This was the domain of Captain Jerry Gray, politically anointed by Governor Ferguson in 1917. A posturing egotist, Gray's mismanagement stirred rancor and rapid turnover in his company, and his meddling in local politics alienated prominent citizens. Some of Gray's men were tough campaigners who knew the country and the enemy and, when not hassled by the captain, could perform creditably. Occasionally they intercepted horsebackers, but they never could catch the notorious Chico Cano, who had confounded Big Bend lawmen for almost a decade.[16]

Two such dauntless Rangers were the brothers Arch and Ray "Pinochle" Miller, who in August 1924 befriended historian Walter Prescott Webb and gave him a tour of their rugged sector. With two others, they were based at Glenn Springs and patrolled the river east of the Chisos Mountains for horsebackers. The adventures of these and other Rangers admiringly described by Webb suggest that in their relations with Mexicans in the Big Bend the six-shooter mentality still prevailed. In one episode, not recounted in Webb's book, on May 14, 1924, Arch and a partner rode down the river from Boquillas to investigate reports of about a dozen Mexicans gathered in a small box canyon. "The result was that hell was popping before we knew it. If you would go there today you would find fourteen dead horses and mules. All the men got away." Arch left unsaid what, if anything, the Mexicans were guilty of.[17]

FROM GOVERNOR HOBBY Pat Neff inherited the concluding stages of a nasty confrontation between labor and management on the Galveston wharves. Pressed by advocates of the open shop, in October 1920 Hobby called the legislature into special session. The result was the Open Port Law, which banned any action that interfered with free trade anywhere in Texas.

The Open Port Law would ultimately be held unconstitutional, but it was on the books when Governor Neff confronted his own labor crisis. On July 1, 1922, defying orders of union officials, 400,000 railroad shopmen and switchmen throughout the nation walked off the job to protest a pay cut. The North Texas rail center of Denison promptly blew up as fourteen hundred workmen of the Missouri, Kansas, and Texas Railroad set up picket lines, harassed employees who did not join them, barred arriving strikebreakers, and vandalized yard facilities. They acted with the sympathy of the townspeople and the town officials. On the night of July 11, as lawmen looked on, a thousand citizens escorted twenty-four employees to the Red River bridge, flogged them, and ran them into Oklahoma.

Adjutant General Barton hurried to Denison to investigate, and the governor himself followed. By this time, as many as one hundred employees and prospective strikebreakers had been flogged and herded across Red River. Neff talked with strikers and local officials as well as railroad executives and concluded that he could not allow lives to be endangered, property destroyed, and commerce paralyzed. "Law and order" must be enforced.[18]

Neff believed this a task for the Texas Rangers. On July 23, the day after he returned to Austin, he ordered the entire Ranger Force on strike duty. Of the forty-eight Rangers, only three remained behind—Captain Aldrich in Austin, a man in Presidio, and one in Mission to care for horses. With the U.S. president and attorney general involved, however, federal authorities thought Neff's measure inadequate.

As the governor sat in his office, a regular army colonel from Fort Sam Houston entered in full uniform, declined to sit, and served notice that he had been instructed to ascertain whether Neff intended to order the National Guard to Denison. "I have arranged to handle the Denison situation with State Rangers," he answered.

"I have not been delegated to discuss the merits of the case with you," declared the colonel, "but to get a 'yes' or 'no' answer." His orders were to remain until he got a "yes" or "no." If "yes," the matter would be left to the state to handle. If "no," "Federal soldiers out of San Antonio will be on their way to Denison in about thirty minutes after your 'no' answer is received by me."[19]

Loath to have federal troops on Texas soil enforcing Texas law, Neff said "yes," and the next morning, July 26, he declared martial law in Denison and surrounding precinct. Colonel Charles W. Nimon and nearly five hundred guardsmen descended on Denison and brought it swiftly under control. Aided by Rangers, the troops remained until Neff lifted martial law on October 21, 1922.

Also on July 26 the governor invoked the Open Port Law in fifteen other railroad cities where violence might occur. To police them, he augmented the regular force by 450 "emergency Rangers," paid for by the railroad companies—a classic conflict of interest scarcely pleasing to the unions. Although reporting to regular Rangers appointed acting captains, the emergency Rangers had been so hastily recruited that they included many incompetents and made constant trouble. With Hamer in the Panhandle, Hickman in Denison and Sherman, Nichols in Marshall, and Wright in Cleburne, the Rangers worked hard at keeping the rails unobstructed throughout Texas until Neff finally canceled the Open Port Law on January 1, 1923. "We damn near ran the trains and everything else," summed up Sergeant Martin Koonsman.[20]

The law-and-order governor had indeed upheld law and order, although in Denison 161 cases were simply stricken from the court docket, and no one was prosecuted for any offense. The price was a six-month diversion of the Ranger Force from normal duties, leaving the boomtowns free to boom and the border open to horsebackers. Forty-five Rangers might well have handled the Denison crisis, but the federal ultimatum left Neff little choice but to declare martial law. Aside from Denison, which required firm measures, by invoking the Open Port Law the state had severely jolted the labor movement in Texas for the second time in two years, and the Rangers and soldiers could be seen as strikebreakers. Not for the last time had they appeared in this role.

EXCEPT IN THE WESTERN part of the state, no less than the rest of the South did Texas practice strict white supremacy, chiefly over blacks but in places over Mexican Americans also. While embracing white supremacy, the Ku Klux Klan did not often single out blacks for special treatment. Racial subordination, segregation, discrimination, and deference—Jim Crow—were simply unquestioned features of Texan culture, and any perceived violation of the social order could instantly transform white Texans into savages. Race riots and lynchings darkly stained half a century of Texas history.

Governor Neff and his Rangers were white Texans and thus white supremacists. But they also stood for law and order, which meant they opposed mob violence against blacks for any reason. Too often local officials shrank from confronting a throng of frenzied citizens. When summoned in time, however, Rangers rushed to the scene and tried to quell the furore.

Lynching was the most horrid and individualized spectacle of the larger context of race relations and race riots. Underlying both was white obsession with presumed black lust for white women. In many if not most instances, although publicized as rape, sexual offenses were secretly consensual and "confessions" either nonexistent or extracted by torture. Many such "rapes" were not sexual at all but convenient coverups for violation of discriminatory social customs.

Lynching bore a long history, but mass rioting originated at the turn of the century. Urbanization, migration of black farmers to cities, the appearance of black urban ghettos, and the rise of successful black businessmen served as catalysts. The Supreme Court's blessing of "separate but equal" sanctified existing Jim Crow thought and practice.

The "Waco Horror" of May 1915 revealed Texans to be as susceptible to mob psychology as people elsewhere. Jesse Washington, seventeen, bludgeoned to death the woman who employed him, and authorities added the charge of rape to murder despite the absence of any evidence. Neither the sheriff nor the judge called for state help, and the judge permitted a farcical prosecution in a courtroom packed with an inflamed armed mob. No sooner had the jury pronounced the guilty verdict than the mob seized the prisoner. Kicking, stabbing, hurling bricks, and stripping Washington naked, they dragged him by a chain through the streets. Hoisting him over a pile of kindling, they slashed off his fingers, ears, toes, and penis, then immolated him as the throng cheered its approval.[21]

Had either the judge or the sheriff called for help, Governor Jim Ferguson almost certainly would have sent Rangers. Time and again one or two Texas Rangers had demonstrated that they knew how to prevent mob action. They simply stood firm, unflinchingly commanded dispersal, and aimed shotguns at mob leaders.

The worst racial outbreak, and an example of effective Ranger work, occurred during the Hobby administration. Blacks returned from World War I with attitudes that contradicted their historic treatment. In the summer of 1919 twenty-five riots erupted in cities both North and South, and seventy-six blacks were lynched, some still wearing army uniforms. Chicago, Omaha, Tulsa, Washington, D.C., Charleston, and Knoxville garnered the national publicity, leaving Texas relatively untouched by the news media.[22]

In Texas the site was Longview, the quiet seat of Gregg County 125 miles east of Dallas. The population numbered seventeen thousand, nearly half blacks. A black man had been whipped, then taken from jail and lynched, for allegedly making indecent advances toward a white woman. An article in the activist black newspaper *The Chicago Defender* described the woman as receptive. (A black Longview school teacher was believed to be the author.) On July 10, when white mobs began to take action, black mobs formed to resist. They clashed and exchanged gunfire. Arson burned out the homes of black leaders. The next morning the sheriff and county judge telephoned Governor Hobby asking for help. By the morning of July 12, one hundred national guardsmen and eight Rangers under Captain William M. Hanson had made camp on the courthouse square. The killing of a black physician, however, stirred more rage. Hobby placed all Gregg County under martial law and augmented the military force to more than 260.

While the military quickly brought the city under control, Hanson and his Rangers conducted investigations. Within two days they had arrested twenty-six whites variously charged with attempted murder and arson, and twenty-one blacks charged with attempted murder. Peace returned to the town. After moving the jailed blacks to Austin for their own safety, both guard and town and county leaders recommended that the governor lift martial law, which he did on July 18.

The Longview riot revealed not only the ugly side of white racism but the effectiveness of judicious leadership. The mayor, county judge, and sheriff acted responsibly. The guard officers acted responsibly. And Hanson and his Rangers acted aggressively and responsibly—for Hanson a bright entry in an otherwise dismal record. And finally, the local authorities wisely dropped the charges against both blacks and whites. Had they been brought to trial, the whites would have been acquitted, the blacks convicted, and racial animosities rekindled.[23]

Governor Neff had few opportunities like Longview to take effective action against violent white racism, although several might have invited Ranger intervention had local officials acted as promptly and prudently as those at Longview. But determined mobs were almost impossible for local peace officers to quell, even when they wanted to. Moreover, mobs consisted of voters, and sheriffs and other officers depended on them for reelection.

An example occurred in Kirvin, forty miles northeast of Waco, in May 1922. This was a rape-murder of a popular young high school student. It was swiftly pinned on three black men, one of whom supposedly confessed. A mob bound one, after repeated mutilations, to the metal seat of a mule-drawn plow and dragged it into a bonfire. Later they threw the other two into the fire. Ironically, the sheriff asked Governor Neff for help only after rumors flew that the blacks planned an armed uprising. Captains Hamer and Hickman converged, not to investigate the executions but to suppress a black revolt. Before their arrival, however, the mayor informed Neff that the danger had passed, and they returned to their headquarters.

In a supreme irony, the murderer turned out to be a white man, and local lawmen had sufficient reason at the time to undertake an investigation. He was never tried.[24]

An incident in 1924 showed that Neff cared about racial violence. On February 26 Booker T. McMillan, a black man, shot and killed a white man in Lufkin. Angelina County Sheriff R. V. Watts arrested and jailed him, but a mob of Lufkin citizens gathered to demand a lynching. The sheriff and six deputies refused and when pressed fired into the crowd, wounding three men and scattering the rest. The governor promptly ordered guardsmen to Lufkin, then dispatched Adjutant General

Barton, Captains Nichols and Aldrich, Sergeant James W. McCormick, and two privates to replace the military. The Rangers kept order until McMillan had been tried and convicted on March 1, then did not withdraw until Captain Nichols had escorted McMillan to the Huntsville penitentiary.[25]

Racist violence was not a battle for any single governor to win. It was part of the Texan way of life, and Neff could count himself fortunate that some of the worst fell to a later governor.

PROHIBITION REMAINED at the top of Pat Neff's agenda. It was not only the law of the land, nation and state, but a deeply felt personal conviction. The smuggling or even transporting of liquor, however, was not Neff's biggest problem. Captain Wright's Rangers worked effectively to head off Mexican horsebackers, and Rangers and local lawmen sought to stem the river of whiskey flowing from Louisiana across East Texas to Dallas and Fort Worth. Neff's most distressing vexation lay in the hundreds of stills springing up virtually everywhere in Texas. Texan drys had been powerful enough to enact statewide prohibition and fuel the drive for national prohibition, but the prosperity of so many moonshiners testified to plenty of wets as well. Except in West Texas, hardly a county did not harbor enough stills to stir appeals for Rangers to root them out. Some sheriffs wanted them out and joined in the appeals, others thought it not worth the effort, and still others accepted bribes *not* to make the effort. Lufkin, Richmond, Denton, San Diego, Clarksville, Marlin, Mesquite—these and many other communities wrestled with or ignored multiplying stills throughout the Neff years.

Of all the distilling centers, Glen Rose proved the most persistent and resistant. Seat of tiny Somervell County, fifty miles southwest of Fort Worth, Glen Rose lay amid rugged, wooded hills replete with springs, ideal for hiding stills. The "mountain moonshine rendezvous," state officials labeled it. Somervell distillers slaked a powerful thirst in Fort Worth, Dallas, Waco, and Wichita Falls. They also paid the sheriff six dollars a month for every barrel of moonshine they produced. Benefiting from the prosperity, citizens wanted no outside interference.

In July 1923 Neff had an undercover agent sent in. Richard Watson, a quiet, friendly youth, ingratiated himself with the still operators and even carried payoffs to county officials. By late August he had gathered enough information for a raid. Rangers Marvin "Red" Burton and R. D. Shumate enlisted lawmen from surrounding counties and on August 25 pounced. In two days of scouring the craggy hills, they destroyed twenty-three stills, confiscated great quantities of whiskey and its makings, arrested and jailed fifty men, and had one shootout in which they killed a prominent leader of a whiskey-running syndicate. The sheriff and county attorney confessed to receiving bribes.[26]

Meantime, Burton also put together the last great raid of the Neff administration on oil boomtowns. In the wake of a major discovery early in 1923 near Corsicana, fifty miles southeast of Dallas, typical boomtowns sprang up all over Navarro County. Undercover agents, including once again Richard Watson, gathered the needed information. Then in February 1924, Burton helped county peace officers organize a series of raids that shut down gambling and vice dens and filled jails with proprietors, gamblers, and bootleggers. Periodic raids through June closed all the illegal establishments. Prosecutors sent many offenders to prison. Citizens ensured that Navarro County stayed clean.[27]

Not so Somervell County. With the venue changed to Cleburne, prosecutions proceeded month after month following the August raids. Citizens grew increasingly rebellious, angrily demanding that the governor leave them alone. In February 1924 prosecutors brought Richard Watson, even then aiding Burton in the cleanup of Navarro County, to testify in a trial in Cleburne. A nighttime shotgun blast took his life. Such was the state of mind in Somervell County.

The raids and prosecutions had struck a powerful blow at the county's distillers but had not won a battle for Governor Neff. Red Burton kept watch as Glen Rose crept back into the moonshine business.[28]

SAN ANTONIO, the largest and oldest city in Texas, hummed with a way of life repugnant to every element of Governor Neff's moral code. All the features of the typical boomtown flourished. Liquor flowed copiously, locally manufactured and imported from Mexico in huge quantities. Gambling, prostitution, and even cockfights thrived. Predominantly Mexican American, also heavily German, embracing a large military garrison at Fort Sam Houston, a popular tourist destination, the city was full of people who loved life as they lived it. If that involved illegal activity, neither the city administration, the police, nor the newspapers objected.[29]

Relying on the same powers that legalized the emergency Rangers mobilized during the railroad strike of 1922, Neff created an emergency Ranger unit of ten men to take on San Antonio. This was Company E, captained by a ten-year veteran of the federal secret service and also a resident of San Antonio, Berk C. Baldwin. Early in September 1923, they took station in San Antonio and went to work. "We've got our hook in at San Antonio," boasted Barton, "and it's going to stay there indefinitely."

Neff rationalized that the "good people" of San Antonio silently acclaimed the hook. The noisy people, however, opposed it noisily. The mayor, police, sheriff's department, prosecutors, and judges complained about the Ranger presence and withheld cooperation. Newspapers editorialized fervidly. Police arrested Rangers in performance of their duties; Captain Baldwin himself faced six grand jury indictments for illegal raids and for destroying whiskey. A movement gathered momentum to persuade the legislature to abolish the entire Ranger Force.

But the governor held firm. Month after month Baldwin and Company E kept San Antonio in a state of constant turmoil, arresting bootleggers and moonshiners, closing gambling and booze joints as well as elite clubs, raiding stills, destroying whiskey and all its ingredients, and even one Sunday afternoon falling on a bloody cockfighting pit and marching 150 men, including policemen and sheriff's deputies, into the city for arraignment.

The company was still in San Antonio in January 1925, when Pat Neff ended his tenure as governor. He could cite some impressive statistics: 41 gambling houses and 33 pool halls closed, together with several "notorious" cockfighting pits; 300 stills seized along with 110,000 gallons of liquor. He could also boast some convictions, 316, all in federal court.

"I sent the Rangers to the Alamo City," Neff had declared, "to assist in enforcing, not the laws of San Antonio, but the laws of Texas." They did not assist because the local law officers neither asked for nor accepted assistance. And Neff's convictions all resulted from violations of the national prohibition law, not the laws of Texas. Few prosecutions and not a single conviction befell the hundreds rounded up for breaking the laws of Texas.

San Antonio dramatized the formidable obstacles confronting Texas Rangers in communities where they were not wanted. Neff understood the difficulties and elsewhere had usually succeeded in maneuvering around them. But San Antonio's offenses, criminal and to him grossly immoral, loomed so large in his mind that he launched a frontal attack rather than try less confrontational measures.

The railroad strike of 1922, Mexia, and San Antonio were Pat Neff's largest battles of peace. With Rangers and the National Guard, he had won the first two. Aides had urged him to declare martial law in San Antonio, but he had thrown the entire burden on less than a dozen Texas Rangers. The battle in San Antonio had not been lost when he left office in January 1925, but neither had it been won.

GOVERNOR PAT NEFF had been good to the Texas Rangers, and they had served him well. Freed of the political burden of the Colquitt, Ferguson, and Hobby administrations, they had grown increasingly professional and effective. With the Canales legislative hearings behind them, they had enjoyed heightened self-esteem. If they still brutalized Mexicans, it did not reach the intensity of earlier years and remained largely hidden from public view.

A cadre of competent captains, not unmindful of politics but intent on professional law enforcement, rebuilt the Ranger reputation and contributed decisively to the rising self-esteem. Aldrich, Hamer, Hickman, Nichols, and Wright all displayed superior leadership. Only Jerry Gray in the Big Bend came up wanting. The captains gave allegiance to the best adjutant general in a generation. Political ambition and Klan connections may have motivated Thomas D. Barton. If so, both failed him; but he proved a supportive and capable chief of the Ranger Force.

The Neff years also marked a significant shift in Ranger orientation. Spurred by national and state prohibition, their principal employment during these years, Rangers concentrated increasingly in East Texas. The Old West Rangers of frontier days evolved into a truly statewide force in practice as well as theory. In fact, two distinct forces took shape within the one: the Border Rangers and the Interior Rangers. Each required distinct skills, and each attracted and developed men adapted to one or the other. Wright's Rangers rode horses through the chaparral looking for Mexican smugglers. Hickman's Rangers drove automobiles in cities and rural areas looking for bootleggers and stills. Either kind would have been a misfit as the other.[30]

The Rangers did not win all of Pat Neff's "battles of peace." Bootlegging, moonshining, stock theft, lynching, and other crimes against which they contended would survive to haunt succeeding governors. But by 1925 these lawmen could genuinely rejoice in the former governor's accolade, "Long live the Texas Rangers!"

[6]

Ma and Pa Ferguson, 1925–1927

THE GUBERNATORIAL RACE of 1924 confronted Texans with a terrible electoral dilemma. Did they want a Ku Klux Klan candidate or a return to the scandals of Fergusonism? The Klan had turned increasingly from hooded violence to politics. The election of 1922 had even sent a Klan-backed candidate to the U.S. Senate.

James E. Ferguson held the Klan in contempt and opposed it vociferously. He had never accepted the validity of his impeachment in 1917, contending that he had resigned before the senate vote expelled him from the governorship and barred him from again holding state office. Even so, he ran for the *federal* office of U.S. senator in 1922 and almost won. He also filed for the gubernatorial race of 1924. On May 17, however, a state judge ordered his name stricken from the primary ballot. He quickly entered the name of his wife, Miriam A. Ferguson–M. A., or Ma, which evoked the sobriquet Pa for the true candidate. The pair ran on a strong anti-Klan platform. The July primary forced a runoff that pitted the Fergusons against Klan-backed Felix Robertson. Although "Farmer Jim" Ferguson reprised his old appeals to the poor–"the boys at the forks of the creek"–the central issue was the Ku Klux Klan.

Mrs. Ferguson's victory in the runoff ensured her election in November and destroyed forever the power of the Klan in Texas.[1]

As Ferguson supporters expected, Mrs. Ferguson served as a figure-head for her husband. In all but ceremonial affairs, he acted as if he were governor and wielded the powers of governor. The Ku Klux Klan had been broken, but Fergusonism reigned in the statehouse. Politics (and maybe money) ruled virtually every decision—appointments, policies, programs, state commissions and agencies, legislative relations, contracts (especially highway contracts), and pardons for penitentiary inmates (3,595 in two years). Scandals revived memories of the first Ferguson administration (1915–17). As Ferguson's attorney had predicted at the conclusion of the impeachment trial, "Fergusonism will be an issue in the politics of Texas every year there is an election held until Jim Ferguson dies." It was.[2]

Most Rangers probably favored the candidacy of Neff's adjutant general, Thomas Barton, even though he flaunted Klan credentials. But the July primary ended his quest, and the Rangers were left with the same choice as other Texans—the Klan or Fergusonism. For the Rangers, Ma's campaign rhetoric left little doubt that her inauguration would end the glory days of the Neff administration. In part as an economy measure but also as a gesture to local authority, she intended to reduce the force, employ it mainly as a border patrol, and withhold Rangers from any locality where not requested or wanted. Fear for their jobs in the political turnover that accompanied every new administration added to their apprehension. Largely but not entirely, Ma and Pa justified the Rangers' anxiety.

FIVE DAYS BEFORE the new governor's inauguration the Rangers got hit with more to worry about than the new regime. On January 15, 1925, district judge R. B. Minor, sitting in San Antonio, ruled the Ranger acts of 1901 and 1919 unconstitutional, and he enjoined the governor from spending any state funds on the Ranger Force. This stunning decision, accepting the argument that the constitution vested law enforcement solely in local officers, originated in a suit brought in December 1924 by

John E. Elgin, a San Antonio attorney and longtime political figure. Like much of the city's leadership and citizenry, Elgin resented the stationing of Captain Baldwin and his Ranger company in their midst with orders from Governor Neff to stay until they had shut down all establishments where gambling and drinking took place, destroyed all stills, cut off all liquor imports, closed all dens of vice, and arrested all violators of the law. Rangers had searched Elgin's home in 1923, and now he fought back. The decision in *Elgin v. Neff*, if upheld, would destroy the Ranger Force.[3]

Only two days after his inauguration, the newly elected attorney general, Daniel J. Moody, appealed Judge Minor's ruling. Arguments and rebuttals, however, took time. Criminals and horsebackers promptly took advantage of the absence of a state constabulary. The new adjutant general, able Mark McGee, interpreted the lower court's injunction as applying only to the expenditure of state funds, not to depriving him of command of the Ranger Force. He instructed captains to take whatever action was necessary and hope some day to be paid. They did, especially Wright and Hickman, although law enforcement weakened significantly.

On February 25, 1925, the Fourth Court of Civil Appeals overruled Judge Minor, and the Rangers were back in business.

THE APPEALS COURT relieved only one source of the Rangers' unrest. On February 20, anticipating the outcome of the appeal, Governor Ferguson and Adjutant General McGee reorganized the Ranger Force to reflect her inaugural address to the legislature. They cut the number of Rangers from fifty-one to twenty-eight and, not surprisingly, abolished Captain Baldwin's Company E at San Antonio. Most of the force would police the Mexican border, they decreed. Except in special cases, moreover, Rangers would be dispatched to a locality only on the request of county officers. These measures, while still disrupting border horsebackers, seriously crippled the ability of the force to combat the rising tide of crime in the interior. Prohibition violators especially enjoyed a new freedom.[4]

The six months the governor took to change the roster of field captains ensured continuing disquietude. Applications and endorsements piled up on her desk. Blasting the politicization of the force, the veteran Captain Will Wright resigned on March 1. In the Big Bend, Captain Jerry Gray also resigned—no loss there. Newly commissioned as a special Ranger, however, he so provoked the Presidio County sheriff that he verbalized why the former captain had been unfit as a Ranger: "Gray is big mouthed; likes to display a gun in his community and is prone to and does stir up trouble and discontent among his neighbors." Finally, on June 30, the highly esteemed Frank Hamer resigned his captaincy. The next day, July 1, he reenlisted as a private in the Ranger Force, with no company specified. Since Mark McGee himself signed the new oath of office and warrant, he must not have wanted Hamer lost and arranged for him to work directly for the adjutant general on special assignments.[5]

Mrs. Ferguson retained Roy Aldrich as quartermaster and Roy Nichols as captain of Company C. Nichols had been a Neff appointee in 1921 but enjoyed strong political support in East Texas, which brimmed with Fergusonites. Almost fifty in 1925, he had excelled as a captain and earlier as a peace officer in Fort Bend County, an army scout on the Mexican border, and longtime policeman and detective in Houston. Captain Aldrich regarded him as one of the state's best lawmen.[6]

A boastful appeal to the governor, backed by a packet of endorsements, won Tom Hickman enough favor to renew his captaincy. In July he moved to Austin to take over Headquarters Company, formerly the domain of Frank Hamer. Company D at Brownsville, Will Wright's old company, fell to William M. Ryan, a Ranger captain from 1917 to 1921. D. E. Lindsey, sixty-two, a former customs officer lacking prior Ranger service, received Company B, Hickman's old company, which was moved from Waco to Del Rio. Finally, in her worst appointment, she replaced Jerry Gray with J. Monroe Fox, fifty-eight. He had captained the Marfa-based company for seven years, 1911–18, until his role in the infamous Porvenir massacre led to his ouster. Despite the reduction of the force and the stringent limits on its employment, the Ranger Force did not suffer seriously from the politics of the Ferguson administration. Ryan did better chasing horsebackers than later critics conceded.

Lindsey did almost nothing. Nor did Monroe Fox, whose association with Porvenir should have barred him even from consideration.[7]

DESPITE THE OBJECTIVE of concentrating most of the Rangers on the Rio Grande frontier, the interior kept the Rangers engaged. Another prospective lynching loomed in September 1925. Three blacks had killed a white man in Panola County and had been brought to Marshall, in neighboring Gregg County, for trial. On the eighteenth, a crowd of people from Panola County gathered to storm the jail and lynch the prisoners. Captain Nichols and the sheriff waded into the mob, arrested a few men, and ordered the rest to leave town "posthaste." They did.[8]

In their principal activity, Nichols and his men labored constantly, in cooperation with local deputies and federal agents, to shut down stills and interdict the flow of liquor from Louisiana to urban centers to the northwest. The latter sometimes involved high-speed auto chases for fifty miles or more, thus highlighting the evolving character of law enforcement. By September 1925 Nichols had made 142 arrests, captured autos used for transport, and seized 10,000 quarts of liquor. The Marshall jail and courthouse, he thought, "looked like a bootleggers' convention."

The Marshall Rangers had also destroyed four stills and arrested twenty-three moonshiners. Three months later, on December 29, 1925, two of Nichols's Rangers, with four local lawmen, closed in on a still operating twenty miles northwest of Marshall. The operators shot it out, losing one killed and others captured. Nichols boasted that the lawmen had seized the ringleaders and stopped "the worst bunch of bootleggers in East Texas."[9]

THE LARGEST CHALLENGE to the interior Rangers in the middle 1920s was the sudden increase in bank robberies, perhaps explained by an expanding highway system that afforded robbers quick escape. Tom Hickman and his men had proved particularly effective in running down bank robbers in the closing years of the Neff administration. They continued to be the specialists during the Ferguson administration.

Hickman's first success occurred in February 1925, scarcely a month after Mrs. Ferguson took office. In the Denton town square, twenty-five miles north of Dallas, local officers had arrested N. A. Story, a suspected car thief, when a big auto packed with gunmen roared onto the scene and opened fire. A gun battle raged around the courthouse until the gangsters drove north and holed up in a cottage belonging to a confederate named Martin. Among them was Yancy Story, brother of N. A. Story. A contingent of Fort Worth officers wanted to storm the house, but the locals, aware that Martin's wife and child were inside and that a college dormitory stood nearby, resisted. At this juncture Tom Hickman flew in from Fort Worth, where he had been visiting friends. With the Storys' attorney he went into the cottage unarmed and negotiated at length, and almost futilely, for the surrender of the gunmen. At last they consented, on condition that Hickman escort them to a safe place where they could make bond. He took them to the Dallas jail.

Hickman suspected that more than auto theft was involved. Further investigation disclosed common links among a series of bank robberies—acetylene torches to cut into bank vaults, an arsenal of weapons, masks, and high-powered autos for escape. He surmised that the gang operated out of Denton County, scene of the February incident, and he sent undercover agents to probe the suspicion. On August 24 Hickman and his Rangers joined with local deputies to raid the Story ranch ten miles south of Denton. They found ample evidence to tie Yancy Story and five men to the robberies, arrested them, and launched them toward indictments for offenses as serious as murder. They were brought to trial in January 1926.[10]

The robberies continued, as they would for years to come. Hickman, increasingly seeking "MOs" (modus operandi) to connect the robberies and using secret agents to penetrate the underworld, continued to concentrate on this form of crime. He discovered one gang using women to scout prospective banks, then transfer the haul from the bandits' car to their own. They also struck at the noon hour, when banks would have fewer patrons.

A tip came to Hickman that this gang planned to hit the Red River National Bank at Clarksville, 125 miles northeast of Dallas, on September 9. With another Ranger and a local constable, he took station across the street from the bank as noon approached. A car drove up and, leaving the engine running, two men, one carrying a suitcase, walked into the bank. In a few minutes they came out. The three lawmen stepped into the street and opened fire, cutting down and killing both men. Whether the robbers were given an opportunity to surrender is unclear. But the suitcase contained more than $30,000, and Hickman and his comrades were widely hailed. The legislature, then in session, commended them, and the Clarksville bank granted a $1,000 reward. The Texas Bankers Association matched the sum and later in 1926 voted a reward of $5,000 for every *dead* bank robber. That offer failed to stem the tide of bank robberies, but it caused bitter controversy in years to come.[11]

FOR YEARS both company and wildcat explorers had searched the Texas Panhandle for oil deposits comparable to those that produced booms in North Texas. They found plenty of gas and even some promising oil, but the lack of pipelines and railroads discouraged serious investment. Gushers in 1924 and 1925, however, attracted a swarm of explorers, who uncovered crude in sufficient quantity to set off a boom. Big companies moved in to create infrastructure and tap the geologically difficult pool.[12]

Hutchinson County lay at the center of the new oil frenzy. It consisted of flat grasslands that had long sustained a flourishing cattle industry and rugged breaks falling to the broad valley of the South Canadian River. To the south, Amarillo furnished the gateway city. Several town sites sprouted on the vast pool, but none prospered like Borger. In March 1926 Oklahoma boomer Asa P. "Ace" Borger and his partner John R. Miller founded the town on the south bank of the river, and within three months it boasted a population of 45,000. To back their quest for wealth and power, they brought in "Two-Gun Dick" Herwig, whose Oklahoma crime syndicate, posing as the law, quickly established control of "Booger Town." All the wickedness of the typical boomtown burgeoned, only with greater intensity.[13]

As early as June complaints of machinery theft reached Governor Ferguson. Sheriff Joseph Ownbey, however, assured the governor that he had four men in the county jail at Plemons already charged with this offense. Reports of murders were false—there had been none in his two terms as sheriff. If the governor wanted to send Rangers, Ownbey would be glad to cooperate. But he thought them unneeded because he believed Borger under as firm control as any oil town.[14]

Late in July 1926, however, the county judge and others at Plemons petitioned Governor Ferguson for Rangers. Her adjutant general, Dallas J. Matthews, who succeeded Mark McGee at the end of 1925, assigned Sergeant J. B. Wheatley and Ranger H. D. Glasscock to report to Sheriff Ownbey and investigate conditions at Borger. They arrived in mid-August. A stroll down the single three-mile street, swarming with humanity, was enough to reveal a host of gambling and booze joints and brothels. Hijackings, a term covering every form of theft from seizure of machinery and vehicles to ordinary street muggings, were daily occurrences. Wheatley and Glasscock had little opportunity to act on their findings, however, for Borger "businessmen" resented their intrusion and complained to Governor Ferguson. Consistent with her policy of heeding local opinion, she withdrew the two Rangers.[15]

With the departure of Wheatley and Glasscock, Two-Gun Dick's mob ran rampant through Borger. On October 1 thieves accidentally shot and killed a fifteen-year-old girl. The federal and state district attorneys joined with the county attorney to appeal once again for Rangers. Meantime five federal prohibition officers, headed by Walter J. Knight and former Ranger Manuel T. "Lone Wolf" Gonzaullas, had worked undercover to identify all liquor dealers. On October 11 Captain Roy Nichols arrived with Sergeant Wheatley and Rangers Glasscock and C. M. Ezell. Joining with the federal officers and the sheriff, they closed twenty dives and arrested fifty violators. The federal agents departed at once, leaving the Rangers to police Borger and dispose of the prisoners.

Sgt. James W. McCormick and Ranger Ray Ballard of Headquarters Company soon reinforced Nichols.

As Borger had no police force and Sheriff Ownbey few deputies, Nichols bore instructions to enforce the law in Borger. Establishing headquarters in a hotel room, he imposed Ranger justice on the town. Guarded by lawmen with machine guns and shotguns, the prisoners were crammed into trucks and driven to jail in Amarillo. "Undesirables" received peremptory orders to leave town, which they did. By the end of October, Nichols declared Borger "100 percent better."

Meantime, in October, Borger incorporated, and the citizens elected John R. Miller mayor. He promised a "first-class" police force. Nichols and his men therefore lifted the occupation and returned to their Marshall headquarters.[16]

Captain Nichols may have cleaned up Borger, but he proclaimed it prematurely. Borger would validate the experience of the Neff administration that once the Rangers departed the bad men came back. Within months, Ma Ferguson's successor would find Borger his most explosive issue.

MA FERGUSON had promised to serve only one term as governor, but only eight months into her term Pa had begun to line up support for another run, and in February 1926 she announced her candidacy. The Fergusons could count on a solid core of "piney woods folks" in East Texas, but voters elsewhere lamented how scandal after scandal dogged the administration. The state highway department proved especially vulnerable, and in the fall of 1925 contracting scandals had raised the threat of impeachment.

The rot in the highway department had been laid bare by the attorney general, who also pursued other signs of fraud and corruption. Daniel J. Moody Jr. had risen rapidly in Texas politics. As youthful district attorney of Williamson and Travis counties, he had prosecuted and won conviction of Klansmen who beat, tarred, and feathered a victim. Moody's prosecution of the Klansmen was a courageous act in 1923. As attorney general, his record of exposing the evils of Fergusonism made him seem a logical candidate to take on the Fergusons in the 1926 election. Honest, able, courageous, a ruggedly handsome thirty-three, "that red-headed whirlwind from Williamson County" entered the crowded field of candidates in May 1926. "Dan's the Man," shouted his supporters. In the July primary he brushed aside the other candidates but fell just short of enough votes to avoid a runoff. Almost the sole issue in the runoff was the evils of Fergusonism, and the campaign was vicious as only Jim Ferguson could make it. Nevertheless, Dan Moody won twice the votes of Ma Ferguson to capture the governorship.[17]

THE FERGUSON ERA of 1925–27 had been a doleful time for the Texas Rangers. The reduction of the force from fifty to thirty, the limits placed on their mission, the wholesale pardoning of convicts, the legal challenge to their constitutionality, the loss of the star captains Hamer and Wright, and the subordination of law enforcement to politics depressed morale. Even so, the Rangers had done as well as the political circumstances permitted. Roy Nichols and his men turned in a superior record fighting violators of prohibition laws in East Texas and taming (at least for the first time) the Panhandle boomtown of Borger. Tom Hickman broke up bank robbing gangs in North Texas. William Ryan and his company conducted a vigorous campaign against horsebackers in South Texas.[18]

Scattered successes, however, could not blur the contrast between the Rangers of the Neff years and the Rangers of the Ferguson years. The force greeted the inauguration of Dan Moody with a sense of optimistic relief and expectation. It was not unwarranted.

[7]
Dan Moody, 1927–1931

AFTER TWO YEARS of the Fergusons, in January 1927 young Dan Moody blew into the statehouse like a fresh breeze. The Texas Rangers saw better days ahead. He named career soldier Robert L. Robertson adjutant general with instructions to give the Rangers special attention. Stressing respect for the law, the governor implied that the Rangers would be deployed wherever he thought necessary—a departure from the Ferguson policy of deferring to local authority. He even urged a salary increase. Not for another two years did the legislature act on that recommendation, but on March 18, 1929, it boosted pay for captains to $225 per month, sergeants to $175, and privates to $150. The law still authorized a force of fifty, but appropriations, especially after the pay raise, never permitted more than the previous thirty.[1]

Rangers also expected the roster of captains to change radically for the better, as foreshadowed on February 2 when General Robertson returned Private Frank Hamer to the rank of captain. The following three months featured hirings and firings, and company relettering and relocation. The final reorganization occurred on April 30, 1927. Ferguson appointees Monroe Fox, William Ryan, and D. E. Lindsey had already been "honorably discharged." Inexplicably, so had Roy Nichols, whose Marshall-based company was disbanded. Although unable to strengthen the force beyond thirty, Moody had created a strong leadership team: Roy Aldrich as quartermaster, Frank Hamer captaining Headquarters Company in Austin, Tom Hickman back in Fort Worth commanding a newly reconstituted Company B, Fox replaced by recall of the veteran Will Wright to take over Company A in Marfa, and perhaps most surprising, Company C at Del Rio assigned to John H. Rogers—the same who as one of the "four great captains" had helped usher the Rangers into the twentieth century. After resigning in 1911, he had served eight years as U.S. marshal for the Western District of Texas. Now sixty-four, he returned for a final three years as a Ranger captain before his death in 1930.[2]

The last of the five companies, D at Laredo, fell to William Warren Sterling, whose later notoriety and fat autobiography have given him special prominence in Ranger history. Thirty-six in 1927, a student at Texas A&M University for two years, a wartime military officer (though not overseas), Sterling was an athletic six feet three, handsome, and a scion of the South Texas ranching elite. He knew the border country intimately as well as its people, culture, and language. He had gained much field experience as an army scout during the "bandit war" of 1915, and after the World War he served as a tough justice of the peace and deputy sheriff in boomtown Mirando City. His horsemanship and marksmanship ranked with the best. He enjoyed strong public support and brought impressive credentials to the Rangers—especially the support of the speaker of the legislature's lower house, Robert Lee Bobbitt of Laredo. Not without reason Sterling enjoyed high self-esteem, and he emerges from his book, published in 1959, as an exemplary leader and lawman.[3]

In this book Sterling decried the influence of politics on the Ranger Force and declared that captains should be appointed on merit alone—a strange contradiction of his boastful gratitude to legislator Bobbitt for sponsoring his captaincy. Left unstated was that in 1921 he had tried unsuccessfully to get on the Ranger Force and in 1925 had all but gained a captaincy at the beginning of the Ferguson administration. Telegrams of opposition, however, informed Mrs. Ferguson that Sterling had run for sheriff of Stephens County in 1922 on the Klan ticket and backed the victorious Klan candidate for U.S. senator. "His record is totally bad," wired another. "Little authority will ruin him." Despite the endorsements of prestigious South Texans, therefore, Sterling fortunately missed the onus of serving as a Ferguson captain.[4]

During his tenure as captain, another reminder of the past shadowed Sterling's character. In June 1922, while running for sheriff at Breckenridge, he borrowed $45 from R. C. Collier to pay a life-insurance premium. Collier himself had to borrow to make the loan. Even after joining the Ranger Force, Sterling continued to ignore requests to repay the loan. This finally led Collier, now Convict 58914 at Huntsville, to complain to the adjutant general that confinement in the penitentiary left him unable to support his needy family and to ask that Sterling be forced to pay his debt. General Robertson replied that he would write the captain about this matter, but the record does not reveal whether the debt was ever paid.[5]

Another dark corner lay hidden in Sterling's background. At Mission in 1915, Frank Warnock feuded with old man Sterling and his two sons, and had shot and killed one of their hands. Frank's son Roland went to visit his father and with two other men stood facing him carrying on a conversation in the courthouse square. Roland suddenly sighted the Sterling brothers round the corner behind his father, who was in shirt-sleeves and unarmed.

"Well, it was done so quick that I didn't have time to warn Papa," related Roland, "but he didn't have a gun on anyway. Both of them come around this corner with automatics in their hands and they hadn't taken no more than about three long, big steps, and they emptied their guns.

"Papa never knew what hit him. They put nine bullets in his back. He fell right across in front of me. When he did, this bullet hit me. It tore a place in my skin and tore my shirt. I thought then that they were trying to kill me too, and I don't know but what they were because they followed me home."

This deed did not mar Bill Sterling's record. The brothers swore that Frank Warnock was reaching for a gun, and a witness backed them up. A jury deliberated for more than eighteen hours and returned a verdict of not guilty by reason of self-defense.[6]

As a Ranger captain and later as adjutant general, Bill Sterling largely lived up to his public image. His book is a treasure of Ranger history and lore. But he was not the paragon of rectitude projected by his reputation and legacy.

In November 1926 Captain Roy Nichols had declared the Panhandle boomtown of Borger cleaned up and brushed the issue off Governor Ferguson's desk. By April 1927 it had landed on Governor Moody's desk. Within three months after Nichols's departure, Borger again throbbed with slot machines, brothels, and more than twenty gambling joints. Hutchinson County sheriff Joe Ownbey took no action and supposedly received frequent payoffs. In late March gangsters killed a city policeman and on April 1 two of Ownbey's deputies. District judge Newton Willis wired Governor Moody "situation desperate" and asked for as many Rangers as could be spared.[7]

The governor promptly telegraphed Captain Hickman in Fort Worth to rush to Borger with four men and ordered Captain Hamer to follow with three from Austin. They carried orders to remain "until the law wins out over the lawless."

In a vigorous campaign of three weeks, the Rangers duplicated the Nichols operation of 1926: slot machines and stills smashed, gambling houses padlocked, prostitutes issued "sundown orders" (twelve hundred left in twenty-four hours), and 124 men arrested. Borger now had a jail of sorts, a frame building next to police headquarters, but it was not big or secure enough. Rangers installed a heavy chain fastened to the main floor beam and shackled prisoners to it until they could be moved to the jail at the new county seat of Stinnett. The "trotline" became a standard feature of Ranger cleanups.

Hamer and Hickman dominated Borger from the day they arrived. Throughout the 1920s the two worked often and well together. Yet they

differed in almost every way except proficiency in criminal investigation. As a team, however, they worked effectively, as Borger swiftly
learned.

Governor Moody warned Mayor John Miller and the county commissioners to root out the crooked officials or he would take action himself. Under pressure from the governor's officers on the scene, the mayor
fired the chief of police and a number of policemen, and Sheriff Ownbey
hastened to explain that he had discharged every deputy named by the
Ranger captains and would cooperate enthusiastically. Some justices
of the peace and county commissioners also resigned. Mayor Miller
and his cronies finally stepped down. Although failing to oust all the
suspect city and county officials, especially Sheriff Ownbey, by early
May the state officers declared Borger "quiet" once again. Two Rangers
remained to watch over the city while the rest returned to their home
stations.[8]

Quiet it may have been, but early in June 1927 the pastors of the
Baptist and Methodist churches warned Governor Moody that the town
had returned to the bad old ways. Meantime, Moody had teamed up
with the federal prohibition administrator in Fort Worth in a joint state-
federal effort to identify a conspiracy to violate the federal prohibition
law in Borger. The federal agent sent to Borger in mid-June 1927 was
Manuel T. Gonzaullas, the former Ranger who had hit Borger dives with
Captain Nichols in October 1926. His investigation, conducted with the
aid of the Borger Rangers, disclosed that the Ranger operation in April
had broken up a massive conspiracy—between city and county officials
on the one hand, and illicit liquor, gambling, vice, and criminal rings on
the other. The witnesses to make a case against these conspirators had
fled, however, either to escape arrest or to avoid murder, so successful
prosecution seemed unlikely. But, Gonzaullas added ominously, some
parties to the broken conspiracy remained, in criminal gangs and in city
and county government. He warned that they might reorganize and set
Borger ablaze once again. Based on this report, the federal administrator closed the case.[9]

Thus inconclusively, Borger Cleanup No. 2 had ended.

MUCH OF THE SCUM the Rangers flushed out of Borger flowed into newly opened fields to the southwest. The vast Permian Basin, underlying seventeen counties of West Texas, began to sprout boomtowns just as Captain Nichols was calming Borger in 1926. The new oil finds occurred in a flat, barren land, sparsely populated by stockmen, that lay west of San Angelo and centered on the railroad towns of Midland and Odessa. The wildest of the wild were McCamey and Wink. Responding to an appeal from the Upton County attorney in January 1927, Governor Moody sent Ranger William H. Kirby to investigate. He turned in an exceptionally thorough report that detailed the usual sordid story of corrupt officials and lawmen connected to criminal rings. If action against these men were not taken soon, Kirby warned, McCamey could become another Borger.[10]

The nearest Rangers, Will Wright's Company A working out of Marfa, were already stretched thin trying to interdict horsebackers and stock thieves in the Big Bend. But the newest oil field fell to Wright. Not until December 1927 could he conduct some tentative raids. Then on February 1, 1928, over the protests of Big Bend citizens, Wright received orders to establish headquarters at McCamey and launch a cleanup campaign such as had occurred in Borger and the North Texas towns. Leaving one man in Presidio, he took the other four to McCamey. For the rest of 1928 and into 1929, his Rangers and federal agents swept through Wink, McCamey, and other lawless towns.

Like his fellow Rangers in other boomtowns, Wright could report impressive statistics in numbers of people arrested, stills destroyed, gallons of liquor confiscated, transport autos seized, illegal joints padlocked, sundown orders issued, and corrupt officials indicted (though rarely convicted). The solution, of course, was at least one Ranger stationed permanently in every oil town. As the district judge in Midland observed, "The gamblers and bootleggers hate the Rangers worse than the devil does holy water." But so long as oil gushed, humanity flocked to the scene, prohibition remained in force, and the Rangers numbered no more than thirty for the entire state, the quandary defied solution.[11]

On the night of January 10, 1928, Eddie V. Hall was driving his yellow Buick roadster northwest on the Sweetwater-Lubbock highway bound for Post. He was an "oil scout" for Gulf Oil Company, constantly on the road checking oil prospects. Just south of Justiceburg he spotted two cars parked facing him on one side of the road and one on the other. They flashed their headlights. The lights revealed an array of men on both sides of the highway holding rifles and shotguns. Fearing hijackers, Hall threw himself flat on the seat, grabbed the bottom of the steering wheel, and hit the accelerator. As he ran the gauntlet, a fusillade ripped into his car, shattered the windshield, tore away part of the steering wheel, and lodged a load of buckshot in his knee. Stopping at a café in Justiceburg, he asked for a doctor. A carload of armed men, two constables and several possemen, drove up and asked why he had not stopped when ordered. Hall replied that they had not held up their hands or given any other sign that they were officers rather than hijackers. One of the posse, who lived in Post, volunteered to drive Hall there to see a doctor. That night and again the next morning the doctor dressed his wound. He had to pay his own bill because the constables contended that his refusal to stop for lawmen made the injury his own fault. Hall's father and sister drove him home to San Angelo, where his own doctor confined him to bed.

Three days later Governor Moody received a telegram from C. C. Phillips, the president of the West Texas Oil Scouts Association in San Angelo. Noting that the bank at Sylvester had been robbed earlier on January 10, he suggested that the constables and possemen, greedy for the reward the Texas Bankers Association had offered for *dead* robbers, had prompted the attack on Hall. They had not sought to identify him, and the condition of the car showed they were not trying to stop it but to kill the driver. Phillips asked the governor to conduct an investigation.

The task fell to the Ranger expert in bank robbery, Captain Tom Hickman. He assigned it to his new sergeant, Manuel T. Gonzaullas. Thirty-six in 1928, Gonzaullas already claimed a distinguished record as a lawman. Born in Spain to traveling American parents, he had been reared in the El Paso area and spoke Spanish fluently. His youthful hero and exemplar was Ranger captain John R. Hughes, based at Ysleta. Gonzaullas joined the Ranger Force in 1920 and served proficiently both on the border and in the North Texas boomtowns. In November 1921 he resigned to accept a higher-paying job as a federal prohibition agent. Although he returned to the Rangers in 1924, he had served the federal administrators so brilliantly that late in 1925 they asked to borrow him back. In July 1927, shortly after his Borger conspiracy investigation, he came back to the Rangers for the rest of his career.

Manuel Gonzaullas not only displayed professional distinction but personal as well. Of medium build but muscular and strong, he dressed and groomed impeccably, loved fancy guns and cars, and harbored a well-deserved high opinion of his talents. Resembling Captain Hickman in vanity, he nevertheless treated all but lawbreakers with courtesy. Like the famous Captain John H. Rogers, he was a devout Presbyterian and carried a pocket Testament. Toward lawbreakers he harbored a visceral hatred that granted no mercy. His two pistols, with trigger guards removed, rested in special holsters that exposed the triggers for instant action. During his long career he is said to have shot and killed twenty-two men and in turn received seven wounds. Although an extrovert, he kept his plans secret and preferred to work alone. "I went into a lot of fights by myself," he recalled, "and I came out by myself, too." Mexican bandits labeled him "El Lobo Solo," and the sobriquet stuck. "Lone Wolf" Gonzaullas became a legend in his own lifetime.[12]

The Lone Wolf traveled to San Angelo and Justiceburg and reconstructed Eddie Hall's calamity in detail. He interviewed all the participants and observers and carefully examined Hall's riddled Buick. He counted three hundred bullet holes, 90 percent in the upper half of the vehicle. If Hall had not thrown himself flat on the seat, the sergeant concluded, he would have been hit about two hundred times in the head and shoulders. The investigation left no doubt in Gonzaullas's mind that had the officers used discretion in attempting to stop Hall's car, the shooting could have been avoided. Both the lawmen and their posse, he concluded, were guilty of assault to murder and should be prosecuted.[13]

Dependent on local initiative, that was not likely to happen. But Eddie Hall's ordeal exemplified but one of many incidents in the continuing quest for dead bank robbers pursued by the Texas Bankers Association. Had Hall robbed the Sylvester bank, the possemen could not have collected the $5,000 reward by arresting him, only by killing him.

Less than a month earlier, with bank robberies a daily occurrence, the most spectacular in Texas history took place at Cisco, a railroad town in Eastland County. On December 23, 1927, four men entered the First National Bank and covered everyone with pistols. They were ex-convicts Marshall Ratliff, Henry Helms, and Robert Hill, and an accomplice, Louis Davis. Ratliff wore a bright Santa Claus costume. They stuffed $12,400 in cash and stacks of nonnegotiable securities into sacks. Before even out of the bank, however, they exchanged gunfire with officers and citizens outside, then got into another shootout in the alley in which they mortally wounded the chief of police and a deputy. High-speed chases followed, first in one car, then in a second, until they bungled the third car by letting the occupant get away with the keys. Abandoning the money sacks and a mortally wounded Davis, the remaining three took to their feet. Spurred by the bankers' association reward, lawmen and possemen all over North Texas took to the field. Captain Tom Hickman appeared in Cisco with bloodhounds, but a mob of possemen had so trampled the area as to destroy the scent.

With stolen autos, the robbers tried to make their way home to Wichita Falls. Another gun battle erupted near South Bend, the Brazos River crossing in Young County, when a sheriff's posse spotted the auto and gave chase. In a roadside exchange of fire, Ratliff went down, but Helms and Hill, with new wounds, raced into the Brazos bottoms. Hickman arrived the next day, to brand the encounter botched because the possemen had been so anxious to claim the reward for the man they thought they had killed, Ratliff, that they let the other two escape.

Hickman wired Fort Worth for an airplane. From the sky Sergeant Gonzaullas scanned the Brazos bottoms where the fugitives, badly wounded and without food, desperately tried to keep under cover. He spotted one in an open field, however, and flew back to Graham to alert Hickman to their whereabouts. Exhausted and hungry, on December 30 Helms and Hill stumbled into Graham and surrendered.

All three stood trial. Hill went to the penitentiary, Helms to the electric chair, and Ratliff set off a tortuous sequence of legal proceedings by convincingly behaving as if insane. In November 1929, trying to escape from the Eastland County jail, he mortally wounded a guard. An enraged mob gathered, dragged him from his cell, and hanged him to the nearest telephone pole.[14]

Every bank in Texas bore a poster proclaiming: "Reward. Five Thousand Dollars for Dead Bank Robbers and Not One Cent for Live Ones." Greed for this reward, in Hickman's opinion, had turned the Santa Claus manhunt into a farce. Crowds of lawmen and possemen swarmed so chaotically that the fugitives repeatedly eluded them until driven by wounds and hunger to give up.

The Texas Bankers Association thus complicated the task of the Texas Rangers by stirring avarice in men with rifles in their hands. But Captain Hamer began to note a more ominous result. Some robbers got killed at night, when the banks were closed. The deeper he dug, the more convinced he became that several men were engaged in luring drunks or unsuspecting youths to banks where local deputies lay in wait. They shot down the dupes, then collected $5,000 from the bankers' association. Hamer tried to persuade the bankers to withdraw or modify the reward offer. They refused.

The reticent, publicity-shy Hamer then took an action altogether out of character. On March 12, 1928, he issued his own press release. Citing three particular cases to back his charges, he concluded: "Here is as perfect a murder machine as can be devised, supported by the Bankers' Association, operated by the officers of the state and directed by the small group of greedy men who furnish the victims and take their cut of the money." It was a disgrace to Texas, he declared, and he challenged the bankers' association to appoint a committee to examine his evidence. The next day headlines all over Texas spotlighted the Ranger captain's damning charges against one of the most powerful organizations in the state.

Hamer next set forth to bring to justice the culprits in the cases he had described in his press release. He secured grand jury indictments of three men in two of the cases and then extracted written confessions. Eventually the bankers relented and modified their offer to suit Hamer's demands.[15]

IN THE ELECTION of 1928 Dan Moody handily won a second term as governor of Texas. The legislature had adopted almost none of his proposed reforms (few governors enjoyed a legislature concerned with more than saving money), but the people liked him, and the two-term tradition remained healthy.

On January 4, 1929, Moody and Adjutant General Robert Robertson decided to retain all the captains appointed in 1927. The strength held at thirty, and the policy of employing Rangers at the governor's discretion continued as in the first term.[16]

BORGER STUBBORNLY refused to stay clean. In 1928 a reform group had won all the Hutchinson County offices except sheriff, still occupied by Joe Ownbey of fetid memory. The new district attorney, John A. Holmes, had made a career of defending criminals during earlier regimes, but now he changed sides. Widely believed to be an incorruptible man of tenacity and integrity, he pursued the criminals as vigorously as he had once defended them. Borger, however, remained in control of the corrupt mayor Glen Pace and the corrupt police chief. In the Borger city elections of April 1929 the Pace ring brought in outside voters, paid their poll tax, and decisively defeated the reform party.[17]

In April 1929 Holmes complained to the governor that he could work effectively only if Rangers resided indefinitely in Borger. Then the booze joints would stay closed. As soon as the Rangers left, all joints opened and stayed open until the Rangers returned. Moreover, Holmes added, this would be the reality so long as Joe Ownbey remained sheriff.[18]

Governor Moody sent in Rangers. On June 28 Captain Hickman, Sergeant Gonzaullas, and six Rangers swept through Borger to enact the familiar routine. Within six hours they and federal agents had destroyed gambling equipment and liquor and arrested thirty-five men. With a statewide force of only thirty, however, they could not remain long. Holmes saw his prophecy fulfilled. As the joints reopened, not only did the sheriff and city police withhold cooperation, but tampered jury lists and reluctant witnesses made prosecutions all but impossible. Thirty-five murders had occurred within the last two years, yet only one conviction had been obtained. Still, Holmes persisted, keeping the officers and mobsters off balance.[19]

On the night of September 13, 1929, Holmes drove home from his office, picking up his wife and mother-in-law en route. He stopped in the backyard to let the two women out, then drove into his garage. He got out and was closing the car door when five .38-caliber bullets blasted through a garage window that had previously been broken out. Three hit Holmes in the head and back.[20]

Headlined throughout Texas, Holmes's murder stirred public outrage. A Borger citizen, noting that the mayor and city commission had been elected by the underworld, declared that everyone knew that the police, sheriff's deputies, and bootleggers had killed Holmes but could not prove it and were afraid to speak up anyway.

Reacting instantly, Moody dispatched Hamer and Hickman with Sergeant J. B. Wheatley and two other Rangers to Borger. They found a rabble of 180,000 "pistol-minded" people, a mayor and police department that had frightened all possible court witnesses into leaving, a sheriff's department unwilling to cooperate, and, as Hamer reported to the governor, "the worst bit of organized crime" he had encountered in twenty-three years as a lawman.

On receipt of Hamer's report, on September 23 Moody ordered Gonzaullas and four more Rangers to Borger. He also called on General Jacob Wolters, who had mobilized the National Guard at Mexia, to go to Borger and determine the need for martial law. Meantime, he had appointed District Attorney Clem Calhoun of Abilene to succeed

Holmes in Borger. In Amarillo General Wolters met with Calhoun and Hickman, then with Calhoun drove to Borger. They found all the people, good and bad, opposed to martial law, but the good people could offer no hope that the conditions of two years could be reversed. "The entire community was in the grip of a frozen terror."

Wolters and Calhoun drove all the way to Austin and sat down with Moody. With Hamer, Calhoun, and Wolters all in favor, on September 28 Moody placed Hutchinson County under martial law. At the same time he suspended Borger police chief J. W. Crabtree, county sheriff Joe Ownbey, and all members of their departments.[21]

Anticipating martial law, General Wolters had been quietly alerting officers for a week to prepare, under a veil of strict secrecy, eighty cavalrymen for an unspecified duty. He and his force steamed into the Borger depot on the morning of September 30 and immediately clamped military occupation on the city. His provost marshal took possession of the city hall, jail, and other offices and disarmed all the local lawmen. Another detail drove to Stinnett, the county seat, and removed Sheriff Ownbey. A veteran of martial law in Mexia, Wolters had complete control of the city and county seat within hours of his arrival.

Wolters then formed a "board of inquiry" consisting of army and civil officers, including District Attorney Calhoun and Captains Hamer and Hickman. The president of the board issued subpoenas to bring in witnesses, and Rangers fanned out to serve them. Mayor Pace, Sheriff Ownbey, and Chief Crabtree all testified, then vanished from the scene. Subsequent witnesses held back, still afraid. Well-known mobsters continued to walk the street. Wolters resolved to get rid of them. By October 10 he had seventeen members of the "organized and entrenched criminal ring" behind bars. They promptly instituted habeas corpus proceedings, but both state and federal judges remanded them to the custody of General Wolters.

Meantime, the Rangers played their part. Private J. W. Aldrich (Quartermaster Roy Aldrich's brother) took over as acting chief of police, Sergeant J. B. Wheatley as acting county sheriff. Within two weeks Rangers had completed the usual routine, shutting down gambling saloons and the red light district, issuing sundown orders, and arresting more than three hundred violators, who endured for a time hooked to the Ranger trotline.

On October 5 a committee of citizens called on General Wolters to ask what he required to end martial law. His response: resignation of the sheriff and all his deputies, the two constables and their deputies, the mayor, the city commission, and all members of the police department; their replacement by men satisfactory to the new district attorney, Clem Calhoun. Mayor Pace and Sheriff Ownbey tried some stalling tactics, but after deliberations involving the district judge and grand jury, all gave in and resigned.

On October 18, 1929, Governor Moody withdrew the military from Borger, and eleven days later he formally lifted martial law. He granted Ranger Charles O. Moore a leave of absence of one year to serve as sheriff of Hutchinson County and sent Marvin "Red" Burton, of Glen Rose liquor fame, to serve as his chief deputy and investigator of the Holmes murder. Alfred Mace, the Ranger who had agreed to become chief of police in Mexia at the end of martial law in 1922, consented to move to Borger and assume the same office. By October 31, Clem Calhoun could report to the governor that peace and quiet prevailed in Borger. Sheriff Moore and his deputies could scarcely find a drunk on the streets. Calhoun had launched a vigorous prosecution of lawbreakers.

Once more, under the expert oversight of General Wolters and Captains Hamer and Hickman, Borger had been cleaned up. Calhoun conceded that some of the old gang were trying to reorganize but doubted they could succeed. Moody worried that ex-mayor Glen Pace might still employ the outside voters holding poll-tax receipts to launch a return to power, and this apprehension seemed partly justified by city elections in June 1930 that awarded Borger's infamous first mayor, John R. Miller, a seat on the city commission. But more influential in preventing a resurgent underworld was the Great Depression, little more than a month in the future when General Wolters pulled out the troops. Borger no longer throbbed as a major oil producer and so no longer offered the market for booze, gambling, and vice that had made it so hard to tame. Neither the Guard nor the Rangers would again be called to clean up Borger.[22]

Working with Clem Calhoun, Red Burton relentlessly pursued the Holmes murder case for more than a year. He assembled what he considered sufficient evidence to convict Borger barber James Hodges and companion Sam Jones, who acted simply as hit men for the chief of police, sheriff, and other officers. Calhoun obtained indictments of the two but never regarded the evidence as strong enough to warrant a trial. In light of Holmes's previous activities, Red Burton's conclusion is persuasive: "My investigation convinced me personally that Holmes was not too far above the balance of the gang of officers at Borger but that he was operating as a lone wolf and he was crossed with the other faction."[23]

THROUGHOUT THE 1920s Jim Crow reigned in Texas as unshakably supreme as in the other states of the Old South. The Longview race riot of 1919, however professionally handled by local authorities and the Texas Rangers, dramatized the barbarity to which white Texans would resort for the least offense, real or imagined, against the entrenched social order. Beatings and lynchings occurred regularly. Sometimes the local lawmen or Rangers headed them off. More often, mobs did their work despite or with the complicity of local police before Rangers could be summoned.

In 1930 Rangers joined with local officers in an imaginative drama to thwart lynch mobs in the eastern Panhandle. On July 11, 1930, Jesse Lee Washington (perhaps related to Jesse Washington of the Waco horror of 1915) had beaten to death Mrs. Henry Vaughan of Shamrock, in Wheeler County. Arrested by Collingsworth County sheriff Claude McKinney, he confessed to the county attorney. With Shamrock mobs threatening to obliterate the black section of town, Wheeler County sheriff W. K. McLemore called on Governor Moody for Rangers. Four were dispatched on July 13 from Austin. Rangers M. T. Gonzaullas, J. P. Huddleston, W. H. Kirby, and Bob Goss hurried to Shamrock, then down to Wellington. They served public notice that the prisoner and all other blacks would be protected "regardless of the cost." On July 16 Sheriff McKinney, disguised as an oil field worker, drove up to the Gray County courthouse in Pampa and, unrecognized, escorted his prisoner into the jail. At once another car, bearing Lone Wolf Gonzaullas and his three comrades from Shamrock, sped to a stop and unloaded a conspicuous display of armament—machine guns, rifles, shotguns, pistols, and grenades. No mob formed to confront such an array of weapons in the hands of determined Rangers.

The next day, July 17, in a carefully timed arrangement with Judge W. E. Ewing, the Rangers and three Pampa deputies drove Washington to Shamrock for arraignment. They arrived at exactly 6:00 PM and emerged five minutes later. Two mobs seeking the prisoner had been led to believe he would be with the Rangers, who easily led them astray while Sheriff McKinney, again garbed in oil field clothing, drove his chained prisoner back to Pampa. Guarded by the four Rangers, Washington remained safely in his cell until escorted to Miami for trial. There on July 28 Judge Ewing sentenced him to the electric chair.

This outcome was never in doubt, only whether Washington would be executed by the state or a mob.

The role of the Rangers infuriated Shamrock citizens. Fifteen women signed a telegram condemning the governor for instructing the Rangers to "kill our fathers husbands and brothers in order to protect a confessed negro rapist and murderer." They were thus left "at the mercy of any negro field hand who runs amuck," and they protested "in behalf of all of the white women of Texas." The sheriff and his prisoner, however, were doubtless grateful for the martial demeanor of the Rangers.[24]

SERGEANT GONZAULLAS and his comrades adopted this assertive approach because of a tragic incident that had happened only three months earlier. One of the most brutish and shameful episodes in the history of Texas, it occurred on May 9, 1930, in Sherman, seat of Grayson County bordering Red River north of Dallas.

Six days earlier, on May 3, field hand George Hughes called at his employer's home to collect six dollars owed him in wages. Told by the man's wife that her husband was in Sherman, Hughes left. He returned forty-five minutes later with a shotgun and, thrusting the woman into the bedroom, brutally and repeatedly raped her as her screaming five-year-old tried to climb on the bed. Hughes pushed the child out of the room and closed the door before returning to the assault. Worried about the child, however, he went outside in search. This allowed his victim to escape across a field and sound the alarm. Deputies arrived to find Hughes wandering around the barn looking for the child. He fired a shotgun blast at them but was quickly in handcuffs. At the jail he confessed the crime.[25]

Newspaper accounts stirred outrage throughout the county, and men rode among the rural families circulating false and exaggerated accounts of the woman's injuries. Heavy rains kept farmers from their fields, and they began to congregate in Sherman. Although assured of a speedy trial, they pressed in ever-growing numbers around the county jail. Rowdy high school boys enthusiastically joined in the demand for Hughes. Only by opening the jail to a few men could local officers demonstrate that Hughes was not held there. Reinforced by whole families from throughout Grayson and adjoining counties, the crowds thronged the muddy streets in an increasingly ugly mood.

Despite some sentiment for moving the trial elsewhere, the victim's family insisted that Hughes be tried in Sherman. District Judge R. M. Carter, young and new to the bench, scheduled the trial for Friday, May 9. On Tuesday, already worried about security, he telephoned Governor Moody and asked for Rangers to back Sheriff Alfred Vaughan and his deputies. Captain Hamer, with Sergeant J. B. Wheatley and Rangers J. E. McCoy and J. W. Aldrich, left Austin by train on Wednesday evening and reached Sherman the next morning, May 8.

On the morning of May 9, with the second-floor courtroom in the courthouse barred to all but parties to the trial, Judge Carter gaveled the court into session. The Rangers and Sheriff Vaughan and several deputies stood guard. Outside, a horde of people clogged the streets. Mothers with children in tow and even babes in their arms sprinkled the mob. A gaggle of teenagers waved an American flag. People surged into the courthouse and filled the stairwell and upstairs hall outside the courtroom. With jury selection complete and the trial about to begin, an ambulance arrived, and attendants bore Hughes's victim (who was never named) on a stretcher up the stairs to the courtroom. The sight sent the mob into a frenzy. Some pressed into the courtroom and ran toward Hughes. The lawmen brandished their weapons and forced them back into the hall. Hughes had pleaded guilty and the first witness had taken the stand when the swelling commotion in the hall caused Judge Carter to halt the proceedings. Removing Hughes from the courtroom, he had him locked in a huge two-story vault made of steel and concrete. It was used by the county clerk as an office and secure storage for records.

The double doors to the hallway outside the courtroom gave way under the crush. The Rangers and county lawmen advanced with shotguns and rifles, fired into the air, and hurled tear gas bombs. The mob retreated down the stairs. As the building filled with tear gas, the fire department arrived to raise ladders to second-story windows and evacuate jurors, witnesses, and other participants in the trial.

Twice more a horde streamed up the stairs, only to be driven back by tear gas. A fourth time they made a rush. Hamer gave them a load of buckshot from his shotgun, and they turned back with two men wounded.

Meantime, rumors flew through the crowds that the Rangers had instructions not to fire on them. A newsman made his way up to the second floor and showed Hamer an Associated Press dispatch quoting a message Governor Moody had supposedly sent to Hamer: "Protect the negro if possible, but don't shoot anybody." No such order had been sent, and as Hamer pointed out to the judge, such a restriction would make protection of Hughes impossible. But the throngs below believed it and made ready for another attack.

Emboldened by the report, one of the agitators came to the foot of the stairs and asked Hamer if he intended to give up the prisoner. Told no, the man replied, "Well we are coming up and get him." "Any time you feel lucky," the burly captain answered, "come on, but when you start up the stairway once more, there is going to be many funerals in Sherman."[26]

This warning kept the mob at bay. The sheriff and his deputies went down to the street, leaving the Rangers to guard Hughes. They heard windows shattering below, as people hurled rocks. A high school student flung a can of gasoline through a window. Another dropped in a lighted match. The gasoline failed to catch. Another boy leaped to the window sill, struck a match, and threw it in. The gasoline caught and flared. "Now the damned old courthouse is on fire," he shouted as he jumped down. The fire spread quickly throughout the first floor, swept up the stairs, and ignited the ceiling of the second floor. A sheet of flame cut off the Rangers from the vault and forced them down into the street, where the mob was receding from the heat of the fire. Firefighters hooked hoses to hydrants to attack the fire, only to have the hoses slashed.[27]

After observing the throng for a few minutes, Hamer persuaded a man to drive him and his comrades to a place where he could telephone the governor in private. Finally, in McKinney, thirty-five miles south on the road to Dallas, he made connection. Moody, however, had already ordered guardsmen to Sherman and, unable to reach Captain Hickman, succeeded in talking with Sergeant Gonzaullas in Dallas. The Lone Wolf hurried to Sherman and took station in front of the county jail. With a pistol holstered on each hip, a Thompson submachine gun conspicuous by his side, and a sawed-off shotgun in hand, he confronted crowds advancing on the jail. Buckshot fired over their heads kept them at bay. Eventually, eleven Rangers from Headquarters Company and Hickman's Company B saw service in Sherman.[28]

By late afternoon, with the courthouse a burned-out hulk, responsibility for riot control shifted from local lawmen to the military. About a dozen guardsmen arrived from Denison but retreated to the jail when assailed by rioters. The same fate befell fifty-two more soldiers from Dallas under Colonel Laurence McGee, who debarked from special interurban cars about seven o'clock that evening. Bottles, bricks, and other missiles injured several guardsmen as they attempted to clear the courthouse square, then hurried to the defenses of the jail. A woman in front of the throng attacking the soldiers held her baby aloft and shouted, "Shoot it, you yellow nigger lovin' soldiers; shoot it!"[29]

While part of the mob besieged the guardsmen in the county jail, others went to the gutted courthouse to look for George Hughes. After labored attempts to open the vault, they brought acetylene torches and dynamite. Cutting through to the inner shell, they set off a dynamite charge that blew a steel plate into the room. George Hughes lay on the floor dead, unburned, his skull probably crushed by the plate. Passed through the opening, the body was thrown out a second-floor window. Cheering rioters chained it to an automobile and dragged it through the streets to the black section of the city. Hoisting it on a cottonwood tree, they gathered furniture from a black drugstore and other shops, and kindled a roaring bonfire beneath it. As Hughes roasted, the mob began to plunder and set fire to black-owned businesses. In addition to homes, seventeen business and professional establishments went up in flames. With slashed hoses, the fire department stayed away.

At 4:00 AM on Saturday morning, another rainy day, two hundred more guardsmen from Fort Worth reached Sherman and quickly set the city under firm occupation. A detail cut down the charred body of Hughes but had to turn it over to a white undertaker since both black morticians had been burned out. On Saturday night Governor Moody proclaimed martial law in Precinct 1 of Grayson County and named Colonel McGee to command. More troops arrived on Sunday morning, together with more Rangers. By this day of continuing rains 450 guardsmen, Rangers, and deputies policed Sherman. The surly mobs dispersed, cowed but not chastened.[30]

Colonel McGee kept Sherman tightly locked down by martial law until May 24, when the governor lifted it. During these two weeks Rangers aided local lawmen in investigating the riot and identifying men and some women to bring before a military court of inquiry Colonel McGee established on May 12. The court questioned sixty-six people, jailed twenty-nine, and on the nineteenth laid evidence before a grand jury that handed down fourteen indictments. All the indictments dealt with various forms of rioting, including burglary, arson, and rioting to commit murder. All but one of the accused were young to middle-aged men of no property and little education. Some had court records for bootlegging, cattle theft, and other minor offenses. They hardly represented the mob of several thousand who thronged the streets to watch and cheer them on. Every social and economic class provided the power that drove the riot.

A change of venue to Dallas produced no jurors who would convict a white man in such a case. Another change of venue to Austin brought one man to trial in June 1931. He was convicted and sent to Huntsville for two years. Several times postponed and finally moved north to Cooke County, the remaining cases ultimately fell off the docket. A single man paid the legal penalty for the horrors inflicted by thousands.

But Sherman paid another penalty. Newspapers throughout Texas, the nation, and even in London excoriated the citizens of Grayson County and Sherman for the bestiality displayed on May 9, 1930. The Sherman riot was the worst offense against blacks in the United States in 1930 and the most universally publicized and chastised by the national public. The mayor and other officials reacted defensively, and leading citizens condemned the actions of their fellow townspeople. But even some of them contended that the black man had only got what was coming to him.

Frank Hamer and the other Rangers bore little criticism for their role. In fact, Colonel McGee commended them highly for their cooperation and their investigative skills in rounding up so many people for examination by the military commission. Whether or not Hamer and his comrades returned to Sherman on May 9 or, more likely, arrived on Sunday morning with the final force of guardsmen, they could not have reined in the crowd; more than 250 guardsmen failed at that. Nor could Hamer have foreseen the fire that prevented him from releasing Hughes from the vault, which he could not have done anyway because he lacked the combination to the lock. His shotgun blast and promise to shoot again had driven the mob from the courthouse. But for the fire, he believed, he could have protected the prisoner. Years later the more aggressive Lone Wolf Gonzaullas declared that Hamer should simply have "shot the hell" out of the mob, then at once called for more help.[31]

THAT THE SHERMAN RIOT was as inspirational as embarrassing became apparent on May 18, only nine days after the torching of the courthouse. At Honey Grove, in Fannin County only fifty miles east of Sherman, George Johnson, farm hand, shot and killed his overseer in an argument over debt. Barricaded in a cabin, he held off officers as they riddled the cabin with as many as two thousand bullets, provided by local merchants. A crowd gathered to watch. After two hours, the firing from the cabin ceased. The officers entered to find Johnson dead. As they pulled his body out of the cabin, the watching crowd rushed to the scene, grabbed Johnson by the feet, and dragged him face-down across a muddy field. Imitating the Sherman mob, they chained the body to an auto and dragged it to the black section of Honey Grove. Here they hoisted it head down from a tree limb, drenched it in gasoline, and set it ablaze. Rain finally dispersed the crowd, and a black undertaker cut down the corpse, now headless.[32]

Less publicized than Sherman, Honey Grove represented the kind of incident that scarred the history of white Texas for three generations. The 1920s afforded numerous examples, in a few of which the Texas Rangers got to the scene either before or after the death of the victim. More often, as in Honey Grove, a rabidly white-supremacist citizenry simply took over from the local lawmen and lynched either a live black or a dead one.

THE CLOSE OF Dan Moody's administration found the Texas Rangers back to the high level of admiration, respect, and competence they had enjoyed before the Fergusons came to power. The star players were Captains Frank Hamer, Tom Hickman, and Will Wright. Hamer and Hickman had exceptionally able companies, even though numbering no more than half a dozen men each. They shone especially bright in Borger, in the gathering storm of bank robberies, and even in the Sherman riot, although they felt shame at losing the prisoner they had been sent to protect. In the Big Bend Will Wright had too few men to make much progress against horsebackers in an unforgiving landscape. After his company moved to McCamey, the Big Bend lay even more vulnerable, but the cleanup of McCamey, Wink, and other West Texas boomtowns reflected creditably on the captain and his men. On the lower Rio Grande, Captains Bill Sterling and John Rogers proved competent captains kept from the public glare by routine operations against horsebackers. They did well but gained far less publicity than their more colorful counterparts working out of Austin and Fort Worth.

Like Pat Neff, Dan Moody had relied heavily on Rangers and accorded them full credit when deserved. After the political trauma of the Ferguson years, Moody professionalized and stabilized the force. An occasional scandal marred the record, as when a Borger Ranger unlawfully interfered with a newspaperman. Excepting Hickman and Rogers, most of the Rangers employed rough techniques common to lawmen of the time. Hamer set the example, as did the emerging celebrity Lone Wolf Gonzaullas. In South Texas the record reveals little oppression of border Mexicans such as had led to the Canales hearings of 1919. Both Bill Sterling and John Rogers related well and sympathetically to them. Big Bend Rangers, however, tended to be less mindful of legalities in relations with Mexicans.

The Ranger record of 1921–25 and 1927–31 exhibits the stature the Texas Rangers could acquire when backed by enlightened governors such as Pat Neff and Dan Moody.

[8]

Ross and Bill Sterling, 1931–1933

No GOVERNOR, not even Pat Neff, had treated the Texas Rangers as well as Dan Moody. Ross S. Sterling, taking office in January 1931, trumped them both. A prosperous Houston oil and newspaper executive, he had served Moody well as chairman of the state highway commission. The Great Depression dogged Sterling's administration, and most of his initiatives died in the legislature. But, in a bid for a strong, competent, and honest Ranger Force, he made the extraordinary decision to name a Ranger captain as adjutant general. William Warren Sterling (no kin) not only won the support of the National Guard generals but lifted the Rangers to their highest stature since frontier times.[1]

Bill Sterling looked and acted the part. Slim and muscular, his six-foot three-inch frame dominated the many group photographs in which he posed. A firm, upthrust chin, grim set of mouth, well-formed nose, and blue eyes betrayed a high sense of self-worth. It drew on impeccable political and social connections together with experience as a border rancher, master of horse and gun, army scout during the "bandit war," local lawman and justice of the peace, and a four-year term as a Ranger captain. He dressed smartly, either in western garb or business suit.

Leaving the National Guard to the generals, Sterling concentrated on the Rangers. He intended to keep the force clean, competent, and well regarded by local authority and the people. This meant recruiting good men and paying enough to keep them. It meant appointment and promotion based on merit rather than politics. He believed that no man should be named captain who had not served two years in the ranks. That politics powered his own rise to captain and adjutant general, and that he had no previous Ranger service, reflected not personal hypocrisy but the system that he sought to reform.[2]

Selection of the captains proved the first test, and the governor accepted all of the adjutant general's recommendations. Four captains drew reappointment: Frank Hamer of Headquarters Company, Will Wright of Company A, Tom Hickman of Company B, and Alfred Mace of Company C. Mace had been appointed captain of Company C in November 1930, following the death of the veteran John H. Rogers. Fifty-four and a hefty 248 pounds, Mace had served as a Ranger under Captain John R. Hughes in 1902–3, but his record now rested on his success as the police chief who had kept Mexia and Borger tamed. To his old Company D Sterling assigned Sergeant Light Townsend, fifty-seven and a stubby five-eight. Friction had marred their relationship, and Townsend expected to be fired. But Sterling regarded him as the right man for the captaincy, which he was.[3]

Surprising everyone, Sterling dropped longtime quartermaster Roy Aldrich, whom he regarded as a scheming, dishonest power grabber. The intensity of Sterling's hatred emerges in several pages of often-trivial denunciation in his book. Aldrich "had obtained his knowledge of the Rangers and 'Texus' . . . from copious reading of wild West and pulp magazines. He did not look like a Texan, talk like a Texan nor think like a Texan, for he was not a Texan." Sterling's contempt is offset by Aldrich's fine record in both field and office, but Sterling replaced him with a good man, Sergeant Charles O. Moore, who had distinguished himself in Borger.

Thus the adjutant general administered the Rangers through a cadre of highly qualified and experienced captains of undoubted reputation.

When Light Townsend died of a heart attack in May 1932, Sergeant J. B. Wheatley of Headquarters Company, another Ranger of superior ability, took over Company D.[4]

ON OCTOBER 3, 1930, Columbus "Dad" Joiner brought in a promising oil well in East Texas, near Kilgore. Joiner was not an oil man but a lease man of sloppy, ethically questionable business habits. From Depression-ridden farmers eager to sell, he had assembled a block of mineral leases. Based on the rosy pronouncements of a pseudogeologist, he hoped to get rich not on oil but on leases. His derrick, assembled from pieces of junk, sucked up enough oil to encourage the hope. H. L. Hunt, an oilman of higher business acumen and ethical standards, bought into the leases. By January 1931 further drilling had confirmed the existence of a major oil field and set off the rush Texans had come to know so well.

In fact, Dad Joiner had drilled into the largest known oilfield in the world at that time—42 miles long and 6 to 14 miles wide, embracing 140,000 acres. It lay east of Tyler, with Kilgore on the western edge and Longview on the northern. Longview was a small modern town that served as county seat of Gregg County. Kilgore, Gladewater, and Henderson (in Rusk County) tapped the vast pool. These were small farm towns with dirt streets, hit hard by the Depression. From all over the nation, wildcatters, scouts for the big oil companies, thousands thrown out of work by the Depression, and the usual parasites (both legal and illegal) swarmed over the East Texas field in a rush that dwarfed Ranger, Mexia, Borger, Wink, and all others of the 1920s.[5]

East Texas confronted the Rangers with a mission they knew well how to handle. The Sterling administration had been in office hardly a week when, on January 28, 1931, Gregg County sheriff Martin Hays asked for state aid in coping with the boom. After a brief visit, Captain Hickman agreed, and early in February he posted Sergeant Lone Wolf Gonzaullas and Rangers J. P. Huddleston and Bob Goss in Kilgore. For a month they worked closely with Sheriff Hays and the Longview and Kilgore police chiefs to round up gamblers and other lawbreakers while running some five hundred panhandlers out of the area.

Early in March Adjutant General Sterling sent in reinforcements: Hickman and the rest of B Company, and Captain Mace with two of his men from Company C. Working with local officers, the eleven Rangers made a thorough sweep of Kilgore and surroundings. Within twenty-four hours, they had arrested five hundred suspects, closed a dozen brothels, two saloons and a gambling house, and confiscated large quantities of narcotics.

Kilgore lacked a jail, so Hickman requisitioned a local church and installed the familiar trotline, a logging chain attached to the pulpit. Handcuffed to the chain, suspects awaited interrogation and, for forty of them, transfer to the Gregg County jail in Longview. Among these were murderers and bank robbers as well as the usual gamblers and whiskey sellers. All others of dubious respectability received sundown orders.

Leaving Sergeant Gonzaullas in charge, Hickman stationed Bob Goss at Kilgore, Dan McDuffie at Gladewater, and Hardy Purvis at Henderson. The Lone Wolf kept the trotline in the church, and through the spring and summer months he and his men, together with the local officers, continued to purge the oil fields of unlawful characters and their establishments. The net snared some prominent bootleggers and hijackers as well as boomtown riffraff.[6]

Lone Wolf Gonzaullas vividly remembered his assignment to East Texas in 1930–31.[7] At Kilgore and Gladewater he found little towns of five hundred people that multiplied into the thousands almost overnight. "The influx was hardly believable," he marveled.

> They'd push you off the sidewalk, fist fights, people were having fights on the street, . . . they'd fight and then go out in the mud and fight there and everybody's standing there watching 'em and let 'em fight. And knife fights and every kind of thing, because they were rough necks and all kind of elements in the field. But there was lots of mud, . . . wooden sidewalks and shack towns. And lots of prostitutes, lots of gamblers, and . . . there were some legitimate merchants and there was lots that came in to try to clean up during the boom.

145

Most clearly Gonzaullas remembered the mud, as heavy rains swept the area in the early months of 1931. He and his two men used both horses and auto, but the mud made auto travel often impossible. Horses sank to their bellies in mud, forcing the rider to cross his legs over the saddle. Mud covered both horse and rider, and Gonzaullas at times rode up on the wooden sidewalks to dismount. Between rainstorms, though, the roads swirled with dust so thick it limited visibility.

As in earlier boomtowns, a great criminal fraternity descended on East Texas. The first Ranger objective was to "pick up the big shot criminals as fast as they hit there before they could get bedded in and built in the place." The test was simple—look at their hands:

> Whenever they'd see us coming along they'd put their hands out in front of them. We'd look at their hands, if their hands was real smooth we knew they wasn't a working man and if they were real rough, like a working man's hand, why we just told 'em, "Well go ahead about your business." Now if they were real smooth and they looked like they were pimps or gamblers or thugs or some kind of outlaw then we immediately put 'em on the chain.

The smooth-skinned variety, whether big time or small time, invariably headed for the red-light district as soon as they reached town. So did escaped convicts. Periodically, therefore, Gonzaullas and local officers raided the tent city of prostitutes, rounded up the usual suspects, and hauled them up to the trotline. "And the mud got so bad you know, down in that area that we had to march 'em up the side of the hill at the railroad track and march 'em on the railroad track." On Saturday nights the trotline held as many as one hundred men. About once a week, they were loaded into the back of a truck and hauled to the jail in Longview.

Gladewater finally got a jail of sorts—a stockade of logs surrounding a "bull pen" in which the prisoners, though still fastened to a trotline, had more freedom of movement. The bull pen also enclosed a "snorten pole," a long post driven into the ground with a ring dangling a chain fastened to the top. "And if you're real rough and tough they let you stand up by yourself . . . where they can watch you, you can't pull that thing out of the ground."

Gladewater was also the scene on July 7, 1931, of a tragedy that sad-dened the entire force. The chief of police had fired Jeff "Tiny" Johnson, a longtime jailer who vowed to kill him in revenge. Drunk and seeking a confrontation, Johnson walked down the main street with his Winchester. With Deputy Everett Hughes at the wheel and Ranger Dan McDuffie in the front seat and two Gladewater policemen, Bill Dial and J. H. Leach, in the back, the officers drove toward the man. McDuffie said, "Let's stop right here and let me get out and I'll go up and talk to him and get the damn gun off of him and take him home." Hughes agreed too late. A bullet smashed through the windshield, struck the steering wheel, and ricocheted into McDuffie's stomach. In the back seat Bill Dial grabbed his pump shotgun and "he hangs out the side of the car and takes an aim on this jailer who's up the street about 50 feet . . . has a dead aim on him and pumps him full of lead. I think he hit him five times before he hit the ground and he kills him deader than hell." McDuffie died in the ambulance before reaching the hospital. He was the first Ranger killed in the line of duty since 1921. To the Lone Wolf, this showed that "life was not worth a damn in the oil field."[8]

Gonzaullas recalled that "we got along pretty good with everybody because we didn't take no back talk, we handled and enforced the law very strict, but we still used common sense and good judgment." Even so, the Rangers sometimes got tough. "We had to slap a few of 'em every day or so to let 'em know we were running things over there and they'd try you out, there's always a lot of tuffies who just say, 'well I'm going to try him out,' and you'd have to give 'em a whipping or something. And we had to muss a few of 'em up."[9]

EAST TEXAS presented the Rangers with a new challenge—oil producers who operated illegally within a dauntingly complex body of law and regulation. The Rangers could deal with hijackers, bank robbers, and other criminal elements more harmful than gamblers and whiskey sellers. But the East Texas strike revealed one massive pool, which meant that all wells drew on the same source. Producers therefore rushed to get as much as they could as quickly as they could. Ultimately the pool supported thirty-two thousand rigs, with twenty-four on a single town lot in Kilgore. The pool thus yielded immense quantities that drove down prices, imperiled the market in a worldwide Depression, and threatened ruin to producers everywhere. Voluntary cooperation of operators in limiting production proved impossible.

Regulation fell to the Texas Railroad Commission. It tried to cap the field's output by imposing proportionally calculated limits on producers—proration. Weak, lacking experts and an enforcement mechanism, the commission tried and failed. Some operators sought court injunctions against the commission, alleging violation of federal laws barring combinations in restraint of trade. Others simply defiantly continued to pump. By July 1931 East Texas producers were selling for prices that ranged from ten to two cents a barrel.

Tempers ran high. Frightened producers threatened aggression against producers who exceeded their proration limits. In August 1931 a special session of the legislature enacted a law mandating "conservation" of natural resources by outlawing "waste," then so weakened it as to provide almost no remedy. Influential oilmen all over the state joined with local lawmen to appeal for martial law as the only means to avert chaos and violence. On August 16, 1931, citing "insurrection" against state conservation laws, Governor Sterling proclaimed martial law in Gregg, Upshur, Smith, and Rusk counties. Once again the veteran general Jacob F. Wolters took command.[10]

On August 17, the first of a series of rainy, soggy days, the general and twelve hundred guardsmen flooded the four counties. At his request, the governor had pulled ten Rangers from other companies to join the four already in the area. The Rangers possessed arrest authority, Wolters explained, and could be used where his soldiers encountered defiance. With the Rangers riding horseback with the troopers, within twenty-four hours Wolters had closed down the entire field, and he kept it closed until September 5, when sufficient calm had been restored that an effort could be made to enforce the proration limits of the railroad commission.[11]

They were not effectively enforced. The commission, divided and ineffectual, proved unequal to the task. Violators resorted to a host of

ingenious ways to escape detection. Martial law stirred bitter controversy throughout the state. But most decisive, the federal courts declared
martial law unconstitutional, setting off months of legal wrangling that
eventually led to the Supreme Court. By early 1932, the governor had
lost and withdrawn most of the guardsmen.

Some remained to join with the Rangers in working on another task
for which they were unprepared—"hot oil." Rogue producers devised
imaginative techniques and devices not only to exceed railroad commission limits but to divert oil from other wells. "Slant holes" were the
most prominent. Although all the wells tapped a single huge pool, the
oil mixed with an ocean of salt water at 3,650 feet below the surface.
This ocean migrated slowly from west to east, which meant that each well
drew differing amounts at different times. (Wells pumped both oil and salt
water; the two had to be separated and the water pumped back down
to maintain geological stability.) Depending on the flow, a slant hole
drilled from one well to its neighbor could often steal its profits. Rangers
and soldiers searched for wells rigged to pump oil secretly or slant into
neighboring rigs and garner great profits even in a depressed market.
Both Rangers and guardsmen scored some successes, but not many.

Meantime, as hot oil remained an elusive quest, Captain Hickman
and a fluctuating number of Rangers pursued their usual boomtown
mission of sweeping up violators of gambling and liquor laws.
"Sometimes we had to get a little rough," conceded then-rookie Ranger
A. Y. Allee, "but they brought it on themselves."[12]

ROSS STERLING had the misfortune to occupy the statehouse during the
opening years of the Great Depression. Not only chaos, but plunging oil
prices and martial law in the East Texas field rocked his administration.
Cotton prices also bottomed, impoverishing farmers and turning them
against Sterling. All the other ills of the Depression also hurt the governor, but most damaging was the impact on farmers and oil workers,
which jeopardized the tradition of two terms for a governor.

Worse yet, the Fergusons, routed by Sterling in 1930, kept up a continuous barrage of inflammatory criticism and once again excited "the

boys at the forks of the creek." In the 1932 primaries, Sterling faced a tough race with Miriam Ferguson (i.e., Jim Ferguson) and other aspirants. In the first, Mrs. Ferguson led with a plurality, but all the other candidates combined to support Sterling. The runoff thus became a bitter contest between Ross Sterling and Miriam Ferguson.

From the beginning the Rangers had understood the dangers of the Ferguson candidacy. They recalled how shoddily they had been treated in 1925–27, and now they reveled in a supportive governor and one of their own as adjutant general. Ranger regulation and tradition prohibited interference in political campaigns—a ban not always honored. But in 1932 the stakes were simply too high. They abandoned all caution and openly campaigned for Ross Sterling. As Ranger Jim McCoy explained to Bill Sterling, "This is not politics, General. We are simply fighting for the life of our outfit."[13]

Reports reached the adjutant general that an unusual number of transients had appeared in East Texas, especially Gregg County. Because in 132 counties the first primary had recorded more votes than residents who had paid poll taxes, mostly Ferguson votes, Sterling suspected that men were being imported from other states to vote the Ferguson ticket. He called to his office Captains Wright, Mace, and Wheatley and Sergeant Earl McWilliams and sought their opinion of launching a massive raid in East Texas. It would be explained as a move against the usual boomtown targets but in reality would be aimed at unsettling the criminal element and running off "a horde of floaters" brought in to vote for the Fergusons. All agreed.

On August 21, 1932, six days before the runoff, thirty-seven Rangers from all five companies joined with twenty local lawmen at Kilgore. In six squads, they spread out to hit virtually every suspected dive in Gregg County. More such raids had been planned, but Governor Sterling learned of the operation and, telephoning the adjutant general from Galveston, called it off. "A move like that would cost us the election," he declared. "On the contrary," answered the adjutant general, "it will win it. The place is flooded with illegal voters, and they are solidly against you." Fearing accusations of impropriety, however, the governor persisted, and the raids ended.[14]

In the August 27 runoff Miriam Ferguson edged Ross Sterling by less than four thousand votes. Bill Sterling's men in East Texas uncovered evidence of massive election fraud, including a barrel of counterfeit ballots and returns in which votes greatly exceeded poll tax receipts. As the governor challenged the results, the Rangers continued to agitate in his favor. Despite the overwhelming evidence of fraud, both the state senate and the state supreme court allowed Miriam Ferguson's name on the ballot. In November she easily defeated the Republican candidate.

As the former governor later conceded to his adjutant general, "Bill, if I had let you go ahead and knock out those illegal votes in Gregg County, we probably would have won."[15]

Ross Sterling almost certainly would have won. That he did not, and that the Rangers had so blatantly campaigned in his behalf, foreshadowed a fate worse than any Ranger could have imagined.

[9]

Return of the Fergusons, 1933–1935

Aᴠᴛᴇʀ ᴛʜᴇ ɢᴇɴᴇʀᴀʟ ᴇʟᴇᴄᴛɪᴏɴ of 1932 threw the governorship decisively to Miriam Ferguson, she and "Farmer Jim" kept to their
Temple home formulating the policies of the new administration and
considering the mountain of job applications that piled up. By January
18, 1933, when Ma took the oath of office, the fate of the Texas Rangers
had been sealed.

On that day the new adjutant general took office. He was Henry
Hutchings, the guardsman who had served both governors Colquitt and
Jim Ferguson in the same office from 1911 to 1917. He had performed
satisfactorily then, although his true interest lay with the National
Guard. Now, at age sixty-nine, he did little more than carry out the
decisions of the two Fergusons.

The first decision, effective inauguration day, was to fire the entire
Ranger Force of forty-four officers and men. Frank Hamer and some
Rangers had already resigned in disgust, but the other captains had hung
on until their formal discharge on January 18, 1933. The next day the
governor appointed thirty-nine new Rangers, including six captains. As
her appointment files indicate, the personnel decisions had all been

made in Temple during November and December, and it may be sur-mised that Jim dictated the selections, all as political rewards.

Also on January 18, the governor canceled all special Ranger com-missions and began doling out new ones. Almost anyone who asked, if he (or she) could demonstrate Ferguson credentials, gained a special commission. Ultimately she appointed 2,344. The roster included not only those with genuine need but such others as mortician, cook, clergyman, dentist, paper hanger, professional wrestler, liquor dealer, barber, housewife, and even radio singer Kate Smith. Not all performed police functions, of course, but all held police powers and could carry firearms. As senate investigators concluded, "Virtually every night club and gambling house of any size has its special ranger or special deputy sheriff guards."[1]

To her credit, in selecting new Ranger captains Mrs. Ferguson restored Roy Aldrich to his old post as quartermaster. Why Adjutant General Sterling had dismissed the slim, modest, soft-spoken officer remains a puzzle, despite the almost libelous tirade in Sterling's auto-biography. In truth, Aldrich was a remarkable person aside from his superior Ranger record. He was forty-five when he joined the Rangers in 1915. Both as field Ranger and quartermaster, he excelled, leading a Ranger raid in San Antonio as late as 1935, at the age of sixty-five.

Aldrich also gained local fame. Bibliophile, biologist, botanist, zo-ologist, he lived alone on a large spread on the eastern edge of Austin. His plantation house contained a huge library, and he maintained a showplace zoo of Texas plants and wildlife. Throngs of people came to see what grew and roamed in Texas. He remained an Austin institution even after his retirement in 1947 at the age of seventy-eight. He died in 1955.[2]

The other captains were a curious lot, none possessing the abilities and stature of their predecessors. The most experienced field officer, Jefferson E. Vaughan, forty-six, took over Company A at Marfa. He had enlisted in the Rangers in the Big Bend in 1912 and served for eight years. Even as the Canales hearings of 1919 highlighted Ranger misdeeds, however, Vaughan had compiled a record of arrogance and brutality, especially during the rein of the infamous Captain J. Monroe Fox. Protégé of state senator Claude Hudspeth, however, Vaughan kept his commission until 1920, when he resigned to run successfully for sheriff of Presidio County. The sheriff's badge failed to improve his habits or disposition, and he continued to alienate many in the Big Bend.

Hickman's old Company B in Fort Worth fell to Harry T. Odneal, forty-six. A staunch Fergusonite, he had gained appointment as sergeant of Company A in the previous Ferguson administration and had been discharged in May 1927 by the new Moody administration.

No other captain had been a Ranger. E. H. Hammond, thirty-five, took over Company C, now based in Houston. He claimed no experience as a peace officer and listed his occupation as "executive." James Robbins, forty-eight, captained Company D in Falfurrias. He gave his occupation as farmer and claimed three years as a deputy sheriff.

Most bizarre was the new captain of Headquarters Company in Austin, in which Frank Hamer had achieved an outstanding reputation. Fifty years old, heavyset, D. Estill Hamer was Frank's older brother. Lacking a Ranger background, he identified his occupation as "investigator." Of the five Hamer brothers, Frank and Estill had never been close, and Estill probably took as much pleasure as the Fergusons in commanding his brother's old company. Indeed, the Fergusons probably chose Estill primarily as a fitting revenge for Frank's opposition.[3]

Not only in personnel did the Fergusons humiliate the Rangers. At the governor's request, the legislature reduced pay and eliminated longevity pay, effective March 1, 1933. In the general appropriations act, not operative until September 1, the legislators went even farther. They trimmed the strength of the force from thirty-nine to thirty-two; fixed the monthly pay of captains at $150 (down from $225), sergeants $130 (down from $175), and privates $115 (down from $150); confirmed the abolition of longevity pay; and cut the operational budget by half.

Furthermore, the governor looked on the Rangers as principally a border force. Rangers could help county sheriffs as before, but only if asked. They also had to leave when asked. As demonstrated in many locales, especially Borger, corrupt, incompetent, or politically sensitive elected officials wanted no Ranger "assistance." Now all they had to do was tell the governor to keep the Rangers away.[4]

With few exceptions, the Ferguson Rangers composed a sorry lot, and the effectiveness and hence the reputation of the force plummeted. The fundamental flaw was simple incompetence, but there was misbehavior as well. As early as July 1933, a Ranger got into an argument with his Austin neighbor, shot and killed him, and wounded his wife. He paid the penalty of twenty years in the penitentiary.[5]

Ironically, the only company that demonstrated competence and results was Captain Estill Hamer's Headquarters Company. Throughout 1933 and 1934 they contended, often successfully, with bank robbers, murderers, auto-theft rings, gamblers, and prohibition violators. Hamer proved a good captain with good men.[6]

Not so the other captains. In the East Texas oil fields Captain E. H. Hammond's Houston-based Rangers proved such dismal failures at battling hot oil that the companies turned to former Rangers. Lone Wolf Gonzaullas recruited eighteen jobless Rangers to guard the pipelines. Frank Hamer hired on to a Houston oil company as a special investigator. Hammond resigned on August 31, 1934. The next day Governor Ferguson personally elevated one of Hammond's privates, George H. Johnson, to the captaincy. His enlistment in January 1933 showed him to have been a farmer, and the company performed only slightly better under his command.[7]

In the Big Bend, Captain Jeff Vaughan continued to exemplify the six-shooter mentality that had shaped his career since 1912. Company A accomplished almost nothing in heading off smuggling and catching cattle thieves but compiled a record of harassing and brutalizing Mexicans. In July 1933 Sheriff A. E. Anderson of Culberson County declared Rangers unneeded in the Big Bend. A year later, in August 1934, one of Vaughan's Rangers shot and killed a Mexican suspect near Marfa. This led the Presidio County sheriff, J. D. Bunton, to request that all the Rangers be removed "for causing a great deal of [bad] feelings." They were not withdrawn, of course, and Vaughan served out his term without any cooperation from local peace officers.[8]

In Fort Worth, where Tom Hickman's Company B had functioned so effectively for a decade, Captain Harry Odneal now and then helped local officers raid gambling dives, but illness could be offered as justification for providing virtually no leadership. On April 28, 1934, as the city newspaper recounted, Odneal "stood in front of a mirror in . . . his home and sent a bullet through his brain." Four days later Governor Ferguson lifted Private Leon P. Hannah to the captaincy. At a youthful twenty-eight, he had enlisted in January 1933, citing previous experience as an inspector for the state highway department. As captain, he failed to improve on Odneal's record.[9]

No captain or company proved more worthless than Captain James Robbins and Company D, based at Falfurrias. This was Bill Sterling's old company, and a ranchman quizzed Sterling about what had happened to the Rangers. He had asked Robbins for a Ranger and been turned down with the reply, "I don't have a man who can ride horseback." This was true. The camps that had been established to cut off liquor-smuggling horsebackers had to be abolished because of the lack of horsemen.[10]

Not that the company remained inactive. A committee of the state senate investigating the explosion of crime in 1934 discovered that operators of gambling houses, saloons, and brothels had been bribing Robbins to leave them alone. Others, perhaps uncooperative, had been run out of the region and their establishments taken over and run by the Rangers themselves. In the summer of 1934 Robbins raided a gambling den competing with his own, confiscating cash, furniture, and even the building. The owner rushed to his other establishment, in a rural area, only to find that Robbins had already taken possession of it too. Two days later Rangers burst into the owner's home brandishing machine guns, drove him out, and left it for Robbins to occupy as his own home. On August 10, 1934, he was arrested in San Antonio and charged with theft and embezzlement. Ultimately he served an eight-year term in the penitentiary.[11]

THE EFFECTIVENESS OF the Texas Rangers tumbled at the very time that an eruption of crime featuring a new breed of criminals employing equally new techniques swept not only Texas but the entire Midwest. With high-powered automobiles and high-powered weaponry, celebrity gangsters sped from state to state robbing banks and stores, murdering, kidnapping, stealing autos, and indulging in any crime that struck their fancy. They dramatized the impotence of the Texas Rangers as crime fighters.[12]

Even before being ruined by the Fergusons, the Ranger Force had failed to keep up with changing times. The traditions of the frontier Rangers lingered well into the twentieth century, in part because they remained relevant in West Texas and along the Mexican border. They were not relevant in East and North Texas, where the modern criminals operated.

Ranger armament had never changed. Each Ranger still bought his own Colt six-shooter and Winchester rifle, hardly a match for the array of arms and munitions used by the gangsters, who favored the Thompson submachine gun and Browning Automatic Rifle (BAR), backed by superior rifles, pistols, and shotguns. For the Rangers, arms other than the standard issue came from their wallets or from philanthropists. A donor presented Tom Hickman's Company B in Fort Worth with four Thompson submachine guns and "riot kits" containing tear gas bombs and gas masks. The other companies had to rely on firepower that would have been familiar to the Rangers of the 1870s.[13]

West Texas Rangers still furnished their own horses, while those in the East drove their own cars or rode the railroads. The state furnished forage for the horses and helped maintain private vehicles. No official autos enabled Rangers to seek or pursue gangsters traveling in the most powerful cars made. Early in 1932 Sergeant Gonzaullas acquired an eight-cylinder Chrysler coupe equipped with bulletproof glass and a machine gun mounted on a swivel next to the driver. Who paid for it is not apparent, and in any event it demonstrated less practicality than it did the Lone Wolf's flamboyant personality.[14]

Rangers lacked even the primitive communication systems other emerging state police forces were developing. No radios linked cars with one another or with headquarters. The telephone and telegraph remained the swiftest mode of communication. Nor did the Rangers keep up with other states in adopting such technological advances as fingerprinting, ballistics, criminal identification, intelligence gathering and sharing, and other scientific methods.

Low pay and miserly operating budgets crippled the force as they had from the beginning. Likewise, a strength that varied from thirty to fifty could not hope to cover a state the size of Texas. The new highway patrol, created in 1929 in the state highway department, numbered 120. Limited to enforcing highway and vehicle laws, however, the patrol could not substitute for Rangers as a state constabulary.

Many regarded the Texas Rangers themselves as obsolete, colorful reminders of the Old West but an expensive anachronism in the modern world. The Fergusons bolstered that opinion by so ravaging the effectiveness and public esteem of the Ranger Force as to highlight the obvious choices: abolish or reform.

TEXANS OF THE 1930s lived with the government their forebears had created in 1875. Drafted mostly by cotton farmers angry over the Civil War and Reconstruction, and determined to keep government and taxes out of their lives, the constitution adopted in 1876 described a small, weak government headed by a virtually powerless governor. Most important initiatives had to be framed as constitutional amendments and thus not only adopted by the legislature but approved by the voters. Reform came slowly or not at all.

The Great Depression fueled such a reform: reorganize and downsize state government to reduce its cost. In May 1931 the legislature created a joint committee to pursue this goal. The committee turned for help to a Chicago firm specializing in public administration and finance, Griffenhagen and Associates. By November 1932 they had begun printing a series of thirteen slim volumes covering every aspect of Texas government. They had all been submitted to the legislature by February 1933, in time for consideration during the regular session. Part 3, dealing with law enforcement, appeared on January 10, 1933, even before the Fergusons took over the statehouse.

The Griffenhagen report sketched the huge challenge to law enforcement in Texas, including its vast size, its coastline, the Mexican border, the urbanized East and the sparsely settled West, primitive transportation, and other features that made the state an inviting haven for criminals. Virtually everything about law enforcement and criminal justice in Texas attracted their criticism: sheriffs and constables dependent on politics and the fee system, courts burdened by a host of paralyzing legal technicalities, the legislature for inadequate support of law enforcement, the National Guard, the highway patrol, and the Texas Rangers.

Addressing the Ranger Force, the report faulted the legislature for paltry appropriations and the absence of legislation that would enable the Rangers to keep pace with other states and adapt to changing social and economic conditions. They sketched other weaknesses, including politics, but their recommendations did not envision a large role for the Rangers.

To the Griffenhagen experts, the Rangers were not the central element of a system that ought to be consolidated. They urged the legislature to create a Department of Public Safety (DPS). In this agency, the highway patrolmen would be equipped with full police powers and converted into *the* state police force. The Rangers, however, boasted a tradition and role in Texas history that must not be lost. Thus the new organization would include a Bureau of State Police and Bureau of Texas Rangers, but the Rangers would be largely confined to the south and west and to the kinds of service "to which their history and traditions best adapt them." Clearly, the old highway patrol would become the statewide constabulary and the Rangers relegated to a minor role in the border country.

To serve both state police and Rangers, the state needed a crime laboratory and a radio communications system. DPS would include these divisions as well as an administrative bureau charged not only with personnel and logistics but centralizing the criminal records of the state and keeping in touch with local and federal peace officers.

Griffenhagen and Associates effectively described conditions, deficiencies, needs, and solutions. Most were enlightened, some impractical, and as it predictably turned out all politically unacceptable. The Fergusons ignored the law enforcement volume, and the legislature took almost no action on any of the thirteen volumes. It did, however, form a senate committee to investigate crime in Texas, which conducted wide-ranging probes through the summer of 1934. In many ways the committee was more critical of state and local institutions than Griffenhagen, and it set forth its findings in more detail. Concluding that criminal law enforcement had broken down in Texas, the committee recommended twenty-four changes in the state penal code and urged that a Department of Public Safety such as envisioned by the Griffenhagens be established. The report had been published in ample time for consideration by the legislature that would convene in January 1935.

Although attracting little interest in the Ferguson administration or the legislature of 1933–34, the report on crime, followed by the report of the senate investigating committee, brought together in coherent form much of what sheriffs, police chiefs, Rangers, legislators, and other experts had been saying for a decade. It laid the groundwork and established momentum for desperately needed reforms in the way Texas sought to enforce state laws.[15]

As IF TO UNDERLINE the strictures of the Griffenhagen report, columns of newsprint daily proclaimed the exploits of the gangsters ravaging the Midwest and South. John Dillinger led the pack. In fact, national attention focused almost entirely on him. The other gangsters were as inept as the corps of handsome young college graduates assembled by J. Edgar Hoover in a newly energized Bureau of Investigation, an arm of the Department of Justice, to wage a federal war on crime. In later years Hoover made certain that the public remembered not only Dillinger but Baby Face Nelson, Machine Gun Kelly, Pretty Boy Floyd, Bonnie and Clyde, and Ma Barker (a pathetic recluse who exerted no control over her sons) as masterful criminals run down by his masterful FBI. He even fabricated some stories himself. By the mid-1930s, however, the big-name gangsters had been eliminated, and Hoover's inexperienced men had transformed themselves into experienced lawmen.[16]

Contrary to popular belief, Bonnie Parker and Clyde Barrow rarely made headlines in a national press preoccupied with John Dillinger. Only in Texas did the pair achieve celebrity status. Both born in Dallas and in their early twenties, Bonnie and Clyde ranged widely in half a dozen states but struck often enough in Texas to gain them top billing. They held up banks, stores, and gas stations, stole autos, drove long distances at high speed, were obsessed with guns and loaded their cars with an arsenal of arms and ammunition, and killed indiscriminately. Sometime accessories in crime were Clyde's brother Buck, Ray Hamilton, Joe Palmer, and Henry Methvin.

As implicit in the Griffenhagen report, local police, county sheriffs, and the Texas Rangers proved ineffective in pursuit of Bonnie and Clyde. Governor Miriam Ferguson vowed to turn the Rangers on the pair, a comic announcement in light of what she and Jim had done to the Ranger Force. In January 1934, however, Bonnie and Clyde set in motion a serious effort to run them down.

The gang had fallen apart. Buck Barrow had been killed by lawmen the previous summer, and Hamilton, Palmer, and Methvin had wound up in the Texas Penitentiary in Huntsville. Learning that their confederates were working on the Eastham Prison Farm, forty miles north of Huntsville, Bonnie and Clyde hid .45-caliber automatics on the edge of the field, then got word to their friends where to find them. On January 16 Hamilton and Palmer drew their weapons and opened fire on their guards. Clyde and an accomplice, hidden nearby, swept the field with fire from Browning Automatic Rifles. One guard fell mortally wounded while others took cover or fled. Hamilton, Palmer, Methvin, and a fourth man piled into a car and, with Bonnie at the wheel, sped from the scene.[17]

Angry and embarrassed, Lee Simmons, the general manager of the state prison system, vowed to end the rampage of Bonnie and Clyde. On February 1, 1934, after obtaining the sanction of the state prison board, he drove to Austin and talked with the governors Ferguson. He proposed to create a post of special prison investigator and find the right person to run down Bonnie and Clyde. He had decided on Frank

Hamer, but before approaching him he had to clear the touchy issue with the Fergusons. They not only agreed but authorized Simmons to use their clemency powers as a weapon if needed. At once Simmons enlisted Hamer for the task.[18]

Hamer did not proceed with the secrecy Simmons describes. In Dallas, Deputy Sheriff Bob Alcorn, the only lawman who could identify Clyde Barrow, joined Hamer. They had already picked up enough clues to lead them to Bienville Parish in northwestern Louisiana. Henry Methvin's parents lived on a farm near Gibsland, ten miles southwest of the parish seat of Arcadia, and Bonnie and Clyde were using a vacant farmhouse in the piney woods nearby as an occasional hideout.

In Arcadia on February 19, less than three weeks after embarking on the search, the two Texans met Sheriff Henderson Jordan, an able lawman who was already ahead of them. He had been approached by a family emissary, John Joyner, with word that Henry Methvin would turn on Clyde and Bonnie in return for a full pardon from the governor of Texas. A special agent of J. Edgar Hoover's Federal Bureau of Investigation had also found his way to Arcadia. All four lawmen met with Joyner, and Hamer agreed to obtain a document, signed by Governor Ferguson, promising to pardon Henry Methvin if his actions led to the capture or death of Bonnie and Clyde.

Agreeing to a betrayal proved easier than carrying it out. Hamer obtained Governor Ferguson's signature on the clemency pledge, which was turned over to Joyner. But weeks passed before the wide-ranging pair returned to their Gibsland hideout under circumstances that would enable Methvin to set in motion his role in the plan. Meantime, as the FBI receded into the background, Hamer gained more partners.

On April 1, 1934, Easter Sunday, Clyde, Bonnie, and Henry lounged in a stolen Ford on a dirt road close to its intersection with Highway 114 near Grapevine, northwest of Dallas. They were waiting for others to gather for an Easter celebration at the Dallas home of Bonnie's mother. Three motorcycle patrolmen passed on the highway. Two, E. B. Wheeler and H. C. Murphy, turned back to check out the parked Ford. Before they could even dismount, Henry popped out of the rear seat and emptied a clip of steel-jacketed rounds from a BAR into the lead officer, Wheeler. As he toppled from his cycle, Murphy, his first day on the job, grabbed for his shotgun. Barrow raised his own sawed-off shotgun and blasted the patrolman to the ground. To finish him off, Methvin pumped more lead into the prostrate form.[19]

Outraged by the murder of the patrolmen, highway patrol chief Louis G. Phares demanded a role in the pursuit of Bonnie and Clyde, indicating that it did not enjoy the secrecy Simmons believed. Hamer chose one of his old Ranger comrades, B. M. "Manny" Gault, to whom Phares issued a patrol commission. Also, Deputy Alcorn wanted one of his colleagues on the team. Ted Hinton, another veteran of a clash with Bonnie and Clyde, enlarged the Texas party to four. In Arcadia, Sheriff Jordan and Deputy Prentis Oakley made six.

The four Texans waited impatiently in a Shreveport motel. Finally, on May 21 Joyner informed Sheriff Jordan that Bonnie and Clyde were at the hideaway and that Henry would slip away from them that night in Shreveport under circumstances that would not arouse suspicion. When such a separation occurred, the three had earlier agreed to rendezvous at the hideout near Gibsland. A single gravel road, used mainly by logging trucks, led into this heavily forested country. By 9:30 PM on the twenty-first, the six lawmen had hidden themselves behind brush piled up beside the road. Across the road Henry's father, Iverson Methvin, had parked his logging truck and removed a wheel as if repairing a flat tire.

All night and all the next day and night the officers waited, their stockpile of heavy weapons primed for use. On the morning of May 23, almost ready to give up, they heard the high-pitched sound of a speeding auto. Only Clyde Barrow would drive so fast on a primitive gravel road. Sheriff Jordan arranged his posse in a rank from left to right: Hinton, Alcorn, Oakley, Jordan, Gault, and Hamer. Each had a BAR, a twelve-gauge shotgun, and two Colt .45-caliber automatic pistols. Jordan and Oakley wanted to try to take the couple alive. One of the Texans replied, "Ain't no way that boy's going to give up. He's done shot his way out of a dozen battles. He ain't doing it again."

As the tan Ford V-8 drew near, Deputy Alcorn peered through a pair of field glasses. "It's him boys. This is it—it's Clyde."[20]

The car eased to a stop next to Iverson Methvin's apparently disabled truck. As Bonnie and Clyde turned to talk with Methvin, he suddenly clutched his stomach and ran into the woods as if sick. It was the pre-arranged signal. But as a logging truck approached, Barrow slowly guided the car forward to open the blocked lane.

Deputy Oakley, excited and fearing another escape, stood and fired two rounds from his BAR into the moving car. Barrow's head jerked back. The other officers quickly rose and opened fire with their automatic rifles and shotguns. A barrage of lead smashed into the car and laced the interior. The riddled Ford coasted down the road and ran into a ditch. The lawmen sprinted to the car, weapons ready, but the hail of gunfire had torn up both Bonnie and Clyde. Bonnie sat slumped with her smashed head in her lap, her body gushing blood from many wounds. Clyde's bloody head dangled through the big steering wheel. The bullet-shattered car, stuffed with a huge cache of weapons and ammunition, served as the first coffin for the notorious pair of murderous outlaws who had already achieved legendary renown.

FRANK HAMER returned to Texas an acclaimed hero—*the* man who had patiently and skillfully traced Bonnie and Clyde to Louisiana, arranged a place to take them, and led the posse of five associates who had gunned them down. Newspapers and magazines extolled the feat and heaped praise on the famed lawman. Thanks largely to the respected historian Walter Prescott Webb, who published his history of the Texas Rangers a year later, Hamer remains in both scholarly and popular perception the man who ran down Bonnie and Clyde.[21]

Hamer did not run down Bonnie and Clyde. Within three weeks after commissioning, he and Deputy Alcorn had joined Bienville Parish sheriff Henderson Jordan at Arcadia, Louisiana. Thereafter, Hamer's major role was to obtain Governor Ferguson's pledge to pardon Henry Methvin if his betrayal of his two friends worked. Simmons claims to have obtained the governor's signature, but Hamer took it back to

Louisiana. Through March, April, and until the final scene on May 23, 1934, Sheriff Jordan guided the effort to get the outlaw pair. He welcomed the help and firepower of the four Texans, but he remained in command. He enlisted the help of Henry's father and set up the ambush as soon as he learned that Henry had carried out his part of the plan. Hamer, Gault, Alcorn, and Hinton deserve recognition for their part in the feat, but Henderson Jordan made it happen.

(Henry Methvin of course merits credit for betraying Bonnie and Clyde. Although armed with a clemency document in Texas, he had committed crimes in Oklahoma, where justice finally overtook him for complicity in the murder of two lawmen.)

Frank Hamer's widely publicized fame as the man who got Bonnie and Clyde had two effects. Although out of the Rangers for more than a year and working under a commission from Lee Simmons, he was usually identified as a Texas Ranger. Despite the ineptitude of the Ferguson Rangers, Frank Hamer recalled the past glories of the Texas Rangers and restored them to the affection of Texans. Hamer's perceived triumph in ending the career of Bonnie and Clyde, moreover, coincided with rising interest in providing Texas with a more effective system of law enforcement. It gave prominence to the Griffenhagen report and the senate investigation of crime. It helped lay the groundwork for the significant reforms that would be set in motion as soon as the Fergusons left the statehouse.

[10]

The Department of Public
Safety, 1935

B Y TEXAS STANDARDS, James V. Allred was a liberal. He ran for governor in 1934 with the blessing of President Franklin D. Roosevelt. Texas had not been as hard hit by the Great Depression as other states, but enough Texans welcomed federal relief programs to greet Allred's candidacy with favor. Moreover, oil prices had not sufficiently rebounded to create the wealthy oil barons who in a few years would drag Texas to the political far right.

A short, vigorous man of thirty-six, endowed with sharp political instincts and a superior intellect, "Jimmie" Allred had practiced law in Wichita Falls, functioned for a time as district attorney, and served two terms as attorney general when he launched his bid for the governorship in 1934. A campaign issue that he promoted with zest was creation of a modern state police force such as recommended in the Griffenhagen report. He won the runoff by a slim margin.

With his experience as attorney general, Allred well knew the weaknesses of the Texas criminal justice system. He had no sooner declared his candidacy early in 1934 than he assembled a working group to draft legislation for a state police agency. Heading the group was a close friend, Dallas lawyer Albert Sidney Johnson. A war veteran and National Guard officer, Captain Johnson had been severely injured by a brickbat in 1930 when the lynch mob at Sherman attacked guardsmen sent to restore order.

Johnson and his group drew not only on the Griffenhagen report and the report of the state senate's committee investigating crime; the Sheriff's Association of Texas submitted its own plan, the work of a legislative committee headed by the association's president, Sheriff J. B. Arnold of Beeville.

Of special influence were the ideas of Tom Hickman, longtime captain of the Fort Worth-based Ranger company, fired by the Fergusons in 1933. The flamboyant Ranger veteran had carefully studied the fledgling state police systems of New York, New Jersey, Pennsylvania, and Oregon. His rodeo travels in Europe had afforded opportunity to observe European models. A series of articles in the *Dallas News* set forth his proposals.

Johnson himself had studied the state forces of New York, Pennsylvania, Michigan, and Illinois. Presumably he and others of the group read a book by Bruce Smith, *The State Police*, published in 1926. It analyzed in depth the organization and operation of existing state systems and set forth solid guidance for the Texans.

Even before the runoff in July 1934, Johnson had provided Allred with a draft bill for the legislature's consideration.[1]

Jimmie Allred thus came to office in January 1935 with a bill already in hand to send to the legislature. It was introduced in the Senate by Senator W. E. H. Beck on January 24, 1935. Only the day before, Adjutant General Carl Nesbitt had announced that Tom Hickman had been restored to his old command of Ranger Company B in Fort Worth.

GOVERNOR ALLRED and his adjutant general, Carl Nesbitt, did not wait for Senator Beck's bill to make its laborious way through the legislature before reorganizing the Rangers and bringing them back from the torpor of the Ferguson years. On January 23, 1935, Nesbitt canceled all special Ranger commissions and discharged all the Ferguson Rangers except quartermaster captain Roy Aldrich, Sergeant Sid Kelso, and Private Fred Holland. Recruitment of replacements began at once. Only eleven of the thirty-six incoming men were Rangers before the Ferguson administration, and some of the rest entered with the political blessings that Allred had vowed to eliminate.

Among the new privates were four who, almost certainly by prior arrangement, emerged as captains within the following weeks: James W. McCormick, Fred L. McDaniel, William W. McMurrey, and Richard C. "Red" Hawkins. McCormick boasted an outstanding record as a lawman, partly as a Ranger, dating from 1920. McDaniel wore the Archer County sheriff's badge. Both hailed from Allred's home city of Wichita Falls, a circumstance surely of consequence. Hawkins, a Galveston officer, counted two terms as a Ranger under Captain J. J. Sanders, 1911–15. A South Texas rancher with six months experience as a customs officer, he could hardly have gained a captaincy without strong political backing. Enlisted as a private but "overlooked" in naming new captains was the veteran Will Wright, now sixty-seven, whose Ranger service began in 1901 and who had performed longer and more effectively as a captain than any other. Despite the political overtones, Tom Hickman and the other Allred captains represented a huge improvement over the Ferguson captains.[2]

THE FIRST BIG CHALLENGE to Jimmie Allred's hard line on crime happened even before his inauguration as governor. Just before Christmas 1934 a gun battle in a San Augustine hardware store killed four men, a vivid reminder of the crime wave that had plagued this far corner of East Texas for several years.[3] A complaint to Governor Ferguson had brought several Ferguson Rangers to town, but they did nothing more than tattle on the complainers. It remained to the new governor to take action, urged to move quickly by his private secretary. This was Ed Clark, a San Augustine native who himself had suffered an assault and robbery in his own hometown.[4]

"I decided if it was to be done without unnecessary slaughter," Allred later declared, "McCormick was the man to do it." Of course

McCormick was in Wichita Falls, waiting to be sworn in as a Ranger private on inauguration day. Nevertheless, in the last week of January 1935, McCormick, now a captain, with Rangers Leo Bishop and Dan Hines, drove into San Augustine.

Resting in the Piney Woods on the Louisiana border, San Augustine County had changed little since the Civil War. Its economy based on lumber, cotton, and corn, it remained steadfastly rural, hostile to modernization and all other outside influence. Its sparse population was ingrown, occasionally roiled by family feuds, and in recent years cowed by two ruthless families with gangland ties. Murder, assault, rape, robbery, hijacking, extortion, and forgery were only a few of the crimes inflicted on the county. Law officers were pointedly warned to keep their distance, and no citizen dared take note of events much less enter a courtroom as witness or juror brave enough to oppose the mobsters.

McCormick and his Rangers handed the three Ferguson Rangers and twenty-eight special Rangers their discharge papers. The heads of the two crime families made no secret of their identity. The Rangers quickly went into their "tough Ranger" mode. With big hats shading their faces and six-shooters conspicuous on their hips, they publicly insulted, threatened, cursed, and occasionally roughed up the culprits, who scattered to Louisiana and elsewhere. At the same time the citizens received assurance that, so long as Texas Rangers remained in town, no harm would come to them for telling what they knew. They told, as Rangers tapped out their stories on portable typewriters, and they testified.

As early as March 22, grateful townspeople held a mass meeting to express their thanks to the Texas Rangers. It was a joyous festival, replete with parades, street dances, and rodeos—only the first of several throughout 1935. McCormick's company remained headquartered in San Augustine throughout 1935, although the captain left the mission largely to Bishop and Hines, dropping by occasionally to offer encouragement and counsel. Assignments elsewhere frequently left but one Ranger to make good the promise of protecting the citizens. With the gangs broken and parading through court to the penitentiary, one was all it took. At the final festival, in December, grateful citizens presented

McCormick, Bishop, and Hines with a pair of silver-mounted six-shooters holstered on a handsome leather belt with a ruby-inlaid silver buckle. All the pistols were engraved with suitable expressions of appreciation.

By the end of 1936, with court proceedings still under way, thirty-three men had been convicted and imprisoned, with as many more indictments outstanding. Crimes included murder, extortion, cow and hog theft, and forgery. The heads of the two criminal families, the McClanahans and the Burlesons, had been sent to the penitentiary for life.

The swift justice dealt the criminals of San Augustine stood in bold relief to the dismal record of the Ferguson Rangers. With a new state police organization in prospect, San Augustine demonstrated that the Texas Rangers could operate far east of the old frontier but had not entirely surrendered frontier methods.

WHILE CAPTAIN MCCORMICK, Leo Bishop, and Dan Hines cleaned up San Augustine, and as the legislature labored week after week on legislation to establish a state police agency, Governor Allred turned to another target of his war on crime: gambling. Of nearly six million Texans counted in the 1930 census, forty percent lived in urban areas. Many enjoyed gambling and prospered from the business it brought into the cities, especially tourist attractions like San Antonio and Galveston. Statewide prohibition would go the way of national prohibition in August 1935, but the legislature had made gambling illegal, and rural members consistently turned back repeal efforts. Nightclubs featuring gambling and drinking flourished, and city officialdom tended to look the other way, with or without monetary encouragement. Not Governor Allred, who was steadfastly determined to enforce the gambling laws.

During the first four months of his administration, Allred turned the Rangers loose on gambling. City officials rarely asked for state help, but no city lacked a few prominent citizens appealing for him to shut down the establishments, which were widely believed, probably with some cause, to be connected with Chicago mobsters. Dallas, Fort Worth, San

Antonio, Houston, Galveston, Corpus Christi, and Rio Grande City all watched axe-wielding Rangers storm into the clubs, smash gambling equipment and furniture, and confiscate liquor.

By May 1935 the axe raids had ceased. Despite the approval of rural Texans, the legislation taking shape in the legislature specifically banned destructive raids. Quickly, however, the night spots sprang back to life as brazenly (and corrupt) as ever.

ON MAY 8, 1935, after nearly five months of debate, amendment, and conference committee wrangling, Senator Beck's bill finally emerged from the legislature, revised in some aspects but basically intact.[5] It moved the Texas Rangers from the adjutant general's department and the motor patrol from the highway department to a new agency, the Department of Public Safety (DPS). Ultimately of great significance, the law provided for a Headquarters Division in Austin consisting of several bureaus responsible for building a professional crime laboratory, working toward a statewide communications network, establishing a comprehensive training program, and cooperating not only with the Rangers and highway patrol but with county and city officers, agencies in neighboring states, and the federal government.

A three-man Public Safety Commission would oversee the new agency. It would name and supervise the director and assistant director, establish policies and procedures, and install a merit system of recruitment and promotion. No longer would Rangers or patrolmen have to rally political backing every two years; they could make a career in DPS if they wanted and if they could qualify under the merit system.

For the first time in law, the Ranger Force was designated the Texas Rangers. They would be organized as a DPS division and consist of a Headquarters Company of one captain, one sergeant, and four privates and "two companies of mounted men," each with a captain, a sergeant, and fifteen privates. The captain of the Headquarters Company would carry the rank of "senior captain" and command the entire Ranger division.

Clearly the legislators, like the Griffenhagen experts, looked on the Rangers as too treasured in Texas history to be done away with but best qualified to do what they had always done as frontier and border horsemen. Implicit in the law and its antecedents was the role of the motor patrol, now designated the Texas Highway Patrol, as the Texas state police force. The law vested patrolmen, hitherto charged with enforcing state highway laws, with all the criminal enforcement powers of the Rangers. The term "state police" carried such odious historical connotations, dating from Reconstruction, that it could not be used. Moreover, while Ranger strength remained at thirty-six, the law authorized an addition of twenty-seven patrolmen to the existing 118, and in 1936 the legislature granted another eighteen, for a total of 163.

Finally, acknowledging the continuing primacy of local lawmen, all sheriffs, constables, and chiefs of police were made "associate members" of DPS. Also, acknowledging generations of administrative practice, the law authorized three hundred special Rangers, though with severely restricted authority, rigid oversight by DPS, and the surety bonding that had provoked so much controversy in the Canales hearings of 1919. (Later, special commissions would be issued only to men already working full time in law enforcement.)

The law would take effect in ninety days, August 10, 1935.

Meantime, with the law on the books, on May 14 Adjutant General Nesbitt announced a new disposition of the Rangers. He named Tom Hickman captain of Headquarters Company in Austin, Fred McDaniel captain of Hickman's Company B in Fort Worth, J. W. McCormick captain of Company C in the San Augustine hot spot, William W. McMurrey captain of Company D in Hebbronville, and Sergeant Sid Kelso head of Company A in Houston. Roy Aldrich retained his quartermaster captaincy in Austin, and Red Hawkins stood by in Austin on special call by the governor. This disposition of course did not accord with the frontier and border orientation contemplated in the law, but that matter could be left to the Public Safety Commission.[6]

On July 27, 1935, Governor Allred announced his selections for the Public Safety Commission: Dallas attorney Albert Sidney Johnson, George Cottingham, editor of the *Houston Chronicle*, and Ernest Goens, a former district attorney from Tyler. The governor also took the occasion to reiterate his conviction that local officers should be left to do their duty without state interference. When they failed, however, the responsibility fell to the state to step in even if not invited. He hoped that the new agency would prompt the locals to be more aggressive in enforcing the law, especially against gambling.[7]

The public safety commissioners had been meeting informally ever since their appointment, but they gathered in Dallas for the first official meeting on August 11, the day after the new law took effect. They elected Albert Sidney Johnson chairman, and in subsequent months, talking to the press and various service clubs, he became the spokesman and public face of the commission.

Although the commissioners worried a lot about office space at their first meeting, they took another personnel action destined for controversy—Tom Hickman as senior Ranger captain. Already captain of Headquarters Company and the most experienced Ranger on active duty, he was the logical choice. Besides, he had contributed significantly to the DPS concept, and he was a close personal friend of Chairman Johnson.

Not divulged until later: Governor Allred had urged the commission not to make this appointment. Ever since January, he had been trying to get Hickman to shut down an elite gambling club, the Top o' the Hill Terrace, on the highway between Dallas and Fort Worth. But Hickman, reputedly a friend of owner-proprietor Fred Browning and "soft" on gambling, had procrastinated and taken refuge in legalistic excuses for delay.

At the first meeting also, the Public Service Commission confirmed Louis G. Phares, chief of the old motor patrol, as chief of the Texas Highway Patrol. Later in August the commission decided to make Phares acting director of DPS in addition to his post as head of the highway patrol. Like Hickman, Phares would travel a rocky bureaucratic road. Calm, soft-spoken, mild-mannered, a thin-faced man of slim build, silver hair, and horn-rimmed glasses, Phares would prove a competent but dogmatic administrator.

In mid-September Phares announced his choice for assistant director, the highway patrol's captain Homer Garrison Jr. He had made a bright reputation in conducting the patrol training program and had even been loaned to New Mexico to help set up a state police force in that state.

Phares's announcement of the chief of the Bureau of Intelligence grabbed headlines. Currently serving as chief criminal investigator for the district attorney in Gregg County, Manuel T. Gonzaullas, the "Lone Wolf" Ranger of earlier times, brought formidable credentials to the new position. As a federal officer in the 1920s, he had been trained in Washington and New York in fingerprint identification, ballistics, handwriting, and other phases of criminal apprehension. Obsessed with firearms, he assembled a huge collection of pistols and rifles, cartridges, and spent bullets. Under his guidance, the Texas DPS became a national model for ballistic analysis. In addition, said Phares, Gonzaullas would serve as chief of detectives and plainclothesmen.

In creating the Department of Public Safety, the legislature had laid the groundwork for a great leap forward in Texas law enforcement. As usual, however, it provided parsimonious funding. The Rangers and highway patrol brought their appropriations with them. In addition, the department itself received only $36,110 for the first year and $29,710 for the second year. Eight new positions were authorized; the rest of the staffing would be drawn from Ranger and patrol ranks.

Starved for equipment and cramped for space, DPS got off to a slow start. The Bureau of Identification and Records, headed by Chief C. G. McGraw, shared space in the highway patrol offices in downtown Austin with Gonzaullas's Intelligence Bureau, until the latter moved to an army building at Camp Mabry. During this time the two bureaus had to operate three eight-hour shifts because of the lack of space.

McGraw began the fingerprint program with 1,500 prints from the Beaumont Police Department, his previous position. Within a year, he was receiving prints from 225 sources. He also brought to his task skills in analyzing handwriting and typewriters.

Gonzaullas specialized not only in ballistics but moulage casting of footprints, tire treads, and marks left by instruments, and he brought ultraviolet light to bear on blood stains, secretions, inks, and erasure marks. Communications, so vital to police operations, languished because denied appropriations.

By October 1, however, Chairman Johnson could tell the press that the Department of Public Safety had completed its preliminary organization and gone to work. He described several recent cases in which Rangers and highway patrolmen had worked together, and gave details of organization and personnel. In fact, DPS had a long way to go, but it had been firmly enough established to offer the prospect of revolutionizing law enforcement in Texas.[8]

ON AUGUST 10, 1935, all Ranger personnel transferred from the adjutant general's payroll to the new department that so far existed only on paper. For the Rangers the only change was a rising sense of uncertainty and anxiety.

Would the Rangers abandon East Texas and take to horseback in the west? Would they no longer deal with modern criminals and instead chase cattle rustlers and guard the border? Would the highway patrol become the principal crime-fighting unit? Would the Rangers be shoved to the side in a department whose acting director and assistant director came from the highway patrol? Would they lose their special stature and fade into obscurity? They shrank from association with "a bunch of motorcycle jockeys."[9]

Acting Director Phares did nothing to ease the Rangers' suspense. In a press interview on September 8, he declared that he did not want hard-boiled officers. He believed roughness a cover for inefficiency. In the old motor patrol, he had inaugurated a politeness policy. Now he intended to introduce it in the Rangers. Axe-swinging raids had created ill feeling, he declared, and local officers resented the Rangers. He wanted them to behave as courteously and helpfully as the patrolmen. Phares's formula for building DPS: "I'm going to develop the department just like the Texas highway patrol was developed." He could hardly have uttered words better calculated to anger every Texas Ranger.[10]

On another issue, Chairman Johnson sought to quiet Ranger fears. On October 7 the commission met to deal with the issue. They left intact the organization and staffing handed over by the adjutant general, thus ignoring the law mandating three companies. The four field companies would be divided between East and West Texas, thus keeping the Rangers focused not only on cattle theft but also modern gangsters. In addition, the commission strongly urged the Rangers to begin training in fingerprinting, communications, records, and ballistics.[11]

Four days later, to make the commissioners' conclusions public, Johnson told the press that while the ten-gallon hat would continue to prevail in the West, it would be doffed in the East, where Rangers would ride high-powered cars and airplanes instead of horses, and learn to fight with submachine guns. "Rangers operating in the larger towns must be able to get around without being noticed," he explained. "In parts of the state, particularly in the West, the rangers will operate as they have in the past, but in the larger cities their work will be similar in large degree to that of government men [he meant FBI 'G-men']." He should have stopped there, but he added, "Their job is largely to gather information."[12]

Rangers had never seen themselves as mere gatherers of information but as men of action as well. The remark was poorly phrased but essentially accurate. Over the coming years, the Rangers would devote most of their effort to criminal investigation while remaining men of action who often used "rough stuff" and bullets to bring investigations to a climax. They would also master the arcane techniques that the DPS crime laboratories offered.

The Rangers still harbored unrest, but as one remarked, probably expressing common sentiment, "Why, we're still in the horseback stage, while crime travels in 85-a-mile cars."[13]

THE CALLS FOR RANGERS did not abate while the Department of Public Safety took shape. They continued to operate essentially as they had under the adjutant general.

For example, mob violence threatened in Columbus, seat of Colorado County west of Houston. Two blacks, ages fifteen and sixteen, had supposedly raped and drowned a nineteen-year-old honor graduate of

Ranger Ed Gooding, the embodiment of the "Garrison Ranger" of the mid-twentieth century, photographed at Company A headquarters in Houston in 1959. Note the blend of old and new, the western garb and boots, and the automobile that replaced the horse. *Robert Nieman*.

Captain J. J. Sanders typified the hard-bitten captains of 1910–20. Politically appointed, he used strong-arm methods and drank too much. His company worked the Lower Rio Grande. This picture was taken near Brownsville. *Texas State Library and Archives.*

Posse typical of the "bandit war" of 1915 in the Lower Rio Grande Valley. The horse of old had given way to the auto. Rangers, local officers, and vigilantes pursued Mexican "bandits" in such posses. *Center for American History, University of Texas–Austin, CN 11513.*

Headquarters of the Norias division of the King Ranch. On August 8, 1915, a small band of soldiers and ranch hands drove off attacking Mexican Sediciosos. Rangers arrived too late to take part. *Center for American History, University of Texas–Austin, CN 11511.*

Although Rangers had taken no part in the Norias fight, Ranger captain Monroe Fox (*left*) joined two men in dragging the bodies of Mexicans killed in the battle. The picture, posed in a series of different views, gained wide circulation among Mexicans on both sides of the boundary and inflamed hatred of Rangers. *Center for American History, University of Texas–Austin, CN 09503.*

On October 18, 1915, Sediciosos wrecked a passenger train north of Brownsville, killing three and wounding four passengers and trainmen. Long after the raiders had escaped across the Rio Grande, Ranger captain Henry Ransom executed at least four nearby Mexicans. *Center for American History, University of Texas–Austin, CN 09181.*

Ranger Jack Webb clowns with skull of "evaporated" Mexican, displaying the attitude of Captain Henry Ransom's Ranger company during the "bandit war" of 1915. *Center for American History, University of Texas–Austin, CN 09505.*

A primary mission of the Texas Rangers after World War I was cleaning up oil boomtowns. This is Desdemona in 1919. *Texas State Library and Archives.*

During the prohibition years of the 1920s, Rangers kept busy rooting out illegal stills. *Center for American History, University of Texas–Austin, CN 03016.*

Illegal liquor, illegal gambling, and wild boom-owns came together in Mexia in 1922. Governor Pat Neff declared martial law, and Rangers joined with soldiers in restoring law and order. Standing at end of table in black hat and suit is Ranger captain Frank Hamer. *Texas Ranger Hall of Fame and Museum.*

TEXAS RANGERS COMPANY A

In West Texas, Rangers operated much as they always had, mainly on horseback. This is Captain Jerry Gray's Company A. Captain Gray affected gaudy attire and managed to alienate most of his company as well as citizens. *Center for American History, University of Texas–Austin, CN 06061.*

The stellar captains of the 1920s, Tom Hickman (*left*) and Frank Hamer. Both had large egos, but Hickman was flamboyant and outgoing while Hamer was quiet and reserved. *Center for American History, University of Texas–Austin, CN 11481.*

Ma Ferguson twice ran for governor because Pa had been impeached, but he told her what to do. Together, they ruined the Texas Rangers. As governor in 1935–37, however, Jimmie Allred restored the Rangers as an elite body of professional crime fighters. *Texas State Library and Archives.*

The Sherman race riot of May 1930 featured atrocious barbarities and high-lighted Jim Crow extremism. The accused black, George Hughes, is shown here in front of Ranger captain Frank Hamer (in black hat). *Texas Ranger Hall of Fame and Museum.*

Kilgore, center of the East Texas oil boom of 1930–33. *Texas State Library and Archives.*

In 1931 Governor Ross Sterling chose Ranger captain William W. Sterling (no relation) as adjutant general, an unprecedented bow to the Rangers. "General Bill" did a good job, although he loved to flaunt his Ranger image in front of the camera. *Western History Collections, University of Oklahoma Libraries.*

Manuel T. Gonzaullas—"Lone Wolf"—served as a Ranger and federal prohibition agent during the 1920s and 1930s and, in this portrait, as captain of Ranger Company B in 1940–51. Flashy and vain, he was also widely regarded as the finest Ranger of his time. His armored 1932 Chrysler with submachine gun mounted on the dash told much about his persona. *Texas State Library and Archives* (above) and *East Texas Oil Museum Archives at Kilgore College* (opposite).

CAPTAIN M. T. (LONE WOLF) GONZAULLAS
COMPANY "B" TEXAS RANGERS

CAPTAIN M. T. (LONE WOLF) GONZAULLAS
COMPANY "B", TEXAS RANGERS
(Inside, holding butt of Sub-machine
gun in his 1932 Model Chrysler, armor
protected scout car, at Longview,
Texas, 1932.)

Louisiana state troopers stand at site where lawmen gunned down Bonnie and Clyde in 1934. Ranger captain Frank Hamer is widely though erroneously credited with locating the pair and setting up the ambush. He played an important role, however, and took part in firing the fusillade of bullets that riddled the two gangsters and their car. *Texas Ranger Hall of Fame and Museum.*

Columbus High School and had confessed—conforming to the pattern in many cases of fabricated offenses and confessions extracted by torture, if at all. On October 22, Ranger E. M. Davenport helped Sheriff Frank Hoegemeyer escort the two youths to the Houston jail to be held in safety pending a trial. On November 14, however, without calling for a Ranger, Sheriff Hoegemeyer and his deputy drove the boys back toward Columbus for trial. En route they were halted by a mob and made to surrender the prisoners, who were driven fourteen miles to the scene of their alleged crime. The Episcopal rector climbed on the hood of his car and pleaded for law and order, but gave up when someone shouted, "Get another rope." Chained together and screaming, the boys were hanged over an oak limb.

The lynching commanded national attention because of the comments of local officials. The county attorney: "I do not call the citizens who executed the negroes a mob. I consider their action an expression of the will of the people." The county judge approved because he believed the ages of the boys would prevent justice being done.

A United Press reporter editorialized that the new Department of Public Safety had failed to equal the record of the old state Rangers by giving Texas a lynchless year. Because Sheriff Hoegemeyer failed to ask for Rangers to help with the return trip lends credence to the charge that he expected to yield his prisoners.[14]

That Rangers could and would head off a mob if alerted in advance was demonstrated twice in June 1936, both in deeply racist rural counties west of Houston. At El Campo on June 18, Rangers balked a mob of three hundred intent on lynching five black men and four women accused of murder. In Franklin on July 30 four Rangers from Headquarters Company, headed by Mannie Gault, stood guard over the trial of a black man accused of raping a thirteen-year-old girl. Conspicuously armed with machine guns and tear gas, they kept the packed courtroom quiet.[15]

Nor were the horse Rangers idle in the last months of 1935. A surge in theft of cattle, sheep, and goats kept captains Bill McMurrey and Red Hawkins busy. Both had been reared on West Texas ranches, but neither had contended with stock thieves employing fenced holding pens and fast trucks on paved roads. Each captain had six Rangers, McMurrey at Hebbronville, and Hawkins at San Angelo, and they joined with county officers, highway patrolmen, operatives of stock associations, and ranchers and cowboys to combat the menace. They stood night guard in pastures, patrolled main highways and back roads, stopped stock trucks to check ownership, and searched stockyards and marketing centers for stolen animals. The operation testified to excellent cooperation among lawmen but, with no point at which victory could be declared, had to be sustained for month after month.[16]

Preoccupied with all the usual kinds of crime and routine, the field Rangers went about their jobs with an eye cocked warily on Austin. There, over the winter months of 1935–36, a drama played out that would have critical consequences for their future.

[11]

DPS Birth Pangs, 1935–1938

DESPITE THE FRIENDSHIP between Albert Sidney Johnson and Tom Hickman, tension between the two increased in the weeks following Hickman's appointment as senior Ranger captain on August 11, 1935. He traveled extensively without letting anyone know where he could be reached, and he pouted when the Public Safety Commission denied his request to travel to Hollywood to participate in a movie about the Texas Rangers. He did not move from Fort Worth to Austin, station of Headquarters Company. He made no effort to integrate the Rangers as a division within the Department of Public Safety or to exert any other control over the companies he now commanded as senior captain. He did not favor placing the Rangers in the new department, and his relations with Acting Director Louis Phares were frosty at best. Dividing Texas into five Ranger districts, Hickman drew his own as a "shoestring" embracing most of the big urban gambling clubs of Dallas–Fort Worth, San Antonio, Corpus Christi, and Houston-Galveston, and he issued orders that none be raided without his explicit approval.[1]

The simmering friction, hidden from public view, reached a climax early in November 1935. The issue was Governor Allred's gambling nemesis, Fred Browning's Top o' the Hill Terrace between Dallas and Fort Worth, which Hickman had failed to raid despite the governor's constant prodding. After the adjutant general moved Hickman to Headquarters Company in May, his successor in Fort Worth, Captain Fred McDaniel, closed the Terrace and confiscated the gambling equipment, only to see it returned by Tarrant County authorities. After August 11, Senior Captain Hickman's "shoestring" district and orders banning any gambling raids without his authority brought the Terrace back under his jurisdiction. Browning reopened and soon hosted crowds drawn by fine food and drink and, in a basement room, gambling for those so inclined.

In late October Governor Allred summoned Hickman to a meeting in his office. Present also was the governor's secretary, Ed Clark. According to Clark, Allred bluntly informed Hickman he wanted the Top o' the Hill Terrace raided at once. Hickman answered that a search warrant would have to be obtained. "Search warrant hell!" exploded the governor. "You're the first ranger I ever heard of who raised the question of a search warrant. You don't need one when you raid a public gambling house." Hickman said it was a private residence. "Private residence hell," retorted Allred. "You told me yourself you had seen several hundred people being given free liquor there. This has got to be done."[2]

Hickman promised to conduct the raid the coming Saturday night, November 2. Supposedly, only Allred, Clark, Hickman, and Acting Director Phares knew of the plan. Even the two highway patrolmen who accompanied Hickman in plainclothes did not know their mission. One was accompanied by his wife, the other by Doris Wheeler, a DPS clerk and the widow of one of the highway patrolmen gunned down by Clyde Barrow in 1934. She later said that before the drive to Fort Worth the license plates of the car had been changed and at the club entrance the gateman, while waving other cars in line forward, stopped Hickman's car and carefully examined the plates.[3]

Everyone involved, including Browning's dining room patrons, agreed on how Hickman conducted the raid. With the two couples, he entered the room, looked around, and after about five minutes departed.

He later explained that he saw no gambling or gambling equipment and had no cause to remain longer. Two lawyer friends of Allred's were among the diners that night, and they described this scene to the governor. Earlier, one had asked the "house man" why there was no gambling and had been informed that a Ranger raid would take place at 11:30 PM. After Hickman and his companions left, they said, roulette, dice, and blackjack tables were rolled out.[4]

Only four days later, after midnight on November 6, Captain J. W. McCormick and Ranger Sid Kelso also raided the Top o' the Hill Terrace. They knew that Browning had all the front approaches covered with gatemen and buzzers, so they crawled a rainy, rocky mile up to the rear of the building. Crashing the door and down a stairway, they burst into a spacious underground room tunneled out of solid rock. A crowd worked three roulette wheels, four dice tables, two blackjack tables, and more than twenty card tables. McCormick arrested Fred Browning and four of his henchmen, and confiscated $8,000 worth of gambling equipment.

The dramatic, well-publicized raid added to Hickman's embarrassment. McCormick is unlikely to have conceived of this raid or its timing alone. That he was a favorite of the governor, a fellow townsman from Wichita Falls, and his daughter married to a partner in the law firm of Allred's brothers all suggest the origin of the raid.[5]

All five men arrested by McCormick soon went free, taking their confiscated equipment with them.

The three public safety commissioners, disappointed with Hickman's performance as senior captain, had been discussing his replacement before November 2. The failed raid followed by McCormick's successful raid brought the issue to a head. On November 7 the commission and Phares met with Hickman and talked about the Terrace fiasco and Hickman's generally unsatisfactory performance since August. All three commissioners agreed that Hickman would be given until December 1 to find another job and submit his resignation. Meantime, he would be suspended pending further notice.

Two days later, with rumors swirling, Hickman journeyed to Dallas to talk with Johnson about his future. On the train back to Austin,

Hickman vented his troubles to a group of men that included a Waco newsman. From Waco the reporter telephoned Austin and gained official confirmation of the commission's action on November 7. The next day, Sunday, the news hit the papers, and on Monday, November 11, Acting Director Phares served official notice on Hickman that the commission wanted his resignation by December 1. Hickman's response: "I have no intention of resigning."

Johnson and Hickman faced off, whether in Austin or Fort Worth is not clear. Johnson demanded an immediate resignation. As described by Hickman, Johnson declared: "You've got to get out Tom, and find yourself another job. If you don't you'll blow up this thing. We're having a bad time in the commission and if it isn't run as Governor Allred wants it run, we won't be reappointed January 1." "I stopped at the door," said Hickman, "and told him I won't quit. I'll kick the roof off first."

Hickman's refusal to resign made its way into the press, and on Monday night Johnson conducted a hurried conference by telephone with the other two commissioners. All agreed that, in view of Hickman's defiance, he had to be fired immediately. That action became public on Tuesday, the twelfth, together with the appointment of James W. McCormick as senior captain.[6]

The discharge of the veteran lawman and celebrity showman exploded in the legislature, then in special session. Within two days, Hickman's friends had combined with Allred's enemies to produce a three-man legislative investigating committee. Together with a vaguely worded charge to investigate the Department of Public Safety, the legislature allowed a paltry $300 for expenses.

PREDICTABLY, the investigation turned into a political donnybrook. Chaired by Dallas representative Sam Hanna, the committee consisted of two majority conservatives (Hanna and John A. Atchison) and one minority liberal (J. B. Ford). Hanna scheduled the first meeting for the Texas Hotel in Fort Worth, Hickman's home city, on December 3. With a total of $300 available for travel and per diem of members and witnesses alike, and with most witnesses and records available in Austin, this suggested the approach Hanna contemplated. Hickman testified at length, with the focus on the Top o' the Hill raid. Hanna also gave him the opportunity to comment on DPS, which he contended had not taken law enforcement out of politics. He and Phares did not get along, Hickman declared, and Phares opposed the consolidation of the Rangers and the highway patrol. According to Hickman, Phares had told Albert Sidney Johnson that he would "smother the rangers as much as possible." Such was Hanna's aim from the beginning: to demonstrate DPS as Allred's political creature, no matter the turmoil it stirred in DPS.[7]

Hanna scheduled the next meeting for San Antonio on December 13. For years the city had ignored widespread gambling and developed a vigorous resentment of the raids of uninvited Texas Rangers. The young Bexar County sheriff, Albert West Jr., held the new DPS in contempt. Thus San Antonio seemed an ideal location for eliciting more testimony critical of DPS.[8]

The hearings opened in a packed room of San Antonio's Gunter Hotel on December 13. Even before the chairman gaveled the session to order, a scuffle in the hall set the tone. Senior Captain McCormick strode up to Bexar County sheriff's deputy Frank Matthews and slugged him in the face, knocking off his glasses. Matthews had been "popping off," McCormick explained, with derogatory comments about Governor Allred. The two had almost come to a shootout in the Red River country years before, when McCormick was a federal officer and Matthews a Ranger.

In the morning the committee grilled Albert Sidney Johnson and Ed Clark, the governor's secretary, about the circumstances that led to Hickman's discharge. So rowdy did the proceedings become, however, that Hanna declared an executive session for the afternoon. Behind closed doors, Sheriff West and several gambling kingpins vented their anger at Rangers for interfering in a city where they were not wanted.

Governor Allred felt that the two meetings had been designed solely to tar him politically, and he resolved that Hanna would not have the last word. On December 14, the day after the San Antonio session, the three committee members were conferring in the capitol press room in Austin. In burst the governor demanding to testify. Atchison explained that this could only be done in a formal hearing. "I'm ready to testify right now," shouted Allred. "Get a court reporter to take the testimony and ask me any questions you want to." With a reporter summoned from the county court, the committeemen, Allred, Ed Clark, and a flock of newsmen paraded down the hall to a hearing room. Phares and McCormick soon rushed to the room.

In heated language and repeatedly slamming his hand against the desk, Allred spilled out in detail his version of the events leading up to Hickman's firing. After the announcement, the governor said, Hickman came to him and asked him to intercede with the commission. Allred refused, and when asked why, he replied: "To be frank with you, Tom, you have been inexcusably negligent. You have fired men for being less negligent than you have been, and to be most charitable, you haven't done a thing since you have been a ranger. You have laid down on this job, and I am not going to intercede for you."

Pounding the table, Allred ended addressing Hanna and Atchison: "You could have got these facts if you had come to me or any member of the safety commission and asked us." He then entered into the record a written statement of thirteen reasons for dismissing Hickman.[9]

Thus the legislative inquiry sputtered to an inconclusive end. With no more money, the committee never met again.

Despite his fine record as a Ranger captain in the 1920s, Tom Hickman deserved to be fired. He could not step up from field captain to the managerial responsibilities of senior captain. All the reasons submitted by the governor were valid. The Top o' the Hill fiasco was merely the final offense. Hickman could have gone quietly and probably remained a captain charged with showing off the Rangers at the Texas Centennial exhibition in Dallas the following summer. Instead, his vanity led him to defy the Public Safety Commission, which had no choice but to fire him abruptly and publicly.

The new senior captain appealed to the press. Described as a "tall, wiry, story-book type of Ranger," James W. McCormick wore a holstered six-shooter on each hip, "one double action for shooting and one single action for a club." Sometimes he also packed a pistol in a shoulder holster and carried another in his pocket. He basked in his success at San Augustine. He did not have to kill anyone in that operation, he explained, but "had to lay awake nights figuring ways to avoid it."[10]

Plainly, McCormick was a product of the six-shooter culture, a tough captain in the traditional mode, exemplar of the old-time Ranger pictured by most Texans.

"WE HAVE MADE UP our minds that gambling can be stopped," declared Acting Director Phares on December 30, 1935. "That is what we are going to do." In contrast to the axe-wielding raids of early in 1935, however, Rangers would use gentler methods. They would enter suspected clubs in inconspicuous attire, pistols in shoulder holsters, and appear as patrons while they watched for violations of the law. If they observed any, Rangers hidden outside would enter to arrest both proprietors and patrons. If necessary, women with pistols in their jeweled purses would accompany the men.[11]

Taking issue with his boss, Senior Captain McCormick disdained "Rangerettes," as they were quickly dubbed. "A couple of good Rangers," he boasted, "can keep these places closed. With a little time, a few Rangers could stop gambling in Chicago." "Ranger Bill" Sterling had an even more biting comment: "That's the last blow to Ranger traditions. Too bad! Too bad!" Despite the ridicule, Phares appointed four Rangerettes.[12]

When Phares served his blunt notice on gamblers, he had just returned from Houston, where he tested his new offensive over the New Year's holiday weekend. Resplendent in a tuxedo, he positioned Rangers also decked out in tuxedos in several clubs while sending plainclothesmen into others. Allred's "Purity Squad," combining the "sit-it-out" policy with soft words, courtesy, and hints, discovered few gambling places. Most that specialized solely in gambling had already shut down. Clubs that offered food and drink as well had purged their establishments of gambling equipment. Those that had not were promptly closed. The opening shot of the war, at least, had seemed to vindicate Phares's softer approach, so contrary to the usual Ranger image.[13]

By the end of 1936, in its first report to the governor, the Public Safety Commission conceded that the campaign against gambling had proved unpopular in many cities and had made political enemies. But the commissioners vowed to continue to enforce the laws so long as the legislature kept them on the books.[14]

In fact, Phares's war on big-time gamblers had already begun to languish. Once again the commission and DPS found itself mired in a controversy even more bitter than the Hickman ordeal. This time the storm centered on Louis Phares himself.

ON APRIL 7, 1936, Albert Sidney Johnson called a press conference to announce the Public Safety Commission's decision to appoint Louis Phares as director of the Department of Public Safety. He had done "an admirable piece of work," and the time had come to reward him by making him director. "We feel now that the organization of the department . . . has been completed. Chief Phares has been put to every test and has met them all."[15]

The storm broke the next day. The Sheriffs' Association of Texas had their own candidate, Sheriff J. B. Arnold of Beeville, and had asked the commission to delay action until a nomination could be filed on April 13. Then word spilled out that the vote for Phares had been two to one. D. D. Baker, who had replaced Ernest Goens when he resigned in October, lost the argument for a delay. In protest he resigned, and rumor had Senior Captain McCormick intending to resign also.[16]

Predictably, the voluble young sheriff of Bexar County, Albert West Jr., weighed in at once. Phares's appointment was a slap in the face to every sheriff in Texas by Governor Allred. "Phares has never co-operated with local officers. The state police and rangers are fighting each other. The sheriffs of Texas cannot and will not co-operate with him because we do not trust him and do not respect him."[17]

Two days after the announcement, April 9, the sheriffs' association opened their annual convention in San Antonio, thus providing a forum for continuing ferment. Sheriff West continued to harangue volubly and intemperately, but calm seemed imminent when McCulloch County sheriff Love Kimbrough, president of the association, wired Governor Allred on April 12. The sheriffs still regretted the commission's action in appointing Phares, he said, but they would cooperate with the Department of Public Safety. On April 16, however, Kimbrough declared that his telegram had been misinterpreted as an agreement with the appointment of Phares. Far from it, he said. He concurred in all that Sheriff West had said and "[I] still agree that Phares is not fit for the job."[18]

The controversy raised two issues, which confronted the public safety commissioners with a dilemma even if they failed to recognize it.

First, should Louis Phares have received the appointment? As acting director, as Chairman Johnson asserted, he had done a remarkable job in organizing the Department of Public Safety. But he was blunt and abrasive, dogmatic, a product of the highway patrol, said to be opposed to consolidation of the patrol with the Rangers, and determined, as Hickman contended, to "smother the Rangers as much as possible."

Phares probably would not have had to smother them. As he built the highway patrol into a state police agency that enforced criminal as well as highway laws, the handful of Rangers would have reverted to horsemen policing the border and the western cattle ranges. They might well have ultimately dropped off the organization chart.

Albert Sidney Johnson should also have perceived that, regardless of Phares's administrative achievement, no one from the highway patrol was likely to gain the allegiance of the Texas Rangers. Nor could a Ranger hope for the backing of the highway patrol.

Second, could a sheriff function as director, as proposed by the sheriffs' association? As the commissioners doubtless recognized, sheriffs lacked the qualifications. They operated within restricted boundaries, commanded too few deputies and too little funding, usually enjoyed limited tenure and thus experience, and knew virtually nothing about the elaborate scientific techniques developing within the DPS laboratories. Sheriffs had to be creatures of politics or court voter displeasure. And too many sheriffs, as a Round Rock editorial phrased it, were "as much under the control of the lawless as they are in control of the law."[19] Finally, a sheriff might have been able to get along with the Rangers but could never hope to command a disgruntled highway patrol.

THE OPPOSITION TO the appointment of Louis Phares to head the Department of Public Safety did not subside. The sheriffs kept up a constant drumbeat of antagonism that all but ended cooperation—although the local officers swiftly came to appreciate the services they could obtain from the crime laboratories in Austin. Albert Sidney Johnson and his colleagues needed only a month to observe the damaging impact on the growth and functioning of the new agency. On May 9, 1936, they asked for Phares's resignation and, according him high praise, sent him back to run the highway patrol.

This time the commission got it right, drawing neither on the Rangers nor the highway patrol for a new director. They named to the post Lieutenant Colonel Horace H. Carmichael of the National Guard. He had served as assistant adjutant general during the Moody and Sterling administrations, and had been restored to the post when Allred took office. Forty-eight, a combat veteran of the war, an experienced administrator, a respected public servant, a man with few if any enemies, Carmichael pursued a policy of "discipline through loyalty." Homer Garrison Jr., preoccupied with conducting patrol training programs, had aroused no Ranger animosity and remained assistant director. Even the hypercritical Sheriff West approved Carmichael.[20]

Chairman Johnson also announced that the Texas Rangers—i.e., Senior Captain McCormick—would now report directly to the Public Safety Commission. In effect removing the Rangers from DPS altogether, this manifestly unworkable gesture to Ranger discontent could not have been seen as more than a temporary arrangement, buying time. At least, that is the way it turned out. On June 25, 1936, the commission called McCormick to Dallas and proposed that he yield the title of senior captain to Director Carmichael and take over a new company, which would be stationed at his hometown of Wichita Falls. McCormick pondered this proposition for more than a month before accepting. Johnson announced it on July 30, 1936.[21]

The idea appears to have been Carmichael's. He asked for the title, and he intended that it be more than honorary. Horace Carmichael, director of DPS, now regarded himself as a Ranger even though not holding a Ranger commission. The five captains reported directly to him, bypassing Assistant Director Garrison. Determined to restore the Rangers' self-image and effectiveness, Carmichael truly functioned as senior captain.[22]

In the autumn of 1937 Carmichael published an article titled "We Rangers: Lawmen of the Frontier." The "we" bespoke his self-identity as a Texas Ranger, and his article was a paean to Ranger traditions. The 1937 model, Carmichael noted, combined the old skills of running down rustlers with new methods of scientific crime detection. The 1937 Ranger, rather than meting out justice himself, had to gather evidence for a jury. "In the past no one looked closely into rough justice. Today the Ranger must not only get his man, but he must bring him in."[23]

To Carmichael belongs the credit of launching the modern Texas Rangers toward their ultimate status as the elite law enforcement arm of the state of Texas. No longer would anyone look to the highway patrol as more than a body of troopers policing the expanding system of state highways. They exercised their new police powers only in the absence of Rangers or in aid of Rangers.

ON APRIL 1, 1938, the Public Safety Commission unanimously voted to remove Louis Phares as chief of the Texas Highway Patrol, to take effect on July 1. According to Phares, the charge had been "incompatibility and failure to cooperate," but speculation centered on his resentment over losing the DPS directorship and his complaints about being saddled with extra responsibility without the manpower to deal with it. When Phares stepped down on July 1, the highway patrol's Captain Fred Hickman (a cousin of Tom Hickman's) took over as chief.[24]

LOUIS PHARES LOOKED on his dismissal as the culmination of three years of persecution, motivated by Governor Allred's determination to keep the Department of Public Safety under his political thumb. Albert Sidney Johnson, not Phares, actually ran DPS on behalf of the governor and made decisions that shredded the merit system into a "farce and travesty." Phares had no say in the choice of department heads. He was relegated to the sidelines in the Hickman controversy. Senior Ranger Captain McCormick, Allred's protégé, was "openly insubordinate" and repeatedly ran to the governor with the slightest matter that displeased him. Returned to the highway patrol, Phares received assurances from Horace Carmichael, an old friend of Johnson's, that he extolled Phares's achievement in organizing DPS and would not interfere with his administration of the highway patrol. Yet the two clashed repeatedly over law and policy as Carmichael, at Johnson's behest, withdrew one function after another from Phares's agency.

Even though publicly lauded by Johnson and named by the Public Safety Commission director of DPS, Phares regarded Johnson, acting for Allred, as the prime villain in politicizing the new agency, pushing him aside as he sought to organize it, and finally shoving him out of the highway patrol. At least this is what he wrote in laborious detail in a twenty-one-page typescript intended for release to the press. There is probably truth buried in his emotional rhetoric, but it never found its way into print.[25]

Phares deserves credit for organizing DPS as acting director, credit amply and repeatedly bestowed by Albert Sidney Johnson. Phares's blustering self-defense, however, discloses that in many ways he destroyed himself. Publication would have stirred partisan rancor and controversy that would have left his reputation far more severely damaged.

ON SEPTEMBER 24, 1938, driving his automobile on Austin's Barton Springs Road, Director Horace Carmichael suffered a heart attack. His car crashed into a post of a gasoline station. Attendants ran to the scene and found him sitting motionless at the wheel. At age fifty-one, his life-less body was pulled from the car.[26]

Assistant Director Homer Garrison, thirty-seven, immediately moved up to acting director of the Department of Public Safety. Three days later the Public Safety Commission made the appointment permanent.[27] Eleven days later Ranger captain S. O. Hamm was named assistant director.

[12]

Homer Garrison, 1938–1968

Homer Garrison came out of the highway patrol and could well have reignited Ranger disaffection. However, his solicitude for Ranger concerns quieted apprehension over his highway patrol origins, and his delegation of Ranger supervision to his assistant director, former Ranger captain S. O. Hamm, maintained the groundwork laid by Horace Carmichael. On January 1, 1940, however, Captain Bill McMurrey resigned as head of Company D in Hebbronville, and Hamm elected to return to the Rangers as his successor. Two days later the Public Safety Commission elevated Fred Hickman from chief of the highway patrol to assistant director.

Homer Garrison knew what that would mean to the Rangers. For two years they had reported to a former Ranger; now he had left and the two top men came from the highway patrol. Insulated by Hamm, Garrison had incurred no enmity among Rangers, and he moved swiftly to head off Ranger resentment. On January 4, 1940, he issued an order instructing all Ranger captains to report directly to him, bypassing Hickman.

Like Carmichael, Garrison had proclaimed himself a Texas Ranger. And so he remained for twenty-eight years.[1]

HOMER GARRISON SEEMED an unlikely candidate for a high state job. Malaria forced him out of high school in the tenth grade. In 1920, at the age of nineteen, he gained appointment as a deputy sheriff of Angelina County, based in Lufkin, and thus embarked on his lifelong career. In 1929 he joined the old motor patrol as a license and weight inspector and quickly rose through the ranks to lieutenant, then captain of the new highway patrol. His record, especially in conducting highway patrol training courses, led the Public Safety Commission to choose him as assistant director of the Department of Public Safety when it began organizing in the fall of 1935. Immediately after Horace Carmichael's death in 1938, the commission named Garrison director.

He looked and acted the part. Aside from the potential in his record, his stature and personality made him an ideal choice. At six feet two and a robust 190 pounds that grew to 210 by the 1960s, he appeared even taller in the high-heeled cowboy boots he usually wore. A layer of severely combed-back graying hair crowned a bespectacled countenance featuring high forehead and square jaw. At his desk he wore a business suit with a small pistol in his pocket. Away from his desk, which was often, he affected conventional western garb, with broad-brimmed hat. On ceremonial occasions he strapped on a pair of embellished Colt revolvers or automatics.

Garrison's imposing physique and one-man-rule style of management intimidated no one. His engaging personality made everyone his friend. Soft-spoken, smiling, quietly gracious, unpretentious, authoritative but not authoritarian, his easy manner put people quickly at ease. He reached out to make everyone his friend, whether rookie Ranger or patrolman, high-ranking official, the governor, or legislator. He constantly reminded field personnel that he kept his door open and no one needed an appointment. When they took him up on it, he sat in congenial conversation as long as his schedule permitted.

As the years passed, the director introduced repeated innovations in departmental methods and capabilities. He upgraded the crime lab; he persuaded the legislature to increase appropriations and the size of the Ranger Service; he developed wide-ranging training programs that strengthened and maintained Ranger effectiveness; he gradually built a communications network that placed Rangers and patrolmen in high-powered automobiles in radio touch with superiors, one another, and local lawmen; he kept politics for the most part out of DPS, although not entirely; he persuaded the legislature to fund a new headquarters building in Austin to replace the crowded, unsuitable rooms at the National Guard's Camp Mabry. DPS moved there in 1953.

Homer Garrison's reputation grew yearly, not only in Texas but in the nation and overseas. While never close friends, he and FBI director J. Edgar Hoover maintained cordial relations and exchanged complimentary letters. Such was Garrison's prestige and effectiveness that his job never came under political peril. His relationship with the Public Safety Commission was solid, although the commissioners had little influence on his style or policies. Successive governors relied on and paid tribute to him, and he took care to respond to their every request. Garrison ran his department with a sure hand from the beginning, but by the 1950s, as one of his Rangers remarked, in Texas he was "Mr. Law."

The Rangers had come to venerate Homer Garrison without reservation. No one expressed it more powerfully than the thirty-year veteran Lewis Rigler, who retired in 1977:

> I have never spoke to one Ranger who served under Homer Garrison who didn't idolize the man—none. And he loved the Rangers. . . . He wore a Texas Ranger badge, signed his name Director of the Department of Public Safety and Chief of Texas Rangers, attended every Ranger function from a lowly company meeting up. And of equal importance, the Rangers considered Garrison a Ranger. He had the love and respect of the Rangers that no other colonel has ever come close to. Check his grave in Austin, he is surrounded by Rangers.[2]

DESPITE WIDESPREAD APPREHENSION, merger of the Texas Rangers into the new Department of Public Safety did not condemn them to extinction or obscurity. Thanks to Horace Carmichael, they lost none of their traditions or elitism. Their mission remained the same: suppression of riot and insurrection, and enforcement of the criminal laws of Texas, chiefly through assistance to local peace officers. The old methods did not suddenly turn irrelevant, although some changed and new ones took shape.

Even so, the Department of Public Safety created a new breed of Rangers. Most importantly, the Public Safety Commission's supervisory role cushioned DPS personnel from the governor's control. The reality did not always reach the ideal, but now a man who qualified and could survive the scrutiny of a captain and Colonel Garrison could make a lifelong career as a Texas Ranger without enduring a political test every two years.

As a result, the Ranger Service came to consist of professional peace officers seasoned by experience, kept up to date with training courses in the latest concepts of criminology, crime-laboratory science, and weaponry, and motivated by the special traditions and pride conferred by more than a century of history. The leadership of Homer Garrison reinforced all these attributes, and the huge pool of applicants for each vacancy enabled him to select the best qualified by experience, physical stature, intelligence, and commitment. Likewise, promotion depended on a man's record, his seniority, a captain's patronage, and the director's approval.

Two innovations marked the new Ranger Service. First was paper-work. Rangers had always been notorious for the absence or brevity of their reports. In January 1936 the Public Safety Commission decreed that Rangers submit a weekly report accounting for every hour of every day, not only criminal work but expenses and travel whether by auto-mobile, train, or horseback. Likewise, with the increasing number of criminal investigations that landed in court, case reports grew fatter and more detailed as prosecutors demanded evidence strong enough to convict.[3]

Second was the distribution of the little force of Rangers in a rational statewide organization. Each company was assigned a geographical region and its headquarters fixed in a particular city. Each Ranger of the company then took station at a town in the region and stood respon-sible for the number of counties assigned him. The first distribution was ordered in June 1936, when the service comprised only four companies and thirty-six men. Subsequent increases added more companies. At the height of Garrison's tenure in the late 1950s and early 1960s, the service numbered fifty-two men divided into six companies: Company A at Houston, Company B at Dallas, Company C at Lubbock, Company D at Corpus Christi, Company E at Midland, and Company F at Waco.[4]

Rangers operated with an independence unknown to typical police forces. They had to because they were so thinly dispersed over such large regions. But more important, independence formed the bedrock of Colonel Garrison's philosophy. "We get results by relying on individual initiative. We simply tell each Ranger to enforce the law in his area. How he does it is up to him." The captains put this philosophy into effect.[5]

A hallmark of DPS policy was cooperation. Cooperation varied from one jurisdiction to another, but for the most part the state and local officers sustained cordial and mutually helpful relations. Rangers brought a level of experience usually lacking on the local level, and their crime laboratories provided vital aid obtainable nowhere else. Their statewide powers, moreover, allowed them to operate across city and county boundaries. Local peace officers, on the other hand, usually had the pulse of the community, knew people and places, and could call on shadowy informers. For their part, Rangers understood the political environment in which sheriffs and police worked. These officers often had to look the other way to avoid offending powerful interests or, more ominously, the electorate. Rangers did not object unless major crime went untended. Once DPS professionalized the Rangers, cooperation contrasted starkly with the boomtown years, when rogue sheriffs wanted no Ranger intruding into their jurisdiction.

A mixed record marked relations with the Federal Bureau of Investigation. Rangers admired the professional "gangbusters" that J. Edgar Hoover had begun shaping in the early 1930s. They too were career professionals. With some agents, moreover, Rangers got along well, to the benefit of both. With others they did not. The FBI's institutional habits of intruding on state and local prerogatives without notice, of sharing only such information as they wanted while demanding all that the state and local officers knew, and of claiming undeserved credit irritated most Rangers, no matter how closely they worked with individual agents. By contrast, most Rangers and local lawmen freely shared information, and the Rangers gained friends and cordial cooperation by fading into the background and letting local peace officers profit from the publicity of jointly produced successes.

The DPS Rangers, backed by the crime laboratory, took on an increasing load of criminal investigation. Crime burgeoned throughout the nation, especially after World War II. Major crime by individuals, impromptu gangs, and organized networks based both in and out of Texas so preoccupied the Rangers that they resented distracting duties of lesser consequence. In 1936, for example, thirty-six Rangers handled 255 cases, while in 1956 fifty-one Rangers were called on to make 16,701 criminal investigations.[6]

Major crime occurred mostly in urbanized East Texas. Stock theft and smuggling remained the scourge of South and West Texas. As a result, the service divided roughly into western Rangers and eastern (or "city") Rangers. Although the abilities called for by each overlapped, they were sufficiently specialized that little interchange of personnel occurred.

In West and South Texas, duties and methods recalled earlier times. Automobiles and radios facilitated operations, but horses still played a critical role in rugged areas lacking roads. Now, moreover, rustlers and smugglers also relied on motorized transportation. The typical western Ranger, however, dressed and worked much like his predecessor.

In East Texas, Rangers rarely resorted to horseback but traveled in high-powered automobiles, and after World War II, airplanes and helicopters. Their targets were gangsters who robbed, raped, bludgeoned, kidnapped, forged, embezzled, and murdered, and the investigative techniques needed to capture and convict differed little from those of city detectives. City Rangers wore broad-brimmed hats and high-heeled boots, but only when they wanted to appear conspicuous. As often, their success depended on looking like ordinary citizens.

Finally, now that they were career professionals, the select few who met Colonel Garrison's standards, most DPS Rangers grew so committed to their jobs, so loyal to Garrison and the service, so conscious of their superlative reputation in and beyond Texas, that they became workaholics. For many, dedication bordered on obsession. Day or night, sick or well, they responded instantly to a sheriff's call for help. Whatever time and effort a case needed, they invested with grim determination. Glenn Elliott devoted seventy to one hundred hours to a typical work week. "My wife never does cook supper for me," remarked Elliott, because she never knew when he would come home.[7]

As Ed Gooding recalled of his service in Houston-based Company A in the 1950s, he and everyone else had ulcers. "We lived on cigarettes and coffee with an occasional sandwich thrown in." Captain Johnny Klevenhagen had half his stomach removed before he died at age forty-six. His successor, Captain Eddie Oliver, endured the same operation, as did Sergeant (later captain) Pete Rogers.[8]

Homer Garrison was as proud of his Rangers as they were of him. Not all lived up to his ideal, but combined with tradition, legend, public reputation, and demonstrated success, the ideal spawned a tight-knit camaraderie, a deeply embedded sense of elitism, and pride in wearing the badge of the Texas Ranger.

ALTHOUGH REPORTING TO the Public Safety Commission, Homer Garrison maintained cordial relations with the governor, especially the governor's private secretary. If he disagreed with a governor's policies or actions, he did not voice it; and he conscientiously responded to every request of a governor that he look into an issue.

Garrison served the DPS founding father, Jimmie Allred, only three months before a new governor replaced him in January 1939. Flour merchant W. Lee O'Daniel, although an astute businessman, had made himself a hillbilly celebrity with a radio program that featured country music, God, and folksy homilies, as well as promotion of "hillbilly flour." "Please pass the biscuits, Pappy" was the signature line of his radio program, carried by the most powerful stations in Texas. His appeal to rural voters and corporate backers alike gained him the nomination (and hence the election) without a runoff.

Pappy O'Daniel's clownish and unpredictable behavior, while commanding the affections of poor farmers, so confounded Austin's political establishment that his programs went nowhere in the legislature. Even so, his veto pen devastated legislation. He cut the DPS appropriation in half, wiping out the entire Bureau of Narcotics, the salaries of two Ranger captains and five Ranger criminal investigators, and the annual ammunition fund. Austerity ruled DPS throughout the O'Daniel years.[9]

Pappy O'Daniel so embarrassed the Democratic Party that leaders wanted to be rid of him. The opportunity came in April 1941 when U.S. senator Morris Sheppard died. Legislators plotted to install O'Daniel in the vacant seat to get him out of Texas. State law, however, required the governor to appoint a successor until a special election could be held. O'Daniel, happily anticipating senatorial distinction, needed to name someone to hold the seat but not contest him for it. He turned to Andrew Jackson Houston, son of Sam Houston. Tottering in dotage at eighty-eight, he had no sooner taken the senate oath than he died. O'Daniel easily won the election.[10]

For Homer Garrison, the O'Daniel governorship was not a happy time. With subsequent governors, however, he endured less stress. Coke Stevenson, Beauford Jester, Allan Shivers, Price Daniel, and John Connally were all conservatives who sometimes promoted policies or measures that doubtless disturbed Garrison. But he faithfully served them, never crossed them, and consistently earned their praise.

MANUEL T. GONZAULLAS, the dashing "Lone Wolf" of earlier times, served DPS in Austin for five years, 1935–40. As chief of the Bureau of Intelligence, he combined his talents as criminal scientist and criminal investigator to erect an exceptional unit. With his mastery of ballistics, fingerprinting, moulage casting, handwriting, documents analysis, and microscopic examination of human hair, blood, shreds of fabric, and any other specimen that might offer evidence, he had developed a staff whose capabilities were the envy even of the FBI. At the same time, he supervised a small cadre of criminal investigators operating mainly as undercover detectives. In their first year alone, his men solved 140 of 142 cases, including 56 murders.[11]

But the "Lone Wolf" was bored and wanted to return to the Rangers. On February 4, 1940, with the approval of Colonel Garrison, Gonzaullas exchanged places with Captain Royal B. Phillips, head of Company B in Dallas.[12] Rumor suggested that another motive came into play. Throughout his career, Garrison remained extremely sensitive to any potential threat to the Rangers' image. Besides unpopularity with his men, Phillips was said to harbor personal characteristics that may have led the colonel to want him safely buried in an Austin office. If so, Gonzaullas's desire to return to the field provided convenient cover.

For the next eleven years, Gonzaullas commanded his scattered company but also, like other captains, undertook case work of his own.[13] At the same time, he oversaw a company that rarely numbered more than a dozen, with two or three in the Dallas office and the rest positioned in towns throughout the fifty-eight counties of his region in North and Northeast Texas. He supported his men when essential and praised them when deserved; but he expected each man to handle his case load without calling for help unless he had to. At their first meeting, he instructed Lewis Rigler not to bother him with little problems. Three weeks later Rigler thought he had a big problem and took it from his Gainesville station to Dallas. Gonzaullas blew up: "Now, by God, I told you to take care of the problems yourself. Now get out of here and go do it."[14]

Inspired by their captain, the Rangers of Company B made it the most active and effective of all. Belying the implication of the weekly reports, not all of their work consisted of unexciting routine such as following leads, interrogating suspects, or brainstorming with sheriffs and deputies. Their cars carried an arsenal of weapons, and sometimes they had to use them.

Ranger Jim Geer, based in Vernon, near Wichita Falls, afforded an example. For more than six months, he and local officers had been trying to break up a ring of thieves stealing oil-rig equipment and machinery. On January 27, 1948, Geer joined Wilbarger County sheriff Ed Luttrell and Vernon police chief Walter Suttle to drive to Lawton, Oklahoma, chasing down a lead in this case. While in the Oklahoma sheriff's office, they agreed to take a mentally deranged woman back to Vernon and to keep watch for a 1941 Chevrolet just reported stolen.

With Sheriff Luttrell at the wheel and the woman in the front seat, the other two officers sat in the back. En route they overtook the stolen vehicle, as confirmed by the number on the Oklahoma license plate. The sheriff sounded his siren, but the driver hit the accelerator and fled. For seventeen miles the chase continued. Seated on the left, Geer cranked down his window and fired two warning shots into the air. When that produced no effect, Chief Suttle lowered his window and emptied his pistol trying to hit a tire. The two then changed sides, and Geer fired at the tires. His third shot took effect. The driver lost control, swerved into a ditch, then across the road into the opposite ditch, then back into the highway to spin around three times before coming to a stop. A man jumped out, ran across the highway, vaulted over a fence and fell down, recovered, and resumed running. As the sheriff's car glided toward a halt, Geer leaped out, found footing on the right fender, and, clinging to the car frame with one hand, fired at the fugitive. One shot felled him. The bullet sliced through his right shoulder, disabling him. A doctor at a Burkburnett hospital patched up the man, and Geer and his companions held him until a Lawton deputy arrived to take custody.

The man proved to be one Dorsey L. Reddix, thirty years old and a longtime hardened criminal. He had not only stolen the automobile but had served three sentences in the Texas State Penitentiary at Huntsville.

The three Texas officers had left Vernon for Lawton at 3:00 PM, and they turned over Reddix to the Oklahoma deputy at 11:00 PM. This was but eight hours of a day that began long before 3:00 PM, a typical Ranger workday.

Furthering the accolade Captain Gonzaullas passed on to Homer Garrison, Geer and his fellow local officers had the satisfaction of breaking the case that called them to Lawton on January 27. The very next day they recovered much of the stolen oil pipe and equipment, which prompted the chief investigator of the regional oil and gas association to advise Colonel Garrison of Jim Geer's hard work and success and express his certainty that Geer "will uphold the tradition of that grand old organization known as the 'Texas Rangers.' "[15]

Jim Geer had several such violent encounters. Some Rangers put in thirty years without ever firing a shot, except at targets. Others used their weapons more often than the weekly activity reports suggest. Throughout his career, Gonzaullas fended off questions about how many men he had killed, seventy-five affording the unlikely number most often cited. Two may have been a more likely count. To one reporter Gonzaullas replied, "Just write that I found it necessary to kill several. But I will says this: I would rather be tried for killing six outlaws, than to have one of them tried for killing me."[16]

Ever the showman, Gonzaullas decided to retire when he turned sixty and apply his talents to radio, television, and motion pictures. To a blaze of national publicity, he stepped down on July 31, 1951. For the next five years he and his devoted wife, Laura, lived in Hollywood and circulated with stardom. He served as technical advisor for the television series "Tales of the Texas Rangers" and for some Hollywood westerns. Despite his well-known vanity, he turned out to be camera shy. Returning to retirement in Dallas, he remained active in Ranger circles and in arranging material for the book he never wrote. Cancer took his life on February 13, 1977, age eighty-five.[17]

Long before then, Homer Garrison explained at least part of the secret of Gonzaullas's success: He "was a master of planning and he was always ready for any eventuality. When he went on a case he figured that anything might happen and he planned for it. He also gave thought to what he would do if he were in the other fellow's place."

"In my opinion," the colonel declared, "Captain Gonzaullas will go down in history as one of the great Rangers of all time." He has, and arguably he was *the* greatest Ranger of all time.[18]

WORLD WAR II badly burdened DPS and the Texas Rangers. By August 1944, 264 DPS employees served in the military, leaving gaping holes that hurt law enforcement coincident with the rise of crime produced by the many military installations in Texas. They not only attracted criminals but produced their own from the uniformed ranks. Rangers considered tracking deserters who often turned to crime legitimate duty, as well as apprehending escapees from German prisoner-of-war camps fleeing to Mexico. Surveillance of the large German-American population of Texas, on the other hand, was rightly viewed as a waste of time.

Both prison and POW escapees posed a massive problem for the undermanned agency. Like DPS, the Texas Department of Corrections lost prison guards to the military, and escapes from prison farms soared. By the end of 1943 DPS had helped search for 255 escaped convicts and 142 POWs. Many of the 262 military deserters stole cars, hijacked motorists and merchants, and committed burglaries and other crimes. Colonel Garrison had gained an increase of the Ranger Service to forty-two, but the department's wartime figures reflect cooperation among the Rangers, highway patrol, local officers, and military police.[19]

War's end allowed DPS to flesh out its ranks, principally the highway patrol. Both Rangers and highway patrol now included combat veterans who brought newly gained special skills to law enforcement. They enhanced the strength and effectiveness of the department.

FOR ALMOST TWO DECADES at midcentury, Bob Crowder reigned as the most effective and beloved of Ranger captains. Not surprisingly, he had been schooled by no less than Manuel T. Gonzaullas. When he retired in 1951, Crowder moved up to captain of Company B in Dallas.

A native of Rusk County, a veteran of the U.S. Marines, the Dallas Police Department, and the Texas Highway Patrol, Robert A. Crowder gained the tutelage of Gonzaullas in 1937 in the DPS Bureau of Intelligence. He won his Ranger badge in 1939 and in 1940, when Gonzaullas took over Company B, again came under his old mentor, who groomed him for sergeant and then, in 1951, for captain.

According to Lewis Rigler, one of Crowder's men, "Bob looked like a Ranger. He stood six feet three inches tall, weighed about 200 pounds, and was in many ways a handsome man." He also looked like a Texan—"tall, angular, and a somewhat swarthy, leathery complexion." Rigler called him an outstanding leader, "the type of man others just naturally wanted to follow. He exuded a confidence with which few are gifted, but he was never conceited or pompous with it."[20]

Although Crowder worked and supervised many cases, he is remembered chiefly for one that displayed his canniness and courage as a peace officer.

On April 14, 1955, Crowder had just returned from lunch when he took a telephone call from Homer Garrison. A riot had broken out in the maximum security unit of the Rusk State Hospital, 120 miles southeast of Dallas. This unit housed inmates diagnosed as criminally insane. Led by a powerfully built young man named Ben Riley, eighty convicts in the segregated black section of the unit had seized ice picks and anything else that could serve as a weapon, beaten several especially brutal "bouncers"—convicts charged with keeping order—and taken two hospital attendants and a doctor hostage. Colonel Garrison suggested that Captain Crowder "ought to get down there." Widely known as a high-speed driver, Crowder jumped into his new Oldsmobile, pushed it to the limit, and pulled up to the electronic gate of the hospital ninety minutes later. Several hundred highway patrolmen and local lawmen milled around outside the double row of high fences. Riley had served notice that an assault would cost the hostages their lives. He had also agreed to meet with a Ranger captain if he represented the state government.

Riley had already allowed himself to be interviewed by a local newsman. Almost hysterically, he had complained of primitive cells, bad food, brutal treatment, and conditions vastly inferior to those in the white part of the maximum security unit. Quickly briefed on these grievances, Crowder got on the telephone to Riley. "Do you want to speak to me?" Crowder asked. "Yes," said Riley. "I'm ready to come in there," declared the captain, "but I don't want no foolishness." "Me neither," answered Riley. "I want to tell you one thing," the Ranger added. "I'm not comin' in unarmed because you've already got three people over there as hostages and I don't want to be the fourth one—and I'm not going to be. I just want to tell you this. If somethin' goes amiss, I know who's going to fall first."

Bob Crowder walked alone across the compound as the throng of officers watched apprehensively. Outside the door to the unit he confronted Riley, armed with an ice pick and scissors. For twenty minutes he listened as the inmate poured out complaints of degrading treatment. All this time, highway patrolman Jim Ray lay about fifty yards distant with the crosshairs of a sniper rifle trained on Riley's chest. (Ray would make his name as a Ranger and ultimately as Chief of Criminal Law Enforcement for DPS.) Crowder confined his part of the dialogue to warnings that the rioters had done wrong and were not helping their cause. To Riley's demand to meet with the head of the hospital, however, Crowder promised to get him a hearing. He then ordered Riley to bring his followers out, stack their weapons in a pile, and release the hostages. Meekly they complied. Riley got his hearing (although probably no improvement in living conditions), and the riot was over.

Colonel Garrison asked Crowder what had taken place between him and Riley. "Aw, boss, I just told them to cut out that stuff." Years later he elaborated: "Now if, when I got down there, it hadn't worked that way, I don't know what the story would have been. But I know one thing. I had two .45s with eight shots in each of them, and that's about as far as I know."[21]

CLINT PEOPLES had less success in talking down a mental case without violence. Captain of Headquarters Company in Austin, Peoples boasted an outstanding record. However, his mountainous ego, conspicuously displayed, drew ridicule and even contempt.

On the morning of May 15, 1955, Peoples and Glen McLaughlin, chief of the Bureau of Intelligence, were driving to Oklahoma to participate in a conference on law enforcement. Just north of Waco, the police radio broadcast that Limestone County sheriff Harry Dunlap had been killed near Thornton and that an insane man held off officers from his hilltop farmhouse. Peoples also had a heavy foot and covered the hundred miles to Thornton in a little more than an hour. He found about forty lawmen and a hundred onlookers on the scene.

Ranger James L. Rogers briefed the captain. The farmer, N. J. Tynes, had been treated for psychosis but had periodic demoniacal spells. The night before, seized by one, he had shot his friend and neighbor off his tractor. That evening Sheriff Dunlap and two deputies approached the house but were driven off by gunfire. The next morning Ranger Rogers and two highway patrolmen joined them. They worked out a plan of attack. Rogers sprinted to a ditch in back of the house and fired a tear gas cannister through a window. Dunlap shouted for Tynes to come out and surrender. The back door swung open, and Tynes fired two quick rifle shots. Both caught Dunlap between the eyes. The officers fell back. Rogers called a Ranger at Belton and asked him to see if the army at Fort Hood would send an armored car. Such was the situation when Peoples and McLaughlin reached the place about noon.

The first task, Peoples decided, was to retrieve Sheriff Dunlap's body. As the other officers sprayed the house with heavy gunfire, Peoples, Rogers, and a deputy sheriff raced forward, grabbed the body, and dragged it to safety.

Although one of the highway patrolmen occasionally caught Tynes in the telescopic sight of a sniper rifle, Peoples insisted that he be taken alive if at all possible. About 2:30 PM an army sergeant drove up in an armored half-track. Peoples and Falls County sheriff Grady Pamplin, an ex-Ranger, climbed in and drove toward the house. Peoples intended to fire enough tear gas rounds into the house to flush Tynes out. Captain Bob Crowder had raced down from Dallas, and he and Rogers took station behind some sheds in the front ready to rush the house once Tynes emerged. Circling the house, Peoples fired one cannister after another through the windows. After half an hour, he directed the driver to pull up to the back porch. At this point Peoples accidentally set off a cannister and filled the vehicle with tear gas. He and Pamplin rose to get air. Tynes fired, knocking off Peoples's hat. The two lawmen hit the ground running, returning fire. Crowder and Rogers charged the front.

From the back porch Peoples fired another cannister through the screen door. It hit Tynes in the left forearm and nearly severed his hand. Crowder and Rogers rushed into the kitchen from the front, to find Tynes sprawled on the floor. He rose and smashed his head into Rogers's stomach. Rogers fired, hitting him in the right shoulder. Bloodied and gasping for air, he nonetheless struggled with the four officers until they subdued him.

A sniper bullet probably would have been quicker and more merciful, but Peoples wanted to take the man alive. He did, only to have him die in the hospital even as the friend he had shot from the tractor recovered. The standoff made a gripping story, and the media made the most of it. Peoples undoubtedly enjoyed the publicity, but he and McLaughlin, after cleaning up in Crowder's Dallas office, drove all night to address the law enforcement conference.[22]

REORGANIZATION BROUGHT Bob Crowder's tenure as captain of Company B to a close.

In fact, the Department of Public Safety stood in urgent need of reorganization. For almost twenty years the legislature had added functions, personnel, workload, and of course new units to the department. By 1955 the organization chart resembled a stylized tree, with hefty limbs sprouting horizontally from a single trunk. Thirteen separate units, including the highway patrol and Texas Rangers, reported to the director and assistant director perched atop the organizational tree trunk. Only a leader of Homer Garrison's talents could make it work.

In 1955 the nonprofit Texas Research League undertook a study of DPS. By the end of the year the league had fed draft portions of the study to Garrison for comment. He liked what he read. So for the most part did Captain Clint Peoples. But he singled out for withering criticism the league's proposed restructuring of the DPS field command. Six regions would contain both Rangers and highway patrol, as well as license and weights, driver's license, vehicle inspection, safety education, communications, and a basic crime laboratory. A single officer, with the rank of major, would command all personnel in the region. Each of the regions would have one of the six Ranger companies, whose captains would report to the major.

Peoples argued that this system simply would not work. The missions, methods, and cultures of the Rangers and highway patrol were so different that one could never be commanded by the other. Homer Garrison rejected the argument. The offending provision remained in the report, submitted to the Public Safety Commission on January 27, 1957. The legislature responded with a brief, simple law enacted in May 1957, to take effect on September 1, 1957. It made no reference to the Texas Research League's report but merely authorized DPS to undertake any reorganization desired so long as it did not add to the number of divisions existing in 1957.[23]

The reorganization, essentially as proposed by the Texas Research League, went into effect on September 1, 1957. One puzzling aspect remains unexplained, since no DPS records of this issue remain. First, anticipating legislative approval of the report, in October 1956 Colonel Garrison brought Captain Bob Crowder to Austin as "chief, Texas Rangers." The Texas Research League's report made no provision for such a position, but it may be speculated that Colonel Garrison negotiated it with the report's authors. The report contains an organization chart portraying the "de facto organization" in 1955 as modified by a 1956 addition of the new Ranger post. But the final report made no mention of such a position, and in fact it could not well have been fitted into an organization in which the regional commanders reported to an assistant director for field operations. When the legislature gave DPS authority to reorganize as it wished, Crowder's title vanished. He then accepted the post of regional commander in Lubbock, effective September 1, whether by choice or pressure from Garrison is not evident. In any event, Crowder almost at once discovered that he preferred his old Ranger company.[24]

The second measure untreated in the report is the abolition of Headquarters Company in Austin and the creation of Company F in

Waco, with Clint Peoples its captain. Presumably this was to provide a Ranger company for the new Waco region. (A suspicion lingered that Garrison found this a convenient way to get the politically powerful Peoples out of Austin.) Much to his displeasure, Peoples moved to Waco and organized Company F. He reported to Major Walter J. Elliott of the highway patrol. They maintained a cool relationship at best. Every Ranger detested the new arrangement. Most had come out of the patrol, and none wanted to return to the "uniformed service." All over Texas, sheriffs and police chiefs protested, and legislators took note.

For Peoples, the climax came as Christmas approached. Major Elliott informed him that Rangers would be needed to help the highway patrol during the holiday season. Peoples responded: "Chief, I like you very much, but as long as there is a breath in my body I'll not assign a Ranger to a patrol car to work traffic."

The crisis passed quickly. Three days after Christmas Colonel Garrison teletyped all field officers that the Public Safety Commission had decreed that effective January 1, 1958, Ranger captains would no longer be responsible to the regional commanders but, as before, directly to Homer Garrison and Assistant Director Joe Fletcher. On January 3 the colonel summoned all these officers to Austin to explain the new system. After the meeting broke up, Garrison approached the captain of Company F. "Clint," he said, "I have to agree with you. This was one bad mistake."[25]

MEANTIME, Crowder's sergeant, E. J. "Jay" Banks, had taken over Company B as acting captain, a title he held until September 1, 1957, when he gained the permanent captaincy. Arthur Hill transferred from the Big Bend as Banks's sergeant.

As Glenn Elliott remembered, "Jay was a very high profile type person. He was always on the cover of a magazine or newspaper." He even stood as the model for the statue of the ideal Texas Ranger that graced the terminal lobby of Dallas's Love Field. Still, he was not Bob Crowder, and his men did not leave the record of praise they heaped on Crowder. Nor did Sergeant Hill think highly of Banks.[26]

Like Crowder, despite starring in a string of well-publicized cases, Jay Banks is mainly remembered for one bloody event.

Gene Paul Norris, the "smiling killer," was an Oklahoma gangster with a long record of murder, burglary, bank heists, and sadism. He seemed to enjoy killing, and the slightest provocation could trigger his revenge, often preceded by torture. Big-time criminals hired him as a hit man. Lawmen credited him with about fifty homicides. The FBI kept track of the comings and goings of Norris and his sidekick, William Carl "Silent Bill" Humphrey.

In March 1957 Norris drove to Fort Worth from Oklahoma. He had conceived a scheme for robbing the payroll of the branch of the Fort Worth National Bank at Carswell Air Force Base. Norris knew that James E. Papworth, who ran a collection agency out of a Lake Worth office on the northwestern edge of the city, had served prison time with John W. Taylor, former manager of the branch bank who had been convicted of embezzlement. Norris demanded (or proposed) that Papworth get a floor plan and other inside information about the bank from Taylor. Papworth delivered, handing over the floor plan and the name and address of the cashier, Mrs. Elizabeth Barles.

The plan was for Norris and Humphrey to seize and doubtless murder Mrs. Barles and her twelve-year-old son John early on the morning of the scheduled payroll delivery, Tuesday April 30, 1957. What Norris wanted was Mrs. Barles's auto and bank keys. Her car, bearing a base entry sticker, would get them onto the base, and the keys would get them into the bank. There they would wait for the payroll couriers to arrive with $500,000 in cash, tie them up, and return to pick up their own car at Mrs. Barles's residence.[27]

First, Norris had unfinished business in Houston. The mission was to carry out a twenty-year-old vow: a revenge killing of gambler John Brannan, whose testimony in 1937 had sent Norris's brother to prison for ninety-nine years. On April 17 Norris and Humphrey entered the Brannan home, threw blankets over the heads of Brannan and his wife, and with hammers pounded their heads to a pulp. Police discovered the deed the same night, and before long they and Company A Ranger captain Johnny Klevenhagen had enough evidence to support arrest warrants. Aside from pistols that linked the two to recent robberies, police had twice spotted Norris's souped-up green 1957 Chevrolet in Brannan's neighborhood and had once given chase, only to be outrun by the powerful Chevy.

Hardly had the Carswell bank scheme been worked out than the FBI knew about it, alerted by a tipster whose identity was never confirmed. Captain Banks later identified the informant as Papworth himself. In Fort Worth the FBI, Texas Rangers, Fort Worth police, and Tarrant County sheriff met to work out a plan. They knew where Norris and Humphrey were holed up and set up a listening device connected from their motel room to one next door. Thus they knew exactly what the two gangsters planned.[28]

The law enforcement response to Norris's design exemplified the longtime Ranger policy of cooperation with other agencies. Company B's acting captain, Jay Banks, worked smoothly with Tarrant County sheriff Harlon Wright, Fort Worth chief of police Cato Hightower, and FBI special agent in charge W. A. "Bill" Murphy. The FBI tracked Norris and Humphrey from Houston to Fort Worth, where they arrived on Saturday April 27. With the surveillance link in place, they learned that Norris and Humphrey intended to make a dry run of escape routes on Monday afternoon. Officers laid plans to apprehend the two hoodlums then. Banks called Johnny Klevenhagen in Houston and invited him to take part. The captain grabbed his shotgun and arrest warrants, and sped north to Fort Worth.

On Monday afternoon, April 29, the local officers converged on the Lake Worth community where Mrs. Barles lived. They had three cars. Captain Banks drove his new high-powered Dodge with Captain Klevenhagen, Chief Hightower, Sheriff Wright, and city detective captain O. R. Brown. Banks's sergeant, Arthur Hill, with Ranger Jim Ray and city chief of detectives Andy Fournier, manned a second car, with Ray at the wheel (he had been a Ranger for only two weeks but a highway patrolman for twelve years before that). In the third were Ranger Ernest Daniel and city detectives George Brakefield (later a Ranger) and sheriff's deputy Bobby Morton.

Banks's car contained the top law officers because they would man the ambush. Posting Sergeant Hill and his two Rangers at "Casino Beach," an amusement park a short distance up Meandering Road from the Jacksboro Highway, Banks and his carload of four other officers drove two miles southwest down Meandering Road to Mrs. Barles's home. She and her son had been moved elsewhere on Sunday. There the lawmen lay in wait.[29]

The FBI spotted the two men in Fort Worth and followed them until Hill saw them turn onto Meandering Road. "Take over, Rangers, we are out of it, now," the FBI radioed.

Hill swung in behind at a distance, but the scheme had gone awry. A Cadillac and the green Chevy had turned right off Meandering Road onto a residential street. Hill's car turned too, maintaining a discreet distance. The officers saw a man get out of the front car and get in the second. They misinterpreted what they saw. Actually, the first car was Papworth's, and he was taking Norris to show him the location of the Barles house. Humphrey followed in the Chevrolet. Papworth, according to his confession, had second thoughts and deliberately took a wrong turn. An enraged Norris, hurling threats, ran back and got in the car with Humphrey. At this time they spotted Hill's car behind them. Swiftly turning in a driveway and backing out, they sped back to Meandering Road and swerved northeast toward the Jacksboro Highway. Banks and his Dodge full of locals, alerted by Hill's radio, swiftly took up the pursuit.

Suddenly Humphrey veered left off Meandering Road and bumped across an open pasture toward the Jacksboro Highway, which here ran almost parallel and about a quarter-mile from Meandering Road. Banks followed. Humphrey smashed through a fence, bounced across a ditch and headed up the four-lane Jacksboro Highway. Banks kept on his tail.

Meantime, Sergeant Hill, with Jim Ray driving, raced back up Meandering Road to the Jacksboro Highway. At the left turn Ray miscalculated and found himself speeding north in the southbound lanes of the Jacksboro Highway. Soon they had pulled abreast of the two cars across the median. But Ray slowed to cross into the northbound lanes and fell behind. The third car, monitoring the radio traffic, now joined the chase, close behind Ray.

The pursuit reached speeds of 120 miles per hour, sirens wailing. Norris leaned out and exchanged fire with the three officers hanging out the windows of Banks's car. The race slowed none as they streaked down the main street of Azle, scattering autos and pedestrians but avoiding collisions.

A mile and a half south of Springtown, now in Parker County, Humphrey swerved right onto a country road, spraying mud across the highway. This was probably not a sudden decision but part of the escape plan earlier mapped. Banks turned too, but spun in two complete circles before recovering, headed in the correct direction. A light rain fell, making the caliche-based road slick as it twisted along the banks of flood-swollen Walnut Creek. Bullets and blasts from Klevenhagen's shotgun continued to slice the space between the vehicles. Suddenly Humphrey took a curve too fast, slid on the rain-slick road, plowed into a ditch, and smashed into two trees. Both gangsters leaped from the car and ran toward the creek, firing pistols at Banks as he sought to bring his Dodge to a stop. With the car crossway on the road, the officers piled out firing with all the weapons at their command, Klevenhagen with his shotgun. Banks grabbed his M-3 (an army M-1 converted to fully automatic, with a large clip), but the magazine fell out, and he had to run back to retrieve it.

The two fugitives fired from behind the creek bank, then struggled to cross the creek. Bullets downed Humphrey, whose body washed up on a small flood-made island. Norris, screaming laughter, backed across the creek firing at the lawmen, all of whom sprayed bullets from every weapon they had. Banks let go the entire clip of his rifle. As he later stated, "The bullets started stitching Norris and he didn't have enough hands to stop up the holes. He died, screaming like a baby, on the banks of muddy Walnut Creek." Norris fell backward in the mud. All the officers later maintained that they did not know who had downed Norris, but the consensus awards the distinction to Banks and his automatic rifle.[30]

At this moment Ray topped a little hill at high speed and saw Banks's car broadside across the road. He hit the brakes, swung in a complete circle, and came to a stop three feet from the side of the other vehicle. As Ray rolled out, Klevenhagen shouted, "I'm out of ammunition. He's getting away, give me a gun." Ray pitched him his own shotgun. The third pursuit car rolled to a stop. But the firing had ended, and the bodies of both gangsters could be seen in and across the creek, about thirty yards apart. Norris had slipped back down the slope, his feet in the creek. Fearing he would be swept away by the floodwaters, Sergeant Hill dragged the body back up the hillside.

Attendants at the Fort Worth funeral home where the corpses were taken told the press that Norris took sixteen hits, mostly in his chest and body, Humphrey twenty-three in his mouth, chest, and left leg. "He shot him to pieces," concluded Jim Ray of Banks's burst of automatic rifle fire. Chief Hightower declared that the death of Norris enabled him to clear nine murder cases from his books.

Banks and his fellow officers had ended the rampage of two of the deadliest criminals in Texas history. The furious chase of twenty-five miles had put many citizens at risk. Even the sheriff had urged Banks to call off the pursuit, to no avail. After years, they finally had two of the most-wanted and deadliest criminals cornered, and Banks intended to get them. He and his colleagues did.[31]

The operation testified to the merit of agency cooperation and revealed the planning skills of the Rangers as well as their ability to push an auto chase to the limit and prevail in an exchange of gunfire.

JAY BANKS SERVED three more years as captain of Company B. On March 2, 1960, Homer Garrison called him to Austin and informed him that he would have to be let go. The explanation was failure to shut down gambling in Fort Worth. Rangers knew this was merely a cover story, that the real reason lay in personal misbehavior likely to bring discredit to the service. The Ranger rumor mill throbbed with speculation but never let the theories become public. Jay Banks charged that the real reason was to make way for Bob Crowder to return to the captaincy of Company B, which he did, serving as effectively and with as much respect and affection of his men as before 1957. He retired in 1967 and died in 1972 at the age of seventy-one.[32]

INCIDENTS LIKE JAY BANKS's grand drama climaxing in a burst of gunfire happened rarely, but it happened often enough to maintain good press for the Texas Rangers. More usual was hard, frustrating investigation that consumed much time but frequently led nowhere. It also led to quieter triumphs in which the fugitive surrendered without resistance and ultimately found his way to the penitentiary at Huntsville.

Rangers regarded crime fighting as their central mission. Any other assignment interfered with that mission and awarded criminals a bonus. Yet other assignments occupied as much as half of a Ranger's time and effort and drew him away from criminal investigation and pursuit. Even though such tasks were genuine law enforcement duties, they diluted what he believed to be his true purpose and should be the responsibility of other lawmen.

[13]

Gambling . . . and Other Distractions

G AMBLING HAD LONG BEEN OUTLAWED in Texas, and the legislature, dominated by rural members, refused to legalize it. However, increasingly urbanized Texans gambled, and so did visitors from elsewhere. City officials tended to tolerate gambling because the electorate wanted them to. Rangers rarely intruded unless invited, which was almost never. They regarded crackdowns as a distraction from fighting major crime, certain to anger city officials and many citizens, nearly always no more than a temporary fix, and properly the domain of local officers. Yet gambling violated Texas law, and when clergymen appealed to the governor, or an attorney general sought publicity to aid his gubernatorial ambitions, Rangers had to take on the gamblers.

In Fort Worth a crusading clergyman finally prompted Captain Manuel T. Gonzaullas to raid the area's most notorious gambling establishment. Fred Browning's Top o' the Hill Terrace, located on the highway connecting Dallas and Fort Worth, had been an irritant to the Rangers ever since Tom Hickman's failed raid of 1935.

Near midnight on August 11, 1947, the Lone Wolf struck. With Rangers Bob Crowder and R. L. Badgett and Special Investigator Dub

Naylor from Austin, he approached the mansion in the same way Captain J. W. McCormick and Sid Kelso had in 1935, crawling up the rocky slope in the rear. When an attendant opened the back door for some patrons, the lawmen raced to get in before the door closed. They surprised the operation in full swing, arrested Browning and his attendants as well as fifty patrons, and confiscated all the expensive equipment. Owner, attendants, and patrons stood before a justice of the peace the next morning. Browning paid their modest fines. Gonzaullas smashed all the equipment.[1]

Fort Worth officialdom had always been lax about gambling, and Browning was soon in full operation again. The Top o' the Hill offered fine food and drink and an array of gambling machines until Browning's death in 1953. In a supreme irony, by the following year it had reopened as a Baptist theological seminary. But for fifteen years Top o' the Hill dramatized Ranger frustration at being pulled off criminal cases to raid gambling dens. They usually reopened at once.[2]

Besides the Dallas–Fort Worth complex, San Antonio, Corpus Christi, Houston, Beaumont, and Port Arthur had their recurring gambling flare-ups. But overshadowing all was Galveston Island, which came close to being one huge gambling palace.

The "Free State of Galveston" had flourished since the early 1930s, when Sicilian immigrants "Big Sam" and "Papa Rose" Maceo and their family virtually took over the island. Their homegrown syndicate established such plush gambling emporiums as the Hollywood Supper Club, the Turf Club, and the Balinese Room. The Maceos dominated politics, controlled all officialdom, allied with the bankers, employed much of the citizenry, turned back encroaching Mafia dons, encouraged the spread of one of the world's biggest red-light districts, and reigned as benevolent civic fathers. They permitted other gamblers to operate so long as they understood whence came the permit. Casinos and walk-ins proliferated from one end of the island to the other. The Maceos brought big-name bands and entertainers such as Frank Sinatra and Bing Crosby to their clubs. Vacationers came from all parts of the nation, and every business prospered, even during the Great Depression.

Periodically, Ranger Company A, based in Houston, pulled off a raid. A battle-scarred veteran who walked with a limp, Hardy Purvis captained the company for twenty years. He retired at the end of 1956, and his sergeant—John J. Klevenhagen—took over the next day. "Something down deep was driving him like a man possessed," remarked Ranger Ed Gooding. Rangering obsessed him, and he devoted himself to it totally. Slender, gaunt, with menacing eyes and explosive temper, Klevenhagen mastered every weapon, piloted the DPS aircraft assigned to Houston, and formed a redoubtable team with Harris County sheriff Buster Kern. The "Gold Dust Twins," they were labeled.

Rangers regarded Galveston raids a waste of time. Courts would not convict, and gamblers reopened at once. Yet when Austin pushed, the Rangers dutifully complied. The toughest challenge was the monarch of them all, the Balinese Room. It sprawled on a pier jutting into Galveston Bay, with a long enclosed passageway from shore to club. This was called the "Ranger Run" because it provided the minute or less needed to conceal all evidence of gambling. When the Rangers rushed into the dining room, the band often struck up "The Eyes of Texas," and the master of ceremonies introduced the Texas Rangers.

By 1957 both Maceos had died, and no one had risen to similar power. The Balinese Room burned in 1954 but was promptly rebuilt with even more opulence. But of largest influence, Ben "Bugsy" Siegel had built the Flamingo casino and hotel in Las Vegas, Nevada, launching the city that would become the mecca of legal gambling and celebrity entertainment and put Galveston out of business.

But not without one more sustained Ranger offensive, this one set off by another ambitious attorney general, Will Wilson. In the spring of 1957 he sent an undercover team to compile a list of sixty-five places to target for a single massive Ranger raid. As Wilson and a cadre of assistants gathered in Klevenhagen's office on June 17, Rangers Ed Gooding and Pete Rogers went to Galveston's lone honest judge and, based on Wilson's evidence of "probable cause," received search warrants. Back in Houston, they found an office full of glum raiders. News of the raid had been leaked by one of the Rangers, said the attorney general, and the raid was off.

Klevenhagen sprang from his chair and shouted: "Don't you dare accuse my men of leaking information! You better clean up your own back yard before you start accusing my Rangers of anything!" Asked what he meant, Klevenhagen answered by explaining how the leak had come out of the attorney general's own office.

As the embarrassed Wilson slunk back to Austin, Klevenhagen put his men on the Galveston streets. They found no gambling, of course; all the equipment had been hidden because of the leak. On June 19, however, Gooding and Rogers happened to look into the old Hollywood Supper Club, long closed. Stacked to the ceiling they saw every variety of gambling device. "Man, we've found their stash," exclaimed one of Wilson's agents.

In the following days other parts of the stash turned up, until more than $2 million in gambling equipment had been confiscated. Klevenhagen quipped that it ought to be dumped into Galveston Bay. Although he then set about smashing and burning, Wilson learned of the wisecrack and ordered it done. Much of the loot did end at the bottom of the bay, prompting the Army Corps of Engineers to threaten litigation for fouling "their" ship channel. Klevenhagen had opposed the idea, and when queried he dryly answered, "I don't know what you're talking about. I burned all the slot machines I was responsible for."[3]

Klevenhagen adopted a new tactic. The Balinese had closed, but others remained open, with gambling rooms discreetly hidden. Each evening one or more of these places numbered two Rangers among their dining patrons. The Rangers entered in full western regalia, with holstered pistols conspicuous on their hips and badges on their chests, then sat through the evening. Nervous customers slipped out quickly and soon quit coming. Gradually business slumped.

Worked to death, Klevenhagen died in November 1957, but Captain Eddie Oliver continued the operation. It was too much for an eight-man company, so Colonel Garrison sent help from other companies, one outsider to accompany an A Company Ranger in every evening visit. For three years, until the end of 1960, the nightly routine shrank the gambling business to near extinction.[4]

By 1961, thanks to the rise of Las Vegas as the gambling capital of the nation and the quiet persistence of the Texas Rangers, Galveston had lost its lure. Not only Galveston but other Texas gambling centers also suffered the Las Vegas effect, and gambling rarely drew the Rangers away from their central mission of crime fighting.

DEALING WITH labor walkouts put Texas Rangers to a far more unwelcome test than benign gambling raids. Looking back on his first strike in 1957, Glenn Elliott wrote: "I did not think then, or now, that a Ranger has any business working a strike. No matter what we do, we lose."[5]

He was right, and all Rangers shared the sentiment. At a strike site, their mission was to prevent violence, damage, and destruction. Restraining aggressive pickets, often with force, cast the Rangers as allies of management. Failure to prevent damage prompted management to brand Rangers as friends of the union.

Urbanization and industrialization powered the rise of unions in Texas, especially during World War II and its aftermath. Big corporations fought the movement, and rural Texans and their legislators acclaimed Governor Pappy O'Daniel's strident campaign against "labor racketeers." After the war, in the perception of conservative Texans, they became "communist labor racketeers."

Rangers seemed especially to side with management when they prevented strikers from interfering with workers who wanted to work. This was a central issue when Captain Manuel Gonzaullas with Rangers Bob Crowder, Ernest Daniel, and A. L. Barr policed an eleven-week strike against the Rogers-Wade Furniture Factory in Paris in the early months of 1941. Pickets had in fact used violence against strikebreakers, but the four-man team put a stop to that. Maintaining the stance of neutrality, Gonzaullas told the press that "the rights of the strikers to peaceful picketing and all other legal means will be upheld just as firmly as the legal rights of the company." Even after the company and the union reached an agreement, the Rangers delayed a week or more to ensure peace. Thus the Rogers-Wade strike tied up a captain and three Rangers for nearly three months.[6]

In September 1947 blistering charges fell on the desk of Governor
Beauford Jester. Gulf Coast oil workers had struck, and Texas Rangers
were abusing them. In particular, the strikers against operators of the
wells in South Texas protested Ranger brutality. This big land of sand
and chaparral southwest of Corpus Christi fell to Company D, led by an
acting captain, Alfred Y. Allee.

Bred to the Rangers—his father and grandfather had been Rangers
and his son would become one—Allee was a tough, gruff, thickset
holdover from earlier times. He had joined in 1931 and, except for the
two years of Ma Ferguson's administration, had covered the South
Texas counties ever since. Born and reared on a South Texas ranch, he
knew guns, horses, cattle, and the Mexicans who made up 90 percent
of the area's population. "I spoke Spanish before I learned English,"
he once quipped. In fact, he signed up the first Hispanic Ranger in the
service, Arturo Rodriguez, who later observed: "They said back then
that Capt. Allee had Mexican blood—on the tips of his boots." Mexicans
both feared and respected Allee, but anyone who provoked him might
discover in him a strain of Johnny Klevenhagen's "short fuse."[7]

Allee's men thought highly of him even as they carefully avoided
antagonizing him. "He was an outstanding captain," said one, "a good
captain back in his times. He worked with a rough element and I didn't
think he was so rough with them." Rodriguez added his telling estimate:
"The whole country was changing, and bless his heart, Cap tried to
change. But he was from the old school and he didn't know how to."[8]

Governor Jester called for an explanation of the oil workers' charges.
Allee responded with a detailed accounting of the wells and pipelines
the strikers had wrecked but mentioned nothing of Ranger violence. He
himself had been accused of attacking a union officer, Arthur Hajecate,
but did not address that either.

He could have explained without reproach. Hajecate had approached Allee from behind, grasped his shoulder, and swung him
around, at the same time exclaiming "You can't . . ." He never finished
the admonition, for Allee slapped his back so hard it knocked the breath
from him. Yes, he could, Allee said, and would if necessary. He added

that anytime Hajecate wanted to talk, prudence dictated that he not touch him.[9]

The episode came at an embarrassing time for A. Y. Allee. He was acting captain of Company D anxiously awaiting appointment as full captain. He soon had his captaincy and retained it until his retirement in 1970. The oil strike was not the last controversial incident of his career.

No strike duty burned more vividly in Ranger memory than Lone Star Steel—actually two strikes, one in 1957 and the second in 1968–69. "The Ranger became the bastard in this strike situation," recalled Lewis · Rigler of the 1957 strike. "The union didn't like him; the company didn't like him."[10]

Located near Daingerfield, in northeastern Texas, Lone Star Steel was a big outfit, employing 4,300 workers, of whom 3,300 belonged to the United Steel Workers union. On September 21, 1957, defying their officers, 2,700 union members walked off the job in a wildcat strike called to protest grievance procedures. E. B. Germany, the Dallas financier who owned the company, detested organized labor and vowed never to compromise. He promptly began hiring scabs to replace the strikers. Rangers and highway patrolmen converged to keep the peace.[11]

Infuriated by Germany's intransigence and the continued operation of the plant by scabs, the strikers repeatedly broke the peace. They cut fences, shot into houses, burned buildings, killed cattle, vandalized trucks and autos, set off dynamite bombs, and threatened people. Captain Jay Banks came down from Dallas but left Sergeant Arthur Hill to command the operation. Soon afterward, the strikers made a bad mistake. Seeking to shut down the plant by blowing up the pipe that furnished gas to the buildings, they mistakenly blew the pipe servicing the community of Pittsburg. With an entire town deprived of gas at the onset of winter, public sentiment turned against the walkout. On November 3 the strikers called off the strike. Germany hired some back, but many lost their jobs altogether.

Day after day, under Hill's supervision, Rangers and patrolmen had put in long hours policing the streets and catching a few hours of sleep

in a Daingerfield motel. That they did not altogether succeed in preventing violence and damage angered Germany and his managers. That
they tried at all angered the strikers. The Lone Star strike left festering
rancor in management and labor as well as law enforcement officers. It
laid the groundwork for another and worse outbreak.

"A STRIKE GONE MAD," headlined the *Dallas Morning News* during the
210 days of the Lone Star Steel strike of 1968–69. On October 27, 1968,
about two thousand union members walked off the job, to protest working conditions rather than wages. Once again, citing Vietnam wartime
contracts, management refused any compromise; E. B. Germany had
given way to George Wilson, who vowed to continue production as
workers vowed as emphatically to shut it down.

Morris County's sheriff had only two deputies, and he called for help.
During the seven months of the strike, six to twenty-six Rangers and
forty-six highway patrolmen worked the scene. At one time or another
nearly every Ranger in Texas served at Lone Star. Captain Bob Crowder
drove over from Dallas to take command.

Crowder adopted his usual low-key approach. He called together the
leaders of both management and labor, and informed them he had come
only to prevent violence and enforce the laws of Texas. "I told them we
were there to protect both sides, the people coming, the people going,
and we weren't going to take sides."[12]

Even so, management and labor alike inflicted violence and destruction. The strikers broke out their guns and used them freely. Dynamite
destroyed or damaged many trucks hauling equipment to and from the
plant, especially after Wilson began to bring in materials and food for
housing scabs on the fenced plant grounds. A bomb turned up at a mess
hall fixed to explode at lunch but was discovered in time. Rangers Glenn
Elliott and Bob Mitchell (the only two to work the entire strike) found
and defused it before it went off. Drive-by shootings at night targeted
houses and automobiles. Ranger Lewis Rigler counted at least two hundred beatings and stabbings, together with four severely injured guards.
The murder of a strikebreaker stirred more angry hostility. Rangers

arrested more than thirty culprits, but none was ever tried. No jury would convict.[13]

Crowder kept calm, even as strikers shouted curses, drove nails in his tires, shot at him once, and hurled countless bottles and bricks in his direction. As he explained to a reporter, people on both sides were scared. "They've been shot at, rocked, beaten, bumped into, cursed, ambushed, and spit on. Things are tense around here, and these people aren't themselves. They eventually kiss and make up and go back to being decent, law-abiding citizens. And some of them might even have a kind word for the Texas Rangers."[14]

As the newsman observed, however, despite the amiability, "Crowder's whole, lanky being exudes a stern authority." With Bob Mitchell, he demonstrated it early one morning. Dressed as workers, the two drove out of the plant gates in a company pickup truck and headed down a country road, Crowder at the wheel. As soon as they left the plant, a white pickup containing three men fell in behind. Three miles down the road, the truck flicked its lights. Crowder pulled over. The other vehicle drove abreast and the occupants began firing. "I slid over," said Crowder, "and Ranger Mitchell fired three loads of buckshot into their pickup. They lit out and we chased them at 90 miles an hour until they had to stop at a dead end road." Mitchell leaped out of the cab prepared to shoot, but Crowder restrained him. Inside the truck, besides three middle-aged toughs, the Rangers found more firearms, a piece of chain, some rocks, and two jars of moonshine whiskey. Placed under bond by a justice of the peace, they never stood trial.[15]

On May 11, 1969, the union voted to go back to work, bringing to an end the longest and most violent strike in Texas history, nearly seven months. Labor walkouts had plagued DPS ever since its formation, but Lone Star was the worst. Glenn Elliott's feeling about Lone Star could well apply to all strikes that drew in the Rangers. "Our job should have been working murders, bank robberies, and other major criminal cases, not trying to keep two sides apart—especially when both sides down deep wanted to fight."[16]

THROUGHOUT HOMER GARRISON'S ascendancy, white supremacy kept a tight lock on Texas blacks. Even as federal lawmakers moved slowly toward freeing blacks from the most onerous restrictions, state officials, reflecting public opinion, resisted any tampering with the color line. The National Association for the Advancement of Colored People (NAACP) grew stronger and more aggressive, and Texans readily accepted the assurance of politicians that it was, if not controlled by communists, at least a communist front.

Racism centered in East Texas. Few blacks lived in South or West Texas, where racism focused instead on Mexicans. Nevertheless, combined with federal pressures, the issue prompted state leaders to grope unwillingly toward some kind of quiet accommodation that would not antagonize East Texans. Even before the landmark *Brown v. Board of Education* Supreme Court ruling of 1954, a few Texas school districts had begun to plan for integration.

Although not nearly so intrusive as gambling and strikes, Jim Crow sometimes called Rangers away from their crime-fighting mission.

Beaumont, with its teeming docks and shipyards and racially mixed workforce, had a long history of racial violence. World War II crowded the city with both blacks and whites, creating housing and food shortages, and firing racial tensions. In June 1943 the alleged rape of two white women by black men ignited the explosive mix. As many as four thousand whites armed themselves with guns, axes, and other bludgeons and rampaged through the black sections of the city, assaulting residents, pillaging homes and stores, and burning buildings. The acting governor declared martial law, and guardsmen brought the riot under control before Rangers and highway patrolmen arrived.

Nevertheless, Captain Hardy Purvis and his men of Ranger Company A came down from Houston to take part in the ensuing investigation. So even did Colonel Garrison and Bureau of Intelligence chief Royal B. Phillips. They questioned shipyard workers extensively but made few arrests. Garrison explained the outbreak mainly in terms of the wartime expansion of the population. This was indeed a cause, but would not the rape allegations have sparked a riot anyway? It had happened often in the past—and would again in Beaumont in 1948. Moreover, Garrison well knew the mind of the governor, Coke Stevenson (1941–47; he became governor when O'Daniel went to the U.S. Senate in 1941). He was a racist to the core who would not look kindly on action against whites who abused blacks.[17]

Dallas also proved a hotbed. In September 1940 blacks began moving into all-white neighborhoods in North Dallas. A bomb exploded under the home of a black. The homeowners' association called on Governor O'Daniel for Rangers and martial law to avert violence. Colonel Garrison directed Captain Gonzaullas to investigate. He concluded that the Dallas Police Department had the situation well under control. A year later, however, the U.S. attorney general advised Governor Coke Stevenson that repeated complaints had been received from Dallas blacks about the housing situation. Again Gonzaullas investigated, this time submitting a report that described a series of incidents extending from September 1940 to the end of October 1941. The captain attributed these to a few hotheads on both sides and again backed the Dallas police as able to take care of the trouble.[18]

The same kind of trouble erupted a decade later in South Dallas. Again Captain Gonzaullas investigated, describing eight bombings of homes that began in February 1950 and still in June had not been solved. Again, however, he expressed confidence in the Dallas police to keep the racial situation controlled. Whites and blacks were now working in an interracial committee, and he portrayed the Dallas hostilities simply as a reflection of what was happening in cities all over the United States. True, but Rangers, products of segregation themselves, tended to downplay black complaints and leave them to local authority.[19]

SCHOOL DESEGREGATION confronted Texans with a volatile issue, as it did citizens in all the southern states. The U.S. Supreme Court's ruling in *Brown v. Board of Education* in 1954 made integration inevitable sooner or later. In Texas the three leading gubernatorial candidates in 1956 favored barring black children from white schools by any means possible, a conviction shared but not so vocally expressed by the lame-duck governor, Allan Shivers. Ironically, one hundred school districts in the state had already integrated.

Against a background of noisy controversy and maneuvering, the issue peaked in August 1956 at Mansfield, a farming community in Tarrant County a few miles south of Fort Worth. A branch of the NAACP had sprung up in Mansfield, taking its lead from the stronger branch in Fort Worth. Mansfield had an elementary school for blacks—separate but hardly equal—but no black high school. These students were bused to a black high school in Fort Worth. Pursuing their cause in the federal courts through 1955, the NAACP had won rulings that ordered the registration of twelve black students in Mansfield High School for the 1956–57 school year.[20]

Registration was scheduled for Thursday and Friday, August 30 and 31, with a final day on September 4, after the Labor Day weekend and the first day of school. By Thursday the local head of the NAACP had received threatening telephone calls, and three straw effigies painted black had been hoisted. One hung across Main Street splotched with red paint and plastered with racist signs. Another had been run up the flagpole in the front of the high school. A third dangled from the archway above the front door to the school. A crowd of several hundred citizens gathered. Tarrant County sheriff Harlon Wright and four deputies circulated among the people, exchanging loud threats with men shouting their determination to prevent the registration of blacks. None of the black teenagers appeared on Thursday, and by midafternoon the crowd had dispersed.

That night L. Clifford Davis, the Fort Worth NAACP's young civil rights attorney spearheading the case, wired Governor Shivers asking that state officers be sent to Mansfield on Friday. He sent the same telegram to Colonel Homer Garrison, who answered that help could not be provided unless requested by the sheriff. Sheriff Wright had already talked with Captain Bob Crowder, who assured him that men could be sent from Dallas quickly if needed.

Friday morning the mob again formed. This was the day for registering rural students brought in by bus, which included most of the blacks.

Gubernatorial candidate W. Lee O'Daniel, trying for a third term, plunged into the throng. "When I'm governor," Pappy declared, "we're not going to pay any attention to those nine old men in the Supreme Court." A group of angry men surrounded and pummeled Fort Worth assistant district attorney Grady Hight, who had to be extracted by sheriff's deputies and driven out of town.

During the morning, in answer to Davis's appeal for state officers, Governor Shivers issued a press release declaring himself ready to send them in if requested by the sheriff, but certainly not at the call of an officer of the NAACP, "whose premature and unwise efforts have created this unfortunate situation at Mansfield." Later, however, he directed Homer Garrison to dispatch Rangers with orders to arrest any person, black or white, who represented a threat to the town's peace. Before noon Crowder had sent Sergeant Jay Banks and Ranger Ernest Daniel.

By then passions had subsided as word came that the NAACP had advised the black boys not to go into Mansfield because of the probability of violence. The crowd had begun to drift away. Banks and Daniels returned to Dallas.

Tuesday, September 4, was the critical day, the last day for registration and the first day of school. Again several hundred people gathered, although less threatening than on Thursday and Friday. This time security proved adequate. Captain Crowder showed up with Sergeant Banks and Rangers Lewis Rigler, Ernest Daniel, George Roach, and B. O. Currin, their car trunks laden with riot gear and weapons. Sheriff Wright appeared with three deputies. Dallas County deputies stood on alert at the Tarrant County line to rush in if needed. Crowder told newsmen, "We are not expecting any trouble. I do not think any Negroes will try to enroll."[21]

He was right. The temper of the mob had persuaded not only the NAACP but the students themselves that riot and bloodshed portended. The teenagers decided they would far rather continue to attend congenial black classes in Fort Worth than hostile classes in Mansfield. Crowder is said to have received orders from Governor Shivers not to escort the black students into the school. Had they tried to enter, he and his men, backed by sheriff's deputies, would have rolled out their arsenal and tried to prevent violence.

Jay Banks made the state and Ranger position explicit a week later, when a similar crisis hit Texarkana Junior College, where two blacks tried to enroll under orders from a federal court. Again Crowder sent his sergeant and Rangers. Explained Banks: "Our orders are to maintain order and keep down violence. We are to take no part in the integration dispute and we are not going to escort anyone in or out of the college."

The Mansfield crisis was a prologue to Little Rock's Central High a year later. At Mansfield the students did not try to register, while at Little Rock they defied the mob and sought to register. When the Arkansas National Guard failed to escort them through the raging mob, President Eisenhower federalized the guard and sent in the regular army to provide the escort. Mansfield directly influenced Little Rock because it brought a reluctant Eisenhower to recognize his responsibility to enforce federal court orders and because the NAACP drew lessons from Mansfield that led to the selection and training of stronger, more determined young blacks to challenge the racial bar in Little Rock.

Looking back on Mansfield years later, Jay Banks described the mob as "just 'salt of the earth' citizens who had been stirred up by agitators," by which he meant the Fort Worth NAACP. He even credited the hanging effigies to "agitators," presumably bent on tarring the citizens as violent extremists. And still bitter over the abrupt end of his Ranger career, he said "the Captain" (Crowder) dropped by briefly for a picture-taking session, then left for Austin.[22]

Banks's opinion reflected attitudes toward integration and white supremacy common in Texas. Many Rangers undoubtedly shared these views. But large numbers of Texans favored school integration and took positive steps toward making it happen. Some Rangers may have agreed with them. Banks was unusual in setting his thoughts to paper. Others did not.

Nine years later, faced with loss of federal funding authorized by the Civil Rights Act of 1964, the Mansfield school district gave in. The first black students registered in September 1965.

POLITICS CONTINUED to tie up Rangers frequently. Few counties entirely escaped the prospect of voting irregularities or even violence, but South Texas glowed constantly as a hotbed. This was the heartland of "boss rule," with each county dominated by an Anglo (or sometimes Mexican) boss who controlled the votes of the Mexican majority. Paternalistic reciprocity characterized the relationship. It worked peacefully until the railroad to Brownsville, opened in 1904, brought a flood of immigrants who transformed the region into an agricultural bonanza. Most were political progressives outraged by boss rule.

Cameron County's Jim Wells long reigned as the strongest boss, but by the 1910s even he had been overtaken by Duval County's Archer "Archie" Parr, the "Duke of Duval." By the early 1930s, Archie Parr had begun to pass his mantle to his son George, the "Second Duke of Duval."

Both father and son held absolute power over the land, people, and government of Duval County and exerted strong influence in surrounding counties, especially neighboring Jim Wells County (named for Cameron County's political boss). The formula, according to a recent historian, was simple: "(1) control the election of every local public official; (2) use local government to provide jobs and handouts for your friends and to punish your enemies; (3) help yourself to as much tax money as you wish." When necessary, the Parrs backed these principles with intimidation, violence, bribery, fraud, forgery, and even murder. Few citizens dared incur Parr disfavor, especially at the polls.[23]

No governor had ever been able to bring down Archie Parr, although William P. Hobby almost succeeded in 1919. To George Parr, the only serious danger arose from the federal Internal Revenue Service. By 1950 he had gained greater notoriety than ever because he "found" the crucial ballot box that threw the 1948 senatorial race to Lyndon Johnson instead of former governor Coke Stevenson. A critical radio commentator paid with his life—shot on the streets of Alice by a deputy sheriff whose illegal activities he had exposed.[24]

George Parr owned all the judges in Duval and Jim Wells counties save one. Governor Allan Shivers had appointed Sam Reams state district judge to fill an unexpired term, and when he was unseated by Parr's candidate in the 1950 elections, the state canvassing board, reacting to evidence of flagrant fraud, refused to certify the election results. Reams remained on the bench, and in April 1952 he impaneled a grand jury to look into election irregularities. For a change, Parr now confronted a judge and a grand jury he did not control.

With the 1952 primaries approaching, moreover, the newly organized Freedom Party challenged Parr. He harassed and intimidated its suspected adherents. He wore the sheriff's badge, and his pistolero deputies broke up opposition party meetings and carried out his every wish, no matter how violent. At this point, learning of threats to the grand jury, Governor Shivers sent in the Rangers.

The assignment fell to Company D, Captain A. Y. Allee, headquartered at Carrizo Springs. He detested George Parr and all he stood for as much as Parr reciprocated the feeling. On May 6, 1952, Allee dispatched Rangers Joe Bridge and Charlie Miller to the Duval county seat, San Diego, with instructions to check into a motel and take station at the courthouse. Both were physically imposing and veterans of border service. They parked their car in front of the courthouse, dragged two chairs to the closed door of the jury room, and sat. "They made no show of force," observed a newsman, "just sat there in their high-heeled boots, khaki pants and big hats, with guns on hips." Inside, the jurors examined the evidence of election fraud laid out by Judge Reams, then adjourned until after the coming primary election. Rangers could ensure their safety inside the jury room but not outside.[25]

Based in their motel room, Bridge and Miller patrolled Duval County during the weeks before the July primary. Visiting the little towns, dropping by cafes for a cup of coffee, making themselves everywhere conspicuous, the two kept Parr and his minions nervous while ensuring a peaceful campaign. Even so, Parr's slate of candidates swept the election and ousted Judge Reams.

Bridge and Miller left—but only temporarily. Parr had decided that Jake Floyd, an outspoken attorney in Jim Wells County, had to be eliminated. At dusk on September 8, 1952, a hired hit man drove up to

Floyd's home in Alice and blasted the man leaving the front door. Buddy Floyd, Jake's grown son, fell dead. Rangers returned to Duval County, not only to investigate the murder but to maintain a continuing presence. Bridge and Miller served sporadically, but Rangers from other companies also rotated in and out of the county, including Klevenhagen, Peoples, Purvis, Banks, and others. They identified the murderer, but he had quickly sought haven in Mexico.

At the same time, sparked by Attorney General Price Daniel, a team of lawyers and accountants descended on San Diego to rummage through county records, many of which had disappeared. They were soon joined by federal investigators from the Post Office Department and the Internal Revenue Service. By January 1954 they had put together a formidable case against George Parr.

The continuing presence of the Rangers and the state and federal agents had given Parr a bad case of anxiety. On January 16, 1954, in Alice, he brandished a pistol at a reporter for a Spanish-language newspaper, Manuel Marroquin, who had written articles critical of Parr. Encouraged by the Rangers, Marroquin took Parr to Jim Wells county court in Alice, where he was charged with illegal gun carrying.

Waiting in the courthouse corridor to post bond, Parr and his nephew Archie, now sheriff of Duval County, encountered Allee and Bridge. Archie and Bridge exchanged insults. Bridge slapped Archie, who at once drew his pistol. Allee plunged in and twisted the gun from his hand. George Parr now joined the fray. Allee, still bullish at forty-eight, smashed George across the ear and dragged both men into the courtroom. "I'm tired of the way you pistol-whipping people are carrying Winchesters over there in Duval County," Allee declared. "I want it stopped!" "I'll stop," replied a seemingly chastened George Parr.

He did not stop. In the weeks following, word circulated that the Rangers had been threatened and that Parr had imported two Mexicans to murder Allee. A month after Parr's promise, his county attorney, Raeburn Norris, laughed contemptuously at Allee in the street. With Parr and others looking on, Allee beat up Norris. Then he walked over to Parr and spat out, "If anything happens to my men, I'll hold you directly responsible." As for Norris, his thrashing was personal. Norris "has been trying to humiliate me and damage the respect which the people down here have for the Texas Rangers."

For his earlier encounter with Allee and Bridge, Parr had both indicted for assault to murder. To push the prosecution, he engaged the famous New York lawyer Arthur Garfield Hays. Quizzed by Hays about his troubles with Parr, Allee answered in candid detail and replied to a final question about his nemesis: "I just don't like him or anything he stands for. I have no intention of killing George Parr, or of being killed, but if anything happens to me or my Rangers, I would hold him directly responsible!"

As Allee stepped down, Hays bowed and stated, "I want to pay my respects to Captain Allee. He is an honest man!" The next day, withdrawing as Parr's attorney, Hays entrained for New York City. Parr thereupon dropped his charges. Outside the courtroom, Allee told reporters: "I just don't like George Parr or nothing about him. He's a dangerous man who would do anything under the sun, and I don't treat a tiger like I do a rabbit. I'm not sorry I hit Mr. Parr."[26]

More setbacks for the boss lay in the future. The Texas Supreme Court overturned the election of Parr's winning candidate for Judge Reams's district judgeship. In the 1954 primary in July, Texas Rangers kept close watch on the polling places, and a number of Parr candidates lost, including Sheriff Archie Parr. Worse, the state and federal cases against Parr went to court, with perhaps as many as two hundred of his lackeys facing indictment.

On the federal front, the Department of Justice, the Post Office, and the Internal Revenue Service had built strong cases against Parr and his cronies, with Texas Rangers helping federal agents as well as state. In a calculated gamble, federal prosecutors decided to base their attack on mail fraud. Tax notices had been mailed to taxpayers and taxes paid by mail—a limited postal use but a window on the whole slimy mess of fraud and theft smeared over all the agencies and officials of county government. Appalled by the revelations, on July 17, 1957, the district court's jury swiftly found Parr and ten associates guilty. The flashy

Houston lawyer Percy Foreman handled the appeal, but on April 6, 1959, the Fifth Circuit Court of Appeals upheld the convictions. Foreman at once headed for the U.S. Supreme Court. The justices acknowledged that the defendants had been guilty of a "brazen scheme to defraud by misappropriating, converting and embezzling the District's monies and property," and they spelled out the elements of the scheme. But state law required that tax notices be sent out, so this was not illegal and was merely incidental to the array of state laws that had been violated. By a six to three majority, the Supreme Court reversed all the convictions.[27]

So the reign of George Parr did not verge on collapse. Not for another fifteen years did that moment occur.

EXCEPT FOR PARR, to be dealt with again in future years, by the mid-1960s Homer Garrison's Rangers had put most of their no-win political calls behind them. They had not abolished gambling, but thanks to Las Vegas, Nevada, they had no more lengthy, pointless distractions like Galveston. Jim Crow ceased almost entirely to occupy them; federal law had shot down that ugly bird. And strikes and union troubles had also become largely a matter of the past—with one great exception, an exception that would push the Texas Rangers to the brink of extinction.

That dark time coincided with the changing of the guard. Cancer struck Homer Garrison, and he died on May 7, 1968. In thirty years as director of the Department of Public Safety, he had transformed the old-time frontier Rangers into an elite body of professional crime fighters, admired throughout the United States. They had their own distinctive methods, a blend of old and new that reflected exactly what their colonel wanted. More than any other person, Homer Garrison created a Ranger service responsive to the needs of the twentieth century.

[14]

Latino Uprising

ALFRED Y. ALLEE had captained Company D since 1947. Product of a South Texas ranch, he had been reared in the border culture. He kept his headquarters at Carrizo Springs, near his ranch. He understood border Mexicans, treated them benignly so long as they knew and kept their place, and even upheld the cause of certain individuals. Short and blocky, turning paunchy as he neared sixty, bushy white eyebrows sprouting from "a face like a sunburned potato," an unlit cigar dangling from his mouth, he projected the image of the old-time frontier Ranger. He acted it too, as when he slapped George Parr, the Duke of Duval, and beat up one of his stooges. Still, he resorted to violence only when provoked (easily), not as a pattern. He got along well with South Texas sheriffs, some of whom bore Spanish surnames. To a man, Allee's Rangers respected and loved their captain. He strongly supported them and stood up for them when they got in trouble. His central aim, as he often proclaimed, was simply to enforce the law.

No one could have been more surprised than Allee himself when in the late 1960s he emerged as the very personification of all that critics found wrong with the Texas Rangers. To them he exemplified an outfit that had outlived its time and ought to be relegated to the history books.

THE 1960s threw not just Captain Allee but the entire Ranger force into a troubling new era in the nation's history. The counterculture movement, with its hippies, rock festivals, protests, and drugs, discomfited the Rangers. But it served merely as backdrop to trends of more direct effect. Civil rights laws brought new hope, and new turmoil, to blacks. Other laws and federal court rulings reinforced this landmark legislation by imposing on all law enforcement officers a host of rules for handling suspected criminals. The Supreme Court's Miranda decision of 1966 alone seemed preposterous: the spectacle of a Ranger apprehending a suspect and reading a list of "rights" printed on a card stood in glaring contrast to the way Rangers usually conducted an arrest. To all Rangers this amounted to "coddling" criminals. A succession of DPS directors echoed the Ranger attitude by inveighing against a "permissive federal judiciary" that fueled a rising crime rate.[1]

Aside from civil and criminal rights, Captain Allee confronted another developing strand of national life: the political awakening of Mexican Americans throughout the Southwest. His domain was South Texas, overwhelmingly Mexican American in population. County and city officers had kept these people in their historic subordination, with solid backing of Allee and his Rangers. In the 1960s that dynamic began to change.

Mexican Americans returned from both world wars to discover that they still did not enjoy the benefits of American citizenship. They organized to seek those benefits for themselves. In 1929 several such organizations spawned by World War I combined to form the League of United Latin American Citizens (LULAC), and in 1948 World War II veterans formed the American G. I. Forum of Texas. Members of both generally enjoyed middle-class social status and income and mainly wanted integration into mainline American society. They resorted primarily to legal tactics and won some significant court victories, such as an end to school segregation, the white primary, and the poll tax.

They also laid the groundwork for the emergence of more activist organizers in the 1960s. These young people, unlike LULAC and other advocacy groups, targeted the entire Hispanic electorate, mostly poor laborers, and worked to get them to the polls. They called themselves "Chicanos," and their tactics featured belligerent confrontation with Anglo officcholders, backed by the threat of mass demonstrations verging on violence. The Political Association of Spanish-Speaking Organizations (PASSO) grew out of the "Viva-Kennedy" clubs of the 1960 election. It fractured along moderate-militant lines, which eventually led to its demise. Altogether militant was the Mexican American Youth Organization (MAYO) founded in San Antonio in 1967. MAYO aimed explicitly at displacing the elected Anglo incumbents from school boards and city and county governments.[2]

The leading founder of MAYO was a youth of twenty-three who had found his calling three years earlier in Crystal City, seat of Zavala County. In 1963, only nineteen and barely out of high school, José Angel Gutiérrez had emerged as an articulate leader in an effort to overthrow the entrenched Anglo domination of the city and school board. The son of a middle-class Mexican doctor who had been well regarded by the Anglo community, José was twelve when his father died in 1957. That marked the young man's sudden transition from respected citizen to Mexican trash. At once he knew how his ethnic compatriots lived and felt. Bright, ambitious, hard-working, he excelled in high school and grew more and more angry at the discrimination and oppression practiced by the Anglo leadership. He resolved to do something about it.[3]

The "spinach capital of the world," Crystal City boasted a Del Monte cannery that employed many of the Mexican Americans. These were unionized workers, and Teamster leaders of the AFL-CIO in San Antonio joined with the militant wing of PASSO to mobilize the city's Mexican American electorate.

Alarmed, the Anglo officials called for the reassuring presence of Captain Allee. Gutiérrez already knew the captain. "I remember when I was 17 years old," he later recalled. "I saw Allee knocking some of my friends around outside my house. I told him to stop it and he started in on me. He slapped me and kicked me." In 1963, his menacing demeanor discouraging violence, Allee let the political process work itself out. The slate backed by the Teamsters and PASSO overthrew the Anglos and took over the city government.[4]

Crystal City portended an awakening majority long suppressed by a ruling minority. Though never intimidated by anyone or anything, Allee had come up against a new breed of Mexican American, both in Latino people and in the person of young Gutiérrez. More important, Crystal City spread alarm throughout the Anglo community of South Texas.

Stimulated and instructed by his success in Crystal City, Gutiérrez moved to San Antonio, acquired a master's degree in political science, and in 1967 took the lead in founding MAYO. For more than a decade his aggressive style would energize Chicano electoral campaigns throughout South Texas and torment the Texas Rangers for years after Captain Allee retired. (Henceforth, it seems appropriate to term the Mexican American population "Latino" and the militant portion "Chicano.")

IN 1966–67 Captain Allee confronted another challenge reminiscent of Crystal City. The new front lay in Starr County, resting on the Rio Grande in the Lower Valley. The influx of immigrant farmers lured by the railroad in 1904 had destroyed the old relationship between majority and minority and, as the valley prospered as an irrigated bonanza of fruit and vegetables, brought further oppression to the majority.

The growers and packers relied on Latino workers paid scarcely fifty cents an hour. In 1965 César Chávez and the National Farm Workers Association, an AFL-CIO affiliate, had successfully struck grape growers in California, and in June 1966 they lent encouragement and leaders to a National Farm Workers Organizing Committee (NFWOC) that attempted to unionize the Lower Valley laborers. Wildcat strikes hit eight corporate growers, mainly La Casita Farms, a major melon producer near Rio Grande City. Poorly organized and undermined by "commuters" from Mexico, the strikes quickly collapsed. Not, however, NFWOC, whose California leader, Eugene Nelson, called for a march on Austin to demand that the legislature set the minimum wage at $1.25.

"La Marcha" lifted the farm strike from an almost unnoticed local affair to one of national prominence. Strung out on the highway from Rio Grande City to Austin, the bedraggled mass of poor Latinos began marching in July and aimed to reach Governor John Connally's doorstep on Labor Day. Tracked by state and national media, they aroused the support and sympathy of liberals everywhere, exacerbated the rancorous divide between Texas conservatives and liberals, raised the usual conservative suspicion of communist inspiration, and caught the attention of Washington politicos.

Governor Connally gave the march even higher visibility by driving to New Braunfels, fifty miles south of Austin, and informing the leaders that he would not be home on Labor Day and so would not talk with them. Attorney General Waggoner Carr, running for the U.S. senate seat of liberal Ralph Yarborough, made matters worse by warning against the infiltration of "agitators and extremists." Angry, the marchers shouted "Viva la huelga!" (Long live the strike!) and pushed on to Austin, where Senator Yarborough and other liberal officials met them and made supportive speeches.[5]

Emboldened by the success of "La Marcha," union organizers continued their agitation throughout the winter, as some crops were planted and others harvested, and as more veterans of the grape strike arrived from California. They had to tread carefully because of state statutes that severely restricted union activity.

Until November 1966 Starr County sheriff's deputies and detectives of the Missouri Pacific Railroad, which carried the growers' produce, enforced these statutes, although court records cite few incidents giving rise to union complaint. In early November, however, someone fired a railroad trestle, and County Attorney Frank R. Nye (also attorney for La Casita Farms) asked Colonel Homer Garrison to send Rangers to help local officers keep the peace. Nye had also obtained warrants for the arrest of ten union leaders for secondary picketing of a La Casita packing shed. On November 9, Captain Allee and his Rangers served these warrants, the first and last specific act attributed to them in subsequent litigation before May 1967.[6]

Throughout the winter months Rangers assisted local officers in overseeing the strikers. According to Allee, he and only nine Rangers composed Company D. He kept four in the Lower Valley, rotating them periodically. He himself did not remain on the scene, and his men were outnumbered by regular and special sheriff's deputies.[7]

Both the U.S. Commission on Civil Rights and the Texas Advisory Committee to the commission held hearings in 1967 and 1968. Both panels were composed of people sympathetic to the plight of the impoverished workers, and the witnesses were Anglo and Latino participants with a loathing of the Rangers. Except for specific events of May and June 1967, their conclusions severely faulted Allee and his Rangers in general terms.

The U.S. commission, echoing its 1968 hearings in San Antonio and the state committee conclusions, declared that

> Rangers conferred with and acted on behalf of the growers and joined with local law enforcement officers in attempting to break the strike and denying the strikers and strike sympathizers their legal rights. More than a hundred arrests were made of farm workers and union sympathizers on such charges as trespass, unlawful assembly, secondary boycott, illegal picketing, abusive language, impersonating an officer, and interfering with the arrest of another.[8]

No particulars supported the allegation that Rangers participated in trying to break the strike, although they plainly favored the growers. Nor did particulars indicate whether Rangers used excessive force in making arrests. If so, they infringed legal rights; if not, they merely enforced the laws then on the books.

In May and June 1967 Rangers and deputies made further arrests, but Captain Allee himself took the lead in two widely publicized incidents that lent substance to the general charges. On May 26, at Mission, Rangers arrested ten picketers for trying to block a train carrying produce. In the evening, as the streets filled with several hundred people, the Reverend Edgar Krueger arrived with his wife and son. A valley minister, he had been asked by the Texas Council of Churches to observe and report on the strike. He approached Captain Allee and asked on what charges the ten men had earlier been arrested. The exchange grew acrimonious, and when Krueger began to urge bystanders to resume picketing Allee had been provoked enough to accost the clergyman. Both recounted highly different versions of what happened next, but Krueger, his wife, and two others wound up in the back seat of Ranger Tol Dawson's car, to be driven to Rio Grande City and charged with secondary picketing. Because it was more sensational, Krueger's story dominated press coverage, and in essentials it prevailed as one of the stipulations of fact later accepted by the federal court. Allee's denial of Krueger's version received scarcely any publicity.[9]

Although Krueger's description appears exaggerated in many respects, Allee's portrayal of the second incident arouses skepticism if not wonder. On June 1 Magdaleno Dimas, a union man with a long police record (and who had an encounter with Allee when he took the Kruegers into custody), supposedly brandished a gun at a special deputy outside a La Casita packing shed. Looking for him that night, Allee and Ranger Tol Dawson, their car lights off, followed another car bearing two union men. It stopped at the home of Kathy Baker. Dimas had just emerged with a rifle in hand. When he spotted Allee, he dropped the weapon and ran inside. Lacking any search or arrest warrant, Allee and Dawson summoned a justice of the peace and sat in their car to await him. When he arrived, he filled out a blank warrant and handed it to them.

Sending Dawson to the rear of the house, Allee cradled his double-barreled shotgun and knocked on the front door. Getting no response, he kicked it down. Inside he saw Dimas sitting at the kitchen table with Benito Rodriguez, a union friend also dogged by a long police record. Allee ordered them to take their hands from beneath the table and put them on top. When they failed to obey, he kicked over the table and tapped Dimas "lightly" on the side of the head with his shotgun, the only time he touched either, he testified. Then, as he told a magazine writer, "they just stampeded." In their haste to escape, they stumbled over furniture, ran into each other, collided with an open door, and collapsed on the floor in a tangled heap.

So Allee testified in court. Hospitalized for five days, Dimas was examined by three doctors, who told of bruises all over his arms and body. A laceration required four stitches to close. An X-ray revealed a blow to the back so severe as to curve the spine away from the point of impact. Two of the three diagnosed a brain concussion. Rodriguez also sustained cuts and bruises all over his body and a broken finger. The judges dryly commented on the difficulty of believing that two grown men could produce such injuries by running into each other.[10]

The Krueger and Dimas incidents afforded particulars for the generalities alleged by the state and national civil rights inquiries. They were the only two cited to support allegations of Ranger brutality. The state committee and national commission focused not only on Ranger misbehavior. They also questioned the constitutionality of the state laws governing labor unions and strikes, pointed out serious procedural lapses in the manner in which persons arrested were processed by the county authorities in Rio Grande City (none ever stood trial), criticized the dispatch of Texas Rangers to enforce any laws among a people who had detested and feared them for more than a century, and made much of the scarcity of minorities in DPS and their complete absence from the Ranger ranks. Even so, the state committee ended its list of eleven proposed reforms by recommending "that the Texas Rangers as a law enforcement agency be abolished and the officers integrated into the State Highway Patrol."[11]

With the melon harvest over and enjoined by a state court, the second strike collapsed before the end of June 1967. The NFWOC ended its organizing efforts. Agricultural conditions in the Lower Valley remained as before the two strikes. Over the next decade, however, the issue played itself out on two fronts. First, a movement gained momentum to abolish the Texas Rangers. Second, the NFWOC, AFL-CIO, assembled a class-action suit in federal court. Seven plaintiffs were listed, including the NFWOC, Dimas, Rodriguez, Kathy Baker (whose home Allee invaded in quest of Dimas), and others injured in one way or another. Heading the list was Francisco Medrano, whose particular complaint is not apparent, but he gave his name to the suit. Defendants were Allee,

Rangers Jack Van Cleve, Jerome Preiss, and Tol Dawson, and six local officers and officials. *Medrano v. Allee* would not reach a definitive conclusion until 1976.[12]

THE TEXAS RANGERS had come under attack at times in the past but never as furiously as in the years following the farm strike. As the federal civil rights commission and its state advisory committee pursued their inquiries, they kept alive the drumroll that had begun as early as May 1967. Press attacks gained momentum. In summer conventions, the Texas AFL-CIO, PASSO, LULAC, and other liberal groups called for abolition of the Rangers or at least their withdrawal from the Lower Valley. "Connally's strikebreakers," Senator Yarborough labeled the Rangers.[13]

Governor Connally denied sending in the Rangers. That occurred at Colonel Garrison's orders. Garrison contended that DPS had investigated the charges of brutality and found them "totally false and unfounded." He also lauded Allee as "one of the truly great all time Rangers." Allee himself shrugged off the storm: "There's been someone raising hell about the Rangers as long as I can remember, and they've never hurt 'em yet."[14]

In May 1968 cancer relieved Colonel Garrison of further responsibility, but his successor, Colonel Wilson E. Speir, adopted the same stance. Appearing as a witness in the federal civil rights hearing at San Antonio in December 1968, he found himself questioned principally about the lack of minorities in DPS, an issue invariably linked by critics with Ranger behavior in the farm strike. Speir answered ineptly and unpersuasively. He did, however, enter a formal statement in the record denying any misdeeds in the Lower Valley and labeling the allegations in the press and the testimony before the commission as so "vague and indefinite" as not to warrant rebuttal.[15]

The newspaper campaign continued into the 1970s, although now and then a paper leaped to the defense of the Rangers. The Rangers themselves seemed unperturbed by the controversy. The issue erupted with fury in the spring of 1972, during the race for governor. Outspoken candidate Frances "Sissy" Farenthold ignited a press and political storm when she appeared to make abolition of the Rangers a platform in her campaign. At once she backed off and simply called for their withdrawal from South Texas. But she had already injected a "rally-round-the-Rangers" response in her opponents, including the winner, Uvalde rancher-banker Dolph Briscoe.[16]

After Sissy Farenthold's electoral defeat, the turmoil seemed to subside, although an occasional press item kept it alive. In September 1970, reaching the mandatory retirement age of sixty-five, Captain Allee had stepped down, although not without a parting flourish: "This civil rights. That's the dog-gondest business I ever heard of. We haven't done anything to be abolished for."[17]

Steady, competent, respected, exuding none of Allee's bravado, Captain John M. Wood took over Company D, moved its headquarters to San Antonio, and hewed to the primary mission of the Rangers: criminal investigation. With help from Austin, he added two Latinos to his company, Rudolfo (Rudy) Rodriguez and Ray Martínez. As an Austin police officer, the latter had killed the infamous Charles Whitman, the sniper who shot down forty-five people (fourteen killed, thirty-one wounded) from the University of Texas tower in 1966. Both proved competent Rangers and outstanding criminal investigators.[18]

By 1976 the call for abolishing the Rangers had quieted; it never had a chance in the first place. It had only quieted, however, not expired. As late as 1981 LULAC still called for abolition, and the subject would rise again in future years.

Coincidentally or not, 1976 was the year when the class-action suit filed as *Medrano v. Allee* in 1967 finally reached the end of the intricate judicial process.

MEDRANO V. ALLEE required four and one-half years to make its tortuous way through the U.S. district court. Sitting in Brownsville, three federal judges heard the testimony and arguments. The plaintiffs, acting on behalf of the entire class of organizers and strikers, alleged that law enforcement officers had deprived workers of their constitutional rights by selective enforcement of statutes and that these statutes were unconstitutional. On June 26, 1972, in a thick document densely packed with tedious legal terminology and reasoning, the judges ruled.

After setting forth the stipulations of fact, the court found five of the six state statutes under which law officers acted violated the First and Fourteenth amendments to the Constitution. Held unconstitutional were the mass picketing law, the secondary strike and boycott law, the breach of peace law, the abusive language law, and the unlawful assembly law. Only the law banning obstruction of public streets survived judicial scrutiny.

The plaintiffs had also sought an injunction prohibiting law officers from enforcing the laws. Having ruled five out of six unconstitutional, the court readily enjoined their enforcement. It went a step farther, however, and permanently barred any future interference with the civil rights of the plaintiffs and the class they represented.

At its simplest, the decision declared five Texas statutes unconstitutional. They had been on the books for many years, the judges observed, reflecting an earlier era. The ruling then enjoined law enforcement officers (not just Texas Rangers) from enforcing the unconstitutional statutes and interfering with the civil rights of strikers.

Such were the actionable parts of the decision. As if to lend substance to Senator Yarborough's quip about "Connally's strikebreakers," however, the judges issued a more stinging rebuke than contained in the actionable ruling:

> Looking at the circumstances as a whole, it is the conclusion of this Court that the unjustified conduct of the defendants had the effect of putting those in sympathy with the strike in fear of expressing their protected first amendment rights with regard to free speech and lawful assembly. The conclusion is inescapable that these officials had concluded that the maintenance of law and order was inextricably bound to preventing the success of the strike. Whether or not they acted with premeditated intent, the net result was that law enforcement officials took sides in what was essentially a labor-management controversy.[19]

The State of Texas, representing the defendants, appealed to the U.S. Supreme Court, where the case now became *Allee v. Medrano*. The Supreme Court disposed of the case in two years. Arguments occurred on November 13, 1973, and the ruling was published on May 20, 1974. Justice William O. Douglas wrote the majority opinion. The question of constitutionality had become moot because the legislature had repealed or greatly narrowed the offending statutes. However, Douglas gave even greater emphasis to the lower court's opinion of the behavior of law officers, finding a "pervasive pattern of intimidation" and asserting that "in this blunderbuss effort the police not only relied on statutes the district court found constitutionally deficient, but concurrently exercised their authority under valid laws in an unconstitutional manner." This pattern justified the lower court in extending the injunction to cover any future violation of civil rights.

Justice Douglas did not carry the entire court with him. Justices William J. Brennan, Potter Stewart, Thurgood Marshall, and Harry A. Blackmun signed on. But Chief Justice Warren Burger, joined by Justices Byron White and William Rehnquist (Lewis Powell not participating), concurred in part but dissented in part. Scanning the brief list of stipulated actions, these justices saw only isolated instances of police misconduct, not a pattern. "Judging by the infrequency of occasions of enforcement of such laws," Burger wrote, "the strike did not become an object of obsessive interest with the law enforcement personnel in Starr County." These justices, accordingly, did not sanction the lower court's injunction. Captain Allee would have agreed.[20]

Armed with the Supreme Court decision, the district court had now to issue a "final judgment." On June 24, 1976, the court put an end to what had once more become *Medrano v. Allee*. Amid the pages of verbiage, one new element stood forth: a list of five specific actions Texas Rangers and Starr County authorities (and by extension all other enforcement officers in Texas) were prohibited from taking. The injunction could not have distressed many officers. It specified actions under laws that had already been declared unconstitutional and removed from the books, and laws and procedures still valid and applicable with or without the federal injunction.

Rangers could take some comfort from the minority dissent of three Supreme Court justices, but the district court and the Supreme Court had found that peace officers in Starr County had conspired with the growers to break the strike. Legally the judgment stood. A reader of the stipulations of fact, however, may side with the majority or the minority. So qualified was the outcome, and so devoid of procedural consequence, that the Rangers could regard themselves as enduring little more than a slap on the wrist. As Ed Gooding observed, a Ranger had no business working a strike. "It puts us in a lose-lose situation. No matter what decision we make, one side or the other is going to claim we were biased for the other side." After 1976, moreover, Rangers did not work strikes if any way could be found to avoid them.[21]

FOR JOSÉ ANGEL GUTIÉRREZ, Crystal City remained the focus of his political efforts. The Latino slate that had captured the city government in 1963 proved incapable and plagued by factionalism. With middle-class Latino support, the Anglos regained control in 1965. A Chicano revolt centering in the high school, protesting the composition of the cheerleading squad, led in 1969 to a student strike that, with federal mediation, ended in acceptance of most of the demands of the students and their parents. Still, positions on the school board and in the city government eluded Gutiérrez and his associates.

The Mexican American Youth Organization provided Gutiérrez a stump for his activism. MAYO, however, was a nonprofit organization with chapters throughout South Texas. It could promote social justice and agitate for overthrow of elected Anglo officials. It could not, however, field its own candidates. The success of the school strike provided the spark for what had been a MAYO objective from the beginning: the formation of a genuine political party. "Raza" had been part of MAYO terminology from the beginning. Literally, it translated as "race," but in the Chicano rendering it meant "people" of Mexican

American ethnicity. In Crystal City on January 17, 1970, Gutiérrez and three hundred Chicanos established La Raza Unida. In April 1970 elections, the fledgling party entered candidates in Crystal City, Cotulla, and Carrizo Springs. Fifteen won, bringing La Raza two city council majorities, two school board majorities, and two mayoralties.[22]

Throughout the struggle for control of Crystal City and its schools, the Anglo leaders had decided not to call in Texas Rangers. They might inflame an already incendiary encounter. After the April 1970 elections, Raza Unida officials controlled the city council. They wanted no DPS presence at all and said so. On June 10 the council passed a resolution declaring Crystal City off-limits to both the Rangers and the highway patrol, and sent copies to Governor Preston Smith and DPS director Wilson Speir. The colonel simply acknowledged receipt of the resolution.[23]

Crystal City had not seen its last Texas Ranger.

THAT RANGERS MIGHT be capable of constructive work in South Texas became evident in February 1971. Allee had retired, and Captain Wood had sent a rookie Ranger, Jack Dean, to McAllen with a typical Ranger command: "Go down there and get along; make a point to establish liaison with everybody in the Valley."

He did, and on February 6, 1971, it paid off. MAYO organized a peaceful march of some two hundred to four hundred Chicanos to protest brutality by the Pharr Police Department. It remained peaceful until reaching police headquarters, when Chief Alfredo Ramirez called in two fire engines manned by Anglo firefighters who turned high-pressure hoses on the crowd. "That made everybody go berserk," said an observer, "it was a full-fledged riot." Chief Ramirez at once sent out a call for help.

Jack Dean raced the three miles from McAllen to Pharr to find the infuriated mob hurling rocks and bottles at the police station, and the streets swarming with neighboring police, sheriff's deputies, and state troopers. The Pharr police were trapped in their own station. Dean took charge, mobilized the outside officers, and swept the streets surrounding the police station free of demonstrators. A man lay on a sidewalk, dead with a bullet in the back of his head. Dean's subsequent investigation disclosed that a deputy had fired in the air, and the bullet had ricocheted off an overhead gutter.

In the police station Dean found an enraged Chief Ramirez. The mob leaders were holed up in a building, he said, and he intended to arrest them all. Dean counseled delay. "If we hit that place, it'll blow up again." Ramirez accepted that wisdom, and the sun set on a tense, restless town.

MAYO organized another protest demonstration, to take place on March 9. In the preceding weeks, Dean labored to get leaders on both sides talking to each other. Even so, he feared another explosion. This time eight hundred Chicanos began the march, and as many more joined en route to the grave of the man shot on February 6. Here a Catholic priest conducted a Mass. To everyone's relief, the day passed peacefully. Both the priest and the mayor credited Ranger Dean with opening channels of communication that had been blocked in the past. "He was easy to communicate with," judged the priest, "mature in judgment, and professionally capable."[24]

After Pharr, Jack Dean's career had no direction to go but up. More important, he represented a transitional generation of Rangers, cherishing the old while looking forward to the new and adjusting accordingly.

HAVING TAKEN THE CITY, José Angel Gutiérrez set his sights on the county. Zavala County grew not only spinach but cattle as well. That meant enough Anglo ranchers to create a political complexion more difficult to overcome than the city's heavily Latino makeup. Nevertheless, Raza Unida filed candidates for offices that would come into play in the November 1972 election.

As the county seat, Crystal City contained both county and city government. The city council might enact resolutions commanding DPS to stay out, but the county, still a bastion of the old order, felt no such inhibition. Sheriff C. L. Sweeten, anathema to Chicanos, called for help whenever he wanted. And of course DPS held statutory authority to operate anywhere it wanted.

Over the next several years, most Crystal City assignments fell to the Ranger based in Uvalde, fifty miles to the north. He was an erect, muscular six-footer who looked every inch like a Ranger should, sworn in by Homer Garrison himself in 1966. A protégé of Captain Allee, he could be fully as tough if he had to, but he preferred talk to violence and possessed a proficiency in criminal investigation. For an Anglo, Ranger Jackson bore the improbable name of Joaquin, a selection he could never explain but that often served him well in dealings with Latinos. He would need all his talents to contend with the turmoil that continued to roil Crystal City.[25]

Election day, November 7, 1972, found an Anglo judge at each polling place, but Raza observers watched over every move of the judges. Joaquin Jackson was literally the lone ranger in Crystal City on this day. He sympathized with what Gutiérrez sought while emphatically disagreeing with his methods. Even so, he intervened when an Anglo election judge tried to expel Raza poll watchers and a noisy throng threatened violence. The Ranger worked out a compromise that left one Raza observer in place, and the mob accepted the outcome. Despite the threat, the election passed without violence, and despite the odds Raza Unida scored two victories: Ray Pérez barely nosed out a longtime Anglo incumbent as county attorney, and José Serna decisively defeated Sheriff Sweeten.[26]

Although Gutiérrez detested Texas Rangers, he developed a grudging respect for Joaquin Jackson. He characterized Jackson as "the only decent Ranger in an old-fashioned kind of way. One could cut a deal with Jackson and he would honor it. Not that it was legal or that he was doing us a favor; he was simply being practical and doing the best he could under the circumstances."[27]

The 1974 general election offered the next chance for Raza Unida to capture Zavala County. The county judge and two seats on the commissioners court would be on the ballot. (The judge presided over the commissioners court; together they represented the county equivalent of the city's mayor and city council.) Meantime, however, Raza Unida kept both Crystal City and Cotulla in chaos as school board elections

approached in April 1973 and again in April 1974. Raza partisans heck-
led speakers, intimidated and even beat up teachers and students, and
staged raucous demonstrations. Both Rangers Joaquin Jackson and
Rudolfo Rodriguez strove to contain the pandemonium, stood guard
at polling places, and headed off disruption of the commissioners court
meetings. They could do little, however, to remedy the attacks on
students and teachers. The county attorney, the Raza candidate elected
in 1972, would not bring charges against Raza militants.[28]

The November 1974 general election gave Raza Unida a good chance
of capturing Zavala County. José Angel Gutiérrez ran for county judge,
the most powerful post in county government, and Raza candidates
contested two seats on the commissioners court held by Anglos.
Apparently without disorder, so overwhelming was the Chicano vote,
Raza triumphed. Gutiérrez ousted the longtime county judge, Irl Taylor,
and the two open commissioner seats fell to the Raza challengers.
Now José Angel Gutiérrez occupied the pinnacle of Zavala County
government and commanded a majority of the commissioners court.
Raza Unida controlled county, city, and school.

For the Texas Rangers, the new order opened a new chapter in
relations with Raza and the institutions it commanded.

AS COUNTY JUDGE, José Angel Gutiérrez used all his powers to punish
Anglos and to reward his Raza Unida followers—a practice entirely
within the Texas political tradition. Jobs went to party members. Only
party members need seek any government service—county or city.

Captain Wood soon found himself plunged deeply into Crystal City
and Zavala County affairs. The Raza slate had been in office less than
eight months when confronted with an insurgency: about twenty former
activists had banded together as the Barrio Club with the aim of seizing
power at all levels of government. The club claimed the city council,
the school board, and the urban renewal agency. With this split came
reports of misuse of urban renewal and school funds. Curiously these
anti-Gutiérrez officials had enacted another council resolution commanding DPS (Rangers and highway patrol) to stay out of town, then

within a month had asked for a Ranger investigation of corruption. Joaquin Jackson found himself in the midst of a probe that would last more than a year.[29]

As evidence of massive fraud and theft accumulated, the attorney general fielded an investigative task force, and Captain Wood backed Joaquin Jackson with additional Rangers to help. The team plowed through financial records, construction contracts, payrolls, and property inventories. Gutiérrez protested the team's presence, to no avail. By September 1976, a special grand jury had handed down indictments of several officials, whom Jackson placed under arrest. The investigation continued.[30]

Rangers and attorneys had not only to pursue the corruption probe but worry about the potential for violence. As Jackson had reported, the Barrio leaders had appointed their own chief of the city police and had named a cadre of "special police," who wore sidearms and might get into a shootout with the Raza sheriff's deputies, one of whom was the ousted city police chief. Lending worry to that development, Wood discovered that Gutiérrez himself had driven to San Antonio and purchased two automatic pistols and a rifle with scope, together with a quantity of ammunition.[31]

Further preoccupying DPS with Gutiérrez, a former Raza city councilman whom the judge had jailed for "abusive language" to a peace officer testified in a San Antonio courtroom that in 1974 Gutiérrez had tried to hire him and others as hit men to eliminate enemies. On November 12, 1976, this brought Ranger Jackson to Austin to confer with top DPS officials. Paired with Ranger Dan North, Jackson left with orders to dig up the truth of this allegation. The two questioned a series of men who had been approached by Gutiérrez or who had heard him threaten assassination, including a scheme to kill former sheriff Sweeten. All conceded that Gutiérrez had been drinking when he broached the idea, and several explained that at drinking parities he indulged in loud talk about paying someone to get rid of his enemies. The Rangers concluded that, with the possible exception of the threat to Sweeten, the threats represented no more than "drunk talk."[32]

Infighting, scandal, corruption, constant scrutiny by the attorney general and DPS, and finally the imprisonment of Raza's state leader on drug charges led finally, in the 1978 election, to the collapse of the party. Throughout these years, however, Gutiérrez kept his respect for Joaquin Jackson. "When I became county judge," he recalled, "we worked well together even when I was under his investigation and his surveillance. He knew I wasn't crooked or a dope dealer.... He was always straight and honest in his dealings with me, and I with him."[33]

For eight years Raza Unida had cut a stormy swath through Texas politics, especially South Texas politics and society. Its methods, reflecting those of the black and red power movements of the same years, angered and frightened all but the most liberal Anglo Texans. Like its companion movements also, Raza Unida left not only a disturbing memory but a positive legacy. By the 1980s, the place of Latinos in Texas society began to show marked improvement. Like blacks and Indians, Latinos would end the century with much left to achieve, but even José Angel Gutiérrez could not deny the progress since the 1970s.

That bellicose activist, mellowing slightly with age, added a PhD to his master's degree, gained a law degree, wrote four books, and in 1982 joined the faculty at the University of Texas at Arlington as a professor of political science. Years elevated him to distinguished rank as teacher, author, editor, and lecturer. Of his decade of activism he recalled:

> The generation that succeeded us got the benefit of us confronting racism head-on. And, to their credit, a lot of gringos stopped being racist. Maybe they still are privately, but not in their policies. Most people now are at least civil and polite. It's not politically correct to be a bigot in public.[34]

About the Texas Rangers, José Angel Gutiérrez doubtless never changed his mind. For him as for his people, they remained the detested *rinches*. But undeniably they had played a large part in the movement he led.

[15]

Change, 1965–1985

CHANGE COMES to all institutions, especially bureaucracies. For the Department of Public Safety and the Texas Rangers, stressful change hit during the darkest years. The Lower Valley farm strike, the Latino awakening, the drive for abolition of the Rangers, the litigation that led all the way to the Supreme Court and branded the Rangers strikebreakers, the continuing probes of the federal and state civil rights agencies, and the unwelcome fallout from the "permissive federal judiciary" kept the state lawmen under constant critical scrutiny by the public. But behind this shield of negative publicity, other major changes took place—some good, some bad, all unsettling to the Texas Rangers.

CANCER STRUCK THE most vicious blow to the Texas Rangers. While managing the Department of Public Safety, Colonel Homer Garrison battled the deadly disease. Although presiding over a huge department that included the state highway patrol, license and weights, and a host of units charged with tasks added by the state legislature over the years, he identified most intimately with his sixty-two Rangers. So did the public. As for the Rangers, to a man they loved Homer Garrison, and to a man they had shaped themselves in the character and image he desired. That the Rangers even existed in 1968 they owed to Homer Garrison, but the distinctive "Garrison Rangers" began to dwindle after 1968. The expansion of DPS had curtailed the time the colonel could devote to Rangers, and direct oversight of the units charged with criminal law enforcement had fallen to the assistant director. Even so, Garrison's door remained open to any Ranger who wanted to drop by and talk.

On May 5, 1968, Homer Garrison died at the age of sixty-seven.

After four months as acting director, Assistant Director Wilson E. "Pat" Speir got the nod from the Public Safety Commission and on September 16, 1968, took over as DPS director. Pat Speir came out of the highway patrol, a veteran since 1941 who had risen through every rank from trooper to lieutenant colonel and assistant director. In 1935 that background had set off a Ranger revolt, but by 1968 the Rangers were well entrenched and had worked directly with Speir since his elevation to assistant director in 1962. They got along well, and Speir often boasted of his pride in the excellence of the Rangers.

Fifty-one in 1968, Speir impressed a magazine writer as tall, raw-boned, broad-shouldered, with strong, angular features and weather-textured skin, articulate in a quiet sort of way, but a vocal defender and champion of the Rangers. He was also bluntly candid in expressing opinions, no matter how unwelcome or impolitic. Rangers considered him one of their own.[1]

Still, Pat Speir was not Homer Garrison, in management style or reputation. While insisting on individual initiative in both captains and Rangers, Garrison ran a one-man regime. He rarely consulted the Public Safety Commission, and he dealt directly with captains and even Rangers. Speir also emphasized individual initiative, but he delegated authority to subordinates and therefore was administratively remote from the Rangers.

COLONEL SPEIR had more subordinates to whom to delegate authority because Homer Garrison himself had been pondering reforms that would make DPS less unwieldy and difficult to manage. Governor

Connally's chairman of the Public Safety Commission, Clifton Cassidy, agreed. Youthful manager of a savings and loan association, Cassidy moved aggressively to assert the authority of a commission that he believed had been too often ignored by Colonel Garrison.

Early in 1968, therefore, before Garrison's death, a major restructuring introduced a new level of supervision into DPS. A traffic enforcement division brought together the highway patrol, license and weights, and other units concerned with traffic. A criminal law enforcement division encompassed the narcotics service, the intelligence service, the motor vehicle theft service, and the Ranger service. By September 1, 1970, the Rangers numbered eighty, up from sixty-two in Garrison's time.

Narcotics and intelligence retained many agents in Austin headquarters, but only two Rangers worked from there. Ranger captains reported directly to the chief of the criminal law enforcement division. This arrangement also impressed Chairman Cassidy as unwieldy. He urged the legislature to restore the old post of senior captain, who would supervise the company captains and report to the chief of criminal law enforcement. On November 1, 1969, Clint Peoples yielded command of Company F in Waco and received the title of senior captain.[2]

Not all Rangers liked or respected Clint Peoples, but they directed their wrath at Cassidy. For one thing, he had insisted on mandatory retirement at age sixty-five, which forced out sixty-five DPS officers, including eight Garrison Rangers. But his gravest offense was to bring in an outsider as the first chief of criminal law enforcement. Dallas detective Jack Revill had figured prominently in the investigation of the assassination of President Kennedy and was believed to be Cassidy's man in DPS, bypassing Colonel Speir to report directly to the chairman. Cassidy also shook up the narcotics service and drove out the chief and six agents. Turbulence rocked DPS, in part caused by the shift from Garrison to Speir but in large part because Cassidy insisted on managing instead of setting policy.

Or so investigative reporters concluded, largely by talking with state legislators, who had reliable sources of information in DPS and especially the Rangers. In fact, disgruntled Rangers were said to have engineered the legislative attack on Revill. Senator E. V. "Red" Berry, once arrested by Revill for gambling, demanded his resignation. Revill resisted for seven months as other legislators backed Berry. Finally Revill gave up and returned to Dallas.[3]

From the Ranger perspective, the outcome could not have been better. On June 21, 1969, a veteran Garrison Ranger assumed the helm of criminal law enforcement. Jim Ray had come to the Rangers from the highway patrol in 1957 and proved an outstanding, well-liked officer. He moved to his new post from the captaincy of Company C in Lubbock. Captains now reported to a senior captain in Austin who reported to a chief of criminal law enforcement who had been a distinguished Texas Ranger for twelve years. Jim Ray in turn reported to Colonel Speir through the assistant director, Lieutenant Colonel Leo Gossett.[4]

THE FEDERAL Fair Labor Standards Act dated from 1938, but the Rangers had paid no attention to it until the early 1970s, when it became a major issue. Especially crippling were requirements for overtime and compensatory time. How could a Ranger punch a time clock when criminals did not? Rangers worked a case night and day until reaching a resolution. "It was ridiculous," said Max Womack, "and brought hardship on the rural counties that depended on me to work cases." In fact, most Rangers simply doctored their time sheets. As Glenn Elliott observed, "You'd have to lie, and then if a case you were working on went to trial, they'd get you on the witness stand and shove your time sheet in front of your face and make a fool out of you in front of the jury."[5]

The issue would not go away. DPS repeatedly changed the regulations until the late 1980s. Company meetings invariably cited overtime procedures as a major factor in the level of morale.[6]

NEITHER COLONEL SPEIR nor criminal law enforcement chief Jim Ray had much liking for Senior Captain Clint Peoples. His exaggerated vanity, his posturing in the public spotlight, and his political ties into the legislature were irritating. But in the fall of 1973 they began to sniff unethical if not criminal misbehavior, and that they could not tolerate. Hollywood producers wanted to do a television series about the Texas Rangers similar to a popular series based on the FBI, and they had cultivated a relationship with Peoples that disturbed Speir. He felt so strongly about it that he assigned Jim Ray himself to conduct an investigation.

Ray flew to Los Angeles and set up a long interview with the two leading producers. He learned that Peoples had duped the two men into believing that only he, through technical advice and access to the Ranger archives, could make the production happen. He expected a "finder's fee" for a contract with himself and a salary of $500 per week. Left unclear was whether Peoples intended to remain with the Rangers while earning this salary.

In any event, Peoples had obviously lied to the producers by representing himself as the only one who could provide the services needed. In any event, also, Peoples must have seen the coming crash. He quickly used his connection to Republican senator John Tower to have his name nominated for the post of U.S. marshal for the Northern District of Texas. With that appointment assured, on January 31, 1974, Peoples submitted a two-page letter to Speir recounting his distinguished career and requesting retirement effective March 31.[7]

Captain William D. Wilson, Peoples's assistant supervisor, promptly applied for the senior captain's position and got it. With his new assistant, James L. "Skippy" Rundell, he provided the Rangers eleven years of competent leadership. Described as a blunt-spoken "mountain of muscle" and "bull of a fellow," "hard as a barrel of nails but soft as a puppy dog," he made no secret of his dislike of horses and airplanes. In fact, he made no secret of anything. Asked his opinion, he gave it, whether tactless or indiscreet. For the Texas Rangers, Bill Wilson was a pleasing change from Clint Peoples.[8]

BY THE CLOSING YEARS of the 1970s, criticism of DPS and the Rangers had receded. Although Speir, Peoples, and Wilson denied that the bad publicity set off by the farm strike and the movement to abolish the Rangers had any effect on the force at all, it did indeed. DPS, and especially the Rangers, grew increasingly sensitive to press criticism of hiring methods. As Garrison Ranger Ed Gooding recalled, "In those days, becoming a Ranger was totally different from what it is today. There were no written tests, no interview boards, no nothing. If the captain had an opening in his company and he wanted you to be his Ranger, you became a Texas Ranger. That was it." In 1971 written tests and interview boards were adopted. To pin on a Ranger badge, one had to demonstrate qualifications and beat out fierce competition.[9]

The federal and state civil rights agencies that scrutinized the state's criminal justice system in the wake of the farm strike made much of the Rangers' lack of ethnic diversity. The highway patrol had begun to make progress in recruiting blacks and Latinos, and in 1973 its academy graduated the first two woman troopers, one black and one white. In 1975 DPS set in place a plan for recruiting women and minorities.[10]

The Rangers made no such plans. Interviewed about minorities in 1979, Senior Captain Wilson answered with his customary candor. Blacks? "We've never had a colored to pass the exam. . . . They just don't, well, there's no interest. It's not that big a deal you know." Women? Long, uncomprehending stare. "We've had inquiries, but never one to take the exam. Probably because of experience requirement. We'll hear from them, I'm sure." Frowning, "We'd certainly have no choice but to consider it." Wilson was right, the Rangers would hear from women, but not until after his time.[11]

GARRISON RANGERS commissioned in the colonel's last years aged as a new generation began to filter into the ranks. The young men were just as dedicated as the old, but they had a better sense of the changing times, a changing institution, and tightening restrictions on law enforcement methods. As usual, most came from the highway patrol, but they had scored high on written tests and survived a tough interview by a board of officers that had to choose from scores of applicants for the rare vacancies.

Many of the old-timers had a hard time adjusting to the new circumstances. Some even held the newcomers in contempt. Sid Merchant voiced their opinion: "I'd go a month at a time without seeing my captain. And things worked, because the old captains would back you. My captain, Jim Riddles, had balls as big as two brass bathtubs. Cap Allee was mean as a snake, but damn it, he stood up for his men. Those fellows left, and the ones who came in after them were all caught up in covering their asses."[12]

That was unfair to such captains as D Company's John Wood and his successor Jack Dean, to A Company's Grady Sessums, and above all to F Company's Bob Mitchell, widely regarded as the best of all of the new breed of captains. Some of the old breed did not turn out as well, especially B Company's G. W. Burks, whose management style and sometimes bizarre behavior stirred resentment among his men, reprimands from his superiors, and company performance ratings embarrassingly lower than those of other companies.[13]

An inquiring newsman, Dick Stanley, perceptively caught the difference between the two generations in 1979 when he drove to the Lower Valley, still the territory of Company D. Here he interviewed Frank Horger in McAllen and Bruce Casteel in Harlingen. Both agreed that strikes such as the farm troubles of 1967 were no longer a Ranger priority. "The highway patrol handles them now," said Horger, a protégé of Allee and veteran of the 1967 strike. "Rangers would only inflame a strike situation," commented Casteel.

Stanley rode with Horger, fifty-two, from McAllen to Rio Grande City. Horger's unmarked car was a 1979 Chrysler Newport, and he never exceeded the federal speed limit of fifty-five as traffic sped past. A twelve-gauge shotgun nestled under his legs along the front seat, covered by a cloth wrapper. The trunk contained a 30-30 AR-15 automatic rifle and a Schmauser submachine gun, together with the varied crime-scene kit stowed in all Ranger vehicles. His trousers belt held a .45 automatic pistol. As they drove, Horger chain-smoked cigarettes and drank Tab. He complained of low pay and said his wife had always had to work to lift the household income.

"Since 1967 we've changed the image a lot," he conceded. "No more gabardine uniforms, no more gun belts. And we don't kick ass anymore.

Haven't done that for years. Not worth having a charge of violating civil rights hung on you." He accepted the new methods, he said, but doubted their long-term worth. He did not want to talk about it further, except in a moment of intense feeling about strikes. "I don't hold with people coming onto private property and refusing to let others go to work." Asked about the future of the Rangers, Horger drove silently for a long time, then said: "They'll be better trained and younger, I suppose. I don't know if they'll be as dedicated or work as hard as some of us old-timers."

Bruce Casteel, thirty-seven, divorced and remarried, foreshadowed the future. A veteran of the highway patrol, slender, with a natural swagger, blown hair brushing the tops of his ears, he took his assignment fully mindful of the 1967 farm strike. "Nobody instructed me how to act; they said 'Do your best.' But I kept a low profile at first and I've never tried to dress the part, either." Unlike Horger, he accepted the low pay because he had always wanted to be a Ranger. The Ranger heritage—perhaps what Horger meant by dedication—did not affect Casteel. "As I told a local civic club," he said, grinning, "sure, I'll take on a riot alone. One riot, one Ranger. Sure, with fifteen hundred state troopers behind me." He had already picked up what Garrison Rangers such as Glenn Elliott, Ed Gooding, and Lewis Rigler had learned: "You get more by being mindful of the personalities, the politics, than by bulling your way in and throwing your weight around."[14]

Bruce Casteel not only represented the future, he was the future. Highly esteemed, proficient in hypnosis and other specialties, skilled in working with local officials, he would rise to sergeant, captain, assistant senior captain, and finally, in the late 1990s, senior captain. By then the Frank Horgers had retired, and the Texas Rangers had been transformed.

COLONEL PAT SPEIR retired on December 31, 1979. The way had already been paved for his successor. James B. Adams, fifty-four, had been assistant director of the FBI, but he retired after twenty years when he failed to get the top job. He returned to his home state of Texas, where he had served in the Texas legislature and worked closely with the Rangers as FBI Special Agent in Charge (SAC) in San Antonio. Still, Rangers instinctively distrusted outsiders, especially from the FBI. But Republican governor William Clements had recruited Adams to return to Texas and wait for Speir's retirement. Adams took over on January 1, 1980.[15]

Adams knew that the Rangers, now ninety-four in number, worried that he would try to make them over in the image of the FBI. Aware of their long history and their tradition of individualism, he understood that he could not do that even if he wanted to. A Ranger captain, he declared, made more decisions in a month than an FBI SAC made in a year. Rangers trained from their first day to make individual decisions, whereas FBI agents worked within a highly structured environment.[16]

Adams held the Rangers in high regard, gave them full support, and worked for more Rangers and higher pay. As he told a television interviewer, "They have been well trained in many of the technical areas in which they have to deal, and I think that today, without a doubt, they continue to render a tremendous service, especially in the more rural areas."[17]

Rangers reciprocated the feeling. Even though Adams brought some Washington bureaucratic innovations with him, he did not try to remake the Rangers. Their first worries dissolved in a widespread conviction that ranked him second only to Homer Garrison as director. As former Company D captain Jack Dean told Robert Nieman, "Adams is only about five feet four, but his brain is about ten feet tall."[18]

Colonel Adams's FBI background gave him another reason for taking special interest in the Rangers. Since 1975 the FBI had been cut back by one thousand agents. That left a void in intrastate coordination of federal crime fighting as agents had to concentrate more heavily on interstate crimes such as transportation of stolen vehicles and other property across state lines. Adams looked to the Rangers to pick up the slack left by the loss of so many agents.[19]

The Rangers had a hard time meeting this challenge. FBI agents continued the practices that had long angered Rangers. Agents withheld important information but demanded all the Rangers gathered, and often they cooperated superficially if at all. In July 1981 Company D captain Jack Dean drew up a three-page chronology of a burglary investigation involving Rangers, San Antonio police, and the FBI. Burglary was normally a state offense, but the FBI took over on a federal pretext. Agents failed to share information. They broke promises. They called a press conference in which Dean and the San Antonio police chief were kept in the background. And they ended by promising that the burglar would spend five years in federal prison, only to have the penalty reduced to probation. So institutionalized had the FBI's concept of "cooperation" become that such instances continued even in the shadow of the former assistant director of the FBI.[20]

Adams applied himself to introducing reforms rather than remaking his department. Since the 1960s, the federal government had become obsessed with fashionable new tools for improving management. They went by a number of labels and acronyms, but Management by Objectives—MBO—proved the most popular. Most federal agencies, including the FBI, tried to put them in place, with varying success. Adams brought the concepts to DPS.

He moved at once, in September 1980, to introduce a system defining statements of mission, goals, and objectives for each supervisory level of DPS. In October 1983 he called for semiannual status reports on progress in achieving mission, goals, and objectives. This system took the label "Results Management Expectations." Dutifully the Ranger companies, the senior captain, and the chief of criminal law enforcement compiled and submitted twice-yearly status reports. Always averse to paperwork, Rangers accepted the new requirements reluctantly, and sometimes captains reported that it adversely affected morale. Except for the listing of outstanding cases and other events, moreover, the reports took on a verbal repetitiveness that revealed how superficially their authors treated the task. Even so, Colonel Adams expressed himself pleased with the results of Results Management. And despite the extra burden imposed on the Rangers, they never faltered in their admiration of the director.[21]

COLONEL ADAMS served for seven years, retiring on May 31, 1987. Leo Gossett, who had been assistant director for more than twenty years, took over the directorate for one year, then gave way to Joe E. Milner. In fact, after Adams, the public face of the Texas Rangers, and the self-image of the Rangers, focused not on the succession of directors or even, after Jim Ray's retirement in 1978, the chief of criminal law enforcement. The senior captain, chief of the Texas Ranger Service, took on more visibility, both to the public and to the Rangers themselves.

From 1983 to 1985 Senior Captain Bill Wilson valiantly battled cancer, had half his stomach removed, and finally conquered the disease with chemotherapy. Although his assistant, Captain H. R. "Lefty" Block, frequently had to fill in for his boss, Wilson continued a perform as the respected senior captain. Finally, in January 1985, he retired at the age of fifty-five. Lefty Block took over as senior captain, and Company E captain Maurice Cook moved from Midland to become assistant supervisor.[22]

The Adams directorate marked an era of vigorous reform, of a Ranger Service pleased with the chain of command, and after so much bad publicity a decided improvement in press coverage and in the public's opinion of the Texas Rangers.

After Adams, the DPS director, more and more preoccupied with highway traffic and narcotics, grew increasingly remote from the field Rangers.

[16]

Highs and Lows, 1970s

COLONEL ADAMS LIKED to refer to the Rangers as "felony investigators." That they were, as specified by law. Most investigations proved routine, unexciting, and laborious. They involved interviews with a host of witnesses, informants, or others thought to have relevant knowledge. They also involved meticulous gathering of crime-scene evidence. And they involved following many leads that went nowhere. Above all, they challenged Rangers to assemble sufficient grounds for a prosecutor to take a case to court and persuade a jury. As often as not, no matter how certain Rangers were of guilt, the evidence fell short of convincing a prosecutor or a jury, or the case collapsed on legal technicalities. Few setbacks proved more discouraging to a Ranger than to know who committed a crime but see the criminal escape justice. Of course, these conditions were not unique to the Texas Rangers. All criminal investigators, local, state, and federal, also labored under them.

From the beginning of the Department of Public Safety and the emergence of Rangers as felony investigators, perhaps the most serious distraction from major crime originated in fraud and corruption—not that fraud and corruption were not major crimes. Such cases were so numerous, time-consuming, and devoid of substantive outcome, however, that they added up to a burdensome distraction. Hardly a county among the 254 in Texas did not experience at one time or another, or repeatedly, official wrongdoing, although the South Texas counties held the lead. Ranger files are full of requests for investigation of fraud or theft by sheriffs, deputies, policemen, auditors, fiscal officers, mayors, county commissioners, and other city and county authorities. The requests came from local officials, such as district judges or prosecuting attorneys, and thus could not be avoided. A related priority was the constant call on Rangers to oversee local elections, often being instructed by judges to impound ballot boxes. Investigation of other, more serious crimes took second priority to such requests.[1]

In the three decades between 1970 and 2000, the Texas Rangers varied the routine of investigation with dramatic shootouts. They scored some major victories in gunfights and in routine investigations, as well as some that rose above the routine. They also stumbled into some embarrassing situations that gained critical publicity.

A MODERN CHASE in the tradition of frontier horseback Rangers catapulted Ranger Tom Arnold into newspaper headlines. A Company B Ranger based in Dallas, he had spent two long days and a short night in assignments all over North Texas when, at 10:15 PM on Wednesday, October 13, 1971, he received a call from his captain, G. W. Burks, ordering him to join with Sergeant Lester Robertson and Ranger Howard "Slick" Alfred in aiding Euless police in a manhunt. Arnold set forth at once for Euless, a suburban community on the eastern edge of Fort Worth.

The drama had begun only minutes earlier when Euless police sergeant B. E. Harvell spotted a car being driven slowly west along Highway 183, as if casing buildings. As it turned north on another highway, Harvell switched on his flashers and stopped it. He walked toward the driver, who rolled out with a pistol in hand. Harvell sprang to the cover of the vehicle and fired through the rear window. The fugitive fired back, jumped behind the wheel, and roared off. Harvell shot four more times, then took up the pursuit. At an intersection the car turned east and stopped. A woman got out on the passenger side and ran into a ditch. Harvell reloaded his pistol. The man leaped from his car and fired again on the officer, three shots hitting the patrol vehicle. The chase resumed until suddenly the street ended in a pasture, and the driver ran into the field and disappeared.

Sergeant Harvell picked up the woman who had abandoned her companion and learned who he was: Huron Ted Walters, fifty-three, a dangerous gangster with a forty-year record of violent crime and prison time, who had just robbed a liquor store and shot the proprietor. Harvell's radio transmission not only brought three Texas Rangers to the scene but stirred up police and sheriff units all over the area. Ultimately fourteen police agencies entered the fray, and sirens and red flashers converged from all directions. They ringed the area as throughout the night lawmen scoured the lightly populated area on foot. At 4:00 AM many of the officers called off the search, Robertson and Alfred among them. Arnold stayed to aid in a daytime search of a broader area.

As feared, Ted Walters seized hostages in their isolated home: Hoyt Houston, forty-nine, a construction executive; his wife Mary; and their five-year-old daughter Jana. Their fifteen-year-old daughter Pamela was in her bedroom dressing for school when she saw what was happening, crawled out a window, and ran to a neighbor to call Bedford police. Walters forced his hostages into their 1969 Mercury sedan, with Mrs. Houston at the wheel, Jana in the center, and Hoyt wedged sideways with his back against the passenger door. Walters himself climbed in the back seat and placed the muzzle of a twelve-gauge sawed-off shotgun against Hoyt's head.

At 7:30 AM Tom Arnold met the Houstons' car, made a quick U-turn, and, joined by Euless and Bedford units, gave pursuit. The fugitive car was quickly boxed, but the ominous shotgun prevented any interference. The caravan proceeded north more than five miles to Grapevine. As Mrs. Houston tried to turn west on Highway 114 toward Southlake, Arnold and a Euless cruiser forced her into a field and onto a county road. Another Euless unit took station broadside at the end of a stone bridge across a small creek. This brought the Houston auto to a halt, with Ranger Arnold stopped thirty feet in the rear. But still the shotgun remained pointed directly at Houston's head.

With only the left rear window rolled down, Arnold and other officers, keeping their distance, tried to persuade Walters to surrender, Arnold talking over his public address mike. Walters answered with silence. Arnold concluded that Walters would not give up and would end by killing the hostages. Summoning a state trooper, Arnold asked him to get his scoped 30.06 rifle from his car trunk. Opening the driver's door of his vehicle, Arnold rested the rifle on the top rim and lined up Walters's head in the crosshairs of the scope. He could not fire, however, so long as the shotgun nudged Houston's skull.

Meantime, two officers on foot worked their way along the creek toward the hostage scene. Sensing movement, Walters turned to look, raising the shotgun momentarily from its position. Quickly Arnold made sure the scope still sited Walters's head and pulled the trigger. The bullet smashed the rear window of the Mercury, preventing Arnold from seeing its effect. Sprinting forward, he pulled his pistol. The car's roof concealed all but Walters's lap, in which the shotgun rested with his finger still on the trigger. Taking no chances, Arnold pumped four .45 slugs into Walters's chest. Only when stooping to look in did Arnold see that his rifle shot had hit the back of Walters's head and, in exiting, turned his face into a mass of red pulp. The standoff had lasted about fifteen minutes.

At the rifle shot, the Houstons hastily slipped out of the front seat and ran away from their car. Not surprisingly, their gratitude to Tom Arnold was effusive. So was Captain Burks's commendation. However, Arnold's hard work and dedication to duty either declined from this peak or somehow he ran afoul of the erratic Captain Burks. His status report for March 5, 1984, carried this cryptic notice: "Unsatisfactory performance complaint lodged against Ranger T. E. Arnold carried into this period and was resolved by his retirement November 30, 1983."[2]

COMPANY B RANGER Glenn Elliott, stationed in Longview, had been trying to nail Charles Robert Mathis for seven years, ever since he got out of the army in 1963. Forty in 1970, slender, with a long, menacing face, big ears, and heavy black hair and eyebrows, Mathis looked like what he was—a seasoned gangster. Elliott had arrested him for several offenses over the years, but each time he evaded justice.

Elliott's chance came in 1970, when he apprehended Larry Fyffe, a sometime accomplice of Mathis's, for stealing televisions and radios. To head off the consequences, Fyffe made a deal with Elliott and his colleague Bob Mitchell. He would team up with Mathis and serve as an informant.

In December 1970 Fyffe reported that Mathis intended to steal a bulldozer on Sunday, December 20. Although he did not know which of three dealers, he thought Mathis inclined toward a John Deere company in Dallas. Rangers staked out all three on that Sunday, but Elliott chose the Dallas site.

Elliott, Mitchell, Red Arnold, and Max Womack waited all Saturday night and Sunday morning inside the shop building. They knew that Mathis normally phoned his intended target to make sure no one was there. If anyone answered, he turned back. About 11:00 AM the telephone rang, and the Rangers knew they had staked the right place.

At noon both Mathis and Fyffe appeared in the back compound. The officers watched as Mathis hot-wired a big truck designed to haul heavy equipment. He then started a bulldozer and began to back it up a ramp onto the truck bed. The Rangers dashed out. Looking back over his shoulder as he maneuvered up the ramp, Mathis failed to see them until they confronted him at the base of the ramp and shouted "Stop, police." He quickly stood and pulled a pistol from his belt. That signaled a barrage of shotgun fire from the four Rangers. The blasts propelled Mathis into the air and thrust him into the steering clutches. As he fell to the ground the dozer, its treads still turning, tangled Mathis and tipped off the ramp on top of him.[3]

The killing had taken place within Dallas city limits, and in January 1971 a Dallas grand jury ruled the shooting justifiable homicide.[4]

Nine years later Glenn Elliott found himself entangled by the Mathis affair in a bizarre and unscrupulous quest for preferment by high federal officials in Texas. U.S. Attorney John Hanna wanted to be governor of Texas and was running for state attorney general, while FBI SAC Niles Duke wanted a triumph that would elevate him in the FBI hierarchy. His notion of such a triumph, as he confided to fellow agents (who passed it on to Elliott), was "to hang a Ranger scalp on my belt."

These two contended that Elliott had withheld vital information in a federal racketeering probe of Gregg County sheriff Tom Welch and had in fact been party to his malfeasance. They also got Larry Fyffe and Mathis's two sons to swear that they had witnesses who had seen Elliott accept payoff money from Mathis and also that the Rangers had planted a pistol on an unarmed Mathis after they killed him in Dallas. The two federal officials leaked their charges to the newspapers, which gave them headlined play.

They picked the wrong scalp. It rested on the head of one of the most widely regarded Rangers in Texas and adjoining states, a man of unblemished honesty and integrity, and a man careful to keep meticulous records of his actions. He had indeed shared with the FBI all he knew about the Welch case and could prove it. Hanna and Duke wisely abandoned that part of their scalping foray, but they persisted for two more years in trying to build a case that Elliott had set up Mathis for murder. Elliott challenged Hanna to subject Fyffe and the two boys to polygraph tests. One refused, one failed, and one turned in inconclusive results. Hanna and Duke finally had to conclude that their three witnesses lacked credibility and that a case could not be made of the Mathis affair that would get them anywhere close to a Ranger scalp.[5]

Such on occasion was the nature of federal-state cooperation.

GARRISON RANGERS and their successor generation esteemed the history and traditions of the Texas Rangers. They had long pondered some way to commemorate their past. Waco real estate agent James R. LeBlond came up with an idea in 1963: incorporate a commemorative center in an extensive beautification program planned for the south bank of the Brazos River. With city and matching federal funding, the complex began to take shape in 1967, when Governor Connally and other dignitaries assembled to watch Homer Garrison turn the first spade of earth. Plans called for a vaguely suggestive log-and-stone replica of the 1837 Fort Fisher that once stood on the site. The building would front on the new Interstate Highway 35 where it crossed the Brazos River. Behind, a landscaped city park would contain tourist cabins and picnic areas. Fort Fisher would provide the headquarters office of Ranger Company F and space for the Homer Garrison Memorial Museum displaying weapons and other artifacts of Rangers past and present.[6]

This undertaking proved just the beginning. As 1973 approached, Rangers prepared to celebrate their sesquicentennial. With the sanction of the legislature, Clint Peoples, then captain of Company F at Fort Fisher, chaired the Texas Ranger Commemorative Commission. The goal: expand the Fort Fisher complex by adding a Texas Ranger Hall of Fame. On August 4, 1973, Governor Briscoe turned another first spade of earth for the enlarged complex, declaring it a hall for heroes of the past and the future.

He spoke truly. The Garrison Museum expanded to include more artifacts and exhibits in addition to tributes to Hall of Fame entries selected each year by an advisory group. It graphically recorded the past, but as the decades passed it recorded the unfolding history Governor Briscoe foretold. Especially important, the museum added an archive to which Rangers could donate personal and official papers for historical research.[7]

As dark clouds at times shadowed the Rangers, some critics viewed the Hall of Fame as pompous breast-beating, but they did not deter the thousands of people who flocked each year to view the exhibits.

TALL, ERECT, GRIM-VISAGED, Captain Pete Rogers had been a Ranger for twenty-seven years, all in Houston. He returned from World War II a highly decorated combat pilot and helped launch the DPS aircraft program. Although seen as a "city Ranger," he and his scattered company dealt not only with rural crimes but increasingly with the murders, maiming, and other offenses committed by inmates incarcerated by the Texas Department of Corrections (TDC). The state penitentiary stood at

Huntsville, only seventy-five miles north of Houston, and satellite units sprouted all over southeastern Texas. Although TDC bloodhounds often aided Rogers in pursuits in the swamps and forests of his region, prison crimes accounted for a growing burden on Company A.

The phone call that reached Rogers from Huntsville early on the afternoon of July 24, 1974, was not another routine request for help. Warden Howell H. Husbands reported that San Antonio drug lord Federico Gómez Carrasco, twenty-seven, and two fellow inmates had seized the third-floor library and classroom of the Walls Unit, were armed with powerful automatic pistols, and held enough hostages, including women, to make a crisis of the first magnitude. As Husbands later said of his call to Rogers: "I knew we had to have help and we needed a bunch of it. I thought, hell, with him we can cross any river."[8]

TDC director Ward J. "Jim" Estelle, a prison administrator of long experience and high competence, a Texan who looked more like a Ranger than a jailer, flew quickly to Huntsville from a speaking engagement in San Antonio. By the time of his arrival, about 3:00 PM, much had been learned, primarily through the courageous prison chaplain, Father Joseph J. O'Brien. He had volunteered to enter the library and talk with Carrasco. There he found that Carrasco's revolt aimed solely at escape; that his two accomplices were Ignacio Cuevas and Rudolfo Dominguez, both emotionally unstable and of low mental order; and that the rooms contained about fifty inmates, one prison guard, and ten library and school employees, including seven women. With O'Brien continuing to act as intermediary, and finally remaining as a hostage himself, the standoff resolved itself into the release of all the inmates and the retention of eleven "civilian" hostages, four inmates who volunteered to stay, and the three determined escapees.

Warden Husbands's office served as the "Think Tank." Jim Estelle presided firmly as the decision-maker. Aiding him in plotting strategy and tactics were Husbands and other top prison staff; the FBI SAC from Bryan, Robert E. Wiatt, who happened to be in Huntsville interviewing an inmate; and Ranger captains Pete Rogers and G. W. Burks. DPS in Austin had ordered Burks from Dallas to Huntsville to join Rogers, and he had arrived decked out in shiny cowboy boots and a pair of ivory-handled pistols holstered on his hips. Rogers had brought Sergeant Johnny Krumnow and two others, and Burks had half his company in tow. The first decision in the Think Tank was to accept the offer of Carrasco's attorney, Reuben Montemayor, to fly his plane over from San Antonio and serve as telephone intermediary between Estelle and Carrasco.

The ordeal that played itself out in the next eleven days subjected the hostages to unimaginable horrors and the thinkers in the Think Tank to emotionally draining explorations of strategy. Beyond an assault that would inevitably cost the lives of some hostages, no option presented itself except to stall and talk. Through Montemayor the thinkers dealt with an erratic, unpredictable, thoroughly ruthless rebel ready to kill the hostages and die if not granted his freedom. For the thinkers, especially the decision-maker Jim Estelle, freedom was the one demand beyond consideration. Even if hostages died, Carrasco would never leave the prison alive.

Day after day the tense standoff fed national public attention and concern. Huntsville overflowed with newspeople and television cameras and lights. Carrasco let his women hostages talk with their families by telephone, which heightened media interest. Day after sweltering day in the relentless July heat and humidity, the negotiations dragged on, the hostages suffering gnawing fear, erratic and terrifying treatment, and a growing feeling of hopelessness. In the Think Tank, Estelle granted such demands as he could—television, food items, custom-made steel helmets, handcuffs, and other items that did not further Carrasco's ultimate goal—while denying any concession that might encourage or aid escape.

An idea with possibilities came from Carrasco himself: he wanted a well-equipped armored car driven to the foot of a ramp leading to the third floor. The thinkers in the command post agreed, well knowing that they would never open any gate to allow the car to exit and that hostages might be killed. From inside the library came another idea, from one of the "volunteer inmates," Stephen Ray Robertson: build an improvised box-shaped shield in which to maneuver down the ramp to the car. Carrasco bought into this scheme only reluctantly, until the hostages pitched in to erect such a vehicle. After two days of labor, the "Trojan Horse," or "Trojan Taco," emerged. It was constructed of two long blackboards on castors, book shelves fixed to the ends, cardboard skirts below the sides to cover legs and feet, and a double layer of law books and encyclopedias taped to all four exposures to provide armor. Weighing seven hundred pounds, it would shelter Carrasco, Dominguez, and Cuevas together with four hostages.

Estelle and his colleagues knew of Carrasco's plan because he had released one of the women to explain it. Estelle ordered officers not to fire at the shield as it inched down the ramp but try to topple it with high-velocity fire hoses brought in by the Huntsville Fire Department. Even so, they positioned plenty of firepower in strategic locations. Pete Rogers assembled a thirteen-man assault team and, with Burks and Wiatt, worked into a position at the front of the second floor dining room under the library entrance. By 9:00 PM on the eleventh day, August 3, the ordeal reached its climax.

In the library Carrasco ordered the final touches to the contraption. A volley ball net twisted into a rope encircled the vehicle, and one of the volunteer inmates handcuffed all the hostages to it except those chosen for the interior. Each of the three inmates, reaching over the left shoulder of a female captive, handcuffed his left wrist to her right wrist and with his right hand jammed a pistol into her back. Father O'Brien entered first, Cuevas and Novella Pollard next, Dominguez and Julia Standley next, and Carrasco and Yvonne Beseda last. Awkwardly, the cumbersome Trojan Taco exited the library and inched slowly around three bends before hanging up on the fourth and final turn that would give access to the ramp.

It stalled close to the assault team. Rogers, Burks, Wiatt, and DPS intelligence agent Winston Padgett burst from hiding and yelled "Drop your guns! Hold it right there!" At the same instant came the order, "Hit the hoses!" Three streams of 250-psi water slammed the vehicle. The outside hostages responded to the shout to "Get down!" Over the deafening noise of the fire-hose attack, four shots rang out. Padgett called to Rogers, "It's gone bad!"

It had. Dominguez had fired three bullets into Julia Standley's back, and Carrasco had pumped one into Yvonne Beseda's heart. A fifth caught Father O'Brien in the arm and splintered into his chest. Cuevas fainted, pulling Novella Pollard to the ground with him. The hoses suddenly lost power, dooming the hope of knocking the Trojan Taco over with water pressure. Through gun slits, Carrasco and Dominguez opened fire on their assailants, knocking down Wiatt, Rogers, and Burks, who were saved only by their bulletproof vests. Officers dragged them inside and helped them back to their feet. They dashed back out to join swarms of other officers firing at the gun slits.

Firefighters restored the water pressure, and another blast hit the vehicle without turning it over. It signaled Carrasco, however, that he had lost his gamble. He fired a bullet into his own brain. Ranger sergeant Johnny Krumnow found an aluminum ladder in the building and with several other officers rammed the side of the Trojan Taco so vigorously that it finally toppled on its side, spilling bodies on the ramp.

Badly wounded, Father O'Brien had fallen on top of Dominguez, who jabbed a pistol into his back. Spotting Wiatt and Padgett, recalled O'Brien, "I rolled over and hollered, 'Shoot! He's got a gun!'" Padgett bestrode the two and put a bullet into Dominguez's head. When he moved, Padgett fired again, and Bob Wiatt sent a round into his neck.

"It looked like a slaughterhouse," according to Wiatt. Dead or dying were Carrasco, Dominguez, Standley, and Beseda. Severely shot up was Father O'Brien. "This guy's chest looks like a junkyard," observed a doctor, but O'Brien would recover to relate his graphic memories of the battle.[9]

An unnamed inmate later stirred a controversy by charging that Rangers had executed Carrasco and Dominguez without cause, but Father O'Brien's emphatic denials quieted the brewing contention. "It was no time for the Marquis of Queensbury rules," he declared. "You had people shot and it was time for the Rangers to shoot."

That seems a fair appraisal. More to the point is the validity of the scenario hatched in the Think Tank for ending the standoff. Short of letting the rebels go free, never discussed as an option, the Trojan Horse scheme offered a risky way out even though a peril to the lives of hostages. A direct assault on the library, the only other alternative anyone could suggest, ensured the death of hostages.

But, as Padgett had shouted, "It's gone bad." Two women died as a result.

GEORGE PARR RETAINED his iron grip on Duval County, even though his manifold crimes had been exposed in federal and state courts in the 1950s and he owed his freedom to a legal technicality. A chance witness fell to federal prosecutors in 1972, and U.S. Attorney for the Western District of Texas William S. Sessions resolved to try once more to end the Duke of Duval's plundering of county revenue. Sessions and his capable assistant, John E. Clark, formed a tireless, determined, aggressive pair that, aided by a talented cadre of investigators and tax experts, went after Parr not on the failed mail fraud charges of the 1950s but on the income taxes he had not declared on the millions stolen from county coffers.

Through 1972 and 1973, the Sessions team exposed a federal grand jury in San Antonio to compelling evidence of these millions. It was hard-won. No cooperative witnesses could be found in Duval or surrounding counties. Subpoenaed witnesses resorted to a range of stratagems to withhold bank and county records and their own knowledge of what transpired. Troves of official records went missing. Parr controlled every elected and appointed official in Duval County, and none dared cross him. No citizen would say or do anything that might offend him. The prosecutors' task was daunting, always frustrating, and frequently disheartening. Yet a grand jury angered by the crimes of the Parr dynasty returned the indictments prosecutors sought. The trial of George Parr began on March 4, 1974, in Corpus Christi. Two weeks later the jury deliberated less than three hours before finding him guilty on all counts of income tax evasion.

A month later Sessions and his team went after Duval county judge Archer Parr, George's nephew and heir apparent, and as brazen a crook as his uncle. During the Duke's trial, Archer had lied under oath so thoroughly and repeatedly that he stood trial for perjury. A jury convicted him as swiftly as another had convicted George.[10]

After obtaining the conviction of a third official, the federal officers decided to turn the rest of the cesspool in Duval County over to an eager John Hill, attorney general of Texas. He and his staff and the Rangers had stood aside while the federal cases proceeded, even though both federal and state laws had been breached. Federal law barred sharing of evidence until the courts had ruled. Now Sessions turned over all his evidence, and Hill fielded a task force of attorneys, accountants, and Rangers to crush the rest of Duval County officialdom.

But not before the Rangers had a related high-profile investigation to conduct. George Parr had been free on bond for a year pending the outcome of his appeal. On March 24, 1975, the appeals court ruled against him. Fearing that he might make a break for Mexico, prosecutors moved swiftly to get his bond revoked and take him into custody. But Parr had disappeared, by all accounts heavily armed. FBI agents, U.S. marshals, Texas Rangers, and Duval county officers searched the county. On April 1 a DPS helicopter spotted Parr's car parked in a remote corner of his sprawling ranch. Inside, officers found Parr on the floor, a .45 automatic pistol beside him and a .45 bullet in his brain.[11]

For the next three years, under Captain Wood's supervision, Rangers of Company D aggressively investigated county officials not only in Duval but also in neighboring Jim Wells and Zavala counties. Assigned to the attorney general's task force, Rangers George E. "Gene" Powell, Ray Martínez, and Rudolfo Rodriguez turned in exceptional records as investigators. Other Rangers rotated in and out of South Texas, including Captain Wood himself. Nearly every election, whether primary, county, or school board, mobilized most of Company D to stand guard at polling places and impound ballot boxes. One after another the crooked officials fell before the attorney general's relentless task force. By 1978 the Parr machine lay in ruins, leaving a history of unparalleled corruption dating from the turn of the century. Although the Texas Rangers played little part in the federal trials that brought down George

Parr in the early 1970s, they contributed crucially in 1975–78 to smashing the machine he had headed.[12]

THROUGHOUT the 1970s San Antonio Company D had wrestled with Latino uprisings in Zavala and other counties, rampant corruption in George Parr's Duval County, and a host of other investigations of fraud and theft all over South Texas. Under the steady, competent guidance of Captain John Wood, the unit's Rangers turned in an extraordinary record. In the fall of 1978, Wood retired.

On November 1, 1978, Jack O. Dean took over Company D. As a one-year rookie seven years earlier, he had made a name for himself by quieting the clash between Raza Unida and the Pharr police, and since had risen rapidly. Most of his service remained on the lower Rio Grande, but he came to San Antonio from a stint with Captain Bob Mitchell in Waco.[13]

Dean had been captain only seven months when hit with a crime that shocked the nation. On the morning of May 29, 1979, an assassin shot and killed federal judge John H. Wood (no kin to Captain Wood) in front of his San Antonio condominium. For almost a decade, the FBI, in tandem with the Drug Enforcement Administration, had been hounding the Chagra brothers of El Paso for alleged drug dealing. By 1978 they had amassed enough evidence, often by odious if not illegal means, to bring Jimmy Chagra to trial. Judge Wood was to preside.

"Maximum John" was but one of many epithets applied to Judge Wood. Not only did he routinely impose the maximum sentence, he was a judicial tyrant who from the bench openly insulted defense lawyers, witnesses, and anyone else who incurred his displeasure, and he consistently displayed abysmal ignorance of the law and courtroom procedure. Virtually the entire West Texas bar held him in contempt. So did the judges of the Fifth Circuit Court of Appeals, who reversed as many of his decisions as they upheld. Regardless of how flawed the evidence collected by the FBI, Jimmy Chagra knew he had no chance of evading the maximum sentence Maximum John would throw at him. He hired a hit man.[14]

Before May 29 had ended, Captain Dean had a DPS task force at the crime scene; besides himself, it consisted of three Rangers, a narcotics agent, and an intelligence agent. San Antonio police had also converged. The FBI SAC, Tony Morrow, formed a multiagency task force and that night announced that FBI deputy director James O. Ingram would assume command. Ingram brought with him from Washington a formidable contingent of agents and quickly let it be known that, while he welcomed all possible information, the Rangers and city police could consider themselves no longer parties to the investigation. Even so, they were. Dean's task force continued to gather evidence, question informants, and comb DPS files for leads. He passed on all findings to the FBI.

A few days after the murder Dean received a telephone call from a man whose voice he recognized as out of his past but who would not identify himself. All he would say was "Charles Harrelson was in San Antonio the day Judge Wood was killed." Jack Dean knew Charles Harrelson, whose profession was robbery and murder for hire. For four years in the Lower Valley Dean had grown to know him very well, as he worked to get him convicted of murder—not his first. The ostentatious Houston lawyer Percy Foreman defended Harrelson with some successes, but after 1974 Harrelson did time in both Huntsville and Leavenworth. In September 1978, seven months before Judge Wood's murder, Harrelson walked free from Leavenworth.[15]

Dean shared his insights with the FBI's Ingram, who questioned him closely about the criminal Dean knew more about than did any lawman. Dean also provided Ingram with DPS mug shots of Harrelson. Ingram thanked Dean, dismissed him as no longer needed, and then launched a search for Harrelson. In August 1980 the FBI got him—from the Van Horn police. They had seized him standing next to his Corvette on Interstate 10, shouting cocaine-induced rantings, and holding a pistol to his head. On the way to jail he confessed to the murder of Judge Wood—and also of President John F. Kennedy.[16]

Dean continued to work the case even as the FBI pulled together enough evidence to convict Harrelson of Wood's murder. The verdict, in December 1982, sent Harrelson to a federal penitentiary with two life sentences. Years later his son, movie celebrity Woody Harrelson, tried hard to get his father out, but in prison he remained.

Assassination rarely struck down a federal judge. The Wood murder therefore set off a nationwide media craze, and the apprehension and conviction of the assassin brought it to a climactic burst. In the summer of 1981 the new San Antonio SAC, Jack Lawn, visited Dean's office and thanked him for his help in the case, in particular his identification of Charles Harrelson. That was all the recognition Captain Dean received. But for his lead, the FBI might never have ended the case. Yet the media spotlight fixed solely on the FBI, which never let the public know that Dean or any other state or local officers had been involved.[17]

THE DECADE OF achievement that lifted the Texas Rangers from the morass of the move to abolish them neared its close with an incident of public embarrassment. Rangers had consistently abhorred politics but in June 1979 found themselves enmeshed in a nasty squabble of state legislators.

Lieutenant Governor William P. "Bill" Hobby had nearly succeeded in ramming through legislation to separate the days on which the 1980 presidential and state primaries were held. Liberals widely interpreted this as a move to promote the presidential ambitions of former governor John Connally. But Hobby had the votes, and the only way opponents could head off the legislation was to deny the Senate a quorum and let the ticking clock doom its passage. On Friday morning May 18, 1979, twelve senators failed to show up.

Dubbed by Hobby the "Killer Bees," the senators made headlines and stoked waggish editorials. A furious Hobby ordered DPS to round up the bees and drag them into the capitol. Reluctantly, troopers and Rangers spread out in a perfunctory effort to meet the lieutenant governor's demand.

Sunday morning, at the residence of Houston senator Gene Jones, his brother Clayton bent to pick up the newspaper only to be confronted by Ranger Charles Cook of Company A. "Is your name Jones?" Cook inquired. When assured it was, Cook announced that he had orders to take Jones to Austin. Flown to the capital and immediately identified by the senate sergeant-at-arms as the wrong man, Clayton Jones was back in Houston by 1:30 PM.

Ranger Cook believed he had been deliberately set up and treated to statewide ignominy by the press. In fact, before leaving with Cook, Clayton had stepped back inside and given the high sign to his brother, who fled out the back door. Clayton asked Cook if he didn't think he might be making a mistake, but did not correct him when repeatedly addressed as "Senator Jones." Cook judged this as deception, as it undoubtedly was. Clayton conceded that as soon as addressed as senator, he grasped the situation. "I was hacked off pretty bad at first," he said, "but then went along with their game"—undoubtedly to give his brother time to find refuge elsewhere.

"I feel I've been made the laughing stock of the whole state," Cook told a reporter. "But I was just doing my job."

Newspapers made a farce of the affair. Cook and the Rangers suffered acute discomfort as Texans laughed at them. And Colonel Pat Speir endured a public tongue-lashing by Lieutenant Governor Hobby over the failure of DPS to round up the absent senators. But the Killer Bees won. They returned to their seats Tuesday morning, May 22, too late for Hobby to get his bill enacted.[18]

DESPITE THE EMBARRASSING FINALE, the decade of the 1970s restored Ranger distinction from its low point during the farm strike fallout and the movement to abolish the force altogether. This outcome may be attributed partly to the solid support of Colonel Pat Speir but mainly to the leadership of Garrison Rangers who had worked their way up to command positions. The exemplary record of Senior Captain Bill Wilson and such captains as John Wood, Jack Dean, Bob Mitchell, and Pete Rogers gave new faces and new prestige to the Texas Rangers.

[17]

Highs and Lows, 1980s

THE 1980S SPOTLIGHTED the Texas Rangers with some headline-grabbing exploits, but the less-noted routine investigations continued.

The approach of the 1982 election revived memories of the Duke of Duval as warnings of election fraud poured into Austin. Captain Jack Dean's men joined with both federal and state officers in a task force to probe allegations in Duval, Hidalgo, Brooks, and San Patricio counties. The drive lasted two years, mainly in Duval County, and produced eight indictments but not much more. Ranger Rudy Rodriguez earned special praise from the FBI. Voter fraud had become so embedded in the political culture of South Texas that task force members must have despaired of ever stamping it out.[1]

Seemingly unavoidable and a core mission for Rangers was running down bank robbers. Throughout the early 1980s, Company B joined with federal and local officers in an attempt to stop a string of robberies throughout North Texas. In May 1984 they caught a man and woman responsible for thirteen stickups, only to confront another sequence. Captain Burks kept the investigation alive but could not stem the wave of heists.[2]

In fact, like voter fraud in South Texas, bank robberies posed a continuing challenge. Rangers could expend much time and effort and occasionally score a success, but the crime, especially in and around the cities, would never be suppressed.

BY THE 1980s, drugs had become the pleasure of choice for many of the nation's youth. Texans, especially in the more heavily populated east, succumbed to the temptation. Not only were drugs illegal, they motivated a wide range of crimes. For lawmen summoned to a crime scene, a first thought was that somehow drugs were involved.

So it was on Saturday morning, September 24, 1983. Summoned by the Kilgore police department, Ranger Glenn Elliott of Longview had joined local lawmen in Kilgore's Kentucky Fried Chicken restaurant. At closing time the night before, the staff—three college boys and a middle-aged woman—had been abducted and $2,000 taken from the cash register. Another middle-aged woman who had dropped by for a visit had also gone missing. While the lawmen scrutinized the building, a call came through that an oil field worker had discovered five bodies in a grassy oil lease several hundred yards from a state highway seventeen miles south of Kilgore, in Rusk County. Elliott and the locals hastened to the scene, where they found four corpses side by side in a neat row, face down, with bullets in the backs of their heads. A fifth had tried to run away and been shot down.

The KFC murders kindled national attention. They also preoccupied Ranger Elliott and his colleague Stuart Dowell. They and local officers found scattered spots of blood on a wall at the restaurant, analysis of which identified some that did not match that of any of the victims. They also deduced that the victims knew their abductors and that more than one had to have been involved to control five scared captives. The latter was confirmed by two calibers of bullets recovered from the bodies. As for motive, speculation at once raced through the communities that a drug deal had gone bad, but Elliott disagreed. "I believe it was a simple act of robbery by druggies looking for cash to buy drugs." Witnesses to the robbery then had to be eliminated.[3]

Elliott and Dowell helped the sheriff's deputies of Rusk and Gregg counties and the Kilgore police round up all the known "druggies" and question them closely. They developed many leads, most of which led nowhere. On September 29 Captain Burks arrived, but with hard, tedious work supplanting the first burst of publicity, he soon returned to Dallas. Thereafter Elliott and Dowell furnished the Ranger participation in the multi-agency investigation. Balancing three other murder cases, including an eerily similar murder at a Mount Pleasant Pizza Hut, they still managed to devote almost full time to the KFC case.[4]

The KFC killings did not recede from the public mind, nor did the failure of investigators to find the killers. Glenn Elliott thought they had one culprit, Jimmy Mankins, but the Rusk County prosecutor believed the evidence inadequate. Two more suspects, unnamed in the press, were Darnell Hartsfield and Romeo Pinkerton. A witness placed Hartsfield at the KFC at closing time, and a blood spot on a white box above the cash register matched his. But again, the evidence did not convince prosecutors they could win.

The investigation remained active. In 1988 Rusk County sheriff Cecil West complained, "It's frustrating as hell, no doubt about it. We all agree we know who did it. As far as getting evidence to prove it, though, that's another matter."[5]

Texas attorney general Dan Morales entered the case in 1993, when a conviction in the still-remembered killings would have meant a wealth of positive publicity for the politically ambitious official. Under a change of venue to Beaumont, he sought an indictment of Jimmy Mankins from a grand jury. But the DNA evidence linking him to the crime proved inconclusive, and before completing his presentation Morales suddenly dropped all charges against Mankins.[6]

Glenn Elliott continued to work on the KFC case until his retirement in 1987. The state attorney general's office, however, kept the case alive. DNA testing had now evolved sufficiently to offer hope of resolution. As Rusk County grand juries continued to probe the case, mishandling of the "foreign" blood samples in 1983 stalled progress, as did the disappearance of the witness to Darnell Hartsfield's presence at the KFC on the night of the abduction. Finally, in October 2005, Hartsfield fell victim to DNA. He had denied ever having been in the KFC, yet DNA proved him there and the missing witness had been found. In Henderson, a Rusk County grand jury convicted him of aggravated perjury, and he went to Huntsville for life, the harsh sentence based on his long criminal record, primarily drug offenses. DNA also at last substituted for the broken chain of blood evidence. In the sequence of grand jury proceedings, Glenn Elliott appeared as a crucial witness for the prosecution.[7]

Hardly a month after Hartsfield's conviction for perjury, on November 17, 2005, the attorney general's prosecutors convinced a Rusk County grand jury to indict Darnell Hartsfield and Romeo Pinkerton for murder. Pinkerton sat in the Smith County jail in Tyler on a parole violation. Both had been among the suspects from the beginning. A third had died, and the fourth remains unnamed. The families of the victims and the investigators who have pursued the case for twenty-two years avidly hope for justice at last.[8]

A CHALLENGE the Rangers faced repeatedly throughout their decades as part of DPS was the hostage quandary. Whether kidnapped for ransom or seized as shields in an escape, hostages faced death if their abductor refused to surrender or was provoked by aggressive law officers. Most such episodes involved negotiations, directly or by telephone, and demanded patience, skill, and mastery of the psychology of bargaining with the offender. Particularly demanding were cornered hostage-takers, those so surrounded by officers that only the hostages offered a means of escape. To deal with increasingly common hostage incidents, by the 1980s each Ranger company included a "hostage-talker" specially trained in "talking down" the offender. Waco Company F's talker was Sergeant Bob Prince.

About 1:00 PM on August 28, 1985, the Waco police dispatcher advised Prince that his services had been requested by police in Meridian, a small town in Bosque County sixty miles northwest of Waco. A DPS helicopter set Prince down in Meridian an hour later. Ranger Joe Wilie had already reached the scene, together with about thirty officers of the small Meridian police force, the county sheriff's department, the highway patrol, and the police departments of two nearby towns. Later in the afternoon, Company F captain Bob Mitchell arrived to take charge, bringing with him Rangers John Dendy, Stan Guffey, and Johnny Waldrip. Prince confronted the worst of hostage situations—a taker with three hostages in a small house surrounded by more than thirty law officers.

Meridian police chief Curtis McGlothlin could not tell Prince much. That morning a sinister-looking man with beard and long hair had entered another residence and made captives of a thirteen-year-old girl, Karen Howard, and a five-year-old boy she was babysitting. When the man began to search the house for keys to a van parked outside, Karen grabbed the child and ran from the house two blocks to a friend's house, where the father phoned the police. McGlothlin called in sheriff's deputies and launched a search. About noon a deputy spotted the fugitive and, with two others, chased him on foot to another house, which he entered through the back door. As police sealed off the premises, he went to the front door and informed Chief McGlothlin that he had three hostages. If threatened, he would "pile up some bodies in front of the house." He would say no more than that his name was Bob. The hostages were Mary Lou York, twenty-five, her five-year-old son, and the boy's aunt, Jennie Davenport, seventeen.[9]

For the next fourteen hours, "Bob" tested every skill Prince could summon. The York residence had no phone, so Bob consented to having a local line run in to furnish communication. He and Prince then began a conversation in which Prince sought to calm Bob's agitation, assure him that no one wanted to hurt him and would not try, and talk him into releasing the hostages. He succeeded in establishing rapport and even a guarded mutual trust.

One rule of negotiation was never to make a concession without receiving something in return. Bob wanted cigarettes. Prince had already stirred sympathy for the plight of the young boy and agreed to exchange cigarettes for him. Bob finally consented. The boy appeared on the front porch and Prince, at no small risk, went to a back window and handed the cigarettes to Bob. When Bob later demanded hamburgers and sodas, Prince answered that the boy was crying for his mother, and he would exchange the food for Mary Lou York in the same manner. With Ranger scopes trained on the window, Prince handed the sack of hamburgers to Bob, and a few minutes later Mrs. York appeared on the front porch.

That left Jennie Davenport. Several times before the exchanges, Bob had let Jennie talk with Prince, and she had assured him that all were fine and had not been harmed. Strangely, Mrs. York seems not to have related to any officer what had happened before her release. She could have told them that Bob had struck Jennie when she lunged for the pistol in his back pocket, then raped her twice. After Mrs. York's departure, he raped her a third time. Prince recalled that "we never had any idea that all this was going on. If we had, I would have made another trip to the window. . . . Then either one of the snipers or I would have ended this standoff right then!"

But the tedious negotiations continued late into the night. Bob offered several unacceptable courses of action, and each time, rather than say no, Prince replied that Captain Mitchell had refused. Increasingly the dialogue turned to Bob himself. He vowed never to return to prison, talked of killing himself or forcing the officers to shoot him. Finally, Bob revealed his true name: Jimmy R. Cooper. A quick check by DPS revealed a tough midwestern criminal with a long record, repeated prison terms, and the recent escape from an Illinois jail. He had come to Meridian in the mistaken belief that relatives lived there and, seeking refuge until dark, had accidentally blundered into the hostage deadlock.

Now Cooper wanted to talk with his mother. Prince conditioned that on the release of Jennie, who continued to insist that she was OK. Two Illinois phone numbers brought no answer, but finally, shortly after midnight Prince made contact. Because the negotiations took place on a temporary local line, Prince could not connect Cooper with his mother. But he relayed her pleas to give up and promised that, if he did, he would make certain he could talk directly with his mother.

Shortly before 6:00 AM Jennie Davenport walked out of the house and across the street. Cooper no longer controlled the standoff. The Rangers wanted him alive but were prepared to shoot if he forced them. About fifteen minutes after Jennie's release, Jimmy Cooper placed his pistol on the front porch and walked out with his hands up.

After fourteen tense hours, the crisis had ended. The hostages had escaped with their lives. Prince had demonstrated through long, nerve-wracking hours all the talents of the hostage-talker, and with a range of well-conceived tactics and carefully chosen words had won the standoff.

He fulfilled his promise. At 6:30 AM, in the Bosque County jail, Cooper talked with his mother. He also went to prison for life, convicted of kidnapping, sexual assault, burglary by criminal entry of two homes, and felony possession of a firearm.

The firearm proved of special interest to Bob Prince. Karen Howard's description left the impression that it was a .22 pistol. Actually, it was a .357 Magnum, and a report received after "Bob" revealed his true name came from an Indiana sheriff: "Lordy, if you're in a hostage situation, don't let your hostage negotiator get up close. That's what happened here. He [Cooper] had a hostage and he lured the hostage negotiator up close and shot him in the face." Prince had already faced Cooper at the window twice. He did not return a third time.

AT FORTY, Bob Mitchell had been one of the youngest Ranger captains in history when he took over Company F in Waco in 1974. In eighteen years as captain, he retained the affection and admiration of his men, and emerged as the most competent and widely respected captain in the service. He gave close attention to training his men, building their character, and imparting high standards of personal and professional conduct. Those who went on to other companies took with them his lessons and his example. Nine rose to captain of their own company.[10]

On Friday morning, January 11, 1985, Mitchell was conducting a company meeting at his Fort Fisher headquarters in Waco when a telephone call from the Johnson County sheriff alerted him to the kidnapping of a thirteen-year-old girl at Alvarado, about fifty miles north of Waco and twenty-five south of Fort Worth. "Let's go, let's all go to Alvarado," exclaimed the captain, "y'all" meet there." The Rangers scattered to their cars and roared north.[11]

Amy McNiel was the daughter of Don McNiel, a wealthy director of the Alvarado State Bank. Early that Friday morning, her seventeen-year-old brother Mark had been driving her and her fourteen-year-old cousin to school when two black-hooded men in a stolen car forced him into a ditch, grabbed Amy, and sped away.[12]

In Alvarado, Mitchell went to the McNiel home and found the FBI already on the scene. He then collected his men in McNiel's bank. A morning call from the kidnappers had set the ransom at $100,000 and given notice to await further instructions. Under McNiel's direction, the Rangers counted out $100,000 and bundled it in a bank bag. A series of telephone exchanges between McNiel and the kidnappers proved unproductive. The Rangers spent the night in the bank, waiting. Saturday afternoon three Rangers from Company B showed up. Shortly afterward, the long-awaited call came through: McNiel should take the money and drive to a phone booth near Interstate 30 in eastern Dallas, where he would receive further instructions.

Thus began a chaotic twelve-hour attempt to rescue Amy McNiel. FBI agents had joined with Mitchell in working with Don McNiel. A procession of cars set out from Alvarado about 5:00 PM Saturday afternoon. Mitchell rode in the FBI car, behind McNiel's big limousine. Six Ranger units followed at a distance. A single-engine DPS aircraft piloted by Reginald Rhea tracked the procession from above. Mitchell had assigned Rangers Ralph Wadsworth and Stan Guffey to fly as observers. Two FBI helicopters covered the operation while the plane landed twice to refuel. Through hours of wild confusion on the ground, the occupants of the airplane never lost sight of all that took place below.[13]

At the first stop, McNiel was told on the telephone to pick up I-20 and drive to Tyler, eighty-two miles, and reach another phone booth by a deadline that kept his car speeding at a hundred miles per hour. There, at about 9:30 PM, he received instructions to continue east through

Longview, then turn north to a closed Gulf gas station on I-30 about ten miles east of Mount Pleasant, another eighty miles. From above, Wadsworth and Guffey tracked the "package car" and its train of units following closely behind.

Some Rangers raced ahead to check out the new location. The Gulf station stood in a small, remote, unlighted community. Thinking this might be the drop site, they positioned their units in hidden locations. McNiel arrived, but his car had given out entirely. When the phone rang at 1:00 AM he was instructed to go to the Best Western Motel in Mount Pleasant, but he had to answer that his car would not start. Hoping the kidnappers would show up here instead, the Rangers prowled the vicinity for several hours before Mitchell and the FBI called off the operation and allowed their men to return to Alvarado.

As Johnny Aycock and Brantley Foster prepared to leave, they saw an auto slowly circle the service station, then speed off on I-30 west toward Mount Pleasant. With a walkie-talkie, Aycock managed to get through to Captain Mitchell, still in the vicinity, and report on this vehicle. Jimmie Ray and Joe Wilie drove the only nearby unit and, alerted by Mitchell, fell in behind the suspect vehicle, identified it as a 1983 Buick carrying several people, and radioed the license number, which confirmed that the plate came from a stolen vehicle.

Meantime, Slick Alfred and Johnny Waldrip, sitting in Unit 684 with the command group back at the Gulf station, heard the report and swiftly hit I-30. They passed Ray and Wilie and got on the tail of the Buick. It passed a cattle truck, and as they sped past the truck the Buick took to an exit ramp without the two seeing it. Ray and Wilie, however, made the exit. Above, pilot Rhea kept the fugitive vehicle in sight, and Wadsworth radioed Wilie that it had turned from the exit road to another, stopped, and had its lights switched off. As the Ranger unit approached from the rear, the lights came on and the car sped away.

Ray hit the siren, threw the magnetized portable flasher on the roof, and raced in pursuit through the streets of Mount Pleasant. The Rangers withheld fire because Amy might be in the car, but the fugitives leaned out the windows on both sides and opened fire. Bullets shattered the Rangers' windshield, and several hit the engine, starting a fire.[14]

As the Ray-Wilic vehicle faltered and fell behind, Slick Alfred and Johnny Waldrip had exited the Interstate only to be advised from the aircraft that the Buick had reentered I-30 and was headed west toward Mount Vernon. Alfred got back on the Interstate and resumed the chase. Slick had a new Ford with overdrive, "and I just had it on the floor." Another car with red flasher entered the highway; it was the FBI, on the way home but now responding to radio alerts. Advised by Wadsworth from above, all the Ranger units made haste to join the chase. John Dendy, accompanied by Johnson County sheriff's deputy D. J. Maulder, caught up with and passed Alfred.

Unknown to the pursuers, the Buick's gas tank verged on empty. Spotting a Mini Mart at tiny Saltillo, six miles west of Mount Vernon, the fugitives slowed and exited, raced twice around the lighted station with the FBI and Dendy close behind, then headed into the little town. The car ran out of gas, lurched into the front yard of Frances Avaritt, and knocked down a flagpole. The occupants rolled out, took cover behind Miss Avaritt's Dodge van parked in the driveway, and opened fire with shotguns on the converging officers. Parked on the street, Alfred and Waldrip returned the fire with a shotgun and Slick's .357 Magnum. Dendy skidded into the yard and with Maulder also shot back. The FBI car came to a halt in the driveway immediately behind the van, and when the two agents found themselves in the middle of a gunfight they both hit the floor, their siren blaring and red lights flashing throughout the gunfight.

After about five minutes, the firing slackened as the kidnappers tried to surrender. With covering fire from Dendy, Maulder ran toward the Buick, followed closely by Alfred. Inside, Maulder saw Amy, grabbed her, and turned to Alfred. "Is that Amy?" Slick asked. "And he said 'Yes,' and I said, 'Let me have her.' And I took Amy and took off back to my car and left them with the cleanup there."

By this time the rest of the Rangers began pulling up. Alfred, pistol drawn, crouched behind his car with Amy beneath him. Sergeant Bob

Prince came up. "I got Amy right here," said Alfred. Prince told him to take Amy to the Mini Mart and get in touch with her father. The FBI brought Don McNiel to his daughter. "I just felt privileged that I got to see the reunion," said Alfred. "It was wonderful. The reunion was worth the gunfight, I can guarantee that."[15]

Back at the battlefield, the FBI siren now silent, the Rangers had five kidnappers lying side by side face down. Four were young men, one a young woman. One man had a bullet in his foot, another several in his body, none serious wounds.

The three-day ordeal, which had been kept out of the newspapers by FBI request, commanded national headlines and detailed accounts. The Ranger role in this complicated, dangerous mission, a gamble of lawmen with the life of a young girl, garnered high praise from the press and DPS. All the Rangers, on the ground and in the air, displayed cool professionalism. Slick Alfred received sole credit for the rescue of Amy McNiel, although Deputy Maulder shared in the feat. Both displayed uncommon courage in dashing to the Buick before the firing had entirely subsided.

In rescuing Amy McNiel, the Texas Rangers earned their richest public laurels of the 1980s.

CAPTAIN BOB MITCHELL'S Company F Rangers had ample experience with hostage situations when, almost exactly two years after the rescue of Amy McNiel, another erupted. On January 14, 1987, Johnny Waldrip, posted in Llano, received a call from the Llano County constable's office reporting a kidnapping in Horseshoe Bay. This was a lakeside community of expensive homes on the south bank of Lake LBJ near Marble Falls. Most owners, wealthy urban dwellers, occupied their homes only in the summer, although some families lived there year-round. Waldrip drove to Horseshoe Bay and learned that the victim was Denise Johnson, twenty-two, the maid of prosperous rancher William Whitehead and his family. In the absence of the family, she had vanished after calling Whitehead's secretary to say she was being kidnapped and held in the vacant house across the street. Neither that house or any other yielded Denise Johnson. For a week Waldrip and Marble Falls officers conducted a thorough investigation that turned up nothing. Johnson could not be found, and no one called to make ransom or other demands.[16]

As the Johnson case fell into the background, a more compelling crisis hit. At 3:30 AM on January 22, 1987, Whitehead's two-year-old daughter, Kara-Leigh, was seized from her bedroom. Whitehead phoned Waldrip and reported the kidnapping. Waldrip alerted Captain Mitchell and FBI agent Sykes Houston, then headed for Horseshoe Bay.[17]

At the Whitehead residence, Waldrip drew from the distraught parents the details of the kidnapper's telephone call. Whitehead said he had received a call from the abductor in which he declared, "Listen to me. If you don't want the same thing to happen to your daughter that happened to your maid, you had better listen to me. Here are the rules. Number one, no cops. Number two, I want $30,000 in $20 bills. Number three, don't let your little boy go to school." Before hanging up, he added, "I made hamburger out of your maid, and I'll make hamburger out of your little girl. . . . You have twenty-four hours to get the money together or I'll kill your daughter."

By 6:30 AM Waldrip had brought FBI agent Houston to the Whitehead house for a briefing. They then drove to Marble Falls. As Whitehead gathered the money, Waldrip went to the police department command post. He found Captain Mitchell already there, with Rangers brought in from Waco and scattered stations: Sergeant Joe Wilie and Rangers Stan Guffey, John Aycock, Joe Davis, Jim Miller, and Fred Cummings. More FBI agents had also showed up, along with most of the city police force.

The officers plotted strategy. Whitehead insisted on driving the drop car, but consented to a bold plan in which Rangers would conceal themselves in the car. Whitehead's Porsche appeared too small, so Ranger Fred Cummings arranged with the district attorney to lend his 1987 Lincoln Town Car for the mission. Stan Guffey and John Aycock drew this delicate task. With Bill Whitehead at the wheel and the two Rangers hidden, they returned to the residence and put the Continental into the garage. FBI agent Houston had already slipped in. From Mrs. Whitehead they learned that the kidnapper had called at 2:20 PM and hung up when told that Whitehead was in Marble Falls getting the money. An FBI tracking device, however, identified the caller's telephone number and traced it to the vacant house across the street.

At 9:30 PM Whitehead received his instructions: within one minute position the drop car in the driveway across the street facing the garage, place the ransom on the front seat, leave the engine running, the driver's door open, the lights on, and run back home at once. Kara-Leigh would be left in the front yard as the culprit left. Otherwise, in one minute and forty-five seconds she would be dead.

All afternoon and evening the FBI's Houston and the Rangers had worked to keep an agitated Whitehead calm. Now they had to stop him from a panicky run to the garage. Guffey and Aycock quickly took position in the car. The backseat cushions had been removed, and the men lay side by side on the floorboards, Guffey's head behind the driver's seat, Aycock's behind the passenger seat and his body at the back of the compartment. At their direction, Whitehead placed the briefcase containing the money on the passenger floor rather than the front seat. The Rangers shut down the interior lights and covered themselves with a blanket. Whitehead drove the auto across the street, parked in front of the garage, and immediately departed.

In less than a minute, the Rangers heard footsteps. They felt something placed on the driver's seat and a voice say "Move over, baby." The following movement alerted them that Kara-Leigh sat in the passenger seat. The voice then entered the car, picked up the briefcase, and thrust it between the front seats to what he thought was the back seat. It came down on Aycock's stomach. Shouting "Police!" the two lawmen rose. "Oh, God damn," was the answer. As the suspect tried to back out of the Lincoln, he twice fired a .44-caliber Magnum through the rear side window. Guffey fired back twice, even as one bullet hit him in the head, the other in the neck. At the same time Aycock fired four rounds through the front window and windshield. He then reached into the front seat and dragged Kara-Leigh into the back. Seeing his target stumbling toward the garage, pistol still in hand, Aycock continued to fire until the kidnapper fell dead, six bullets in his body.

FBI, Rangers, and police converged on the scene. Guffey was bundled into an FBI auto and raced to the Marble Falls hospital, where he was pronounced dead.

A driver's license identified the kidnapper as Brent Albert Beeler, twenty-three, a criminal with a record of forgery, fraud, and drug offenses. He was also wanted for parole violation. A search of the house from which he emerged disclosed nothing, but in a boathouse in the rear lay the bound body of Denise Johnson, apparently suffocated by duct tape applied to her mouth and nose. Beeler had seized her to obtain the keys to the Whitehead's residence and the unlisted telephone number. A search of other vacant houses revealed one in which Beeler had stayed during the week between Johnson's abduction and the kidnapping of Kara-Leigh Whitehead.

Once again the Rangers had freed a kidnapped victim held for ransom. The case of Kara-Leigh, however, scarcely represented the triumph of Amy McNiel. The first Ranger since 1978 to die in the line of duty, Stan Guffey left a wife and four children. At forty, a nineteen-year veteran of DPS, eight as a Ranger, he was esteemed by his colleagues and fellow citizens as a strong, quiet, cheerful, friendly man. Funeral services in Brady, his home station, drew law officers from all over Texas. The Texas legislature passed a concurrent resolution paying tribute to a man mourned by all DPS. Stan Guffey's death marked as low a point in recent Ranger history as Amy McNiel had marked a high point.[18]

"I'LL TELL YOU. I've been to two county fairs and a hog-calling, and I've never seen anything like this." So declared Ranger Phil Ryan of his three-month ordeal in a Montague County jail. A member of Lubbock-based Company C, he worked out of Decatur covering four North Texas counties bordering Oklahoma. He had aided Montague County sheriff W. F. Conway in identifying and arresting the killer of two women—Henry Lee Lucas. At Lucas's arraignment on June 11, 1983, he blurted out that he had killed at least one hundred others in many states since he had killed his mother in 1960. He had done time in and out of prison and mental institutions, and had been on the loose since his release from a Michigan prison in 1975.

As the number escalated to 150, Ryan repeatedly interviewed Lucas. "The first night to sit there and listen to someone talk in detail about all those murders. . . . We went until 4 in the morning. . . . In one night he goes through forty murders, what they (the victims) said, what he said, where he stabbed them, how he stabbed them. . . . It can't help but affect you if you value human life."

As Ryan later observed, the mounting number of confessions produced "just this feeding frenzy on the part of law enforcement—and the media. Henry is a bigger liar than he is a murderer. I believe that he killed his momma. And I know personally that he killed Kate Rich and Becky Powell," the cases Ryan had worked. Beyond that, "I wouldn't bet my paycheck on anything that Henry said that's uncorroborated."[19]

As Ryan noted, Lucas's confessions, in gory detail, set off a furor in the press and police agencies throughout the nation, most of which had unsolved homicides on their books. In October 1983 Ryan met with more than eighty officers from twenty states who gathered for three days in Monroe, Louisiana, to compare notes and wonder how many cases Lucas's confessions would clear. They recognized him as a monumental liar, but concluded that he and his traveling companion, Ottis E. Toole, might be linked to as many as ninety-seven killings in thirteen states. Already, they viewed twenty-eight as confirmed, including nineteen that had produced warrants or indictments based on his confessions.[20]

For the first time in his sordid life, this scruffy little man with an eyelid that drooped over an ill-fitting glass eye had everyone's attention. He became the star of a two-year saga. He reveled in telling of his childhood in a dilapidated mountain cabin in western Virginia, one of two sons of a drunken, sadistic, vicious prostitute who had married a legless man who stayed drunk on moonshine most of the time. Henry told of brutal beatings for little offense or none at all. He told of being routinely forced to watch his mother ply her trade. And he told of killing his aging mother in Michigan in 1960 in what may have been an accidental slip of his knife as they fought each other over Henry's decision to strike out on his own. He told of linking up in Florida with big, dumb Ottis E. Toole, another loser whose sexual obsessions equaled Henry's but focused on men instead of women. And Lucas recounted seemingly aimless drives around the nation pursuing their obsessions, which featured murder, sex with corpses, dismemberment, and other horrors that tormented Ranger Ryan as he listened.

In Montague County, Lucas had finally led officers to the ashes that had once been Kate Rich, an eighty-year-old widow who had taken him in, and in Denton County to the scattered parts of Becky Powell, his fifteen-year-old "wife," also the niece of Ottis Toole. In September 1983 Lucas pleaded guilty in Montague County to killing Kate Rich, and in November a Denton County jury convicted him of killing Becky Powell. For the first, Lucas drew a sentence of seventy-five years and for the second, a sentence of life imprisonment.

A close friend of Sheriff Conway's also had an interest in Lucas. As early as August 1980 Williamson County sheriff Jim Boutwell had noted the accumulation of unsolved murders of young women along Interstate 35 in his and the string of counties to the north and south. He had persuaded DPS to host a symposium of law officers with such unsolved cases to compare notes and plot strategy. He was especially concerned over such a killing discovered the day after Halloween 1979. In a ditch next to I-35 north of Georgetown, a motorist had spotted the strangled body of a young woman clad only in a pair of orange socks. In public and law enforcement circles, she took the name "Orange Socks."[21]

While Lucas awaited trial in the Rich and Powell murders, Boutwell drove to Montague County and interviewed him. He readily confessed to the murder of Orange Socks. As soon as the Becky Powell trial in Denton ended in November 1983, Boutwell loaded Lucas into his patrol car and drove down I-35 to Georgetown, where District Attorney Ed Walsh intended to seek the death penalty in the slaying of Orange Socks.[22]

For more than a year, Ranger Phil Ryan had functioned as a one-man task force, grilling Lucas and recording his confessions. It was too much for one lawman. Texas needed a task force simply to manage the influx of press and lawmen who wanted to talk with Lucas. Sheriff Jim Boutwell proposed such a task force, and Colonel Jim Adams authorized it. Sergeant Bob Prince of Waco's Company F headed the group, which also included Boutwell and Ranger Clayton Smith. They established headquarters at the Williamson County jail in Georgetown, where Lucas was confined awaiting his trial for killing Orange Socks.

Prince and his colleagues acted mainly as gatekeepers, scheduling interviews, warning all investigators to accept nothing Lucas said that they could not corroborate, occasionally traveling with Lucas and investigators from all over the nation as well as Texas, ensuring that all interviews were videotaped, especially those in which Lucas led officers to locations where he claimed he had killed someone. Many of his confessions betrayed knowledge only the killer could have known, and many of his travels led directly to the murder site. As often, his confessions were quickly identified as bogus. To complicate the task further, he changed his stories, sometimes radically.[23]

A turning point came early in March 1984 when, on a change of venue to San Angelo, District Attorney Ed Walsh prosecuted Lucas on a capital murder charge of killing Orange Socks. The case rested almost entirely on the confession, which defense attorneys charged had been guided by Sheriff Boutwell's coaching. The defense also produced work sheets that recorded Lucas as employed as a roofer in Jacksonville, Florida, on October 31, 1979, and to have cashed a paycheck there on November 2. The prosecution countered by exposing a kickback scheme by which the timekeeper recorded work not performed. Also alleged was that Lucas could have driven the 2,400 miles to Florida, as he often did, in less than two days. Despite the weaknesses in both prosecution and defense, Walsh persuaded the jury to give Lucas the death penalty.[24]

Again the influx of lawmen descended on Georgetown to interview Henry Lucas. Colonel Adams and his associates at DPS began to worry about how much time and how many resources the Lucas investigation consumed. When would it end?[25]

Already the media had begun to question the validity of the task force's work, as in a September 1984 article in *Texas Monthly*. But the most painful blow hit in April 1985, when the *Dallas Times-Herald* ran a series of investigative reports comparing the sites of all Lucas confessions with his locations at the time. Labeling the rush to clear cases based on Lucas confessions a "massive hoax," the reporters accused Prince and other Texas Rangers around the state of helping Lucas to perfect his confessions and made much of the conviction of Lucas based solely on his confession. To make matters worse, Lucas began changing his story again, now denying that he killed anyone except his mother in 1960 and ridiculing the Rangers for believing stories he had concocted to expose their incompetence.[26]

On the heels of adverse press coverage, Sergeant Prince and his associates became mired in that nightmare of all Rangers: politics. Hardly a week after the *Times-Herald* exposé, McLennan County district attorney Vic Feazell persuaded a judge to subpoena Lucas for grand jury hearings in Waco. For almost three months he paraded Lucas before the jurors with his new story of fabricating confessions, and in July the grand jury disbanded without any indictments. Feazell had gained valuable publicity for his contemplated run for attorney general, a race ironically that might pit him against Ed Walsh, Lucas's prosecutor in the Orange Socks case. While he had Lucas in Waco, Feazell lost no chance to scoff at the Texas Rangers.

Sitting in on Feazell's grand jury proceedings was Texas attorney general Jim Mattox, no friend of the Rangers. In the wake of the *Dallas Times-Herald* articles, Mattox had set his staff to work probing the Rangers' handling of Lucas. Mattox enjoyed the publicity as much as Feazell because he had his eye set on the governor's office. The staff met with the Public Safety Commission in January 1986 to give assurances that their work had developed nothing to indicate the Rangers had done anything "illegal." This was the careful phrasing of the final report, issued on May 7, 1986, which characterized the Lucas affair as a "massive hoax" but carefully refrained from criticizing the Rangers except by implication. After the Orange Socks trial, however, Mattox had already revealed his opinion by declaring Prosecutor Walsh and the Rangers as part of the Lucas "charade" and "road show."[27]

Many throughout Texas were less skeptical of the "road show." However many false confessions Lucas signed, plenty proved valid. The weakness of the Orange Socks case raised the possibility that Lucas might get off Death Row, an unacceptable outcome for one who had plainly committed so much slaughter. One who sought another capital conviction was El Paso County's assistant district attorney Bill Moody. Interviews with Lucas in 1984 had made him a prime suspect in the May 1983 axe killing of Librada Apodaca, seventy-two, an El Paso widow. In fact, further investigation turned up the case against Lucas as the strongest in his long line of confessions. His confession was detailed, and he led El Paso officers and Ranger Clayton Smith directly to Mrs. Apodaca's residence, described the crime scene and the murder in terms that only the murderer could know, and told of the items he had stolen and how he had sold them to waitresses at a truck stop east of El Paso. Investigators succeeded in finding the two waitresses, who remembered Lucas and the items he had sold them, which family members identified as having belonged to Mrs. Apodaca. Here was the first case in which independent evidence solidly buttressed the details of the confession.

District judge Brunson Moore happened to be a close friend of Attorney General Mattox. Moreover, he shrank from subjecting the county to the expense and effort of trying a man already in prison for life. "I think we're all a little tired of it," he said from the bench on December 19, 1986, as he accepted a defense motion to exclude the confession from evidence. That left prosecutors no option but to drop the charges.[28]

The Rangers had not been buffeted by negative publicity so intense since the years after the Lower Valley farm strike of 1966–67. Bob Prince in particular felt acute pain at the assaults on his integrity and professionalism. Perhaps easing the pain somewhat, Mattox did not become governor, and neither Feazell nor Walsh became attorney general. In fact, the U.S. attorney conducted an investigation of Feazell for accepting bribes from defense lawyers. Although acquitted by a federal jury, the grievance committee of the state bar sanctioned him, and in January 1988 he agreed to a two-year probationary suspension of his law license. Four months later, in April 1988, the Texas Commission on Judicial Conduct reprimanded Judge Moore for judicial misconduct in his courtroom and in the political arena.[29]

Although the cloud of suspicion hung over Bob Prince and Clayton Smith for years, they deserved none of the opprobrium. They simply got caught up in the media feeding on a serial killer who indeed killed many—no one will ever know how many—but emitted so many false confessions and changes in his story that he did perpetrate a "massive hoax." Investigators from all over the nation rushed to clear unsolved cases, many failing to heed the warnings of Prince and Smith. No credible evidence survives to convict either of slipping from the most rigid professionalism in the handling of an impossible mission.[30]

Those who worried that the flaws in the Orange Socks conviction might one day liberate Lucas from Death Row had good reason for concern. And again politics dropped into the equation. In June 1998 former attorney general Mattox, running for his old job against incumbent Dan Morales, revived the case and had it refought in the press. Morales admitted that it was "not impossible but highly improbable" that Lucas killed Orange Socks. Himself running for reelection, Governor George W. Bush conceded his own doubts about Lucas's guilt and asked the Texas Board of Pardons and Paroles to review the case. In a conspicuously uncharacteristic action, the board recommended clemency, and no less uncharacteristically Governor Bush commuted the death sentence.

And so Henry Lee Lucas, undoubtedly a serial killer who ripped apart, burned, and raped dozens if not hundreds of victims, at last escaped from Death Row. On March 12, 2001, he died of a heart attack at the Ellis prison unit near Huntsville. He was sixty-four.[31]

SENIOR CAPTAIN W. D. Wilson, plagued by cancer in his final three years, retired on January 1, 1985. He died on January 1, 1990.[32]

Wilson's assistant, Captain H. R. "Lefty" Block, replaced Bill Wilson as senior captain on February 1, 1985, and the same day Company E captain Maurice Cook took Block's position as assistant supervisor of the Rangers. Described as a tall, stately man with thinning hair, Block yearned for the old days while recognizing the new. "Back then," he said, "you didn't have to do two days of paper work to seize evidence. We're often frustrated, because one technical error can cost us a whole case." But, he added, "These days, we portray a professional image. We don't play games and tricks any more. We're there to get the job done. I felt the manner in which some cases in South Texas, such as the farmworker strikes, were handled in the '60s and '70s, cost us a lot of respect. In recent history, we've handled similar situations and managed to keep the peace without losing face."[33]

Rangers did not accord Lefty Block the respect and admiration Bill Wilson had enjoyed, probably chiefly because he was not Bill Wilson. Moreover, he had cool relations with some of his captains. But he served without serious misstep for seven years. The same could not be said of his successor.

[18]

Highs and Lows, 1990s

IN JUNE 1992 Maurice Cook replaced Lefty Block as senior captain. By September 1993 he headed a Texas Ranger force no longer subordinate to the criminal law enforcement division but a full division in its own right. As the division chief, Cook had no supervisor between him and the DPS top command.

This move had occurred by legislative action earlier in 1993 and was attributed by many to Cook's ties to state legislators, which rivaled those of Clint Peoples twenty years earlier. That some veteran captains openly favored the move doubtless also had an effect. The separation created bitter feeling in DPS and resentment of Cook's political maneuvering. "He wanted his own little empire, and that's what he got," said one retired Ranger.

Even so, the Rangers themselves welcomed the move. Not only did they intensely dislike the criminal law enforcement chief, but they reveled in the greater independence it afforded. They also welcomed a change put into effect in 1989: all Rangers started as sergeants rather than privates, and all sergeants now bore the rank of lieutenant.

Company C captain Bruce Casteel moved from Lubbock to become Cook's assistant and heir apparent.

Cook evoked the frontier image of the Rangers with cowboy boots and western-cut suits and was fated to have a stormy tenure, not only because of the political intrigues that Rangers abhorred but also because of his tyrannical style. His clerical staff related harrowing tales of abusive actions and hair-trigger temper. Most Rangers despised him, although he retained some supporters. As Joaquin Jackson declared after his retirement: "I don't have any respect for Cook . . . or any of the little group around him who think he's God. There's not many, just a handful."

Cook's relations with his assistant, Bruce Casteel, grew increasingly frigid. Another retired Ranger, an admirer of Casteel, observed that the two captains "differ over quite a lot of things, mainly philosophy. Casteel is 'us' oriented. Cook is 'me' oriented."

The two ranking captains, Bob Mitchell and Jack Dean, chose to retire as Cook ascended, Mitchell in June 1992 and Dean in September 1993. Either would have performed exceptionally well as Ranger chief. Dean gained appointment as U.S. marshal for the Western District of Texas. Bob Prince, formerly Mitchell's sergeant but since 1986 captain of Company A in Houston, moved to Waco to replace Mitchell. C. J. Havrda, another rising star, succeeded Dean in San Antonio.[1]

BY FEBRUARY 1993 Bob Prince, captain of Waco-based Company F, knew of the eight-month investigation the federal Bureau of Alcohol, Tobacco, Firearms and Explosives (ATF) had been conducting of a religious sect called Branch Davidians, more than a hundred men, women, and children based in a sprawling two-story building at Mount Carmel, ten miles east of Waco. The leader, David Koresh, ruled his flock with an iron hand, proclaimed himself Jesus Christ, and vowed to fulfill biblical prophecies by bringing on Armageddon.

ATF's involvement can be explained chiefly by Davidian apostates in the United States and Australia who in 1989 had broken with Koresh, and through books, articles, and television sought to portray the sect as

Architects of the Department of Public Safety. Dallas lawyer Albert Sidney Johnson (*top left*) headed the group that crafted the authorizing legislation, then served as the first chairman of the Public Safety Commission. Louis G. Phares (*right*), chief of the highway patrol, performed ably as acting director and director until ousted politically. Colonel Horace H. Carmichael, named director in 1936 after the dismissal of Chief Phares, quieted Ranger disaffection by appointing himself senior Ranger captain and decreeing that all Ranger captains report directly to him. A heart attack ended his tenure after only two years, in 1938. *Texas State Library and Archives (Johnson)* and *Texas Ranger Hall of Fame and Museum.*

The men who turned the Rangers from Old West lawmen into professional crime-fighters: Horace Carmichael (*left*) and Homer Garrison. They pose here with their vehicles in 1938 in front of temporary headquarters at the National Guard's Camp Mabry near Austin. *Texas State Library and Archives.*

Although usually seated behind his desk clad in a business suit, Colonel Homer Garrison often donned western police attire. He served as director of the Department of Public Safety for thirty years, 1938–68. Continuing Carmichael's practice of having Ranger captains report directly to him, he built a professional force of crime fighters who achieved elite status both in Texas and the nation. All Rangers adored him. *Texas State Library and Archives.*

Rangers Hardy Purvis Jr. (*left*) and Clint Peoples check cattle near Kerrville, 1949. *Texas State Library and Archives.*

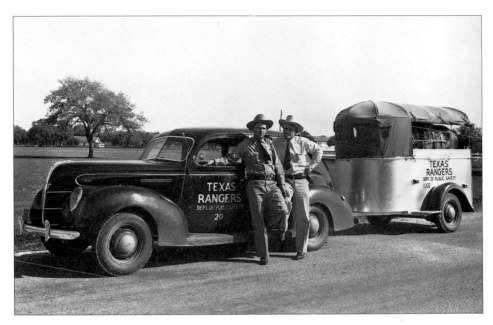

Horses still proved essential in many parts of Texas, but they could now be more quickly transported to rough country. Rangers A. Y. Allee and Ab Riggs stand beside their horse trailer in 1939. Horses proved indispensable in the mountainous Big Bend, here patrolled by two Rangers in 1940. *Texas State Library and Archives.*

Captain Bob Crowder (*in car*) and Sergeant Jay Banks of Dallas-based Company B use primitive communications gear to set up a roadblock, 1951. Note shotgun and sub-machine gun. *Texas Rangers Hall of Fame and Museum.*

Rangers sometimes borrowed armored vehicles from the army but in the 1950s purchased one of their own. DPS Director Homer Garrison (*left*) and Assistant Director Joe Fletcher (*right*) inspect the new weapon. *Texas State Library and Archives.*

After World War II, aircraft aided Rangers in surveillance, transportation, and other tasks. Assistant DPS director Joe Fletcher is on wing, Ranger Doyle Currington standing, 1949. The "Texas Ranger" was the first of an expanding air force. Road blocks and pursuits proved more effective when autos worked with aircraft, 1950s. *Texas State Library and Archives* (above); *Texas Ranger Hall of Fame and Museum* (below).

Prefiguring the Little Rock High School integration crisis of 1957, the Mansfield, Texas, crisis of September 1956 ended when black youth failed to appear for registration. Here Company B sergeant E. J. Banks chats with students. Note effigy of black person hanging over school door. *Texas State Library and Archives.*

In 1957 in Fort Worth, Ranger captain Jay Banks led state and local officers in a wild pursuit of gangsters Gene Paul Norris and William Carl Humphrey. The chase ended with the death of both. Norris's covered body can be seen on the creek bank as officers gather to remove it. Banks, Sheriff Harlon Wright, and Ranger Jim Ray inspect Norris's souped-up green Chevrolet in the ditch where it slid from a slick road and set off a gun battle. *Robert Nieman.*

Clint Peoples boasted a distinguished career in the Rangers, ending with senior captain 1969–73. A mountainous ego alienated many, and his political connections worried others. As evidence of fraudulent dealings with Hollywood producers mounted, he retired and used his connections to gain appointment as a U.S. marshal. *Texas State Library and Archives.*

A. Y. Allee had a longtime reputation as a tough but fair Ranger who did not shrink from strong-arm tactics and enjoyed the respect of his men. As captain of Company D, he figured in the farm workers strike in the Lower Rio Grande Valley in 1966–67 and became the personification of a Ranger force critics believed had outlived its time. *Texas State Library and Archives.*

In 1969 students at Wiley College in Marshall, like students at campuses across the nation, rioted to force changes. The college president asked for Rangers. Robert Nieman titled this photo "A Solution Waiting for a Problem." The problem failed to materialize. *Left to right:* Company B's G. W. Burks, Charley Moore, Glenn Elliott, Sergeant Lester Robertson, Bob Mitchell. *Robert Nieman.*

On the eastern edge of Fort Worth on October 14, 1971, Ranger Tom Arnold joined with local police to box hostage-taker Huron Ted Walters on a bridge. Walters sat in the back seat and held a shotgun to the head of Hoyt Houston, whose wife and daughter sat next to him in the front seat. In this picture, the Houston vehicle is in center, on bridge, Arnold's behind it. Arnold rested a sniper rifle on the open door of his car and waited until Walters momentarily shifted his shotgun from Houston's head, then fired. The bullet smashed Walters's head and face and freed the Houstons. *Texas State Library and Archives.*

Jack Dean performed distinguished service in the Lower Valley before appointed captain of Company D in San Antonio in 1978. He played a critical role in identifying the hit man who killed federal judge John Wood in 1979. The FBI never disclosed Dean's role but took full credit. Dean retired in 1993 to become a U.S. marshal. *Robert Nieman.*

Glenn Elliott, "The Ranger's Ranger," served northeastern Texas faithfully and effectively from 1961 to 1987. *Dan Winters Photography.*

In January 1985 kidnappers seized Amy McNiel, daughter of an Alvarado banker, and held her for ransom. After a wild chase through Dallas, Longview, and Mount Pleasant by Ranger and FBI units, aided by a DPS aircraft and two FBI helicopters, the Rangers cornered the kidnappers in Mount Vernon. After an exchange of gunfire, two of the five kidnappers were wounded and Amy was freed unharmed. Here the handcuffed fugitives are laid out by officers. *Left to right*: Rangers Brantley Foster and Jack Morton, unidentified, Captain Bob Mitchell, Ranger Bill Gunn. *Texas Ranger Hall of Fame and Museum.*

The standoff between Rangers and the Republic of Texas militia in the Davis Mountains of West Texas commanded national attention for a week in 1997. When ROT "ambassador" Richard McLaren finally surrendered, he insisted on shaking hands with Ranger captain Barry Caver, even though handcuffed. After the siege, Company E posed with the ROT flag. Captain Caver (hatless) holds upper left corner.
Captain Barry Caver.

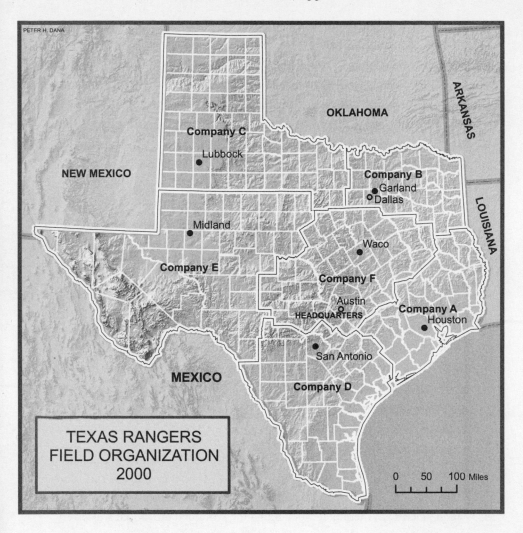

PETER H. DANA

OKLAHOMA

ARKANSAS

NEW MEXICO

Company C

Lubbock

Company B

Garland
Dallas

Midland

Waco

Company E

Company F

Austin
HEADQUARTERS

Company A

Houston

San Antonio

LOUISIANA

MEXICO

Company D

**TEXAS RANGERS
FIELD ORGANIZATION
2000**

0   50   100 Miles

a "cult" and Koresh as the "cult leader." They told lurid tales of brain-washing, rampant corporal and sexual abuse of children, polygamy, drug offenses, and a huge arsenal of weaponry. In June 1992 the *Waco Tribune-Herald* began work on a series relying uncritically on the charges of the apostates. In the same month ATF, with the encouragement of the U.S. attorney's office in Waco, began its investigation.

Koresh almost certainly possessed illegal weapons, the valid grounds for ATF inquiry; but beyond the reports of apostates, agents could not specify how many and what kind or explain why Mount Carmel differed from the scores of gun shows that occurred every weekend throughout Texas. Apparently also, ATF feared absorption into the FBI and wanted to stage a spectacular success—which agents dubbed "dynamic entry" and "Showtime"—before congressional appropriation hearings scheduled for March 10, 1993.

From the beginning, Koresh knew of the investigation. He even invited officers to come talk with him and inspect the compound, but they refused. Instead, in November 1992, they persuaded a magistrate to issue search and arrest warrants. These were "knock only" warrants (i.e., talk before shoot), but in the next seven weeks, at nearby Fort Hood, ATF assault teams, eighty officers in three groups, rehearsed an attack on the compound.[2]

On February 27, 1993, the *Tribune-Herald* published the first of a seven-part series portraying the Davidians as the apostates described them. Fearing that publicity would cause Koresh to prepare for battle, ATF fixed the raid for the next morning, February 28. Learning of the plan, Captain Bob Prince called the ATF commander and asked if Ranger assistance was needed.

> I was told that no, they wanted it to be an all-Federal operation. Thank the Lord. The next morning of course they went in, they did the raid, and of course things went sour on them. I was notified and went out there, and when I got there they were taking the wounded out, and it was a very emotional, traumatic scene. They had been kicked and beaten pretty badly. They had pulled out and kind of in chaos and really didn't know what to do yet.[3]

The raid had in fact been botched. The ATF agents stormed the compound, both on the ground floor and the roof. The Davidians defended themselves vigorously, so vigorously that the ATF withdrew. Prince arrived during a truce arranged with Koresh to bring out the dead and wounded agents. Four had been killed, twenty wounded. Inside, at least six Davidians had been killed and an unknown number wounded.

Four federal officers had been killed, making four homicides in violation of federal as well as state law. The federal agents still had a standoff to handle, but they also wanted the Davidians prosecuted for murder. At the instigation of Assistant U.S. Attorney William Johnston in Waco, therefore, ATF, which had ignored the Rangers from the beginning, now asked Captain Prince to take responsibility for the homicide investigation.

As Prince recalled, the ATF and FBI leaders came to his office and insisted. Prince declined, but the ATF's leader asked who was DPS director. Colonel James Wilson, Prince replied. "Can you get him for me?" Prince rang him on his cell phone. The ATF agent took the phone into the next room, then returned and said, "Colonel Wilson would like to speak to you." Prince took the phone. "Captain Prince, bring in whatever manpower you need to, the Rangers will conduct all of it." "Yes, sir," replied Prince.[4]

Some thirty-five Rangers, one-third of the force, converged on Waco. Because their evidence would be presented in federal court, they were sworn in as deputy U.S. marshals. At once they began interviewing Davidians who had left or escaped from the compound, as well as the ATF agents who had commanded and participated in the raid.

Bob Prince did not supervise the investigation for long. Senior Captain Cook, perhaps fearing Prince too tainted by the Lucas task force, assigned B Company captain David Byrnes to take charge of the investigation. Prince retained Company F until his retirement in September 1993.

For fifty-one days after the failed ATF raid, the FBI managed the standoff. FBI spokesmen conducted daily press briefings in Waco and appeared nightly on television. Because most Americans were appalled by the narrative of Davidian customs constructed by the ATF and FBI based on apostate Davidian propaganda, because they wanted to think well of the FBI, and because the press meekly accepted the FBI version of events, public sentiment overwhelmingly favored the government as against the Davidians.

Throughout March and into April the FBI negotiators sparred with Koresh by telephone, seeking his surrender with all his followers to stand trial for murder and for the alleged firearms offenses. The FBI conducted a strategy of verbal intimidation and physical harassment they called "psywar," psychological warfare. They installed loudspeakers that for six weeks, night and day, blasted the sounds of sirens, crying babies, crowing roosters, rock-and-roll music, Christmas carols, Buddhist chants, the rumblings of railroad trains, and other singular noises. They surrounded the compound with stadium lights that kept it brightly illumined all night. They interrupted electricity and finally cut it off altogether, which also stilled water pumps. Tanks and other military vehicles borrowed from the army at Fort Hood but driven by FBI agents prowled the battlesite, knocking over outlying buildings and crushing parked vehicles.

The tank treads destroyed evidence that Captain Byrnes's Rangers would have found helpful in piecing together what happened on February 28. Although they kept at their task, they often ran afoul of the same FBI intransigence that confounded the news media. As Captain Brynes recalled, if he had to summarize the FBI in two words, "I would say uncooperative and unprofessional."[5]

The negotiations took on a bizarre aspect. Each side spoke a language incomprehensible to the other. The FBI demanded surrender in menacing terms that meant nothing to David Koresh. In turn he spoke completely in Davidian theological concepts, the "Bible Babble" that FBI negotiators could not understand and refused to acknowledge. They brushed aside the advice of specialists in nontraditional religious groups and pushed forward with threat and intimidation that fit into none of Koresh's scriptural formulations.

As the impasse extended into April, the FBI grew embarrassed over the failure to end the siege peacefully. They covered their unease by raising the specter of children abused by Koresh and living in squalid conditions caused by diminishing water supplies. Jonestown was evoked to imply the possibility of mass suicide. Persuaded (again by apostates) that Koresh would never surrender, the FBI drew up plans for driving out the inhabitants by tear gas and, failing that, battering down the walls with army tanks. Newly appointed attorney general Janet Reno resisted a violent solution. Her worries focused on the children, and only when assured that tear gas would cause them no permanent injury did she relent and approve the scheme.

The assault began early on April 19 as combat engineering vehicles (CEVs), tanks modified for demolition by removing the cannon-firing mechanism but leaving the barrels as battering rams, began smashing holes in the walls and releasing tear gas through nozzled hoses bound beneath the demolition barrels. The fine print in the plan Reno approved specified that if any of these vehicles were fired on, then the four borrowed Bradley armored vehicles would join the fray by firing tear gas into all the windows. The CEVs took fire almost immediately, so the Bradleys rushed in. They had no snouts to support tubes and nozzles for spraying gas and had to launch so-called ferret rounds through a front port. These missiles, the size of a football, contained not only the gas but a chemical mix. At least twice in recent FBI history, ferret rounds set off in a closed space had ignited a sudden devastating fire.

The Bradleys had exhausted their four hundred ferrets by 11:40 AM. Twenty minutes later the compound erupted in a fire that leveled it within half an hour. Seventy-six men, women, and children perished. Koresh and a score or more of his acolytes died by gunshot wounds, the rest either of smoke inhalation or of concrete walls pushed over on them by CEVs. The Davidians had chosen mass suicide after all, contended the FBI, preferring immolation to surrender.

Even before the flames died out, the FBI turned the charred ruins over to the Texas Rangers. The next day all relations with the press were abruptly shifted to the DPS public information officer, Mike Cox. An ATF flag flew over the mound of ashes.

Captain Byrnes's investigative assignment suddenly doubled. He now had exclusive control of the seventy-seven-acre Davidian compound, littered with the rubble of battle that included potential evidence.

He divided his Rangers into eight teams that segmented the site into numbered grids and inventoried all material found in each. The FBI had not withdrawn altogether. Each of Byrnes's teams included FBI technical experts (not the tactical agents who had conducted the siege and assault) as well as state troopers and a variety of DPS crime-scene specialists.[6]

The results of Captain Byrnes's investigation figured prominently in the government's next move. The U.S. attorney's office in Waco selected eleven survivors of the Mount Carmel fire to try on federal charges of conspiracy to murder federal officers, attempted murder of federal officers, aiding and abetting the murder of federal officers (for those who had fired no weapons), murdering federal officers, and possession of illegal firearms. After a change of venue, the trial opened in San Antonio early in January 1994.

The prosecution's objective was to prove conspiracy by portraying the Davidian theology as binding all the Davidians together in an armed group intent on making war. The charge of murdering federal officers rested on the contention that Koresh ambushed the ATF when their assault teams attacked the compound on February 28.[7]

Prosecutors quizzed 120 witnesses, including some residents of Mount Carmel who agreed to cooperate, while the defense mainly made its case by cross-examination. Texas Rangers took the stand as prosecution witnesses and introduced into evidence many of the interviews conducted after February 28. These were especially helpful in enabling the jury to reconstruct the sequence of battle. But the most telling testimony concerned firearms. Prosecutors stacked boxes of weapons in the courtroom and paraded one after another before the jury. Ranger sergeants George Turner, Ray Coffman, and Ronnie Griffith, among others, took their place on the witness stand.

The Byrnes teams had retrieved three hundred weapons from the ruined compound. FBI weapons expert James Cadigan said that he had examined them all and discovered forty-eight semiautomatics that had been illegally converted to automatic. A Davidian witness told of two .50-caliber rifles used in the battle with the ATF. Neither they nor the automatics seem to have been among the arms placed in evidence because Coffman and other Rangers conceded under cross-examination that none of the weapons shown the jury was illegal and that most of the grenades were empty shells. Coffman added that of 133 firearms found in the "bunker" (actually a tornado shelter under construction), all but twenty-two had been secured on gun racks.

Prosecutors also questioned expert witnesses and introduced evidence designed to show that the Davidians had deliberatcly fired the compound about noon on April 19, thus committing mass suicide and fulfilling the prophesied Armageddon. The FBI explained that listening devices had been planted inside the compound and that the Davidians had been heard splashing fuel and talking of setting it afire. Defense attorneys succeeded in calling much of this evidence into question.

After seven tedious weeks of testimony, the trial drew to a close on February 23, 1994, and Judge Walter Smith instructed the jury. He included two provisions the prosecution had vigorously contested: under certain circumstances the jury could consider self-defense as mitigation and could substitute manslaughter for murder. Although the jury deliberated for four days, almost at once it split nine to three, the majority favoring acquittal on all charges, with three holding out for conviction of conspiracy. The final compromise: all defendants innocent of conspiracy and murder, three innocent of all charges, seven guilty of manslaughter, five of the seven guilty of carrying a firearm during commission of a crime of violence, and two of firearms violations.

The prosecution had failed to convince the jury that the Davidians bore more guilt than the government itself. But in its effort to reach a compromise, the jurors had misunderstood portions of Judge Smith's instructions. At once he ruled that the conviction of the five defendants of carrying a firearm during commission of a crime of violence could not stand unless paired with a conviction of conspiracy, and he voided those five convictions.

Although seemingly another setback for the prosecution, the distressing spectacle had yet to play out. The hard-line prosecutors went to work on the hard-line judge. On June 17, 1994, Judge Smith pronounced sentence on the eight defendants still in custody. In effect, he upended his ruling that voided conviction for carrying a firearm during a crime. By deciding that five men were guilty of that offense, he reasoned, jurors had automatically found them guilty of conspiracy—a charge all twelve jurors had rejected. He sentenced the five to the maximum for forty years and the other three to lesser but still maximum terms. Gratuitously, he added that on February 28 the first shots had come from inside the compound and that on April 19 the Davidians themselves had ignited the fire that leveled the building. Neither of these statements had been proved at trial nor placed before the jury for decision.[8]

The Branch Davidian saga seemed destined never to end. In the highly charged political climate following the Oklahoma City bombing, both the U.S. House and Senate conducted hearings in 1995 and raked over all the old issues and questions, both answered and unanswered. Litigation flourished. And in July 1997 a documentary film highly critical of the government aired on television and won awards.

Against this background, with wrongful-death suits before Judge Smith, the issue of who started the April 19 fire became crucial. And crucial to that question was whether the FBI had used any incendiary devices in the tank and Bradley attack on Mount Carmel. Although the FBI continued to deny firing rounds of any kind other than tear gas, Ranger investigators knew this to be untrue as early as the weeks after the fire. They had discovered 40-millimeter projectiles that FBI agents on the scene admitted had been fired by the FBI. These could have ignited fuel the Davidians used to power their generator or oil lamps used for light, or they could themselves have been incendiary devices. Captain Byrnes's Rangers had stored 24,000 pounds of battlefield debris in a Waco warehouse and carted off to an Austin warehouse items placed in evidence in the 1994 criminal trial against eleven Davidians.

Filmmakers, attorneys, and others seeking evidence wanted to inspect these warehouses, but the Justice Department had instructed the Texas DPS to refer all such applications to Washington. There applicants were told that DPS held custody. The Rangers found themselves in an untenable position, caught between a federal ban on opening the warehouse doors and federal assertions that only the Rangers held the keys. Public Safety Commission chairman James B. Francis, therefore, asked state attorney general John Cornyn to petition Judge Smith to relieve Texas of responsibility for the tons of metal.

Convinced that the Justice Department and FBI could not be trusted and had consistently covered up their true role at Mount Carmel, Judge Smith responded by ordering all the material in Austin hauled to Waco, consolidated with the rest, and placed under his direct jurisdiction. Anticipating such a move, in September 1999 the Rangers inventoried the contents of the two warehouses. The inventory revealed not only the 40-millimeter shell casings used to knock down doors and the 40-millimeter ferret rounds of tear gas fired from the Bradleys, but also a star parachute flare. All contained combustible potential.[9]

At the same time, on September 9, 1999, rather than entrust further investigation to the FBI, Attorney General Janet Reno asked former senator John C. Danforth to serve as special counsel and lead an exhaustive inquiry that would set the roiling contention to rest. The two specifically excluded the issues of whether the ATF should have conducted the raid of February 28 and whether the FBI should have launched the gas-insertion attack of April 19. Rather, in carrying out these actions, had government agents "committed bad acts"?

Employing seventy-four staff personnel, interviewing a thousand witnesses, reviewing 2.3 million pages of documents, and examining thousands of pounds of battlefield debris, Danforth's team concluded its assignment in fourteen months. Throughout, Texas Rangers aided staff investigators, especially in the matter of incendiary devices.

On November 8, 2000, Danforth submitted his thick report with multiple appendices to Attorney General Reno. In sum, his conclusions absolved the government of all blame and threw it all on David Koresh. When the FBI attacked on April 19, the Davidians fired on agents trying to insert tear gas into the complex. Although the FBI fired three pyrotechnic tear gas rounds, they did not cause the fire. The Davidians themselves spread fuel throughout the main structure, ignited it in three places, and immolated all not killed by their own gunfire. The FBI did not cause the fire.[10]

Voluminous though it was, the Danforth report did not settle the basic questions of whether the ATF raid should have been carried out at all or whether the FBI had properly handled the fifty-one-day standoff and its fiery conclusion. It also left some experts dubious of the origins of the fire of April 19. Nonetheless, the Danforth report stood as the final official conclusion to the long, tragic, tangled chronology that began when the ATF initiated its investigation of the Davidians in June 1992.

The Texas Rangers had figured significantly in the Davidian controversy, beginning with the appointment of Captain David Byrnes to head the Ranger investigation of the ATF raid. Rangers had served as witnesses and submitted documentary evidence to the courts as they dealt with the litigious aftermath. And they had conducted themselves professionally in the sparring over the warehouses containing the tons of rubble collected from the battlesite by Captain Byrnes's teams. Of all the participants in the extended drama, the Texas Rangers emerged with the cleanest record. Captain Byrnes pronounced their work the most important investigation the Rangers had conducted in half a century.[11]

"I THINK THAT we recognize that law enforcement can't be effective unless it's representative of the society it's serving," Colonel Jim Adams answered a newsman in March 1980, shortly after becoming DPS director. "We can recruit applicants today but we do have trouble recruiting blacks, we have trouble recruiting women. We have only seventeen female troopers at the present time. We promote through the ranks so before we get a Ranger that's a female, we have to recruit more female troopers." Some day, he thought, DPS commissioned ranks would represent the public they served.[12]

The recruitment problems were real enough. Not many women aspired to a trooper's uniform, still less a Ranger commission, and black troopers sensed little welcome in the Ranger ranks. The movement to abolish the Rangers in the wake of the 1966–67 farm strike had exposed the absence of Hispanic Rangers, a deficiency the Rangers moved quickly to remedy. During the 1970s Arturo and Rudolfo Rodriguez and Ray Martínez performed well in Latino South Texas. During the 1980s the NAACP held the Rangers up to scorn for a similar absence of blacks. The failure of a highly qualified black trooper, Michael Scott, to breach the white wall stirred enough bad publicity to take him out of the running but smoothed the way for the appointment, in July 1988, of the first black Ranger, Le Roy Young.[13]

Despite Colonel Adams's optimism, women were another matter altogether. Even as the pressures built, few if any Rangers could visualize admitting women to the Ranger ranks. They could not qualify physically; they could not pass the tests; they could not perform punishing tasks in swamps, deserts, and mountains; they could not share the values and traditions of a masculine "band of brothers"; and they just did not belong in a corps composed of tall, muscular white men with a scattering of Latinos and blacks.

Then in 1993 Ann Richards became governor of Texas. Rangers feared the worst. Although she stoutly denied exerting pressure, Colonel James Wilson and all other agency heads had no doubt of her wishes.[14]

But the critical pressures seem not to have come so much from the governor's office as the legislature. Three new members of the House Appropriations Committee took on the issue. Mario Gallegos, Pete Gallego, and Karyne Conley called Colonel Wilson and Senior Captain Cook to the capitol. "We raked them over the coals," said Gallegos. "The low numbers of minorities just stuck out like a sore thumb." If the DPS and the Rangers expected to get through the 1993 legislative session without severe funding cuts, they would have to act boldly. "You hate to write policy through appropriations," explained Conley, "but that's the only way you get people's attention. The Rangers are the last bastion of the good-old-boy system. We sent them a message that their ranks would have to be reflective of the state as a whole."[15]

On August 1, 1993, newspapers reported that nine new Rangers would be commissioned in September: two white men, three Hispanics, one black, an Asian American, and two women. Clearly Cook and Wilson had heeded the threats of the hostile legislators and bowed to political imperatives.

Rangers could accept the male minorities so long as convinced that they had truly qualified. What infuriated them was the service background of the women, which strongly suggested lack of qualifications. Cheryl Steadman was a trooper assigned to the warrants division in Houston. Marrie Reynolds García (an Anglo married to a Latino) was a sergeant in the drivers' license service in San Antonio. DPS spokesman Mike Cox shrugged off the appointments as routine. "This is the result of an extensive testing and interview process. We're delighted to have two women as Texas Rangers, but we consider it just business as usual." Rangers knew better.[16]

Assigned to Company A in Houston, Cheryl Steadman did not last long. In March 1994 she attended an off-duty party held annually by Company A at a Southeast Texas retreat. She said the Rangers got drunk, gambled, told dirty stories, and subjected her to masculine put-downs. A DPS investigation determined the party to have involved only moderate drinking, low-stakes poker, and harsh language that was not directed at her. Steadman regarded this as a whitewash and wanted out of the Rangers. She transferred to the DPS motor vehicle theft division in Houston.

Steadman did not leave quietly, for in June 1994 she gained an ally. The annual selection of new Rangers included two women. One, Christine Nix, was a black woman with extensive experience in the army military police, the Temple police department, and a variety of DPS offices around the state. The other, Lisa Sheppard, a white DPS criminal investigator, turned down the appointment. Senior Captain Maurice Cook had already offended her by carving out a special assignment that isolated her from the Ranger force and otherwise subjecting her to snide indignities. Sheppard and Steadman joined in lodging complaints of sexual harassment and job discrimination with the Texas Commission on Human Rights. Both singled out Cook as the chief abuser.[17]

Steadman had another chance to make her case. On July 11, 1995, the three-man Public Safety Commission convened a formal hearing into her charges of sexual harassment and discrimination. Eleven active and retired Rangers took the stand, including two women, Christine Nix and Marrie García. Both told the commissioners they had suffered no discrimination and liked their job as Rangers.[18]

Even before Nix and García testified, Steadman had stormed out of the room. In fact, hardly any of the Rangers dealt with the issues for which the meeting had been called. Instead, their principal concerns seemed to be what female Rangers should wear and the feeling that Steadman was simply a whiny complainer. The Public Safety Commission ended the meeting by voting unanimously that the Rangers had not been guilty of discrimination or sexual harassment.[19]

The hearing did the Ranger cause no good. The spectacle of wasting the formal hearing in trivialities instead of Steadman's charges of discrimination and sexual harassment reinforced the growing public opinion that the Rangers had not kept up with the times. In fact, the Steadman and Sheppard cases had been handled ineptly.

But the two women then overplayed their hand. With the Texas Commission on Human Rights still to rule on their complaint, in December 1995 they filed suit in federal court demanding millions in damages for "extreme and outrageous conduct" of the Rangers and DPS, for the "severe emotional distress" that resulted, and for the libel, slander, and ridicule to which they had been subjected. In January 1996, as the state attorney general prepared to rebut the charges, the Texas Commission on Human Rights dismissed the allegations as groundless. The federal suits of the two women slowly worked their way through the court system, at each level ending in a ruling against the plaintiffs. Finally, on January 18, 2000, the U.S. Supreme Court turned down Steadman's appeal without comment.[20]

The disposition of the two cases by the courts and the human rights commission ratified the internal investigation of DPS and the avowals of many Rangers as well. Each company held an annual party such as the Company A gathering Steadman had attended, and none featured

317

the wild drunken scenes she had described, nor any other behavior that could bring discredit to the Rangers.

Even after filing suit, the Steadman and Sheppard cases had fallen into the past, largely forgotten by the public. At the turn of century, the Rangers still had only two women, Christine Nix and Marrie García. Nix retired in 2004.

Both active and retired Rangers held mixed attitudes about women. Some fervently maintained that no woman should ever be a Ranger. Others, recognizing the changing times, believed that any woman who could meet the qualifications demanded of men should be admitted.

BECAUSE OF HIS incendiary temperament and handling of the gender controversy, Senior Captain Maurice Cook caused the Rangers almost as much grief as Steadman and Sheppard. In February 1996 anonymous sources within DPS told the Associated Press that Colonel James Wilson had delivered Cook an ultimatum: "retire, resign, transfer, or they'd fire him." Furious, Cook denied that he had any intention of retiring. In June he reinforced his denial by filing suit against the AP, two newspapers, two reporters, the Travis County sheriff, and a Houston attorney, alleging libel and intentional infliction of emotional stress. A month later, on July 26, 1996, Cook announced his retirement.[21]

Cook did not slide silently into oblivion. Two years later he sued DPS itself for wrongfully terminating him—thus confirming the AP's original story. He had been fired, declared Cook, because of his association with "certain groups and individuals, including members of the Texas Legislature." He wanted a jury trial and damages for lost wages, attorney's fees, and mental anguish. If he gained any satisfaction, it did not make the newspapers.[22]

On September 1, 1996, the assistant division chief, Bruce Casteel, took over as senior captain of the 105 Rangers. For four years an opponent and victim of Senior Captain Cook, Casteel blew in like a breath of fresh air. He was liked and respected by the Rangers, dedicated, as one had said a year earlier, to "us" rather than "me." No serious controversy or unfavorable publicity marred his five-year tenure. In fact, one of the most successful operations of half a century occurred on his watch.[23]

ON NOVEMBER 1, 1996, Barry Caver took over Company E in Midland, at thirty-eight the youngest Ranger captain since the formation of DPS in 1935. Tall and muscular, he fitted the image of the traditional Ranger. As the Company C lieutenant, he had made a reputation as a top-flight criminal investigator and an outstanding leader and quickly moved up when Captain Gene Powell transferred to Austin as Bruce Casteel's assistant chief.

In February 1997 Jeff Davis County sheriff Steve Bailey drove to Midland to talk with the new captain. Bailey's county embraced the craggy, forested Davis Mountains and surrounding grasslands, which supported a scattering of cattlemen. The county seat, Fort Davis, lay about twenty-five miles north of Marfa and Alpine. Sparsely populated, the entire county relied on only two lawmen, Sheriff Bailey and one deputy.

In recent years the county had attracted a growing number of residents, drawn by the mountain scenery and temperate climate. Most lived along a road that penetrated a steep canyon southwest of the county seat. One resident in particular had brought Sheriff Bailey to Midland.

Richard McLaren headed one of three quarreling factions of the Republic of Texas. Adherents to this bogus sovereignty contended that Texas had been illegally annexed to the United States in 1845 and remained an independent republic, which they intended to restore by peaceful or violent means. They had already bedeviled state and county governments by refusing to obey state law or acknowledge state officials, as well as by tying up anyone who offended them by filing liens against their personal property. These filings clogged county offices and the courts, and brought on clashes with the state attorney general and even the federal courts.[24]

The ROT movement gained momentum at a time when antigovernment militia groups were sprouting all over the United States. On weekends camouflage-clad men gathered at McLaren's compound to train for a violent revolution should the state not peacefully acquiesce in their demands. Ironically, McLaren and his closest associates had moved to Texas from elsewhere.

Filing liens, talking of war, conducting weekend war games, Richard McLaren had already caused plenty of trouble for his neighbors, for Jeff Davis County, and for Sheriff Bailey. If an emergency did occur, Bailey knew that he and his deputy could not handle it. If it erupted, he asked Captain Caver, would the Rangers take control? Of course, Caver answered, later confirming the promise with Chief Bruce Casteel in Austin.

McLaren billed himself as "ambassador" of the Republic of Texas. His "embassy" lay at the end of a nine-mile dirt road ending in the mouth of a rocky canyon. It was an old house trailer with a scrubby wooden lean-to attached. No one knew how many men guarded the embassy or how they were armed.

Authorities held a federal and a state warrant for McLaren's arrest for filing false liens and other violations of both federal and state law. Although no move had been made against his compound, throughout April his Internet website emitted bellicose declarations of an impending invasion that would be met with armed force.

About 150 neighbors shared the community with McLaren. They had grown heartily disgusted with the martial activities that had ranged up and down the road and throughout the community for four years. The second house from the entrance sat on a knoll affording a good view of surroundings. Joe and Margaret Ann Rowe lived there, and they kept Sheriff Bailey informed of ROT activities. McLaren had often feuded with them and regarded them as "federal moles."

The crisis hit early on Sunday morning, April 27, 1997. Sheriff Bailey stopped a van driven by Robert J. Scheidt, McLaren's "chief of security," for a traffic violation and took him in after finding firearms in the vehicle. ROT struck back. Three of the ROT militia, decked in camouflage and combat gear, stormed the Rowe home firing volleys from rifles. A bullet hit Joe Rowe in the shoulder, and flying glass cut him. The militia, Greg and Karen Paulson and Richard Keyes, now held Rowe and his wife as hostages.

Quickly alerted, Captain Caver called every member of his company, scattered throughout the Company E region, and told them to pack and head for Fort Davis. He informed Chief Casteel in Austin, then passed the word to the highway patrol captain in Midland, David Baker. By late afternoon a helicopter had set both down in Fort Davis.[25]

As he had promised Sheriff Bailey, Caver took control. No one had talked with the hostage takers. From the first residence on the access road, home of a border patrol officer, Caver dialed the Rowes' telephone number. Greg Paulson answered. Caver asked for the ROT demands. Polite, respectful, and entirely unresponsive, Paulson replied that he could take orders only from chief of security Robert Scheidt. Since his morning arrest by Sheriff Bailey, however, Scheidt had sat in a Marfa jail cell (Fort Davis had no jail). Brought back to Fort Davis, he professed to know nothing of what had happened but promised to help in any way he could to resolve the trouble.

Meantime, Caver had talked with McLaren by telephone. Like Scheidt, he denied all knowledge of the kidnapping and declared that he had not ordered it. Even so, in telephone interviews and Internet communications, he took full credit. He held the hostages as "prisoners of war" and would exchange them for Scheidt and a ROT woman who had been arrested in Austin a week earlier. On McLaren's website he ordered militia members throughout the state to start picking up and deporting judges, legislators, IRS agents, Governor George Bush and Attorney General Dan Morales, and in fact any foreigner found in Texas.

On Monday morning, after lengthy negotiation, Scheidt agreed with Caver that he would free the hostages if he could have his van returned and then drive with the Paulsons and Keyes back to McLaren's compound. As Caver conceded, a first rule of hostage negotiation is never to make a deal, but he believed it imperative to get the Rowes released so Joe could be rushed to the hospital. Scheidt made good on his promise. The Rowes were liberated, and Scheidt, the Paulsons, and Keyes drove back into the mountains.[26]

McLaren's public bluster meant nothing on the scene, for Captain Caver now controlled it. His object was to force the surrender of McLaren and all his cohorts, and it seemed unlikely to be attained quickly. In the next few days help arrived in ample measure. The sheriff was already there with Caver and his growing number of Rangers. Eventually Rangers from elsewhere brought the number to thirty-five. The highway patrol poured in men and cars and manned roadblocks. The FBI, border patrol, and U.S. marshals showed up in strength. The fifteen-man DPS SWAT team arrived from Austin. The Texas Forest Service joined, since McLaren threatened to set fire to the forests. Texas Parks and Wildlife sent in game wardens experienced in backcountry tracking. The army provided two Blackhawk helicopters from Fort Bliss, which were used mainly for logistics. From East Texas, the Smith County sheriff sent two armored personnel carriers (APCs), "Bubba 1" and "Bubba 2." Chief Casteel and DPS director Dudley Thomas flew in for a hasty show of support, but they refrained from interfering with Caver's conduct of the mission.

The state forest service introduced Caver to the concept of "incident command," employed throughout the nation for fighting forest and range fires. As Caver later observed, with more than three hundred officers "it was a manpower and scheduling nightmare." The forest service personnel took over the logistics of scheduling, feeding, housing, and sanitation, freeing Caver to concentrate on McLaren. Throughout, Caver was "incident commander," the ultimate authority who reported to no one else.

Caver felt a sense of urgency because weekends usually brought an influx of armed militiamen. McLaren had declared war and summoned an army. Caver felt the standoff had to be resolved before the weekend in case reinforcements in fact responded.

To avoid further kidnappings, on Monday Caver moved his command post to an abandoned volunteer fire station closer to the compound, thus putting the community to his rear. Many residents had left anyway.

Attorney General Janet Reno tried to get federal officers out of the area because Fort Davis bore similarities to Waco. One was the nationwide attention that sent dozens of news and television people to Fort Davis. Like the FBI at Waco, Caver established a press rendezvous in a roadside park a dozen miles distant, where TV cameras had nothing to film but state troopers and their patrol cruisers and Mike Cox dispensed only such information as the captain wanted. Akin to Waco as well were the negotiations, which were conducted with McLaren by telephone. Since commander and negotiator should never be the same person, Caver assigned the duty to Ranger Jesse Malone, a calm, articulate man who could talk sensibly with anyone. Especially like Waco, the talks proceeded in mutually incomprehensible languages. Talking with McLaren was like talking with David Koresh. Malone sought surrender to the state of Texas; McLaren recognized no such entity and could respond only in the tortured language of the Republic of Texas. Also with Waco in mind, Caver desperately wanted to end the siege peacefully, without the opprobrium heaped on the FBI.

Malone made no headway Monday. To McLaren, "surrender" meant the sovereign ROT giving up to a foreign power. In a statement to CNN, he said his only interest was "in getting foreign agents off Texas soil." He also sought intervention by the United Nations to broker a cease-fire.

Tuesday McLaren's Houston attorney, Terence O'Rourke, showed up. Caver let him talk with McLaren, who made no concession but inscribed a bundle of "legal documents" for O'Rourke and placed them in a "diplomatic pouch" on the road near his compound. SWAT team members drove one of the APCs out to retrieve the pouch. Without disclosing the contents of the documents, O'Rourke pronounced them the starting point for negotiations.[27]

Wednesday, as O'Rourke prepared a packet of papers to be returned in the pouch, the ambassador suddenly broke off all communication by telephone or fax. Amid indications that he was summoning militia groups from across the nation, Caver shut down the ROT Internet site and prepared for offensive action. Friday evening he moved his forces closer to the embassy. McLaren took to his ham radio: "Mayday! Mayday! Mayday! Hostiles are invading the Republic of Texas embassy.

We have hostiles in the woods. This is a mayday call for any nation in the world. We are being invaded!" At the same time he warned the invaders, "You're dead meat."[28]

But on this same Friday, ROT solidarity had begun to disintegrate. Caver thought the "embassy" contained about thirteen militiamen, for six of whom he now held felony warrants. Actually, the bedraggled old trailer housed only eight, two of them women: McLaren and his wife, Evelyn, Robert "White Eagle" Otto, Mike Matson, Richard Keyes, and Greg Paulson and his wife, Karen—all from outside Texas. Friday, in another ritual of exchanging diplomatic pouches, Bob Scheidt walked out to place the pouch on the road. Instead, he just kept walking into the arms of the Rangers. "I've had enough of this," he explained. "I could see the handwriting on the wall—what's fixing to happen next—and I don't want any part of that."

Meantime, Evelyn McLaren's two daughters had driven over from Dallas. They wanted to talk with their mother by telephone, but she refused. Friday night Caver told her by telephone how badly her daughters wanted to see her and assured her that she would be treated with dignity and respect if she would surrender. Given the ROT obsession with sovereignty, this promise seemed to weigh heavily in Evelyn McLaren's thinking. On that condition, she promised to come out the next morning. She did.

She was cordially greeted and not handcuffed, and she received the studied courtesy and the respect that meant so much. Captain Caver allowed her to talk by phone with her husband. She told him of her kind treatment and urged him to surrender. She had also brought out another ROT document, a formal cease-fire agreement with stipulations, signature blocks, and the embossed seal of the Republic of Texas. Working by telephone with Chief Casteel in Austin, Caver crossed out the stipulations that could not be accepted and signed the document. Evelyn McLaren called her husband and exclaimed, "He signed it. We've won." Two hours later McLaren and White Eagle Otto drove down the road and surrendered. Although handcuffed behind his back, McLaren insisted on shaking hands with Captain Caver. He had lived up to all his promises, including respect, and the ambassador appreciated that. He too signed the cease-fire.[29]

Not all had come out. The Paulsons had insisted on surrendering the "military way." To them that meant arranging their arms in a semicircle in front of the flagpole and sitting with their backs against the flagpole. Caver worked his way to the canyon rim where he had kept lookouts throughout the siege and observed the Paulsons quietly awaiting arrest in the "military way."

Although two others, Richard Keyes and Mike Matson, had taken to the mountains rather than give up, the siege had ended peacefully. In fact, it had come close to ending violently. Still apprehensive of reinforcements, by Friday Caver had lost patience and advanced his forces in the move that prompted McLaren's mayday call.

> It just got to the point after a week of listening to this guy ramble on and make his threats, no progress appeared [close] to being made. I got tired of it. I had all the people I needed, all the resources with the tanks [from Fort Bliss] and two armored personnel carriers. I knew that I could go in there, but it was just whether or not I wanted to face the heat that was going to go along with it. But I got to the point where, had they not surrendered that Saturday morning, I was prepared to do something that afternoon.[30]

An assault was full of unknowns, except the certainty of facing the heat. Would McLaren turn his firepower against the armor? Were the approaches to the "embassy" mined and booby-trapped? (They were.) Would McLaren resort to some desperate bid for martyrdom through suicide or set fire to the compound and surrounding forest, evoking visions of Waco?

The best explanation of the peaceful outcome lies in the decision Caver made to sign the cease-fire. When Eveyln McLaren told her husband on the phone, "We've won," she provided a clue to Caver's victory. By signing an official document of the Republic of Texas, even though stripped of all unacceptable provisions, in their minds he had acknowledged the validity of the ROT concept. Reinforcing this conclusion, less than a month later Eveyln McLaren called a press conference in Garland, a Dallas suburb, to accuse the state and federal governments of breaking an "international agreement" to end the standoff. After concluding the agreement, she angrily charged, officers swarmed over the embassy. "Then my husband and I and the embassy staff were arrested and incarcerated on bogus charges in violation of this same treaty and agreement. The world is watching."[31]

Two of McLaren's militiamen remained free, somewhere in the almost impenetrable wilderness of the Davis Mountains. On Monday, May 5, Caver began the search for Matson and Keyes. Earlier in the week, the Texas Department of Corrections (TDC), the state's prison agency, had brought in tracking dogs. Handled by TDC lieutenant Eric Pechacek and accompanied by two Rangers, three bloodhounds picked up the scent at once and within a mile flushed and attacked Matson. He shot and killed one dog and wounded the other two. So forested and furrowed was the terrain, however, that the ground party could not find the location. Caver ordered a helicopter to search from above. It circled as Ranger Gene Kea and Lieutenant Pechacek tried to find the fugitive. They spotted him, and Kea opened fire. Matson fired back. Pechacek leveled his deer rifle and dropped Matson, dead.[32]

That left Keyes. Caver's men searched for two more days. But as the captain recalled, the terrain was so treacherous, "I was afraid we were going to get somebody else hurt just looking for the guy, so I decided to call it off. He'd eventually surface."[33]

He did. Authorities thought he would die in the fastness of the Davis Mountains. But they found sleeping bags and other evidence that suggested that sympathizers had aided his escape. A tip to the FBI led, after four months, to Keyes's arrest in the forests north of Houston. He had probably been shielded by ROT sympathizers and handed off from one to another.[34]

In November an Alpine jury, based on a host of charges accumulated before and during the siege, sentenced McLaren to ninety-nine years in prison and Otto to fifty. Tried later, the Paulsons and Keyes also drew prison terms. In April 1998 Richard and Evelyn McLaren and eight associates faced federal mail fraud charges and were convicted. Elsewhere in Texas, other ROT zealots went to prison on various fraud charges. The Republic of Texas seemed destined for extinction. It wasn't. Mostly emitting rhetoric rather than violations of law, it remained alive if not healthy at the turn of the century.[35]

Throughout the seven-day impasse, the Texas Rangers received almost no mention by the press, and Captain Caver only once. The officers were characterized merely as "police" or "troopers," when in fact most of the offensive force consisted of Rangers. A week after the stalemate ended, however, the other participating agencies began heaping praise on the Rangers and Captain Caver. He returned the favor: "Everyone is trying to give me all the credit, but there is no way I could've done it without all the coordination and support between the agencies." He was right, of course, but as incident commander Captain Caver bore the ultimate responsibility and deserved the prime credit.[36]

ALTHOUGH THE RANGER ROLE in the ROT negotiations received almost no publicity as they unfolded, and not much afterward, in fact it represented a decisive success. A company of Rangers, headed by an exemplary captain, had achieved a difficult mission fraught with lethal consequences. Followed in 1999 by the apprehension of railroad serial killer Rafael Resendez Ramírez by rookie Ranger Drew Carter and his partner Brian Taylor, the Davis Mountains represented a bright climax to the Ranger history of the 1990s—and the twentieth century.

Waco and Davis Mountains bracketed a lamentable period in the decade's history. The reign of Senior Captain Maurice Cook, with its legacy of damaging publicity, reflected unfavorably on the Rangers even though most of them held him and his methods in contempt. Further marring his tenure was the nasty ordeal over the scarcity of minority Rangers and the absence of any female Rangers. Although badly handled by Ranger and DPS leadership, the responsibility rests also with the Rangers themselves. Too many failed to recognize the changing times and set their minds against "diluting" the proud corps Homer Garrison had ruled. Thoughtful Texans and their representatives in state government believed that the composition of the Rangers should more nearly reflect the ethnic diversity of the population. If the two women selected as Rangers in 1993 truly qualified, their subsequent behavior brought such discredit on the force as to disqualify them. Male minorities found increasing acceptance, but at this writing (2006) but one female Ranger patiently awaits retirement.

Despite the unpleasant middle years of the 1990s, Captains David Byrnes and Barry Caver, backed by Senior Captain Bruce Casteel, ushered the Texas Rangers into the twenty-first century on a high plane of professionalism.

[19]

A Summing-Up

THE TEXAS RANGERS have served Texas for nearly two centuries. They and their fellow Texans regard 1823 as the founding year and impresario Stephen F. Austin as the founder. Although the year is not supported by credible documentation, the founder definitely had in mind the idea that eventually evolved into the Texas Rangers. Mexican Texas needed more effective fighters than Mexican militia to ward off Indian raids. Gradually men came together informally to "range" the frontiers, then more formally after Texas won independence from Mexico in 1836. Although popularly known as "rangers" and later as "Texas Rangers," not until the twentieth century did any law sanction the term.

The Texas Rangers of modern times have little, at least functionally, to unite them under this designation with their nineteenth-century predecessors. But history, tradition, and legend bind them to the earlier "rangers."

In fact, the Rangers of the nineteenth century served in three distinct roles: citizen soldiers battling Comanche warriors, federalized units of the U.S. Army fighting in the Mexican War, and finally lawmen on the western frontier of Texas. Not until the last incarnation, launched in 1874 when for the first time they became a permanent institution, did they become crime fighters—and then they were the kind of lawmen celebrated in the lore of the American West, rather than the criminal investigators of recent times.

Like the nineteenth-century Rangers of *Lone Star Justice*, the twentieth-century Rangers of *Lone Star Lawmen* revel in the designation and the history, tradition, and legendry it carries forward. Although this is mainly what the men of two centuries have in common, it is powerfully significant. It has made the Texas Rangers known all around the world, and it has infused each generation with the strength and determination to live up to the image.

ASIDE FROM IMAGE and regardless of purpose, the Rangers of two centuries bore another quality in common—leadership. Still today as in the 1830s, the Ranger captain is the elite of the elite. In the nineteenth century, which had its share of bad captains as well as good, the captain whom generations of subsequent captains took as their role model was John Coffee Hays. At the Battle of Walker Creek in 1844, he introduced the Colt repeating pistol to mounted warfare and with ten men smashed a force of seventy Comanche warriors. In the Mexican War, he led outnumbered former Rangers in a string of victories over Mexican lancers.

The nineteenth-century Rangers boasted other distinguished captains—Ben McCulloch, Rip Ford, the "Four Great Captains" of the turn of the century. But none ever displaced Hays as the example.

The key to Hays's success, as to the success of other great captains, was leadership. And the key to leadership was not authoritarian command but command by example. Men respected and followed a captain who provided the example of courage, decision, dedication, aggressiveness, proficiency with arms, and other qualities that define a superior leader.

The twentieth century had its good and bad captains as well. Tom Hickman, Frank Hamer, Bob Crowder, Bob Mitchell, Jack Dean—all excelled as Ranger captains. But the captain whose record, combined with the opinion of others, singles out as the best of the best was Manuel T. "Lone Wolf" Gonzaullas. His services from the 1920s through the 1940s stamped him the most skilled and the most successful—in short, the exemplary leader.

Managerial leadership influenced the performance of the captains and their men, until 1935 the adjutant general, afterward the director of the Department of Public Safety. In the nineteenth century, the name that stands above all is Major John B. Jones. Beginning in 1874, he created the permanent institution—administratively styled the Frontier Battalion—that spawned the Old West lawmen, then nurtured it after his elevation to adjutant general. In the twentieth century, Colonel Homer Garrison has no peer. In his thirty-year reign as director of DPS (1938–68), he not only saved the Rangers from likely extinction but molded them into skilled professional crime fighters.

Jones and Garrison rank with the best captains in the heritage of the Texas Rangers.

IN 1935 HISTORIAN Walter Prescott Webb published *The Texas Rangers: A Century of Frontier Defense.* Still a yearly best seller of the University of Texas Press, Webb's history added to the legend that had already elevated the Texas Rangers to elite status. Hardly a critical word detracted from the heroic posture in which he portrayed the Rangers. Even the atrocities of the Mexican War and the aggressions of Leander McNelly emerged as triumphs over Mexican villains. He detailed some of the events of the decade of the Mexican Revolution of 1910–20 but pronounced no judgments. He conceded, however, that "in the orgy of bloodshed . . . the Texas Rangers played a prominent part, and one of which many members of the force have been heartily ashamed."[1]

As the book made its way through the press in 1935, the legislature authorized the creation of the Department of Public Safety, which brought the highway patrol and the Rangers together in one agency. "Farewell to the Texas Rangers," Webb headed the concluding paragraph of his book. "It is safe to say that as time goes on the functions of the un-uniformed Texas Rangers will gradually slip away and that those of the Highway Patrol will increase." In fact, he sadly looked for the ultimate extinction of his beloved Rangers.[2]

Webb had good reason for his fear. The law creating DPS reduced the Rangers to forty and implied that, rather than lose the Ranger image vibrant in Texan affections, they would do what they had always done: chase smugglers and rustlers on horseback in West Texas. The highway patrol, enlarged and vested with all the law enforcement powers of the Rangers, would probably take over the statewide crime-fighting role of the Rangers. Bitter over this probability and the prospect of serving in an agency whose top officials came from the patrol, the Rangers expected to be gradually extinguished by the "motorcycle jockeys."

Two men saved the Rangers from that fate. The new Public Safety Commission, designed to insulate DPS from politics, chose a director from the Adjutant General's Department, Horace Carmichael. Easing the senior Ranger captain into a new post in Wichita Falls, they permitted Carmichael to require all the company captains to report directly to him. With no highway patrol officer between them and Carmichael, the Rangers recovered their morale and self-esteem, which he constantly reinforced (see chapter 11).

Carmichael served only two years (1936–38) before a heart attack felled him. Ominously, his successor came from the highway patrol. Homer Garrison moved swiftly to head off Ranger disaffection. He restored Carmichael's directive that all Ranger captains report directly to him. For thirty years, from 1938 to 1968, he paid close attention to the Rangers, provided strong leadership, and shaped them into the elite body of statewide crime fighters that Webb had thought would characterize the highway patrol. Garrison also won from them all an extraordinary loyalty and affection (see chapter 12).

"At the time," Garrison later recalled, "I told Dr. Webb the rangers would never be overshadowed and as long as there was a Texas there would be Texas Rangers. . . . He just wouldn't believe me then. As the years passed, I always brought the subject up and asked if he's seen the death of the Rangers yet." Finally, in 1959, Webb came to Garrison's office and admitted that he had been wrong. He intended to publish a second edition of his book bringing the story up to date. "Two weeks before his death [in 1963, in an auto accident], Dr. Webb told me that he was going to write that revision and everything was in order to do it."[3]

It was. Webb had commissioned a graduate student, Thomas Lee Charlton, to write the history of DPS from 1935 to 1957. Webb's partially revised chapter, "The Texas Rangers in the Modern World, 1935–1960," is largely the revised text of this master's thesis. When the new edition of *The Texas Rangers* was published in 1965, however, it merely reproduced the 1935 version without change.[4]

In one respect Webb proved correct. The formation of DPS marked a watershed in Ranger history. On the Rangers of 1935 the stamp of Old West lawmen remained conspicuous. They had adopted some modern trappings, such as automobiles, railroads, telephones, and automatic weapons. Even so, horses still afforded the best transportation in the mountains and deserts of West Texas, and the forests and swamps of East Texas. Politics ruled the composition of the force and often directed policy and employment. Politics and low salaries caused a constant turnover in manpower. The six-shooter culture too often guided recruitment, with character and judgment rating less important than marksmanship and pugilism.

The Garrison Rangers who took shape after 1935 inherited the traditions of their predecessors, but they bore only superficial resemblance. Largely freed of political interference by the Public Safety Commission, they could now make a career as Texas Rangers. Turnover rates fell drastically. Modern crime laboratories brought science and technology to their aid. Training courses introduced them to every facet of criminology. They still occasionally became embroiled in a swift pursuit or a shootout with gangsters, but they devoted most of their time and effort to criminal investigation, usually in support of local lawmen. As a reminder of old times, they retained some of the trappings of the past, such as horses and western garb. West Texas, especially the Big Bend, still needed the old-style Ranger to fight smuggling and cattle rustling. East Texas, chiefly the urban centers, required a different specialist, the "concrete Rangers" who looked and worked much like city detectives.

Whether western or eastern, the Garrison Rangers retained enough of the six-shooter culture to resort to strong-arm methods when they thought necessary.

The history of the Texas Rangers in their second century, therefore, is the history of two very different types of lawmen.

In 1935 POLITICS had always dogged the Texas Rangers, more or less depending on the governor. Only in part because of politics, by 1910, plagued by mediocre leadership, the force had deteriorated to scarcely marginal effectiveness. That year ushered in a decade in which two developments pressed the Rangers to the lowest point in their history. The first was politicization increasing in intensity from governors Oscar B. Colquitt (1911–15) to James E. Ferguson (1915–17) to William P. Hobby (1917–21). The second was the Mexican Revolution, which inflamed the Rio Grande border and imposed an equivocal mission on the Rangers.

After the retirement of the veteran captain John R. Hughes in 1915, company leadership offered no promise of improvement. In South Texas, John B. Sanders was a tough and rough captain who played by his own rules and drank too much. In the Big Bend, J. Monroe Fox turned in a thoroughly incompetent performance. But the worst captain in all Ranger history was Henry L. Ransom, whom Governor Ferguson placed in charge of the Lower Rio Grande Valley during the so-called "bandit war" of 1915.

This conflict, and the years on both sides of 1915, featured the excesses of which Walter Webb described the Rangers of 1935 as "heartily ashamed." The "bandit war" was more a patriotic uprising against years of Anglo oppression than a clash with marauding bandits from Mexico. It occurred within the context of the *Plan de San Diego*, a wild scheme to retake the Southwest for Mexico that held appeal for downtrodden Mexicans and Mexican Americans. Panicked Anglo residents not only turned their local lawmen loose on almost any "suspicious" Mexican but demanded that Governor Ferguson take action too. Thus Captain Ransom arrived in the Lower Valley with orders to end the carnage of the "bandit" raids.

How many innocent Mexicans lost their lives in the rampage against "bandits" has prompted estimates ranging from three hundred to five thousand. Any Mexican deemed "suspicious" by any Anglo could be "evaporated." Captain Ransom had hardly a dozen Rangers, but they set the example for the scores of local lawmen and vigilantes (see chapter 2).

Even so, undeniable evidence convicts Ransom and the captains who followed of murder and other unlawful conduct. They and their men accounted for many of the "evaporated" or persecuted Mexicans who fell victim to Anglo vengeance for the organized forays of fighters for the Plan of San Diego.

Out in the Big Bend, Captain Fox's little company tried to police an international boundary that defied even the U.S. Army. Stock theft and smuggling posed other challenges that his Rangers failed to meet. Like other companies, most of Fox's men reflected inferior leadership that tolerated easy resort to their fists or six-shooters and undue fondness for the bottle. The Porvenir massacre of 1918—fifteen inoffensive Mexicans lined up and executed by Rangers and stockmen—revealed the quality of Fox and his men, and added one more atrocity to the Ranger record of the revolutionary decade (see chapter 3).

Not politics but Ranger brutality led to the legislative hearings of 1919. Brownsville Representative J. T. Canales complained to both Ferguson and Governor Will Hobby of the vicious acts of Rangers. Receiving no satisfaction, he introduced legislation to reform the force. Adjutant General James A. Harley demanded a legislative investigation. It ended in a whitewash, but twelve days of testimony exposed the truth of Canales's charges in terms of individual offenses. For most of the decade, the Ranger Force had been a rogue police force, composed of many brutal men, led by brutal captains, guilty of repeated acts of brutality and lawlessness. The hearings produced cosmetic reforms that avoided the thorough overhaul sought by Canales and closed out the blackest ten years in the history of the Texas Rangers (see chapter 4).

STRANGELY, IF POLITICS crippled the capability and darkened the image of the Texas Rangers in the decade of 1910–20, politics revived their fortunes in the decade of 1920–30. The key ingredient was Will Hobby's successor as governor. Pat M. Neff valued the Rangers as lawmen rather than political tools and laid the groundwork for rebuilding. His platform included a sturdy plank promising improved law enforcement, and he appointed an adjutant general, Thomas D. Barton, who gave close attention and support to the Rangers.

Not surprisingly, leadership on the political level opened the way for leadership on the field level. In stark contrast to Ransom, Sanders, and Fox, the captains of the 1920s led by competence and example. Frank Hamer, Tom Hickman, Will Wright, and Roy Nichols gave definition to the reincarnated Rangers as a viable law enforcement agency. Not even the political setbacks of the Miriam Ferguson administration (1925–27) proved more than a brief interruption. Dan Moody (1927–31) returned the force to the environment of Pat Neff.

The principal employment of the Rangers during the 1920s and early 1930s centered on the raucous boomtowns that swallowed farm villages in the wake of oil discoveries. These towns were wild and lawless and often exploited by lawless lawmen. The Rangers afforded the only means of restoring law and order, and they carried out this mission with a tough pugnacity that later Ranger generations would find hobbled by law and the courts.

Related to cleaning up boomtowns were two other illegalities—gambling and liquor. Rangers repeatedly shut down gambling dens, both in the boomtowns and in big cities. Both national and state prohibition occupied the Rangers in raiding drinking establishments not only in boomtowns and cities but also in seeking out and destroying whiskey stills in mountains and forests.

Less conspicuously, the western Rangers pursued their routine but dangerous mission to apprehend horsebackers—Mexican smugglers whose pack trains bore liquor across the Rio Grande into the United States. This involved hard service, mostly on horseback, in the hostile border terrain, especially the craggy Big Bend. It also involved much more gunplay than confronted the eastern Rangers. Cattle rustling also continued to be a preoccupation, as in the past. Oil boomtowns in the

Permian Basin gave the western officers a taste of what their eastern peers dealt with constantly. Will Wright shone as an outstanding captain, in stark contrast to Jerry Gray (see chapter 5).

THE 1930S SHOOK the Texas Rangers more traumatically than any period in their history. They began with the same high standing Pat Neff had conferred and Dan Moody had continued. With the accession of Ross Sterling to the governorship in 1931, for the first time they flourished under an adjutant general drawn from their own ranks. Bill Sterling supported them solidly and fiercely protected them from politics.

The euphoria did not last long. After only one term, Sterling yielded the governor's office to Miriam Ferguson, with "Farmer Jim" standing behind her to give instructions. Recalling the bleak rule of the Fergusons in 1925–27, the Rangers openly campaigned against another Ferguson term in the 1932 elections. That was a bad mistake. In revenge, Ma Ferguson fired the entire Ranger Force. For the next two years, in composition and effectiveness, the Rangers fell to a nadir almost as low as 1915, scorned and laughed at not only by fellow lawmen but by the general public.

These two years of institutional rot coincided with the first serious examination of law enforcement in Texas. Attorney General Jimmie Allred ran for governor in 1934 on a platform that included a vigorous promise of reform. The result was Allred's victory and the creation of the Department of Public Safety—the landmark that divided the old Texas Rangers from the new.

THE OLD AND THE NEW were not completely different. Colonel Homer Garrison shaped the new Rangers into a band of career professionals, largely insulated from the politics of the past. But elements of the past survived—tradition, pride, history and legend, and the esteem of Anglo Texans. The central mission, however, now became criminal investigation. Population growth, urbanization, and industrialization spawned spiraling crime rates, mainly in East Texas. The Rangers scattered thinly over this part of the state had to deal with a variety and profusion of crimes their predecessors rarely encountered. In the western part of the state, however, duties remained much the same, both in the type of crime and the methods of fighting it.

Reflecting the expectations of Homer Garrison, the new breed pursued their mission with an almost obsessive dedication. Like every organization, the Rangers had their share of deadbeats, but not nearly as many as most. They remained on call twenty-four hours a day, seven days a week, and responded instantly when called. Once embarked on an investigation or pursuit, they kept at it night and day until resolved.

Colonel Garrison emphasized close cooperation. With few exceptions, Rangers and sheriffs worked well as a team in the spirit Garrison intended. Rangers facilitated cooperation by recognizing the political imperatives under which sheriffs worked. Otherwise, as always, they scorned politics even though, like most lawmen, they tended to favor conservative candidates and causes. In part, their conservatism reflected resentment of the expanding body of criminal rights imposed by the Congress and the federal courts.

With the FBI, the record was not so bright. Some Rangers and agents cooperated in the spirit encouraged by Garrison. But as an institution the FBI had few friends among Texas lawmen. The FBI intruded where not needed or wanted, demanded a flow of relevant information from the Rangers but shared almost none of their own, insisted on taking the lead in any case involving other agencies, and grabbed the publicity when favorable while shifting it to others when not. Especially blatant instances of FBI arrogance occurred when the FBI withheld public recognition of the key role of Ranger captain Jack Dean in identifying the hired killer of federal judge John Wood and at Mount Carmel in the Branch Davidian standoff.

IN THE SIXTY-FIVE YEARS from the organization of the Department of Public Safety until the end of the century, three overlapping generations made up the Texas Rangers. Homer Garrison created the first, emphasizing history and tradition while building a professionalism fortified by rigorous training and scientific detection tools. The next generation inherited the Garrison legacy but had to modify practices and attitudes to meet changing times—federal civil rights laws that applied to everyone, including criminals, and the expectations of an increasingly diverse population. The third generation, extending into the twenty-first century, had come to terms with the changing times and most of the inflammatory issues that had roiled the second generation. This third generation also embraced computers and other technological tools that had begun to emerge during the time of their predecessors.

Both the Garrison generation and the one that followed enjoyed a rare camaraderie. Their dedication, their mission, and their pride forged strong personal bonds. Whether good, bad, or mediocre, all felt an extraordinary kinship with one another. They belonged to a family, and they labored to keep internal troubles from public view.

Rangers had always known that labor disputes brought only grief. But they failed to foresee the grief the farm workers strike of 1966–67 in the Lower Valley caused them. Hard-bitten old captain A. Y. Allee, combined with poor Mexican workers, and with the proliferation of civil rights laws and groups, plunged the Rangers into such trouble that they confronted three serious challenges. First, they endured litigation that lasted eight years and ended in censure by the U.S. Supreme Court. Second, the bad publicity generated by the farm strike spawned a movement in liberal groups to abolish the Texas Rangers as relics of the past. Third, the ordeal exposed the total lack of ethnic diversity in the outfit of tall, muscular white men that Garrison had created.

The Rangers shrugged off the movement to abolish them. They knew they commanded too much popular and political support for such a measure to be seriously considered by the legislature. They professed not to be troubled by the publicity, but they were.

Finally, the issue of diversity dogged this generation for years to come. They tightened entry qualifications and in 1969 commissioned the first Latino Ranger, then in 1988, after another spate of bruising publicity, the first black Ranger. As pressures built for a Ranger force reflective of the state's ethnic diversity, Ranger attitudes grew more accepting so long as minorities truly met the stringent selection process.

Gender was another matter. Few if any Rangers believed any woman should ever be given the distinctive Ranger badge. In 1993 political imperatives forced two women troopers on the Rangers. The force handled the crisis clumsily and got hit with several years of damaging publicity.

Except for women, the Rangers entered the twenty-first century with the diversity issue largely resolved. Both black and Latino Rangers gave the force a composition more reflective of the state's population. But the gender issue had not been resolved, in part because of the lack of female applicants.

Despite the turmoil within the second generation of DPS Rangers, at the end of the century the force could look back on all but the first two decades of the twentieth century with pride and satisfaction. The law enforcement record was exemplary. Only the decade of 1910–20 marred it. By 2000 few Texans called for abolition, although many Latinos remained alienated. Aside from the atrocities inflicted in the second decade, little persecution of Mexican Americans is apparent after 1920 except, perhaps, in the Big Bend and, as always, in the minds of Mexican Americans convinced that the Rangers had always abused them.

But not all shared this conviction. As Captain Jack Dean declared, "I always hear of the Mexican dislike for Rangers, especially in South Texas. I found this to be wrong. I was welcomed by nearly all of the people in South Texas. There were and are many who backed the Ranger in the teens because they were attacked and abused by Mexican bandits."[5]

The second generation of Rangers did not yield to the third without some friction, especially during the gender wars of the middle 1990s. Too much computer, too little hard fieldwork, ran some of the complaint. Joaquin Jackson, however, eloquently drew the true comparison: "The contemporary Rangers are every bit as magnificent in their time as my generation was in ours. They aren't better or worse, they're just *different*, mainly because they have to be. The Texas Rangers have adapted beautifully to their time and place, just as they always have."[6]

In many ways the Texas Rangers are unique, but not as state criminal investigators. Every state government includes a criminal investigative arm. In Texas this agency is titled the Texas Ranger Division. It might, as in some other states, bear another name, such as the Georgia Bureau of Investigation. The powers and responsibilities of such agencies are essentially the same in all the states, including Texas. Effectiveness varies from state to state. Some are very good, some less so. None, however, enjoys the history, tradition, legend, and public image of the Texas Rangers. In few states do many citizens even know the name of their own state criminal law enforcement agency, but most people in every state have heard of the Texas Rangers. As Joaquin Jackson observed, moreover, they are very good. They may even be better than any other criminal law enforcement agency in any state.

And as Homer Garrison told Walter Prescott Webb, "As long as there was a Texas there would be Texas Rangers."

ABBREVIATIONS

To ABBREVIATE THE CITATIONS for documents in the Texas State Archives, I have adopted a system that combines record group, box, and folder as here exemplified: 401-406-6. This translates to record group 401, box 406, folder 6.

AAG Assistant Adjutant General

AG Adjutant General

AGD Adjutant General's Department

AGO Adjutant General's Office

AP Associated Press

CAH, UTA Center for American History, University of Texas at Austin

CIS Criminal Intelligence Service

CLE Criminal Law Enforcement

DPS Department of Public Safety

GO General Order

INS International News Service

LPB Letter Press Book

MTG Manuel T. Gonzaullas

Abbreviations

NARA National Archives and Records Administration
RG Record Group
SO Special Order
SWHQ *Southwestern Historical Quarterly*
TRHF Texas Ranger Hall of Fame and Museum
TSA Texas State Archives
TSHA Texas State Historical Association
UP United Press

NOTES

Prologue

1. I have written the first of two volumes of Ranger history: *Lone Star Justice: The First Century of the Texas Rangers* (New York: Oxford University Press, 2002). Standard since 1935 has been Walter Prescott Webb, *The Texas Rangers: A Century of Frontier Defense* (Boston: Houghton Mifflin, 1935; repr. Austin: University of Texas Press, 1965). A thorough history of the origins of the RCMP is John P. Turner, *The North-West Mounted Police, 1873–1893*, 2 vols. (Ottawa: Kings Printer and Controller of Stationery, 1950).

2. As prominent examples, see Samuel C. Reid Jr., *The Scouting Expeditions of McCulloch's Texas Rangers* . . . (Philadelphia: G. B. Zieber, 1847; repr., Austin: Steck, 1935); and George Wilkins Kendall, *Dispatches from the Mexican War*, ed. Lawrence Delbert Cress (Norman: University of Oklahoma Press, 1999).

3. For Gray, Joseph E. Chance, ed., *Mexico under Fire: Being the Diary of Samuel Ryan Curtis . . . during the Occupation of Northern Mexico, 1846–47* (Fort Worth: Texas Christian University Press, 1994), 137, 261–62. For Cutthroat, John S. Ford (Hays's adjutant), *Rip Ford's Texas*, ed. Stephen H. Oates (Austin: University of Texas Press, 1963), 83–85. Taylor to AG, Monterrey, June 16, 1847, *Mexican War Correspondence*, House Executive Document no. 60, 30th Cong., 1st sess. (serial 520), 1178. A biography of Hays is James K. Greer, *Colonel Jack Hays: Texas Frontier Leader and California Builder* (New York: Dutton, 1952). Ben McCulloch is well treated in Thomas W. Cutrer, *Ben McCulloch and the Frontier Military Tradition* (Chapel Hill: University of North Carolina Press, 1993).

4. I have treated this period in *Lone Star Justice*, chap. 5. For a biography of Ford, see W. J. Hughes, *Rebellious Ranger: Rip Ford and the Old Southwest* (Norman: University of Oklahoma Press, 1964). Ford's own papers appear in Oates, *Rip Ford's Texas*.

5. A biography is Chuck Parsons and Marianne E. Hall Little, *Captain L. H. McNelly, Texas Ranger: The Life and Times of a Fighting Man* (Austin: State House Press, 2001). My own treatment, which is less generous, is in *Lone Star Justice*, chap. 9.

6. I have told this story in *Lone Star Justice*, chaps. 12–14.

7. For the broader application of the term *rinches*, see Américo Paredes, *"With His Pistol in His Hand": A Border Ballad and Its Hero* (Austin: University of Texas Press, 1958), 24. William W. Sterling, who was reared in the border setting, makes the same point in *Trails and Trials of a Texas Ranger* (Norman: University of Oklahoma Press, 1969), 510.

8. "Six-shooter culture" is my term. However, the Rangers' excessive emphasis on the six-shooter is a theme that runs through the Texas Legislature's investigation of the Ranger Force in 1919, a source that will be often cited in the following pages. *Proceedings of the Joint Committee of the Senate and House in the Investigation of the Texas Ranger Force*, 1919. The record was never published and may be consulted in manuscript or microfilm at the Texas State Archives or the Benson Latin American Library at the University of Texas at Austin.

Chapter 1

1. A flawed biography is Jack Martin, *Border Boss: Captain John R. Hughes, Texas Ranger* (San Antonio: Naylor, 1942).

2. A fine biography is Paul N. Spellman, *Captain John H. Rogers, Texas Ranger* (Denton: University of North Texas Press, 2003).

3. Lewis L. Gould, *Progressives and Prohibitionists: Texas Democrats in the Wilson Era* (Austin: Texas State Historical Association, 1992), 86–89. Kenneth E. Hendrickson, Jr., *The Chief Executives of Texas* (College Station: Texas A&M Press, 1995), 153–57.

4. Lura N. Rouse, "Hutchings, Henry," in *The New Handbook of Texas*, 6 vols. (Austin: Texas State Historical Association, 1995), 3:803. Service record of Henry Hutchings, 401-199-Hutchings, TSA. (Hereafter, in citations to records in the Texas State Archives, the first number [401] is the record group, the second [530] the box number, the third [15] the folder number.)

5. Service record of John J. Sanders, 401-62-Sanders, TSA.

6. Don M. Coerver and Linda B. Hall, *Texas and the Mexican Revolution: A Study in State and National Border Policy, 1910–1920* (San Antonio: Trinity University Press, 1984), 28. Charles H. Harris III and Louis R. Sadler, *The Texas Rangers and the Mexican Revolution: The Bloodiest Decade, 1910–1920* (Albuquerque: University of New Mexico Press, 2004), 75–77. GO 5, Headquarters Ranger Force, AGO, Austin, October 2, 1911, 401-1183-11, TSA.

7. Service Record of J. Monroe Fox, 401-55-Fox, TSA.

8. The act of 1911, reproducing verbatim the act of 1901, is printed in GO 5, Headquarters Ranger Force, AGO, Austin, October 2, 1911, 401-1183-11, TSA.

9. Telegram, Hughes to Hutchings, Ysleta, April 19, 1911, 401-530-15, TSA.

10. Telegram, Hughes to Hutchings, El Paso, May 9, 1911, 401-531-3, TSA.

11. Coerver and Hall, *Texas and the Mexican Revolution*, 26–27. Harris and Sadler, *Texas Rangers and Mexican Revolution*, 70–71.

12. Hughes to Colquitt, Ysleta, May 12, 1911, Colquitt governors papers 301-52-2; Colquitt to Hughes, May 15, 1911, Colquitt governors papers 301-61-LPB 8, 157. TSA.

13. Colquitt to Hutchings, November 1, 1912 (quotation). See also Colquitt to Hutchings, October 28 and 29, November 1, 1912; and Hutchings to Colquitt, October 29, 1912, 401-534-9, -10, TSA.

14. Telegram, Hutchings to Colquitt, El Paso, May 21, 1912, Colquitt governors papers 301-252-14, TSA. Telegram, Sheriff Payton J. Edwards to Hutchings, El Paso, June 17, 1912; telegram, Colquitt to Hutchings, June 18, 1912 (2); telegram, Hutchings to Edwards, June 18, 1912; telegram, Edwards to Hutchings, June 19, 1912, 401-06-17, TSA. Coerver and Hall, *Texas and the Mexican Revolution*, 50–51.

15. Pvt. C. R. Moore to AG at El Paso, Camp on Pirate Island, May 21, 1912, 401-534-4, -5, TSA. Endorsement of Lt. Clarence A. Daugherty on report of Private Moore, Fort Bliss, June 1, 1912, AGO Texas Ranger Correspondence, vol. 18, box 2R290, Walter Prescott Webb Collection, CAH, UTA.

16. Telegram, Hughes to AG, El Paso, January 30, 1913; Sgt. C. R. Moore to AG, Ysleta, February 5, 1913, 401-534-24, -26, TSA.

17. An excellent overall view is Jerry Thompson, *A Wild and Vivid Land: An Illustrated History of the South Texas Border* (Austin: Texas State Historical Association, 1997). For the King Ranch, see Don Graham, *Kings of Texas: The 150-Year Saga of an American Ranching Empire* (New York: John Wiley & Sons, 2003). The repeated Brownsville flare-ups are treated throughout Harris and Sadler, *Texas Rangers and Mexican Revolution.*

18. These and following paragraphs are drawn primarily from David Montejano, *Anglos and Mexicans in the Making of Texas, 1836–1986* (Austin: University of Texas Press, 1987), chaps. 2–6; Evan Anders, *Boss Rule in South Texas: The Progressive Era* (Austin: University of Texas Press, 1982); and Richard H. Ribb, "José Tomás Canales and the Texas Rangers: Myth, Identity, and Power in South Texas, 1900–1920" (PhD diss., University of Texas–Austin, 2001, chap. 2).

19. Sanders to Hutchings, Brownsville, November 10, 1912; telegram, Sanders to Hutchings, November 10, 1912; Report of Cameron County Grand Jury, November 18, 1912; affidavits of Sanders and Hawkins, November 30, 1912, all in AGO Texas Ranger Correspondence, vol. 18, box 2R290, Walter Prescott Webb Collection, CAH UTA. These documents were not found in TSA. Testimony of T. N. Creager, 353–58; dying declaration of Toribio Rodriguez, 375–76; testimony of Pat D. Haley, 1276–97; testimony of Capt. J. J. Sanders, 1383–95; affidavit of Andrew Uresti, February 12, 1919, 1577–78, all in *Proceedings of the Joint Committee of the Senate and House in the Investigation of the Texas Ranger Force, 1919*, TSA. Hereafter this source will be cited as *TRF Investigation*. An illuminating backdrop to Brownsville political conditions in general and the Sanders affair in particular is Harbert Davenport to W. P. Webb, Brownsville, January 2, 1935, in box 2M260, Webb Collection, CAH, UTA. Davenport was a longtime Brownsville lawyer, present in the city at the time of the Rodriguez affair. Harris and Sadler, *Texas Rangers and Mexican Revolution*, 108–13, treat this incident but read the evidence somewhat differently than I.

20. James A. Sandos, *Rebellion in the Borderlands: Anarchism and the Plan of San Diego, 1904–1923* (Norman: University of Oklahoma Press, 1992).

21. Ibid., chap. 5, but also entire book. A more recent study is Benjamin Johnson, *Revolution in Texas: How a Forgotten Rebellion and Its Bloody Suppression Turned Mexicans into Americans* (New Haven: Yale University Press, 2003). Charles H. Harris III, "The Plan of San Diego and the Mexican-United States War Crisis of 1916: A Reexamination," *Hispanic American Historical Review* 58 (1978): 381–408. For the revelation and content of the plan, see Inspector in Charge E. P. Reynolds to Supervising Inspector of the Immigration Service in El Paso, Brownsville, January 30, 1915, 401-548-10, TSA. The full text is printed in *Investigation of Mexican Affairs*, Senate Executive Document no. 285, 66th Cong., 2d sess., 1920 (U.S. serials 7665 and 7666, continuous pagination), 1205–7.

22. Pizaña and de la Rosa are well characterized in Sandos, *Rebellion in the Borderlands*, 72–75, but see also Johnson *America's Unknown Rebellion*, 88–90.

23. The Vergara incident is well treated in Coerver and Hall, *Texas and the Mexican Revolution*, 65–74; Walter Prescott Webb, *The Texas Rangers: A Century of Frontier Defense* (2nd ed., Austin: University of Texas Press, 1965), 486–91; and Harris and Sadler, *Texas Rangers and Mexican Revolution*, 165–71. Extensive official correspondence is in the AGO Texas Ranger Correspondence, vol. 19, box 2R290, Walter Prescott Webb

Collection, CAH, UTA. Bound in this volume is a series of notes made by Webb from the *Dallas Morning News* during February and March 1914. For Vergara and all the troubles that followed, an excellent source is Rodolfo Rocha, "The Influence of the Mexican Revolution on the Mexico-Texas Border, 1910–1916" (PhD diss., Texas Tech University, 1981). The larger context is set forth in Gould, *Progressives and Prohibitionists*, 116–19. See also *Laredo Times*, March 18, 1914.

24. Brig. Gen. Tasker H. Bliss to Maj. Gen. W. W. Wotherspoon, Fort Sam Houston, San Antonio, March 16, 1914, RG 165, War College Division, file 8958, entry 296, NARA.

25. *San Antonio Express*, December 10, 1914, quoted in Coerver and Hall, *Texas and the Mexican Revolution*, 79.

26. Gould, *Progressives and Prohibitionists*, 129–30.

Chapter 2

1. This important distinction is made by James A. Sandos, *Rebellion in the Borderlands: Anarchism and the Plan of San Diego, 1904–1923* (Norman: University of Oklahoma Press, 1992), 188, n37.

2. Sanders to Hutchings, Del Rio, February 12, 1915, AGO Texas Ranger Correspondence, vol. 19, box 2R290, Walter Prescott Webb Collection, CAH, UTA. Sanders to Hutchings, Del Rio, March 1, 1915, 401-548-23, TSA. *General Laws of the State of Texas, 1915*, 151. Charles C. Cumberland, "Border Raids in the Lower Rio Grande Valley, 1915," *SWHQ* 57 (January 1954): 285–311. Frank C. Pierce, *Texas' Last Frontier: A Brief History of the Lower Rio Grande* (Menache, WI: George Banta Publishing, 1917), 89. A Brownsville lawyer, Pierce compiled a list of killings and other depredations throughout the revolutionary period. Much of his book was reprinted in the congressional hearings of Senator Albert B. Fall: *Investigation of Mexican Affairs*, Senate Executive Document no. 285, 66th Cong., 2d sess., 1920 (U.S. serials 7665 and 7666). See also in ibid. testimony of Lon C. Hill, 1253–54. Hereafter cited as *Investigation of Mexican Affairs*.

3. Pierce, *Texas' Last Frontier*, 89–90. Weekly Report of Border Conditions, July 10, 1915, in *Records of the Department of State Relating to Internal Affairs of Mexico, 1910–29*, M274, reel 46, file 812.00/15517, frames 1126–29, NARA. Each week the army's headquarters of the Southern Department at Fort Sam Houston provided this informative report. The source will hereafter be cited as *Internal Affairs of Mexico*. For the daily activities of Rangers R. W. Aldrich, T. N. Reneau, and L. W. Edwards, see Co. A Scout Reports, July 1915, 401-1186-16, TSA.

4. William W. Sterling, *Trails and Trials of a Texas Ranger* (1959; repr., Norman: University of Oklahoma Press, 1968), 47–48. A biographical sketch is in Charles H. Harris III and Louis R. Sadler, *The Texas Rangers and the Mexican Revolution* (Albuquerque: University of New Mexico Press, 2004), 256–58. See also Service Record of Henry Lee Ransom, 401-61-Ransom, TSA, and telegram, Wolters to Hutchings, Houston, July 19, 1915, 401-550-13, TSA.

5. Testimony of E. A. Sterling, February 13, 1919, *Proceedings of the Joint Committee of the Senate and House in the Investigation of the Texas Ranger Force, 1919*, 1502–3, TSA. Hereafter *TRF Investigation*.

6. Testimony of W. T. Vann, February 7, 1919, ibid., 574.

7. Telegram, Vann to Hutchings, Brownsville, July 16, 1915. Hutchings to Vann, July 27, 1915. Telegram, Sanders to Hutchings, July 28, 1915. All in 401-550-15, TSA. See also Ransom's service record, 401-61-Ransom, TSA. Sterling, *Trails and Trials of a Texas Ranger*, 47.

8. Frank Pierce's list in *Texas' Last Frontier*, chap. 10; and in the Weekly Reports of Border Conditions in *Internal Affairs of Mexico*, M274, reels 47–50, NARA.

9. The best synthesis of the evidence is in Benjamin Johnson, *Revolution in Texas: How a Forgotten Rebellion and Its Bloody Suppression Turned Mexicans into Americans* (New Haven: Yale University Press, 2003), 88–90. See also Sandos, *Rebellion in the Borderlands*, 87–88; and Richard H. Ribb, "José Tomás Canales and the Texas Rangers: Myth, Identity, and Power in South Texas, 1900–1920" (PhD diss., University of Texas–Austin, 2001), 98–104. Harris and Sadler, *Texas Rangers and Mexican Revolution*, 261–62, construct this event differently than I. Military reports are in Weekly Report of Border Conditions, July 31, August 7 and 14, 1915, *Internal Affairs of Mexico*, reel 47, file 812.00/15730, frames 0530–33 and 0544–45; file 812.00/15812, frames 1859–60; reel 48, file 812.00/15908, frame 0016, NARA. Developer Lon C. Hill and Cameron County deputy Mike Monohan (who was wounded) gave their versions to the Fall senatorial committee, January 2, 1920, in *Investigation of Mexican Affairs*, 1255–56 and 1265–68. State legislator José T. Canales (about whom more later) related still another account on February 10, 1919, in *TRF Investigation*, 860–64, TSA. Ransom's monthly scout reports tell where he went but rarely what he did, other than "scout." For August 2, he wrote that he left Harlingen with Sergeant Reneau and Rangers Davenport and Veale, joined Sheriff Vann at San Benito, and scouted to Paso Real, a favorite crossing of Arroyo Colorado. "We returned to camp [at Harlingen] on the 3rd." Total distance fifty miles. Scout Report of Capt. H. L. Ransom for August 1915, 401-1186-6, TSA. Other sources establish the arrival at Los Tulitos of a civilian posse later in the day. Some connect Sheriff Vann with this group. Ransom and his men could well have been in this posse, on their way back to Harlingen. His presence would also lend strength to the concern of several citizens that civil officers might kill the two prisoners unless in military custody.

10. Telegram, Hutchings to Ferguson at Rockport, August 4, 1915, 401-550-18, TSA, tells of the plea of Wells and Kleberg. Exchange of telegrams between Hutchings and Fox, August 5, 1915, and Hutchings to city ticket agent reserving Pullman berth for night of August 5, 401-550-17 and -18, TSA. Monthly Return of Co. B, Capt. J. M. Fox, for August 1915, 401-1262-1, TSA.

11. Scout Report of Capt. H. L. Ransom, Co. D, for August 1915, 401-1186-6, TSA. Testimony of W. T. Vann, February 7, 1919, *TRF Investigation*, frames 561–62, TSA. Sterling, *Trails and Trials of a Texas Ranger*, 32–33. Ribb, "Canales," 104–6. Pierce, *Texas's Last Frontier*, 90, gives the names of the victims as Desiderio Flores and two sons but dates it August 3. Guzman is the name given in Ransom's scout report. There is a slight possibility that two events are involved, but that seems unlikely given other evidence. Harris and Sadler, *Texas Rangers and Mexican Revolution*, 263, interpret this event differently than I.

12. D. P. Gay, "The Amazing Bare-Faced Facts of the Norias Fight," typescript in Harbert Davenport Papers, 2-23/214, CAH, UTA. This detailed and explicit paper was written in 1933 by Gay, who by then was chief inspector of the border patrol in Brownsville.

13. Gay MS (see n. 12), on which my account draws heavily. Johnson, *America's Unknown Rebellion*, 91–92, includes details from authoritative sources unavailable to me. See also Pierce, *Texas' Last Frontier*, 91–92; Sandos, *Rebellion in the Borderlands*, 89–91; testimony of Caesar Kleberg, John A. Kleiber, and Marcus Hines, January 23, 1920, *Investigation of Mexican Affairs*, 1284–85, 1287, 1309–12; testimony of Lon C. Hill, February 11, 1919, *TRF Investigation*, frames 1223–26, TSA; and Virgil N. Lott, "The Rio Grande Valley," typescript, 2 vols., Virgil Lott Papers, CAH, UTA. Fox's August scout report merely records when the men left and then returned to Marfa. Ransom's August scout report is almost day by day, but he leaves out August 8 altogether.

14. A King ranch hand in his late seventies, Manuel Rincones, was captured by the Sediciosos on August 7 and retained as guide until they crossed back into Mexico. He gave his observations in an affidavit recorded by an army officer on August 12, 1915, and entered

in testimony of Caesar Kleberg before the Fall committee, January 23, 1920, *Investigation of Mexican Affairs*, 1284–85. Captain Ransom was also certain of the Carranza connection, as he told Virgil Lott, in "Rio Grande Valley." Johnson, 91–92, and Ribb, "Canales," 106–7, identify de la Rosa as the leader. Others name Pizaña's nephew, and others Antonio Rocha. Thus de la Rosa's presence is in question, even though he was the Plan field general.

15. This is Gay's version, according to the woman's son. Rocha is identified by Marcus Hines, testimony before Fall committee, January 23, 1920, *Investigation of Mexican Affairs*, 1309–20.

16. Gay and others agree on the ranch casualties. The Sedicioso casualties were counted by Manuel Rincones, cited in n14 above. I have assumed that four of Rincones's five dead were those left on the battlefield and that the fifth was the one the Carranza officer killed rather than care for. Gay inflates enemy casualties to twenty-three killed and twenty wounded.

17. The quotation is Gay's.

18. Ribb, "Canales," 312–20. Ribb analyzed and compared all the Norias photographs in the Runyon Collection, CAH, UTA. Lon C. Hill minimized the photo as a mere snapshot in testimony of February 11, 1919, *TRF Investigation*, frames 1223–25, TSA. See also R. B. Creager, February 5, 1919, in ibid., frame 0364.

19. For the blacklists, see testimony of R. B. Creager, February 5, 1919, *TRF Investigation*, frame 355.

20. *Austin Statesman*, August 14, 1915, in Texas Ranger Scrapbooks, CAH, UTA. Fox to Hutchings, Raymondville, August 21, 1915, 401-551-5, TSA.

21. Hutchings to Fox at Raymondville, August 23 and 28, 1915; Hutchings to Sanders at Norias, August 31, 1915, 401-551-6 and -7, TSA. Hutchings to Sanders, September 20 and 24, 1915, 401-551-17, TSA.

22. The full text is in telegram, Garrett to Secretary of State, Laredo, August 26, 1915, *Internal Affairs of Mexico*, reel 48, file 812.00/15929, frames 0097–99, NARA.

23. Testimony of Lon C. Hill, January 22, 1920, *Investigation of Mexican Affairs*, 1262.

24. For example, Weekly Report of Border Conditions, September 18 and October 9, 1915, *Internal Affairs of Mexico*, reel 49, files 812.00/16319 and 812.00/16526, frames 0026 and 0617, NARA.

25. Testimony of William G. B. Morrison, *TRF Investigation*, 17, TSA.

26. Testimony of R. B. Creager, *TRF Investigation*, 380–81, TSA.

27. Peavy as quoted in Johnson, *America's Unknown Rebellion*, 115. Testimony of James B. Wells, February 8, 1919, in *TRF Investigation*, 676–77, TSA. Peavy writes that a fight had occurred earlier on September 28 between "bandits" and Rangers, and that these men had been taken captive. Ransom's September scout report, 401-1186-6, TSA, records that he and detachment "scouted" from Harlingen to Pharr on September 26, which would have placed them at the site sometime during that day. That the victims were captives taken in a fight rather than blacklisted Mexicans rests solely on Peavy's statement. These are undoubtedly the victims identified by Frank Pierce in an early list drawn up for the U.S. consul in Matamoros. J. H. Johnson to Secretary of State, Matamoros, January 26, 1916, Weekly Report of Border Conditions, *Internal Affairs of Mexico*, reel 51, file 812.00/17186, frame 0173, NARA.

28. Lott, "Rio Grande Valley," 24, 66.

29. Telegram, Funston to AG, Fort Sam Houston, August 20, 1915, *Internal Affairs of Mexico*, reel 48, file 812.00/16002, frame 0338, NARA.

30. Pierce, *Texas' Last Frontier*, 95. Weekly Report of Border Conditions, *Internal Affairs of Mexico*, reel 49, file 812.00/16397, frame 0254, NARA. Mary Margaret McAllen

Amberson, James A. McAllen, and Margaret H. McAllen, *I Would Rather Sleep in Texas: A History of the Lower Rio Grande Valley and the People of the Santa Anita Land Grant* (Austin: TSHA, 2003), 479–81. Sterling, *Trails and Trials of a Texas Ranger*, 38–42. Harris and Sadler, *Texas Rangers and Mexican Revolution*, 287–88. Roland A. Warnock, as told to Kirby F. Warnock, A *Texas Cowboy* (Dallas: Trans Pecos Productions, 1992), 49–50.

31. Pierce, *Texas' Last Frontier*, 96–97. Harris and Sadler, *Texas Rangers and the Mexican Revolution*, 290–92. Testimony of John I. Kleiber and W. T. Vann, January 23, 1920, *Investigation of Mexican Affairs*, 1269–77, 1296–1302; and testimony of Kleiber, February 13, 1919, in *TRF Investigation*, 1483–85, TSA.

32. This information came from one Cheno Flores, later arrested by Sheriff Vann. He said he had been kidnapped by the rebels several days earlier. They had organized in Matamoros and picked up five or six men on the Texas side. Flores regained his freedom after the raid, as the rebels scattered. Testimony of W. E. Vann and John I. Kleiber, January 23, 1920, *Investigation of Mexican Affairs*, 1296–1302, 1274.

33. Testimony of W. T. Vann and J. T. Canales, February 7 and 10, 1919, *TRF Investigation*, 562–74, 906–7, TSA. Ransom's October scout report, covering himself and seven Rangers, merely records for October 18 "left Harlingen with detachment of Rangers to investigate wrecking and robbing of train on railroad near Olmito." For October 19 he reports "scouting through brush for Mexican bandits. By trailing and making careful investigation learned that part of the band crossed the river southwest about six miles from wreck. A number of trails were followed east from the wreck to Mexican shacks and into brush in direction of Brownsville. Returned to Harlingen." Scout Report of Co. D for October 1915, 401-1186-6, TSA. Testimony of J. J. Kirk, February 7, 1919, *TRF Investigation*, 599, TSA.

34. Telegram, Funston to AG, Fort Sam Houston, September 16, 1915 (repeating telegram to Governor Ferguson), *Internal Affairs of Mexico*, reel 48, file 812.00/16198, frame 1074, NARA. Funston's letter of November 5 (from Douglas, Arizona, where he was monitoring revolutionary fighting) has not been found. Ferguson sent it to Hutchings but asked for its return, and Ferguson's papers at TSA contain no incoming correspondence, only bound ledgers of letters sent. The content is easily deduced, however, from Ferguson's reply of November 10, Ferguson governors papers 301-76-LPB 18, 262; and from the AG's response of November 16, 401-552-13, TSA. For the directive to Captains Fox, Sanders, and Ransom, see Hutchings to Ferguson, November 19, 1915, ibid.

35. For the relationship between Carranza, the Plan of San Diego, and the United States, see Johnson, *Revolution in Texas*, 99–107; and Coerver and Hall, *Texas and the Mexican Revolution*, 90–91.

36. Consul General Philip Hamed to Secretary of State, Monterrey, October 6, 1915; U.S. Consul Jessse H. Johnson to Secretary of State, Matamoros, October 12, 1915; Funston to AG, Fort Sam Houston, October 21, 1915, *Internal Affairs of Mexico*, reel 49, files 812.00/16469, 812.00/16505, and 812.00/16545, frames 0513, 0584, and 0691, NARA.

37. Sandos, *Rebellion in the Borderlands*, 122–23. Telegram, Garrett to Secretary of State, Laredo, November 24, 1915; Weekly Report of Border Conditions, December 4, 1915, *Internal Affairs of Mexico*, reel 50, files 812.00/16852 and 812.00/16951, frames 0255 and 0552, NARA.

38. U. S. Consul General [illegible] to Secretary of State, Monterrey, December 8, 1915; Weekly Report of Border Conditions, December 14 and 18, 1915, January 5, 1916; *Internal Affairs of Mexico*, reel 50, files 812.00/16946, 812.00/16999, 812.00/17030, 812.00/17112, frames 0543, 0735, 0802, 1196, NARA. Special Agent in Charge Robert L. Barnes to Chief, Bureau of Investigation, Department of Justice, San Antonio, January 22, 1916; telegram, Garrett to Secretary of State, Laredo, February 12, 1916; Funston to AG, Fort Sam

Houston, February 16, 1916; Weekly Report of Border Conditions, April 15, 1916, ibid., reel 51, files 812.00/17212, 812.00/17261, 812.00/17309, and 812.00/17981, frames 0238–39, 0410, 0557, and 1065. Secretary of War to Secretary of State (citing Col. A. P. Blocksom at Brownsville), May 17, 1916; Secretary of State Lansing to U. S. Consul Monterrey, June 8, 1916; Weekly Report of Border Conditions, June 3, 1916; telegram, Johnson to Secretary of State, Brownsville, June 12, 1916, ibid., reel 52, files 812.00/18199, 812.00/18431, 812.00/18336, and 812.00/18397, frames 0429, 0960–62, 0754, 0803–6, and 0903.

39. Clarence C. Clendenen, *Blood on the Border: The United States Army and the Mexican Irregulars* (New York: Macmillan, 1969). Mitchell Yockelson, "The United States Armed Forces and the Mexican Punitive Expedition," *Prologue: Quarterly of the National Archives and Records Administrations* 29 (Fall 1997): 256–62, and (Winter 1997): 334–43. Frank McLynn, *Villa and Zapata: A History of the Mexican Revolution* (New York: Carroll & Graf, 2000), 319–25.

40. This operation is thoroughly documented in a series of dispatches from Funston to the AG, quoting dispatches from Parker, June 17 and 18, 1916, in RG 165, Military Intelligence Division File 9700-19, Records of the War Department and Special Staffs, NARA. See also telegrams, Johnson to Secretary of State, Brownsville, June 17 and 18, 1916, *Internal Affairs of Mexico*, reel 52, files 812.00/18437, 812.00/18462, and 812.00/18453, frames 0981, 1154, and 1142, NARA. Pierce, *Texas' Last Frontier*, 100–102. Sterling, *Trails and Trials of a Texas Ranger*, 44–46 (Sterling was a scout for Parker). James Parker, *The Old Army: Memories, 1872–1918* (Philadelphia: Dorrance & Co., 1929), 424–25.

Chapter 3

1. Robert Keil, *Bosque Bonito: Violent Times along the Borderland during the Mexican Revolution* (Alpine, TX: Center for Big Bend Studies, 2004), chap. 3. Keil was a cavalryman stationed in the upper Big Bend during this period.

2. Joyce E. Means, "Joe Sitter versus Chico Cano: What Really Happened," *West Texas Historical Association Year Book* 72 (1996): 86–104. This is a strange mixture of authoritative data and superficial rambling. Walter Prescott Webb, *The Texas Rangers: A Century of Frontier Defense* (Austin: University of Texas Press, 1965), 498. Throughout his career Sitter was known as Joe Sitters, whether with his consent or not is unknown. However, his birth name was Sitter, as his death certificate and Ranger service record disclose (401-172-Sitter, TSA). I am indebted to Chuck Parsons and Bob Alexander for calling this to my attention.

3. Cano is prominent in the records of the entire revolutionary period, but his persona has been gleaned from scattered references. He is hard to document. Some details are in testimony of R. M. Wadsworth, *Investigation of Mexican Affairs*, Senate Executive Document no. 285, 66th Cong., 2d sess., 1920 (U.S. serials 7665 and 7666, continuous pagination), 1533–35.

4. Wadsworth testimony, ibid. Glenn Justice, *Revolution on the Rio Grande: Mexican Raids and Army Pursuits, 1916–1919* (El Paso: Texas Western Press, 1992), 9. Charles H. Harris III and Louis R. Sadler, *The Texas Rangers and the Mexican Revolution* (Albuquerque: University of New Mexico Press, 2004), 122–23.

5. Fox to AG, Marfa, May 27, 1915, 401-549-23, TSA. Testimony of R. M. Wadsworth (one of Sitter's officers and a member of the posse that discovered the bodies), *Investigation of Mexican Affairs*, 1533–35. Harris and Sadler, *Texas Rangers and Mexican Revolution*, 190–95.

6. Texas Secretary of State John G. McKay to Hutchings, June 2, 1915; Hutchings to Fox at Marfa, June 2 and 5, 1915, 401-549-24, -25. Ferguson to Hutchings, September 22, 1915;

Hutchings to Ferguson, September 24, 1915; Fox to Hutchings, Marfa, September 29, 1915, 401-551-10, -21. Monthly Return of Co. B, Capt. J. M. Fox, for October 1915, 401-1262-1. All TSA.

7. The term is from James A. Sandos, *Rebellion in the Borderlands: Anarchism and the Plan of San Diego, 1904–1923* (Norman: University of Oklahoma Press, 1992), 115. This also is the interpretation of Orozco's biographer: Michael C. Meyer, *Mexican Rebel: Pascual Orozco and the Mexican Revolution, 1910–1915* (Lincoln: University of Nebraska Press, 1967), 131–33. The people involved and the sequence of events are detailed in contemporary customs agency reports and leave no doubt that the men were seen and treated as ordinary bandits by a hastily assembled posse that included no Rangers. Cobb to Secretary of State with enclosures, September 2, 1915, *Internal Affairs of Mexico*, reel 48, file 812.00/16046, frames 0443-50, NARA. See also Weekly Report of Border Conditions, September 11, 1915, ibid., file 812.00/16256, frames 1285–87; and telegram, Culberson County Sheriff John A. Morine to Gov. James E. Ferguson, Van Horn, September 3, 1915; Hutchings to Fox at Marfa, September 4, 1915; Fox to Huchings, Marfa, September 5, 1915, 401-551-12, -11, TSA. For background of the Huerta-Orozco plot and German involvement, see Don M. Coerver and Linda B. Hall, *Texas and the Mexican Revolution: A Study in State and National Border Policy, 1910–1920* (San Antonio: Trinity University Press, 1984), chap. 5.

8. Fox to Hutchings, El Paso, June 19, 1916, Roy W. Aldrich Papers, box 3P157, folder 1, CAH UTA. Monthly Returns of Co. B, Capt. J. M. Fox, are in 401-1262-2, TSA.

9. Ron C. Tyler, *The Big Bend: A History of the Last Texas Frontier* (College Station: Texas A&M Press, 1996), 162–74. Tyler, "The Little Punitive Expedition in the Big Bend," *SWHQ* 78 (January 1975): 271–91. W. D. Smithers, "They Outstayed the Bandits," typescript ca. 1964, W. D. Smithers Collection, box 3J333, CAH, UTA. Telegram, Funston to AG, El Paso, May 7, 1916, *Internal Affairs of Mexico*, reel 52, file 812.00/18073, frame 0094 NARA. Participants testified before the Fall Committee in 1920: *Investigation of Mexican Affairs*, 1060 (O. G. Compton), 1517–21 (C. D. Wood), 1630 (George T. Langhorne).

10. Testimony of James B. Wells, February 8, 1919, J. T. Canales, February 10, 1919, and C. B. Hudspeth, February 10, 1919, *TRF Investigation*, 707, 869–73, 964, TSA. *General Laws of Texas*, 35th Legislature, First Called Session, 1917, 57–59.

11. Lewis L. Gould, *Progressives and Prohibitionists: Texas Democrats in the Wilson Era* (Austin: TSHA, 1992), chap. 7.

12. Ellis A. Davis and Edwin H. Grobe, comps., *The New Encyclopedia of Texas and Texans*, 4 vols. (ca. 1929), 2:1466.

13. Gould, *Progressives and Prohibitionists*, chap. 8, recounts the history of the 1918 election. Ferguson contended that the senate ban did not apply because enacted the day after he resigned the governorship.

14. Richard H. Ribb, "José Tomás Canales and the Texas Rangers: Myth, Identity, and Power in South Texas, 1900–1920" (PhD diss., University of Texas–Austin, 2001), 138–46. Service record of William M. Hanson, 401-56-Hanson, TSA. Hanson to Harley, San Antonio, February 1, 1918, 401-573-23, TSA, is an autobiographical sketch.

15. Keil, *Bosque Bonito*, 25. *Biennial Report of the Adjutant General of Texas, 1917–18*, 56–57.

16. Justice, *Revolution on the Rio Grande*, chap. 2. W. D. Smithers, "Ranching and Fighting Bandits," typescript ca. 1964, Smithers Collection, box 3J333, CAH, UTA. Testimony of participants is in *Investigation of Mexican Affairs*, 1529–31 (Grover Webb), 1629–33 (Col. George T. Langhorne), 1650–51 (Capt. Leonard Matlack), 1540–59 (Sam Neill). *Annual Report of the Headquarters, Big Bend District, 1917–18*, RG 165, Historical Section, 8th Cavalry, Entry 310, NARA.

17. Fox to Johnston, Marfa, December 29, 1917, 401-573-3, TSA.

18. The relations between the cavalry and the town are related in Keil, *Bosque Bonito*, as is the role of the army in the Porvenir affair, chap. 8. An authoritative history, grounded in original sources, is Justice, *Revolution on the Rio Grande*, chap. 3.

19. Drawn from the oath of service of each in his service record, TSA.

20. Keil, *Bosque Bonito*, who was there, describes the scene in the military camp, chap. 8, as does Justice, *Revolution on the Rio Grande*, based on Keil's letters to Mrs. J. E. Walker of Candelaria in 1961, 37–38.

21. This is my attempt to make sense of conflicting sources. A major source is Harry Warren, who was on the scene before dawn. In April 1918 eight Porvenir widows made affidavits for an army officer. Forwarding these to Governor Hobby, Warren wrote his own account of what had happened. *TRF Investigation*, 841–52, TSA. Later, Warren wrote another account, "The Porvenir Massacre in Presidio County, Texas, on January 28, 1918," MS, Harry Warren Papers, B4888, Archives of the Big Bend, Sul Ross State University, Alpine, Texas. Keil, *Bosque Bonito*, chap. 8, relates the events in detail, as does Justice, *Revolution on the Rio Grande*, chap. 3. Keil and Justice have the soldiers searching the houses and turning out the entire population, while the affidavits of the widows make it plain that masked civilians, not soldiers, took only the men and left the women in their homes. Keil has forty soldiers involved, Warren twelve. If the Rangers are to be credited, they left hurriedly after the gunfire, so could not have still been there when the cavalry arrived. See below. Harris and Sadler, *Texas Rangers and Mexican Revolution*, 351–56, treat Porvenir but in a manner that confuses or skirts some of the basic issues.

22. Affidavits of Bud Weaver and John Pool, ca. March 1918; statement of J. W. Pool, Marfa, March 11, 1918, AGO Texas Ranger Correspondence, vol. 20, box 2R290, Walter Prescott Webb Collection, CAH, UTA. These documents are not in the files of TSA. Fox to Harley, February 18, 1918, and Harley's undated statement, *TRF Investigation*, 834–35, 838–39, TSA. None of these accounts makes any mention of the military role.

23. The seven Ojinaga affidavits are in *TRF Investigation*, 1586–1601, TSA.

24. The widows' affidavits are in ibid., 841–52. For good background and analysis, see Ribb, "Canales," 329–36, and Justice, *Revolution on the Rio Grande*, chap. 8. For Langhorne, see Langhorne to Hanson, Marfa, March 12, 1918, AGO Texas Ranger Correspondence, vol. 20, box 2R290, Webb Collection, CAH, UTA. Again, this document has disappeared from the official files in TSA.

25. Fox to Johnston, January 31, 1917, 401-573-20, TSA. Fox to Harley, February 18, 1918, *TRF Investigation*, 834–35.

26. Hanson to Harley, San Antonio, February 8, 1918, 401-573-26, TSA.

27. For Fox's summons to Austin: telegram, Woodul AAG to Fox at Marfa, May 27, 1918; Fox to Woodul, May 27, 1918; telegram, Fox to Harley, Austin, May 31, 1918, 401-575-15, -16, TSA; GO 5, June 4, disbanding the company; Fox to Hobby, June 11, 1918; Harley to Fox at Marfa, July 3, 1918, all in *TRF Investigation*, 836–41, TSA. The eight Rangers of Porvenir were Bud Weaver, A. R. Barker, Max Newman, Allen Cole, Boone Oliphant, J. H. McCampbell, W. K. Duncan, and Clint Holden. The service record of McCampbell, Duncan, and Holden in TSA shows that they resigned from the Ranger Force before the disbandment of Company B. The service record of each of the five still on the rolls in June 1918 bears a notation of discharge effective February 8, 1918. Clearly the discharges were backdated. Whether coincidentally or not, February 8 was the day Captain Hanson wrote the report of his visit to Marfa. On that day, neither Hanson nor anyone else knew enough about Porvenir to have discharged these men. Perhaps the AG wanted the record to suggest that Hanson had taken this decisive action only a week after the massacre, and coincident with his visit to Marfa. I can think of no other explanation for tampering

with the records. As a further complication, the AG's *Biennial Report*, issued December 31, 1918, bore a cryptic notation that "volunteer" Company B had been discharged on February 8, 1918. Although Justice, *Revolution on the Rio Grande*, 36, writes that Fox had an informal "volunteer" Company B composed of about two hundred stockmen, his citations do not document this. No "volunteer" company appears elsewhere in the records.

28. C. L. Douglas, *The Gentlemen in White Hats: Dramatic Episodes in the History of the Texas Rangers* (1934; repr., Austin: State House Press, 1992), 172–73.

29. Justice, *Revolution on the Rio Grande*, chap. 4. Keil, *Bosque Bonito*, chap. 9. Keil was one of Anderson's troopers who reached the scene within hours; he was also a close friend of Glenn Nevill's. Smithers, "Ranching and Fighting Bandits." Smithers was an army packer in the Big Bend during this period. Testimony in *Investigation of Mexican Affairs*, 1510–15 (Ed Nevill), 1629–35 (Col. George T. Langhorne), 1654–55 (Capt. Leonard Matlack). Telegram, Langhorne to CG Southern Department, March 30, 1918, *Internal Affairs of Mexico*, M274, reel 47, frame 0820, NARA. "Ed (E. W.) Nevill," MS, Smithers Collection, box 3J333, CAH, UTA. There are some inconsistencies in these accounts. Nevill's testimony is closest to the event.

30. Testimony of Claude Hudspeth, February 10, 1919, *TRF Investigation*, frames 968–90, TSA. J. D. McGregor to Hobby, Van Horn, April 13, 1918; telegram, Hudspeth to Harley, El Paso, April 15, 1918; Hudspeth to Woodul, El Paso, April 17, 1918; McGregor to Woodul, Lobo, April 25, 1918; Woodul to Hudspeth at El Paso, April 25, 1918, 401-1183-21; Special Ranger W. D. Allison to Harley, Sierra Blanca, August 2 and 28 (2), 1918, 401-576-23, -577-3; Knight to Harley, Valentine, August 14, 1918, 401-576-28; SO 33, AGO, August 26, 1918 (disbanding Co. N); Harley to Knight at Valentine, August 26 and 31, 1918; Knight to Harley, Valentine, August 30, 1918, 401-577-5, TSA. *Biennial Report of the Adjutant General of Texas, 1917–18*, 11–12.

Chapter 4

1. Richard H. Ribb, "José Tomás Canales and the Texas Rangers: Myth, Identity, and Power in South Texas, 1900–1920" (PhD diss., University of Texas–Austin, 2001).

2. Hobby to Chapa at San Antonio, January 5, 1918, Hobby governors papers 301-336-v. 6, 500–501; testimony of Canales, February 10, 1919, *TRF Investigation*, 878–79, TSA. Canales recalled this meeting as occurring in February 1918, but Ribb, 133, n438, shows that he did not reach Austin until March 1; thus the meeting probably took place early in March.

3. "Rules Governing Texas Rangers," *TRF Investigation*, 1583–86, TSA.

4. Hanson to Harley, Brownsville, March 28, 1918; Hanson to AAG Walter Woodul, Brownsville, March 28, 1918, 401-574-13, -14, TSA.

5. Service record of Charles F. Stevens, 401-63-Stevens; Vann to Hanson, Brownsville, April 19, 1918, 401-574-25; Stevens to Woodul, Mercedes, April 25 and May 14, 1918, 401-575-3, -9; Stevens to Woodul, Mercedes, July 15, 1918, 401-576-14; testimony of W. B. Hinkly, February 12, 1919, and Charles F. Stevens, February 13, 1919, *TRF Investigation*, 1331–33, 1436, TSA.

6. Stevens to Harley, Mercedes, April 26, 1918, AGO Texas Ranger Correspondence, vol. 20, box 2R290, Walter Prescott Webb Collection, CAH, UTA; Hanson to Harley, Galveston, April 27, 1918, *TRF Investigation*, 794–98; testimony of John I. Kleiber, February 13, 1919, and James B. Wells, February 8, 1919, ibid., 1487, 685–86.

7. Alba Heywood to Gov. W. P. Hobby, San Benito, August 28, 1918, AGO Texas Ranger Correspondence, vol. 20, box 2R290, Webb Collection, CAH, UTA. Telegram,

Canales to Harley, Brownsville, August 31, 1918, 401-577-5, TSA. *Biennial Report of the Adjutant General of Texas, January 1, 1917, to December 31, 1918* (Austin: Von Boeckman-Jones, 1919), 12.

8. Service records of Bates, Cunningham, and Gray, 401-51-Bates, -54-Cunningham, -56-Gray, TSA. *Dallas News*, April 3, 1918. *Biennial Report of the Adjutant General of Texas, 1917–18*, 11–12.

9. Ribb, "Canales," 162–69. Hanson to AG, San Antonio, October 10, 1918; Capt. William Wright to Acting AG, Rio Grande City, October 9, 1918; Hanson to Harley, San Antonio, October 15, 1918; statements of J. J. Edds, Zaragosa Sánchez, Jesús Sánchez, and Monroe Wells, all October 18, 1918, AGO Ranger Correspondence, vol. 20, box 2R290, Webb Collection, CAH UTA. Hanson to Harley, October 23, 1918; testimony of Capt. William Wright, February 13, 1919; testimony of J. J. Edds, February 7, 1919; testimony of James B. Wells, February 8, 1918, *TRF Investigation*, 780–81, 1519–20, 481–93, 715–17. The October 18 statements of Edds, Zaragosa and Jesús Sánchez, and Monroe Wells, together with statement of Federico Saldana, are also in ibid., 782–88. Starr County Prosecutor R. Oosterveen to Hobby, October 18, 1918, 401-577-19, TSA.

10. Ribb, "Canales," 162–69. Canales tells of the train incident in testimony of February 10, 1919, *TRF Investigation*, 880–88.

11. Charge 16; testimony of Canales, February 10, 1919; testimony of Jesse Dennett, February 7, 1919, *TRF Investigation*, 885–87, 527–28.

12. Canales to Hobby, Brownsville, December 12, 1918; telegram, Hobby to Canales, December 14, 1918; Harley to Canales, December 19, 1918; Canales to Harley, Brownsville, December 21, 1918; telegram, Harley to Hamer at Brownsville, December 24, 1918, *TRF Investigation*, 888–95; Hanson to Capt. and QM H. M. Johnston, Brownsville, November 19, 1918, 401-577-24, TSA.

13. Ribb, "Canales," 146–57. *General Laws of Texas*, 35th Legislature, 4th Called Session, 1918, 12–15. For establishment of the Loyalty Rangers, see *Biennial Report of the Adjutant General of Texas, 1917–18*, 63. The Loyalty Rangers were not established in January, as stated here, but in June, after passage of the Loyalty Act. Hanson did not join the Ranger Force until late January 1918.

14. Ribb, "Canales," 148.

15. Burkett to Hobby, Abilene, September 25, 1917, 401-571-11; Sam McKenzie to AG W. D. Cope, Alice, November 7, 1919, 401-581-10; testimony of Judge Ed C. Hamner, February 4, 1919; testimony of former sheriff Jack Yarborough, February 5, 1919, *TRF Investigation*, 222–26, 446–50, TSA.

16. Joe R. Baulch, "Farmers' and Laborers' Protective Association," *New Handbook of Texas*, 6 vols. (Austin: TSHA, 1996), 2:956.

17. Telegram, Chapa to Hobby, San Antonio, September 2, 1918; attorney E. L. Garmmage to Harley, Rio Grande City, September 9, 1918; Harley to Hon. O. E. Dunlap at Waxahachie, September 14, 1918; Brownsville mayor A. A. Browne to Harley, Brownsville, September 16, 1918, 401-577-7, -8, -12, TSA; Ribb, "Canales," 158–59.

18. Testimony of J. T. Canales, February 10, 1919, *TRF Investigation*, 899–900.

19. For the maneuvering that led to the investigation, I rely heavily on Ribb, "Canales," 181–200. Ribb has thoroughly mined newspaper and legislative sources that I have not consulted. An excellent explanation of the background of HB 5 and the Ranger investigation is Canales to W. P. Webb, Brownsville, January 11, 1935, Webb Papers, box 2M260, CAH, UTA.

20. House Concurrent Resolution 20, February 3, 1919, *General Laws of Texas*, 36th Legislature, Regular Session, 1919, 365. Approved by senate February 7, ibid., 367–68.

21. Ribb, "Canales" chap. 6, covers the investigation in detail, as do Charles H. Harris III and Louis R. Sadler, *The Texas Rangers and the Mexican Revolution* (Albuquerque:

University of New Mexico Press, 2004), chap. 17. I have thoroughly researched the transcript of the investigation.

22. See notes 9 and 10.

23. Two examples: affidavits of Jesús Villareal and Eulalio Benavides, January 20, 1919; testimony of Jesús Villareal and Sgt. J. J. Edds, February 7, 1919; testimony of army scouts Royal Collins and Lee Dickens, February 12, 1919, *TRF Investigation*, 1573–76, 467–78, 493–510, 1341–62, 1362–63, TSA.

24. Capt. Charles F. Stevens to AAG Walter F. Woodul, Mercedes, May 23 and 25, June 2, 1918; Hanson to Harley, San Antonio, May 29, 1918, 401-575-17, -18; Hanson to AG, "Death of Florencio García," San Antonio, January 29, 1919, 401-578-15; Hanson to Woodul, June 6, 1918; W. R. Jones to Hanson, Brownsville, June 4, 1918; statement of G. W. Sterick Jr., Brownsville, June 1, 1918; H. N. Gray to Harley, Brownsville, May 24, 1918; Anonymous statement, Brownsville, May 24, 1918; Cameron County Attorney Oscar C. Dancy to Gov. W. P. Hobby, Brownsville, May 23, 1918; Hanson to Harley, "Florencio García," n.d., ca. May 28, 1918; testimony of J. C. George, February 4, 1919; Oscar C. Dancy, W. T. Vann, and H. J. Kirk, February 7, 1919; H. N. Gray, C. L. Jessup, and Lon C. Hill, February 11, 1919; H. E. Barnes, February 12, 1919; Capt. Charles F. Stevens, Ranger George Saddler, and Ranger John Sittre, February 13, 1919, *TRF Investigation*, 798–815. 284–85, 542–57, 558–59, 597–98, 1059–60, 1094–98, 1149–50, 1365–80, 1431–33, 1531–40, 1544–56, TSA.

25. *San Antonio Express*, February 9, 1919, Texas Ranger Scrapbooks, folder 2, CAH, UTA. *TRF Investigation*, February 13, 1919, 1562–66, TSA.

26. The committee report, dated February 18, 1919, is in *Journal of the House of Representatives of the Regular Session of the 36th Legislature*, 535–39; *Dallas News*, February 21, 1919; telegrams, Harley to R. L. Knight and Dayton Moses at Fort Worth, Everett Anglin at McAllen, Rangers Thompson and Edds at Hebbronville, F. A. Hamer at Brownsville, and W. H. Gilmore at Laredo, February 19, 1919, 401-578-23, -24, TSA.

27. This complicated sequence is well sorted out by Ribb, "Canales," 358–65. The law is printed in *General Laws of Texas*, 36th Legislature, Regular Session, 1919, 263–66.

28. SO 21, Texas Ranger Force, signed Harley by order of Hobby, March 10, 1919, AGO Texas Ranger Correspondence, vol. 21, box 2R290, Webb Collection, CAH, UTA; Harley to Capt. W. L. Barler at Del Rio, March 24, 1919, 401-579-9, TSA.

29. Hudspeth to Harley, May 20, 1919; Harley to Hudspeth, May 25, 1919; Hudspeth to Harley, May 26, 1919, telegram, Harley to Hudspeth, May 20, 1919, 401-579-22, -23, TSA.

Chapter 5

1. Pat M. Neff, *The Battles of Peace* (Fort Worth: Pioneer Publishing Co., 1925). For the Neff administration, see Norman D. Brown, *Hood, Bonnet, and Little Brown Jug: Texas Politics, 1921–1928* (College Station: Texas A&M Press, 1983), chap. 1; and Lewis L. Gould, *Progressives and Prohibitionists: Texas Democrats in the Wilson Era* (Austin: TSHA, 1992), chap. 9.

2. *General Laws of Texas*, 36th Legislature, Regular Session, 263–66.

3. *Report of the Adjutant General of Texas, 1921–22*, 53–54. The judgments are mine.

4. Neff, *Battles of Peace*, 142–43.

5. The most authoritative histories are Charles C. Alexander, *The Ku Klux Klan in the Southwest* (Lexington: University of Kentucky Press, 1965); and Alexander, *The Ku Klux Klan in Texas, 1920–1930* (Houston: Texas Gulf Coast Historical Association, 1962). The Klan operated powerfully throughout the nation in the early 1920s, but violence to enforce morality was most prevalent in the four southwestern states of Arkansas, Louisiana, Oklahoma, and Texas, with Texas in the lead. For Barton's gubernatorial run, see Brown,

Hood, Bonnet, and Little Brown Jug, 214. For Davidson's actions, see ibid., 159; and James R. Ward, "The Texas Rangers, 1919–1935: A Study in Law Enforcement" (PhD diss., Texas Christian University, 1972), 94–97. I cite Ward's dissertation frequently because it is based primarily on official records that, since he worked in the late 1960s, are no longer to be found at the Department of Public Safety and were not transferred to the state archives. For a lukewarm endorsement of the Klan, see QM Capt. Roy W. Aldrich to Buck Singleton, October 18, 1921, in Aldrich Papers, box 3P156, folder 5, CAH UTA. For work of Sgt. J. W. McCormick and Pvt. Lem Lamkin in behalf of Barton, see McCormick to Aldrich, Wichita Falls, June 30, 1923; and Lamkin to Aldrich, Texarkana, July 1, 1923, 401-598-17, -20, TSA.

6. Diana Davids Olien and Roger M. Olien, *Oil in Texas: The Gusher Age, 1895–1945* (Austin: University of Texas Press, 2002), chap. 4.

7. Ward, "Texas Rangers, 1919–1935," 40–49, citing missing official records. For a biographical sketch of Hickman, see Mike Cox, "Cowboy Tom Hickman," in Cox, *Texas Ranger Tales II* (Plano: Republic of Texas Press, 1999), 175–92.

8. Thomas D. Barton, *State Ranger and Martial Law Activities of the National Guard of Texas, 1921 and 1922* (Austin: Von Boeckmann-Jones, 1923), 3–5; *Annual Report of the Adjutant General of Texas, 1921–22*, 53–54. Neff, *Battles of Peace*, 138. Ward, "Texas Rangers, 1919–1935," 52–53.

9. Barton, *State Ranger and Martial Law Activities of the National Guard of Texas*, 6–22; *Annual Report of the Adjutant General of Texas, 1921–22*, 107–8; Jacob F. Wolters, *Martial Law and Its Administration* (Austin: Gammel Book Co., 1930), 81–89; Harry Krenek, *The Power Vested: The Use of Martial Law and the National Guard in Texas Domestic Crisis, 1919–1932* (Austin: Presidial Press, 1980), 59–84; and Kyle W. Shoemaker, "How Mexia was Made a Clean City," *Owenwood Magazine* 1 (May 1922): 21–26.

10. Service record of Francis Augustus Hamer, 401-56-Hamer, TSA. H. Gordon Frost and John H. Jenkins, *I'm Frank Hamer: The Life of a Texas Peace Officer* (Austin: Pemberton Press, 1968). Walter Prescott Webb, *The Texas Rangers: A Century of Frontier Defense* (1935; 2nd ed., Austin: University of Texas Press, 1965), chap. 22. W. W. Sterling, *Trails and Trials of a Texas Ranger* (1959; repr., Norman: University of Oklahoma Press, 1968), chap. 41 (p. 421 for quotes). Robert Nieman, "20th Century Shining Star: Frank Hamer," *Texas Ranger Dispatch Magazine* 11 (Summer 2003), www.texasranger.org/dispatch/11/Pages/Hamer.htm.

11. Lewis C. and Judyth Wagner Rigler, *In the Line of Duty: Reflections of a Texas Ranger Private* (Denton: University of North Texas Press, 1995), 155–62; Kenneth B. Ragsdale, "Hickman, Thomas R.," in *The New Handbook of Texas*, 6 vols. (Austin: TSHA, 1995), 3:586; Service record of Tom R. Hickman, 401-57-Hickman, TSA.

12. Barton, *State Ranger and Martial Law Activities of the National Guard of Texas*, 7.

13. Wolters to Barton, n.d., in ibid., 12.

14. Walter Prescott Webb, "Veteran Ranger Protects Border," *State Trooper* 6 (September 1924): 13–14; Harold J. Weiss Jr., "Wright, William Lee," in *The New Handbook of Texas*, 6:1093; Valls to AG, Laredo, February 11, 1921, 401-584-25, TSA.

15. Ward, "Texas Rangers, 1919–1935," 53–57, citing missing Ranger records; Webb, "Veteran Ranger Protects Border," 13; Wright to Barton, Laredo, September 13, 1921, AGO Texas Ranger Correspondence, vol. 21, box 2R290, Walter Prescott Webb Collection, CAH, UTA.

16. For Gray see his service record in 401-56-Gray, TSA. For Gray's overt involvement in the election of 1920, in which he tried to make all his men vote for former Ranger Jeff Vaughn for sheriff, see N. N. Fuller to Aldrich, Candelaria, February 11, 1920; and Fuller to AG, February 20, 1920, 401-582-11, -12, TSA. Throughout the Neff administration, complaints about Gray turned up on Captain Aldrich's desk.

17. Webb, *Texas Rangers*, chap. 23. Miller to Webb, Marathon, September 30, 1924, box 2M259, Webb Collection, CAH UTA.

18. Neff, *Battles of Peace*, 73–74. My account is drawn mainly from this source; Barton, *State Rangers and Martial Law Activities*, 22–39; and Ward, "Texas Rangers, 1919–1935," 78–81, drawing on missing official records.

19. Neff, *Battles of Peace*, 75.

20. Koonsman interview quoted in Ward, "Texas Rangers, 1919–1935," 81.

21. Patricia Bernstein, *The First Waco Horror: The Lynching of Jesse Washington and the Rise of the NAACP* (College Station: Texas A&M Press, 2005); Philip Dray, *At the Hands of Persons Unknown: The Lynching of Black America* (New York: Random House, 2002), 216–19.

22. Dray, *At the Hands of Persons Unknown*, 245–58, tells of the summer clashes of 1919. In Texas a particularly brutal lynching occurred in Hillsboro in January 1919.

23. Kenneth R. Durham Jr., "The Longview Race Riot of 1919," *East Texas Historical Journal* 18 (fall 1980): 13–24; William M. Tuttle Jr., "Violence in a 'Heathen' Land: The Longview Race Riot of 1919," *Phylon* 33 (no. 4, 1972): 324–33; *Biennial Report of the Adjutant General of Texas, 1919–20*, 27–28; Hanson to AG, July 17, 1919, AGO Texas Ranger Correspondence, vol. 21, box 2R290, Walter Prescott Webb Collection, CAH UTA.

24. The Kirvin story, almost lost to history, has been recovered in Monte Akers, *Flames after Midnight: Murder, Vengeance, and the Desolation of a Texas Community* (Austin: University of Texas Press, 1999). The *Corsicana Daily Sun*, June 23, 1923, carried a long and confusing article about the Kirvin horrors, but the true facts remained buried for years. The *Sun* article is in Scrapbook 1 of MS 4, Manuel T. Gonzaullas Collection, TRHF. Hereafter this source will be cited as MTG Collection, TRHF.

25. Ward, "Texas Rangers, 1919–1935," 114–15, drawing on local newspapers.

26. Ibid., citing missing official records, newspapers, and Marvin Burton interview, 104–8, 139–40; Shumate to Barton, Dallas, August 21, 1923, 401-599-12, TSA.

27. James R. Ward, "Establishing Law and Order in the Oil Fields: The 1924 Ranger Raids in Navarro County, Texas," *Texana* 8 (1970): 38–46.

28. Marvin Burton, "The Story of the Glen Rose Liquor War in 1923," MS 26, Burton Collection, series I, transcripts, box 1, Glen Rose folder, TRHF; M. "Red" Burton, interview by Roger Conger, Waco Historical Society, May 1, 1956, in MS 33, Oral History, Red Burton, TRHF.

29. Neff, *Battles of Peace*, 138–39; Ward, "Texas Rangers, 1919–1935," 98–103, citing missing Ranger records and newspapers; and Walter Prescott Webb, "Lawless Town Gets Ranger Justice," *The State Trooper* 5 (April 1924): 12–13; B. C. Baldwin's service record, 401-51-Baldwin, Berk C., TSA.

30. The point is well made in Walter Prescott Webb, "Texas Rangers of Today," *State Trooper* 5 (March 1924): 5–6, 18.

Chapter 6

1. Charles C. Alexander, *The Ku Klux Klan in the Southwest* (Lexington: University of Kentucky Press, 1965); and Alexander, *The Ku Klux Klan in Texas, 1920–1930* (Houston: Texas Gulf Coast Historical Association, 1962).

2. Quoted in Norman D. Brown, *Hood, Bonnet, and Little Brown Jug: Texas Politics, 1921–1928* (College Station: Texas A&M Press, 1983), 97. For the election and administration, see chaps. 6 and 7.

3. My account draws heavily on two articles historian Walter Prescott Webb wrote in 1925 while he was working on his history of the Texas Rangers: "Fight against the Texas

Rangers," *State Trooper* 6 (July 1925): 11–12, 18; and "Texas Ranger Case Important," ibid., 6 (August 1925): 13–14, 26. Curiously, Webb does not mention this case in his history, published in 1935. See also James R. Ward, "The Texas Rangers, 1919–1935: A Study in Law Enforcement" (PhD diss., Texas Christian University, 1972), 121–24.

4. Ward, "Texas Rangers, 1919–1935," citing missing Ranger records, 125–26. The AG's official report for 1925–26 contains no mention of the Ranger Force.

5. Ibid. Hamer's biographers (who date his resignation in January rather than June) write that after some time even the Fergusons lamented Hamer's loss and appealed to him to return. Gordon Frost and John H. Jenkins, *I'm Frank Hamer: The Life of a Texas Peace Officer* (1968; repr., Austin: State House Press, 1993), 125–26. Walter Prescott Webb, *The Texas Rangers: A Century of Frontier Defense* (1935; repr., Austin: University of Texas Press, 1965), chap. 22, is a biographical sketch of Hamer but omits the resignation altogether. Presidio County sheriff Joe D. Bunton to Gov. Dan Moody, Marfa, February 6, 1928, 401-1184-22; service records: 401-65-Wright, 401-56-Gray, 401-56-Hamer, TSA.

6. Service record of Roy C. Nichols, 401-63-Nichols; Aldrich to Lt. Fred D. Ball of *Dallas News*, June 29, 1921, 401-586-15, TSA.

7. Ward, "Texas Rangers, 1919–1935," 125–26; service records: 401-55-Aldrich, 401-63-Nichols, 401-57-Hickman, 401-62-Ryan, 401-58-Lindsey, 401-55-Fox; Hickman to Gov. Miriam Ferguson at Temple (before inauguration), Waco, January 3, 1925, Ferguson governors papers 301-423-31, TSA. This box and 424 contain applications and endorsements for Ranger positions. D. E. Lindsey inspired a thick packet of endorsements.

8. Ward, "Texas Rangers, 1919–1935," 130, citing Ranger records.

9. Ibid., 128–29, citing missing Ranger records. Walter Prescott Webb and M. F. Kennedy, "With the Texas Rangers," *State Trooper* 7 (October 1925): 11.

10. Ward, "Texas Rangers, 1919–1935," 132–33, citing Ranger records and newspapers; Walter Prescott Webb, "Lone Ranger Gets Bandits," *State Trooper* 7 (March 1926): 9–10, 20; *Fort Worth Record*, August 25, 1925; *Dallas Dispatch*, August 26, 1925, in MS 4, MTG Collection, scrapbook 1, TRHF.

11. Ward, "Texas Rangers, 1919–1935," 135–37, citing Ranger records; Walter Prescott Webb, "Bank Robbers Slain," *State Trooper* 8 (November 1926): 7–8.

12. Diana Davids Olien and Robert M. Olien, *Oil in Texas: The Gusher Age, 1895–1945* (Austin: University of Texas Press, 2002), 149–51.

13. H. Allen Anderson, "Borger, Texas," and "Borger, Asa Phillip," *New Handbook of Texas*, 6 vols. (Austin: TSHA, 1996), 1:649–50.

14. Ownbey to Ferguson, Plemons, June 30, 1926, Ferguson governors papers 301-424-23, TSA.

15. Ward, "Texas Rangers, 1919–1935," 138–40, drawing on Ranger records; AG Dallas J. Matthews to Hutchinson County judge W. R. Goodwin at Plemons, August 12, 1926, Ferguson governors papers 301-424-24, TSA.

16. Ward, "Texas Rangers, 1919–1935," 138–41, drawing on Ranger records; Anderson, "Borger, Texas," 1:650; *Fort Worth Press*, October 16, 1926, in MS 4, MTG Collection, scrapbook 1, TRHF.

17. Brown, *Hood, Bonnet, and Little Brown Jug*, chap. 8.

18. Walter Prescott Webb, "Texas Rangers in Eclipse," *State Trooper* 7 (January 1926): 13–14.

Chapter 7

1. James R. Ward, "The Texas Rangers, 1919–1935: A Study in Law Enforcement," (PhD diss., Texas Christian University, 1972), 145–46. For salaries, see *General and Special*

Laws of Texas, 41st Legislature, Regular Session, chap. 247, 512–13. This law was approved March 18 and effective September 1, 1929.

2. *Report of the Adjutant General of Texas, 1927–28*, 17–19. A biography of Rogers is Paul N. Spellman, *Captain John H. Rogers, Texas Ranger* (Denton: University of North Texas Press, 2003).

3. William Warren Sterling, *Trails and Trials of a Texas Ranger* (1959; repr., Norman: University of Oklahoma Press, 1968).

4. Sterling to AG, Breckenridge, June 1, 1921; Capt. Roy Aldrich to "Dear Bill" at Breckenridge, July 5, 1921, 401-586-9, -17; seven telegrams to Gov. M. A. Ferguson supporting Sterling's candidacy, April 4 and 27, May 24, 25, 26, and June 2, 1925, Moody governors papers 301-424-7, -9, TSA. These included endorsements of two sheriffs and county judge J. A. Brooks, formerly one of the "four great captains." Telegram, Frank S. Roberts to Governor James E. Ferguson [*sic*], Breckenridge, May 23, 1925; telegram, Fred L. Flynn to AG Mark McGee, Mission, May 26, 1925, Moody governors papers 301-424-9, -11, TSA.

5. AG Robert L. Robertson to R. C. Collier at Huntsville Penitentiary, April 18, 1928, Moody governors papers 301-12-folder State Rangers 11/15/27-4/18/28, TSA.

6. Roland A. Warnock, as told to Kirby F. Warnock, *Texas Cowboy* (Dallas: Trans Pecos Publications, 1992), 56–60.

7. Telegram, Willis to Moody, Panhandle, April 1, 1927, Moody governors papers 301-12-folder "Requesting Rangers," TSA. The official papers of the Neff and Ferguson administrations in the Texas State Archives are unhelpful. Moody's papers in the 301 series, however, contain much Ranger material and help offset the disappearance of the Ranger Records from the Department of Public Safety. This account also draws on Norman Crockett, "Crime on the Petroleum Frontier: Borger, Texas, in the Late 1920s," *Panhandle-Plains Historical Review* 64 (1991): 53–56; Ward, "Texas Rangers 1919–1935," 147–51; *Report of the Adjutant General of Texas, 1927–28*, 17–19; and Sterling, *Trails and Trials*, chap. 10. The "first" battle of Borger, before the martial law "second" battle, is well treated in Mike Cox, "The Battle of Borger," in Cox, *Texas Ranger Tales: Stories that Need Telling* (Plano: Republic of Texas Press, 1997), 197–208.

8. Sources cited in n7. Also, telegram, Moody to county judge at Stinnett, April 8, 1927; telegram, Moody to Mayor John R. Miller, April 8, 1927; Miller to Moody, Borger, April 8, 1927, Moody governors papers 301-11-folder Borger 4/5-9/27; resolution of Hutchinson County Commissioners Court, Stinnett, April 9, 1927; telegram, W. Boyd Gatewood to Moody, Borger, April 9, 1927; telegram, Gatewood to Moody, Amarillo, April 12, 1927, Moody governors papers 301-11-folder Borger 4/9-14/27; Miller and city commissioners to Moody, Borger, April 18, 1927; telegram, Ownbey to Moody, Borger, April 20, 1927, Moody governors papers 301-11-folder Borger 4/16-25/27, TSA.

9. Prohibition Agent M. T. Gonzaullas to Assistant Administrator A. R. Butler at Fort Worth, Borger, June 15, 1927; Administrator Frank V. Wright to Moody, Fort Worth, June 24, 1927, Moody governors papers 301-11-folder Borger 6/13-7/27/27, TSA.

10. Telegram, Upton county attorney W. M. Davis to Moody, McCamey, January 19, 1927; telegram, Moody to Davis, January 20; Davis to Moody, January 22; Moody to Davis, January 29; telegram, Davis to Moody, February 5 and 8; telegram, Moody to Davis, February 8, Moody governors papers 301-12-folder Ranger Requests 1/31-4/2/27; Kirby to Moody, May 22, 1927, Moody governors papers 301-12-folder McCamey 5/22-7/18/27, TSA.

11. *Report of the Adjutant General of Texas, 1927–28*, 33; Ward, "Texas Rangers, 1919–1935," 159–63; Moody to AG (copying letter from district judge Charles Klapproth in Midland), January 16, 1929, Moody governors papers 301-11-folder Borger 2/29/28-10/29, TSA.

12. Brownson Malsch, *"Lone Wolf" Gonzaullas, Texas Ranger* (1980; repr., Norman: University of Oklahoma Press, 1998); service record, 401-Gonzaullas, TSA; Bob Stephens,

"Manuel T. 'Lone Wolf' Gonzaullas," *Texas Ranger Dispatch Magazine* 7 (Summer 2002), www.texasranger.org/dispatch/7/Gonzaullas.htm.

13. Gonzaullas to AG Robert L. Robertson, Dallas, January 21, 1928; telegram, C. C. Phillips to Moody, San Angelo, January 13, 1928, Moody governors papers 301-11-folder Ranger Reports, TSA.

14. A. C. Greene, *The Santa Claus Bank Robbery*, rev. ed. (1972; repr., Denton: University of North Texas Press, 1999). Walter F. Pilcher, "Santa Claus Bank Robbery," *New Handbook of Texas*, 6 vols. (Austin: TSHA, 1996), 5:883–84.

15. Walter Prescott Webb, *The Texas Rangers: A Century of Frontier Defense* (1935; repr., Austin: University of Texas Press, 1965), 533–38; Frost and Jenkins, *I'm Frank Hamer: The Life of a Texas Peace Officer* (1968; repr., Austin: State House Press, 1993), chap. 17. Both sources reproduce the text of Hamer's release. Ward, "Texas Rangers, 1919–1935," 156–57, based on missing Rangers records and newspapers.

16. *Report of the Adjutant General of Texas, 1929–30*, 81. Ward, "Texas Rangers, 1919–1935," 163–64, citing Ranger Records.

17. This complicated sequence is explained in Jacob F. Wolters, *Martial Law and Its Administration* (Austin: Gammel Book Co., 1930), 92–93.

18. Holmes to Moody, Borger, April 20, 1929, Moody governors papers 301-11-folder Borger 2/29/28-10/29, TSA.

19. Wolters, *Martial Law*, 94. Ward, "Texas Rangers, 1919–1935," 166–67, citing missing Ranger records.

20. Wolters, *Martial Law*, 94.

21. *Report of the Adjutant General of Texas, 1929–30*, 80; Wolters, *Martial Law*, 95–97; Ward, "Texas Rangers, 1919–1935," 167–69, drawing on missing Ranger Records. The proclamation, September 28, 1929, is in Moody governors papers 301-11-folder Borger 2/29/28-10/29, TSA.

22. Ward, "Texas Rangers, 1919–1935," 166–72, citing Ranger records. Wolters, *Martial Law*, 89–119; Harry Krenek, *The Power Vested: The Use of Martial Law and the National Guard in Texas Domestic Crisis, 1919–1932* (Austin: Presidial Press, 1980), 85–104; SO 259, AGD, October 17, 1929; Calhoun to Moody, Stinnett, October 31, 1929, Moody governors papers 301-10-folder 10/17-11/4/29; Calhoun to Moody, Stinnett, November 8, 1929; Moody to Calhoun, November 13, 1929, Moody governors papers 301-10-folder 10/17-11/4/29; telegram, J. C. Rothwell (*Borger Daily Herald*) to Moody, Borger, June 25, 1930; telegram, Moody to Rothwell, June 26, 1930, Moody governors papers 301-10-folder 11/12/29-12/24/30, TSA.

23. Typewritten MS, Marvin Burton, "The Johnny Holmes Murder Case," MS 26, Burton Collection, series I, transcripts, box 2, Holmes folder, TRHF; Burton, interview by Roger Conger, May 1, 1956, MS 33, Oral History, Red Burton, TRHF. Both typescripts contain ample detail of Burton's service in Borger.

24. Ward, "Texas Rangers, 1919–1935," 179, citing missing Ranger records; telegram, fifteen women to Moody, Shamrock, July 16, 1930, Moody governors papers 301-12-folder Shamrock 7/13-16/30, TSA. The story is reported in detail, with some confusion of dates and the sheriffs of Wheeler and Collingsworth counties, in a series of news items in the *Amarillo Daily News*, July 17 and 29, 1930; *Pampa Daily News*, July 17 and 28, 1930; and *Pampa Times*, July 18, 1930, in MS 4, MTG Collection, scrapbook 2, TRHF. See also *Austin Statesman*, July 15, 1930.

25. Arthur F. Raper, *The Tragedy of Lynching* (Chapel Hill: University of North Carolina Press, 1933), chap. 16; Edward Hake Phillips, "The Sherman Courthouse Riot of 1930," *East Texas Historical Journal* 25 (fall 1987): 12–19; Mike Cox, "The Sherman Riot," in Cox, *Texas Ranger Tales II* (Plano: Republic of Texas Press, 1999), 193–205; Thompson, "Sherman

Riot of 1930," *New Handbook of Texas* 5:1024–25; and Ward, "Texas Rangers, 1919–1935," 176–78, citing missing Ranger records; Malsch, *"Lone Wolf" Gonzaullas*, chap. 9; Frost and Jenkins, *"I'm Frank Hamer,"* chap. 18.

26. Hamer's official report to Governor Moody, May 13, 1930, Moody governors papers 301-12-folder Sherman 5/9-13/30, TSA.

27. Some accounts state that Hughes chose the vault and was left with a bucket of water and the door ajar. Most, however, have the door locked and the combination unknown to the Rangers even had they been able to reach it.

28. After the courthouse was fired, which Rangers reached Sherman when is obscure. The role of Gonzaullas is taken from Phillips, "Sherman Courthouse Riot," 14, based on a 1972 interview with him. Strangely, Gonzaullas's biographer, Brownson Malsch, describes the Sherman affair in detail but relegates the Lone Wolf's role to generalities about his investigative activities. Gonzaullas's stand at the jail makes a colorful story and deserves attention even though mentioned in no other source, including Malsch's biography.

29. Quoted in Raper, *Tragedy of Lynching*, 326.

30. The proclamation is in Moody governors papers 301-12-folder Sherman 5/9-13, TSA. Although Ward, "Texas Rangers, 1919–1935," 176, has Company B of the Rangers arriving on the afternoon of May 9, this seems unlikely. My speculation is that Hamer and his men came back Sunday with Hickman and his men and the final contingent of guardsmen. Gonzaullas's "lone ranger" act at the jail on May 9, recounted forty-two years later, may have been an embellished version of something that happened on this or a later day but went unrecorded.

31. Hamer to Moody, May 13, 1930, Moody governors papers 301-12-folder Sherman 5/9-13/29, TSA. Ward, "Texas Rangers, 1919–1935," 176 n50, citing "closed interview" in Dallas, June 18, 1970. From citations to the same interview associated with other events, it became apparent that the anonymous interviewee was Manuel Gonzaullas. My memo for the record of October 23, 2003, states that by telephone James Ward confirmed Gonzaullas as the interviewee. He wished to remain anonymous because he intended to write a book himself, which he never did. Ward explicitly authorized me to identify Gonzaullas as the source of all quotations attributed to the "closed interview."

32. Raper, *Tragedy of Lynching*, chap. 17.

Chapter 8

1. Sterling's autobiography contains much valuable if self-inflating information: *Trails and Trials of a Texas Ranger* (1959; repr., Norman: University of Oklahoma Press, 1968).

2. Ibid., chap. 21. *Report of the Adjutant General of Texas, 1931–32*, 21–23.

3. Service records of Mace and Townsend, 401-59-Mace and 401-64-Townsend, TSA.

4. Unlike previous adjutant generals, Sterling did not name or discuss personnel in his biennial report, so the selection of captains must be taken from his autobiography, chap. 21.

5. Diana Davids Olien and Roger M. Olien, *Oil in Texas: The Gusher Age, 1895–1945* (Austin: University of Texas Press, 2002), chap. 7; Robert D. Boyle, "Chaos in the East Texas Oil Field, 1930–1935," *SWHQ* 69 (January 1966): 340–52; Julia Cauble Smith, "East Texas Oilfield," in *New Handbook of Texas*, 6 vols. (Austin: TSHA, 1996), 2:772–74.

6. James R. Ward, "The Texas Rangers, 1919–1935: A Study in Law Enforcement" (PhD diss., Texas Christian University, 1972), 191–94. Ward's account relies heavily on missing Ranger records. For the arrival of Gonzaullas and Huddleston, see *Gregg County Oil News* (Kilgore), February 6, 1931; for the arrival of Hickman and his company, see *Kilgore News*, March 2, 1931, both in MS 4, MTG Collection, scrapbook 2, TRHF; Marvin Burton, "The Kilgore Raid," typescript in MS 26, Burton Collection, series I, transcripts, box 1,

Kilgore folder, TRHF; Brownson Malsch, *"Lone Wolf" Gonzaullas, Texas Ranger* (1980; repr., Norman: University of Oklahoma Press, 1998), chap. 10.

7. The following is taken largely from a lengthy interview with Gonzaullas in 1956 at a ceremony held at slain Ranger Dan McDuffie's grave in New Boston, Texas. The interviewer's first name was Stacey but otherwise unidentified. Dan Green, McDuffie's great-grandson, gave the tape to Robert Nieman, who in turn made a transcript available to me. He also deposited it in the TRHF. Hard copy in my possession. Other colorful details are in "How One Man Kept a Boom Town from Going Wild," *St. Louis Post-Dispatch*, May 19, 1931, in MS 4, MTG Collection, scrapbook 2, TRHF.

8. In addition to ibid., see Ward, "Texas Rangers, 1919–1935," 193, citing Ranger records and "closed" interview with Gonzaullus, the source of the final quote.

9. Gonzaullas 1956 interview, n7.

10. Olien and Olien, *Oil in Texas*, chap. 7, deals with the very complex situation that led to martial law. The proclamation is in Sterling governors papers 301-457-1, folder 8/15-21/31. TSA.

11. Ward, "Texas Rangers, 1919–1935," 198–200, citing Ranger records, newspapers, and interviews with Gonzaullus and A. Y. Allee. Sterling, *Trails and Trials*, chaps. 24–25. See also Harry Krenek, *The Power Vested: The Use of Martial Law and the National Guard in Texas Domestic Crisis, 1919–1932* (Austin: Presidial Press, 1980), 139–70.

12. Ward, "Texas Rangers, 1919–1935," citing Allee interview, 200.

13. Sterling, *Trails and Trials*, 255.

14. The quotations are from ibid., 265–66. Sterling writes as if the governor's telephone call reached him in time to call off the operation. However, Ward, "Texas Rangers, 1919–1935," 205–6, citing Rangers records and interviews with participants, documents at least the raid of August 21.

15. Ibid., 266.

Chapter 9

1. *Report of the Adjutant General, 1933–34*, 46; Stephen W. Schuster IV, "The Modernization of the Texas Rangers, 1930–1936" (master's thesis, Texas Christian University, 1965), 21–22. Like Ward's dissertation (see n. 4 below), Schuster's thesis relies on Ranger records at the Department of Public Safety, which have since disappeared. A condensed version was published under the same title in *West Texas Historical Association Year Book* 43 (October 1967): 65–79. Applications for Ranger appointments are in Ferguson governors papers 301-505-1, TSA. A long list of inappropriate recipients of special commissions appears in *Report and Recommendations of the Senate Committee Investigating Crime*, 43d Legislature, 1933–34, 58.

2. Mike Cox, "The Readin' Ranger," in Cox, *Texas Ranger Tales: Stories That Need Telling* (Plano: Republic of Texas Press, 1997), 160–71.

3. Service records: 401-64-Vaughan, 401-60-Odneal, 401-56-Hammond, 401-62-Robbins, 401-56-Hamer, D. E., TSA. The family history is recorded in Robert Nieman, "On the Trail of Bonnie and Clyde: Why Frank Hamer Wasn't Serving as a Texas Ranger," *Texas Ranger Dispatch Magazine* 13 (Spring 2004), www.texasranger.org/dispatch/13/pages/Hamer.htm.

4. *Report of the Adjutant General, 1933–34*, 46. James R. Ward, "The Texas Rangers, 1919–1935: A Study in Law Enforcement" (PhD diss., Texas Christian University, 1972), 210–12.

5. Schuster, "Modernization of the Texas Rangers," 22–23.

6. Ward, "Texas Rangers, 1919–1935, citing Ranger records, details the company record for two years, 217–20.

7. Ibid., citing Ranger records, 216–17; Brownson Malsch, *"Lone Wolf" Gonzaullas, Texas Ranger* (1980; repr., Norman: University of Oklahoma Press, 1997), 120; H. Gordon

Frost and John H. Jenkins, *I'm Frank Hamer: The Life of a Texas Peace Officer* (1968; repr., Austin: State House Press, 1993), 177; service record of Johnson, 401-58-Johnson, TSA.

8. Ward, "Texas Rangers, 1919–1935," citing Ranger records, 215–16, 220, 223.

9. Ibid., citing Ranger records and *Fort Worth Star-Telegram*, 216, 221.

10. William Warren Sterling, *Trails and Trials of a Texas Ranger* (1959; repr., Norman: University of Oklahoma Press, 1968), 519. Ward, "Texas Rangers, 1919–1935," citing Ranger records, 215.

11. *Report and Recommendations of the Senate Committee Investigating Crime*, 43d Legislature, 1933–34, 63–64; Schuster, "Modernization of the Texas Rangers," 23–24. Robbins was not identified by name, but the locale described points to him and his company stationed at Falfurrias.

12. The best history of the gangster years is Bryan Burrough, *Public Enemies: America's Greatest Crime Wave and the Birth of the FBI, 1933–34* (New York: Penguin, 2004). John Toland, *The Dillinger Days* (1963; repr., New York: Da Capo Press, 1995), is also excellent. Burrough, however, wrote after FBI files had been made public.

13. Schuster, "Modernization of the Texas Rangers," 8–9.

14. Ibid., 8. Malsch, "*Lone Wolf*," 116–17.

15. Joint Legislative Committee on Organization and Economy and Griffenhagen and Associates, *The Government of Texas*, Part 3 (Austin: Griffenhagen and Associates, 1933); *Report and Recommendations of the Senate Committee Investigating Crime*, 43d Legislature, 1933–34; Thomas L. Charlton, "The Texas Department of Public Safety, 1935–1957" (master's thesis, University of Texas–Austin, 1961), 12–19; J. Horace Bass, "Griffenhagen Report," *New Handbook of Texas*, 6 vols. (Austin: TSHA, 1996), 3:336–37.

16. Burrough, *Public Enemies*, tells this story authoritatively, making good use of FBI records opened only in recent years.

17. Lee Simmons, *Assignment Huntsville: Memoirs of a Texas Prison Official* (Austin: University of Texas Press, 1957), chap. 13; John Neal Phillips, *Running with Bonnie and Clyde: The Ten Fast Years of Ralph Fults* (Norman: University of Oklahoma Press, 1996), 168–72. In following the pursuit of Bonnie and Clyde, I have relied principally on this work, which is well documented from primary sources.

18. Simmons, *Assignment Huntsville*, 126–27. Phillips, *Running with Bonnie and Clyde*, 180, has Hamer receiving a commission in the highway patrol, but Simmons is the more authoritative, and the patrol chief, L. G. Phares, did not learn until later of Hamer's mission.

19. Phillips, *Running with Bonnie and Clyde*, 182–83. Simmons, *Assignment Huntsville*, 130, citing a watching farmer, credits Bonnie with finishing off Murphy. Simmons also places the pair at this location waiting in ambush to kill Ray Hamilton, with whom they had quarreled.

20. The action and quotations are from Phillips, *Running with Bonnie and Clyde*, 204–6, amply documented from original sources. It diverges in many ways from Simmons's account.

21. Walter Prescott Webb, *The Texas Rangers: A Century of Frontier Defense* (1935; repr., Austin: University of Texas Press, 1968), 538–44. Webb devotes a full chapter to Hamer. For his role in the story of Bonnie and Clyde, Webb relies on an interview with the normally reticent Hamer in July 1934, only two months after the Louisiana ambush. Webb concedes that the interview, although written in the first person, was constructed from notes taken during a two-hour conversation with Hamer. The account relegates the other five officers to supporting roles and, either because Hamer had to protect confidential sources or Webb erred seriously in converting hasty notes into a first-person interview, differs in substantial ways from the version I have given. Hamer's biographers tell the story mainly by quoting verbatim from the "interview" in Webb. Frost and Jenkins, *I'm Frank Hamer*, chaps. 20–22.

Chapter 10

1. Stephen W. Schuster IV, "The Modernization of the Texas Rangers" (master's thesis, Texas Christian University, 1965), 38–41; Thomas L. Charlton, "The Texas Department of Public Safety, 1935–1957" (master's thesis, University of Texas–Austin, 1961), 24–25. These two studies draw on official records in the Department of Public Safety as well as interviews with the major participants in the establishment of DPS. As noted in earlier chapters, DPS destroyed or otherwise lost the AG Ranger records of 1919–35. The DPS records in the state archives contain only one item before 1967, a box of extremely valuable newspaper clippings during the formation of DPS, 1935–36. Presumably, therefore, the official records of 1935–67 cited in these studies suffered the same fate as the records cited by James Ward in my earlier chapters. Schuster and Charlton are essential to this and subsequent chapters.

Bruce Smith, *State Police: Organization and Administration* (1925; repr., Montclair, NJ: Patterson Smith, 1969) probes the strengths and weaknesses of state police forces as they existed in the middle 1920s. The emphasis was mainly on Pennsylvania, New York, West Virginia, and New Jersey. The book not only may be presumed to have provided important guidance for the Johnson committee but is a valuable historical document showing the condition of state forces at the time. It was subsequently updated to reflect a later time: *Police Systems in the United States* (New York: Harper and Row, 1960).

2. Schuster, "Modernization of the Texas Rangers," 37, citing Ranger records and "closed interview" subsequently identified as with Manuel T. Gonzaullas; Charlton, "Department of Public Safety," 21–23; James R. Ward, "The Texas Rangers, 1919–1935: A Study in Law Enforcement" (PhD diss., Texas Christian University, 1972), 228–29; service records of all named in 401-56, -59, TSA.

3. UP dispatch of December 24, 1935, taken from the *Henderson News* of same date. Shortly after the organization of the Department of Public Safety in August 1935, someone subscribed to a clipping service and entered the news clips in a scrap book. The pages, no longer bound, are in box DPS 1980/240, TSA. The items circulated by the wire services—UP, AP, INS—appeared in many newspapers, and the scrapbook clippings often came, as in this instance, from small-town rather than big-city newspapers, in which they usually appeared too. In the absence of official records, these clippings are the best sources for the organization of DPS in 1935–36 and will often be cited. Wire service reporting lends credibility to a story regardless of the paper in which it appeared.

4. This story rests in part on Ben H. Procter, *Just One Riot: Episodes of Texas Rangers in the 20th Century* (Austin: Eakin Press, 1991), chap. 4. Titled "Leo Bishop and the San Augustine Crime Wave," the chapter draws largely on interviews conducted with Bishop in 1968 and 1969. I have also drawn on *Texas Department of Public Safety, August 10, 1935, to December 1, 1936*, Report of Public Safety Commission to Governor Allred, 15; Col. H. H. Carmichael (as told to Westmoreland Gray), "We Rangers: Lawmen of the Frontier, 1937 Model," *Best Action Western Stories*, September 1937, 103; *San Augustine Tribune*, November 14 and December 19, 1935; *Henderson News*, December 24, 1935; AP dispatch in *Brenham Press*, January 23, 1936; and AP dispatch in *Amarillo Globe*, March 16, 1936. The newspapers are clippings in DPS 1980/240, TSA.

Critical to my account has been the aid of Jody Ginn, presently (2005) criminal investigator for the Travis County district attorney's office (Austin). Ginn has exhaustively researched the San Augustine story for years and uncovered evidence hitherto untapped. I am grateful for a detailed, documented commentary on my first draft that he provided me by e-mail on June 6, 2005.

5. *General Laws of Texas*, 44th Legislature, Regular Session, 444–54.

6. *San Antonio Express*, May 15, 1935.

7. *Dallas Morning News*, July 27 and 28, 1935, clippings in DPS 1980/240, TSA.

8. Johnson in *Dallas News*, October 1, 1935, clipping in DPS 1980/240, TSA. Preceding paragraphs draw heavily on Charlton, "Department of Public Safety," 41–50; *Texas Department of Public Safety, August 10, 1935, to December 1, 1936*, Report of Public Safety Commission to Governor Allred; and James W. Robinson, *The DPS Story: History of the Development of the Department of Public Safety in Texas* (Austin: DPS, 1974). Appropriations are in *General Laws of Texas*, 43rd Legislature, Regular Session, 1092–95.

9. Schuster, "Modernization of the Texas Rangers," 52–53, based on interview with Homer Garrison.

10. *Austin American-Statesman*, September 8, 1935; *San Antonio Light*, September 8, 1935, in DPS 1980/240, TSA.

11. Schuster, "Modernization of Texas Rangers," 53, citing interview with Johnson.

12. UPS dispatch, Dallas, October 11, 1935, in *Tyler Courier Times*, same date, DPS 1980/240, TSA.

13. *Shreveport Times*, August 4, 1935, DPS 1980/240, TSA.

14. Allred governors papers 301-1985/024-21, TSA, contains folders labeled "Lynching in Columbus" that hold many letters of protest and a few supporting the mob.

15. *New York Post*, June 18, 1936, in Ralph Ginzburg, *One Hundred Years of Lynchings* (Baltimore: Black Classic Press, 1988), 229; *Austin American*, July 31, 1936.

16. AP dispatch in *Corpus Christi Caller*, December 31, 1935, DPS 1980/240, TSA; Carmichael, "We Rangers," 102, 104–5.

Chapter 11

1. *Wichita Times*, December 13, 1935, quoting Albert Sidney Johnson; *Houston Chronicle*, December 15, 1935, quoting Governor Allred, DPS 1980/240, TSA. These troubles emerged in a legislative investigation dealt with later in this chapter. Mike Cox, "Cowboy Tom Hickman," in Cox, *Texas Ranger Tales II* (Plano: Republic of Texas Press, 1999), 188, tells of the Hollywood venture.

2. *Dallas Herald*, December 14, 1935, quoting Clark's testimony in legislative hearing, DPS 1980/240, TSA.

3. Mrs. Wheeler related the plate-switching and drive to Fort Worth to Governor Allred. AP dispatch, December 14, 1935, in *Dallas Herald*, same date, DPS 1980/240, TSA.

4. AP dispatch, December 14, 1935, in *Dallas Herald*, same date, DPS 1980/240, TSA. The two men were Polk Shelton and Assistant Attorney General Lester King.

5. *Dallas Dispatch*, November 6, 1935, DPS 1980/240, TSA. An unidentified George West paper, November 11, 1935, ibid., described the raid and stated that the two Rangers acted on the "specific, personal instructions" of Governor Allred.

6. This is taken from an unidentified newspaper clipping, Fort Worth, December 2, 1935, DPS 1980/240, TSA. Another version, almost the same, appeared in an AP dispatch, Fort Worth, December 3, in *Austin Statesman*, December 4, 1935, ibid. Johnson tells of the telephone conference call: AP dispatch, Dallas, November 13, 1935, in *Brownsville Herald*, November 15, 1935, ibid. See also Stephen W. Schuster IV, "The Modernization of the Texas Rangers, 1930–1936" (master's thesis, Texas Christian University, 1965), 62–65.

7. AP dispatch, Fort Worth, December 3, 1935, in *Austin Statesman*, December 4, and *Houston Chronicle*, same date, DPS 1980/240, TSA.

8. *San Antonio Express*, December 12, 1935; UP dispatch, Austin, December 12, in *Fort Worth Star*, same date, DPS 1980/240, TSA.

9. AP dispatch, Austin, December 14, 1935, in *Houston Chronicle*, December 15; UPI dispatch, Austin, December 14, in *Dallas Journal* (?), December 15; INS dispatch, Austin, December 14, in *Dallas Times-Herald*, December 15; AP dispatch, Austin, December 14, in *Houston Post*, December 15, 1935, DPS 1980/240, TSA.

10. AP dispatch, Austin, March 16, 1936, in *Amarillo Globe*, same date, DPS 1980/240, TSA.

11. Austin, December 30, 1935, in *Houston Press*, same date; AP dispatch in *Corpus Christi Caller*, December 31, 1935; UP dispatch, Austin, December 31, 1935, in *Fort Worth Press*, same date, DPS 1980/240, TSA.

12. AP dispatch in *Corpus Christi Caller*, December 31, 1935; UP dispatch, Austin, in *Eastland Telegram*, January 10, 1936, DPS 1980/240, TSA.

13. Austin, December 30, 1935, in *Houston Press*, same date; AP dispatch, *Corpus Christi Caller*, December 31, 1935; *Austin Statesman*, January 2, 1936; UP dispatch, Austin, in *Marshall News*, January 2, 1936, DPS 1980/240, TSA.

14. *Texas Department of Public Safety, August 10, 1935, to December 1, 1936*, Report of the Public Safety Commission to Governor Allred, 26.

15. *Austin Dispatch*, April 7, 1936, DPS 1980/240, TSA. See also Thomas L. Charlton, "The Texas Department of Public Safety, 1935–1957" (master's thesis, University of Texas–Austin, 1961), 63–69.

16. AP dispatch, Austin, April 8, 1936, in *Waco Herald*, same date; *San Antonio Light*, April 9, 1936, DPS 1980/240, TSA.

17. *San Antonio Light*, April 9, 1936, DPS 1980/240, TSA.

18. INS dispatch, Austin, April 11, 1936, in *Dallas Herald*, April 12, 1936; *San Antonio Light*, dispatch in *Beeville Bee*, April 16, 1936, DPS 1980/240, TSA.

19. *Round Rock Leader*, May 21, 1936, DPS 1980/240, TSA.

20. AP dispatch, Austin, May 9, 1936, in unidentified San Angelo newspaper, same date, DPS 1980/240, TSA. Charlton, "Texas Department of Public Safety," 68.

21. *Austin American*, July 31, 1936. Charlton, "Texas Department of Public Safety," 72–74.

22. Charlton, "Texas Department of Public Safety," 72–74.

23. H. H. Carmichael (as told to Westmoreland Gray), "We Rangers: Lawmen of the Frontier, 1937 model,'" *Best Action Western Stories*, September 1937, 104–5.

24. Charlton, "Texas Department of Public Safety," 93–95.

25. MS 84, Phares Collection, box 1, TRHF. This typescript is a carbon copy, probably drafted in the spring or summer of 1938, and bears at the top a handwritten notation, "Sunday Aus[tin] Release."

26. *Austin American Statesman*, September 25, 1938, MS 4, MTG Collection, scrapbook 3, TRHF.

27. *Austin Statesman*, September 27, 1938, in ibid.

Chapter 12

1. Thomas L. Charlton, "The Texas Department of Public Safety, 1935–1957" (master's thesis, University of Texas–Austin, 1961), 113–14; James W. Robinson, *The DPS Story: History of the Department of Public Safety in Texas* (Austin: DPS, 1974), 21.

2. The quotation is from interview of Lewis Rigler by Robert Nieman, which Nieman sent me by e-mail on August 3, 2003. Profiles of Garrison are common throughout his reign. I have drawn on my own research of this period and also Charlton, "Texas Department of Public Safety," 98–99; Ben H. Procter, *Just One Riot: Episodes of Texas Rangers in the 20th Century* (Austin: Eakin Press, 1991), 13; *DPS Chaparral*, July–August

1949, 3; "He Heads the Texas Rangers," *Together* [a Methodist publication], August 1961; and Stan Redding, "What is a Ranger?" *Houston Chronicle Texas Magazine*, February 9, 1969, 11. Four good books give the Ranger's perspective throughout: Glenn Elliott with Robert Nieman, *Glenn Elliott: A Ranger's Ranger* (Waco: Texian Press, 1999); Elliott and Nieman, *Glenn Elliott: Still a Ranger's Ranger* (Longview, TX: Ranger Publishing, 2002); Ed Gooding and Robert Nieman, *Ed Gooding: Soldier, Texas Ranger* (Longview, Texas: Ranger Publishing, 2001); and Lewis C. Rigler and Judyth Wagner Rigler, *In the Line of Duty: Reflections of a Texas Ranger Private* (Denton: University of North Texas Press, 1995).

3. Stephen W. Schuster IV, "The Modernization of the Texas Rangers, 1930–1936," (master's thesis, Texas Christian University, 1965), 54–55. Schuster's sources are DPS records that no longer exist. Some Rangers of the Carmichael and Garrison eras, however, kept all their records, both sent and received, and donated them to the archives at the TRHF. I have sampled both weekly reports and case reports. The weekly reports are of value more in showing Ranger routine than adventure. Most of the case reports are excellent examples of investigative reporting.

4. Charlton, "Texas Department of Public Safety," 72–74 (based on missing DPS records); Texas DPS, *Twenty-five Year Review and Biennial Report 1959–60*, January 1, 1961, 27. For a map of the regional commands, see ibid., 26. For statistics of DPS progress 1936–56, see Robinson, *DPS Story*, 28.

5. *Wall Street Journal*, October 15, 1959.

6. Robinson, *DPS Story*, 28.

7. *Longview News*, February 12, 1968. I have examined enough weekly reports in the archives of the TRHF to confirm that typical Ranger weeks involved more than sixty hours and sometimes one hundred.

8. Gooding and Nieman, *Ed Gooding*, 172.

9. Charlton, "Texas Department of Public Safety," 103–4.

10. George Norris Green, *The Establishment in Texas Politics: The Primitive Years, 1938–1957* (Westport, CT: Greenwood Press, 1979), chap. 3.

11. Brownson Malsch, *"Lone Wolf" Gonzaullas, Texas Ranger* (1980; repr., Norman: University of Oklahoma Press, 1998), chaps. 11–17.

12. Charlton, "Texas Department of Public Safety," 114.

13. Although DPS records for the period have disappeared, numerous case reports of Gonzaullas are in the governors papers, RG 301, of Coke Stevenson, Beauford Jester, and Allan Shivers, TSA.

14. Ranger roster in *DPS Chaparral*, July–August 1949; Rigler and Rigler, *In the Line of Duty*, 163. Rigler profiles and pays tribute to Gonzaullas, 162–67.

15. Geer to Gonzaullas, Vernon, January 30, 1948, MS 40, James Geer Collection, 1/18; Gonzaullas to Garrison, Dallas, February 4, 1948, 1/17; Chief Investigator John W. Kelley, Texas Mid-Continent Oil & Gas Association, to Garrison, Dallas, February 3, 1948, 1/7, TRHF.

16. *Longview News-Journal*, February 15, 1957.

17. Malsch, *"Lone Wolf,"* chap. 18.

18. Wick Fowler, "Badmen were Better in Lone Wolf's Day," *Dallas Morning News*, May 25, 1963; Lewis Rigler, as told to Robert Nieman, "Lone Wolf Was Camera Shy," *Texas Ranger Dispatch* 4 (Summer 2001), www.texasranger.org/dispatch/4/LoneWolf.htm.

19. Texas DPS, *Progress Report, 1942–44*.

20. Rigler and Rigler, *In the Line of Duty*, 151–53. My characterization of Crowder draws mainly on this source; Elliott and Nieman, *Glenn Elliott*, 85 ff; and Robert Nieman, "Capt. Bob Crowder," *Texas Ranger Dispatch Magazine* 14 (Summer 2004), www.texasranger.org/dispatch/14/pages/20th_Crowder.htm.

21. In the absence of DPS records, the best source is Procter, *Just One Riot*, chap. 6, based on interviews with Crowder. See also Charlton, "Texas Department of Public Safety," 167–70, based on *Dallas Times Herald*, April 17, 1955; and Robert Nieman, "Captain Bob Crowder and the Rusk State Hospital Riot," *Texas Ranger Dispatch Magazine* 3 (Spring 2001), www.texasranger.org/dispatch/3/Crowder.htm. Interviewed by a journalist, Crowder, in this version armed with only one pistol, gave a slightly different answer about what might have happened: "I don't know how I would have come out with that many against me, had they tried to call my hand, but I know this: I would have taken eight of them with me." Stan Redding, "Tall in the Saddle for 150 Years," *State Journal of Peace Officers* (May 1973):48.

22. Official records having disappeared, this is Peoples's story as told to his biographer: James M. Day, *Captain Clint Peoples, Texas Ranger: Fifty Years a Lawman* (Waco: Texian Press, 1980), 108–10.

23. Texas Research League, *The Texas Department of Public Safety: Its Services and Organization* (Austin, 1957); Texas Legislature, *General and Special Laws*, 55th Regular Session, 1957, chap. 261; Day, *Clint Peoples*, 118–19; Texas DPS, *Twenty-five Year Review and Biennial Report, 1959–60*, January 1, 1961.

24. Texas Research League, *The Texas Department of Public Safety: Its Services and Organization*. Company B's new sergeant, Arthur Hill, recorded in his weekly log conferring in Austin with Chief Crowder in October 1956. Hill Family Papers, courtesy Sharon Spinks. Rigler, *In the Line of Duty*, 154.

25. Day, *Clint Peoples*, 123.

26. Elliott and Nieman, *Glenn Elliott*, 73; Linda Jay Puckett, *Cast a Long Shadow: A Casebook of the Law Enforcement Career of Texas Ranger Captain E. J. (Jay) Banks* (Dallas: Ussery Printing, 1984), 102.

27. Papworth finally confessed his role, although in self-serving terms. He explained the content of the confession to a reporter, and it appeared in the evening edition of the *Fort Worth Star-Telegram*, May 1, 1957.

28. Accounts by participants differ in some major ways. All at the time refused to identify the tipster. Banks named Papworth to a crime writer, Stan Redding, "Top Gun of the Texas Rangers," *True Detective Magazine*, February 1963, a biographical article about Klevenhagen. The surveillance between motel rooms is the recollection of Sergeant Hill, interview by Andy and Sharon Spinks, December 30, 1986, Hill Family Papers, courtesy Sharon Spinks.

29. Most sources have Hill at the intersection of Meandering Road and Jacksboro Highway, the location of the Beachcomber Tavern. Hill's daily log, however, names Casino Beach, and Jim Ray's interview with Robert Nieman, October 18, 1997, identifies a small park up Meandering Road from the intersection.

30. This seems plausible because Norris's wife, who appeared the next day, could have brought murder charges against a named lawman, and this was a simple way to avoid litigation.

31. This episode has been difficult to reconstruct. Vital sources are contemporary accounts of participants in both the morning and evening editions of the *Fort Worth Star-Telegram*, April 30 and May 1, 1957, and the evening paper, the *Fort Worth Press*, both dates. I am indebted to J'Nell Pate of Azle for researching these papers for me and also providing a copy of the relevant portion of a Fort Worth city map of 1957. In later accounts of participants, memories differed both on events and geography. The sources are Banks himself in Puckett, *Cast a Long Shadow*, chap. 19; Hill in interview with Andy and Sharon Spinks, December 30, 1986, and Hill's "Weekly Activity Notebook" for relevant dates, courtesy Sharon Spinks; Redding, "Top Gun of the Texas Rangers";

Douglas V. Meed, *Texas Ranger Johnny Klevenhagen* (Plano: Republic of Texas Press, 2000), chap. 17; Jim Ray, interview by Robert Nieman, October 18, 1997, copy provided by Nieman; also based on Ray is Nieman, "Capt. Johnny Klevenhagen," *Texas Ranger Dispatch Magazine* 10 (Spring 2003), www.texasranger.org/dispatch/10/Pages/Klevenhagen.htm. Meed based his account on the *Houston Post*, May 1, 1957, but wrongly attributed the killing of Norris to Klevenhagen. The accounts of Banks, Hill, and Ray are much more plausible, especially since the crime-scene photograph of Norris's body (which I have seen) belies the notion that he was killed by a shotgun. These later recollections proved valuable in filling in details contained in the contemporary newspaper accounts, especially Banks's account.

32. Puckett, *Cast a Long Shadow*, chaps. 23–24, contains Banks's self-justification.

Chapter 13

1. Gonzaullas to Garrison, September 10, 1947, Jester governors papers 301-4-14/60, Top of Hill, TSA. This file contains detailed news clippings also.

2. *Fort Worth Star-Telegram*, December 12, 1978, in MS 4, MTG Collection, scrapbook 5, TRHF.

3. Ed Gooding and Robert Nieman, *Ed Gooding: Soldier, Texas Ranger* (Longview, TX: Ranger Publishing, 2001), 107–16. Gooding of course was an active participant. I have also drawn on Nieman, paper presented at the Texas State Historical Association convention in Fort Worth, March 3, 2005, copy provided by Nieman.

4. MS 17, Galveston Gambling, 1/6, TRHF, contains a roster of weekly Ranger assignments to Galveston from June 25, 1957, to January 1, 1961, showing the pairing of Rangers from the other five companies with those of Company A.

5. Glenn Elliott and Robert Nieman, *Glenn Elliott: A Ranger's Ranger* (Waco: Texian Press, 1999), 103.

6. *Paris News*, January 24, 1941, and March 2, 1941, in MS 4, MTG Collection, scrapbook 3, TRHF.

7. Quotations: *Dallas Morning News*, July 26, 1968, and March 4, 1996.

8. Ibid., January 13, 1987, and March 4, 1996.

9. Arthur Hajecate, President Oil Workers International Union Local 227, to AG, with copies to Governor Jester and Attorney General Price Daniel, Corpus Christi, September 25, 1947; Jester to Hajecate, September 29, 1947; Hajecate to Jester, October 7, 1947; Jester to Hajecate, October 11, 1947, Jester governors papers 301-4-14/112, DPS 1947 folder; Allee to Jester, Harlingen, September 27, 1947, ibid., 301-4-14/60, oil strike folder; telegram, T. M. McCormick, Secretary-Treasurer Oil Workers International Union, to Jester, Toledo, Ohio, August 10, 1948, ibid., 301-4-14/112, DPS 1948 folder, TSA. Ranger Joe Bridge's son told what had happened: Joe Bridge Jr., *Joe H. Bridge, Texas Ranger, 1936–1956* (n.p. 1988), 47–49.

10. Lewis Rigler and Judyth Wagner Rigler, *In the Line of Duty: Reflections of a Texas Ranger Private* (Denton: University of North Texas Press, 1995), 58–59.

11. In the absence of official documents, my account is derived mainly from Elliott and Nieman, *Glenn Elliott*, 69–73, and Rigler and Rigler, *In the Line of Duty*, 56–61.

12. Stan Redding, "Trouble at Daingerfield," *Houston Chronicle Texas Magazine*, February 9, 1969, 12.

13. Elliott and Nieman, *Glenn Elliott*, chap. 8; Rigler and Rigler, *In the Line of Duty*, 61–68; Redding, "Trouble at Daingerfield," 12.

14. Redding, "Trouble at Daingerfield," 12.

15. Glenn Elliott, *Glenn Elliott*, 105–6, and Stan Redding give different versions of this incident. Redding had contemporary quotes from Crowder. I have combined the most plausible elements of the two accounts.

16. Elliott and Nieman, *Glenn Elliott*, 108.

17. James S. Olson, "Beaumont Riot of 1943," *New Handbook of Texas*, 6 vols. (Austin: TSHA, 1996), 1:448; Thomas L. Charlton, "The Texas Department of Public Safety, 1935–57" (master's thesis, University of Texas–Austin, 1961), 138–39, drawing on Beaumont newspapers.

18. Telegram, K. W. Lorenz, North Dallas Home Owners and Tax Payers Protective Association, to O'Daniel, Dallas, September 3, 1940; Garrison to O'Daniel, September 5, 1940; telegram, Walter White, Secretary NAACP, to O'Daniel, New York, September 17, 1940, O'Daniel governors papers 301-2001/138-102, folder DPS Gen Corres September–December 1940; Attorney General Francis Biddle to Gov. Coke Stevenson, October 15, 1941; Gonzaullas to Garrison, Dallas, November 5, 1941, Stevenson governors papers 301-4-14/171, folder P.S. Dept of, TSA.

19. Garrison to Gonzaullas, June 21, 1950; Gonzaullas to Garrison, Dallas, June 27, 1930, Shivers governors papers 301-1977/081-134, folder DPS special reports, TSA.

20. Robyn Duff Ladino, *Desegregating Texas Schools: Eisenhower, Shivers, and the Crisis at Mansfield High* (Austin: University of Texas Press, 1996). Useful background is in Ricky F. Dobbs, *Yellow Dogs and Republicans: Allan Shivers and Texas Two-Party Politics* (College Station: Texas A&M University Press, 2005), 136–44.

21. Ladino, *Desegregating Texas Schools*, chap. 6. According to her, on October 8, 1956, Sgt. Jay Banks wrote a detailed report of the Mansfield operation to Colonel Garrison. Her efforts to obtain a copy from DPS and the Rangers proved futile. It had been destroyed, she was told. A copy, however, had made its way into the National Archives in Washington. She discusses the report and its fate on p. 173, n62.

22. Linda Jay Puckett, *Cast a Long Shadow: A Casebook of the Law Enforcement Career of Texas Ranger Captain E. J. (Jay) Banks* (Dallas: Ussery Printing Co., 1984), 92–94.

23. John E. Clark, *The Fall of the Duke of Duval: A Prosecutor's Journal* (Austin: Eakin Press, 1996), 23. Background before the 1920s is authoritatively treated in Evan Anders, *Boss Rule in South Texas* (Austin: University of Texas Press, 1982).

24. Clark, *Fall of Duke of Duval*, 64.

25. Bridge Jr., *Joe Bridge*, 50–57, recounts and includes first-hand evidence of Bridge's service in San Diego. The quotation is from a newspaper clipping, May 24, 1954, reprinted on p. 54.

26. Several versions of this story appear in the sources. I have relied mainly on Stan Redding, "A Man to Watch the Rugged Land," *Houston Chronicle Texas Magazine*, February 9, 1969, 28; and James Pattie, "A. Y. Allee: The Man and the Legend," *Texas Parade*, July 1971. See also Clark, *Fall of the Duke of Duval*, 73–74.

27. Clark, *Fall of the Duke of Duval*, 77–85.

Chapter 14

1. See for one of many examples remarks of Col. Wilson Speir at annual meeting, Texas Police Association, Fort Worth, June 12, 1972, 1992/13-1, Speir Speeches, TSA. The theme runs throughout Glenn Elliott with Robert Nieman, *Glenn Elliott: A Ranger's Ranger* (Waco: Texian Press, 1999) and Ed Gooding and Robert Nieman, *Ed Gooding: Soldier, Texas Ranger* (Longview, TX: Ranger Publishing, 2001). The discontent did not quickly abate. Rangers, mostly retired, expressed the same opinion repeatedly in press interviews as late as the 1990s.

2. All these organizations have substantial historical sketches in *The New Handbook of Texas*, 6 vols. (Austin: TSHA, 1996), under the appropriate alphabetical heading, both in print and online. See also under "Mexican American Organizations" and "Crystal City Revolts".

3. Bryan Woolley, "Raising 'La Raza,'" *Dallas Morning News*, July 27, 2003. Gutiérrez tells his own story in *The Making of a Chicano Militant: Lessons from Cristal* (Madison: University of Wisconsin Press, 1998).

4. Surviving Ranger records include none bearing on Allee and his Rangers in the tense developments at Crystal City in 1963. A thorough study is John Staples Shockley, *Chicano Revolt in a Texas Town* (Notre Dame: University of Notre Dame Press, 1974), chap. 2. Gutiérrez's quote on Allee is in *San Antonio Express*, September 9, 1970. See also David Montejano, *Anglos and Mexicans in the Making of Texas, 1836–1986* (Austin: University of Texas Press, 1987), 282–85.

5. Ben H. Procter, "The Modern Texas Rangers: A Law Enforcement Dilemma in the Rio Grande Valley," in Manuel P. Servin, ed., *The Mexican Americans: An Awakening Minority* (Beverly Hills: Glencoe Press, 1970), 212–27.

6. In *Medrano v. Allee*, a three-judge federal panel accepted as established fact a series of specified actions by law enforcement officers. Except for the November 1966 incident, Texas Rangers did not figure in any of these stipulations until May 1967, the month Captain Allee began to attract widespread notice.

7. Ranger assignments are described in testimony of Allee in *Hearing before the United States Commission on Civil Rights, San Antonio, December 9–14, 1968* (Washington: GPO, n.d.), 740–41.

8. U.S. Commission on Civil Rights, *Mexican Americans and the Administration of Justice in the Southwest* (Washington: GPO, March 1970), 17. The state advisory committee's report is *Civil Rights in Texas* (a mimeographed compilation dated February 1970). It is certain that in July 1967 the committee issued a report titled *The Administration of Justice in Starr County*, but I have been unable to find a copy. Excerpts appear in the federal commission report.

9. Both versions appear in the testimony of Krueger and Allee at the San Antonio hearing of December 1968 (n7); Krueger, 418–27, Allee, 735–45. See also Procter, "Modern Texas Rangers," 223–24.

10. This account is taken mainly from the stipulation of fact accepted by the district court judges. Allee was not questioned about the Dimas affair in the San Antonio hearings of December 1968. See also Jane Pattie, "A. Y. Allee. The Man and the Legend," *Texas Parade*, July 1971; Stan Redding, "Abolish the Rangers," *Houston Chronicle Texas Magazine*, February 2, 1969, 30; and Procter, "Modern Texas Rangers," 224–25.

11. *Civil Rights in Texas*, 48.

12. The suit was tried in the U.S. District Court for the Southern District of Texas as *Francisco Medrano et al. v. A. Y. Allee et al.* I am indebted to lawyer-historian Rick Miller, Bell County attorney, for providing the complete texts of the U.S. district and Supreme Court rulings in this case.

13. Redding, "Abolish the Rangers," 30; Paul Reecer, "Ranger Stance Aired," AP dispatch in *Daily Texan*, January 10, 1968.

14. Reecer, "Ranger Stance Aired"; Redding, "Abolish the Rangers," 30.

15. *Hearing before the United States Civil Rights Commission*, 715–34 (testimony), 1211–13 (statement for the record).

16. "Should We Abolish the Rangers?" *Houston Post*, August 20, 1972. Magazines and newspapers afford the principal sources because no DPS records relating to the issue survived.

17. Allee quote: John Kifner (*New York Times* staff writer), "Texas Rangers under Fire," *Stars and Stripes*, May 9, 1970. Probably reprinted from an article in the *Times*.

18. Ramiro Martínez, *They Call Me Ranger Ray: From the UT Tower Sniper to Corruption in South Texas* (New Braunfels, TX: Rio Bravo Publishing, 2005).

19. Case No. 67-B-36, 347 F. Supp. 605, *Francisco Medrano et al. v. A. Y. Allee et al.*

20. *Allee v. Medrano*, 416 U.S. 802.

21. Final Judgment as Modified Pursuant to Remand by the Supreme Court of the United States, Civil Action No. 67-B-36, *Medrano v. Allee*, June 24, 1976. Gooding and Nieman, *Ed Gooding*, 152.

22. Shockley, *Chicano Revolt in a Texas Town*, chaps. 2–6, remains the most thorough and authoritative history of events in Crystal City. For Gutiérrez's account of his rise and the rise of the Chicano movement, see his *Making of a Chicano Militant*. An amusing but not irrelevant book is Gutiérrez, *A Gringo Manual on How to Handle Mexicans*, 2nd ed. (Houston: Arte Público Press, 2001).

23. Crystal City Manager William Richey to Col. Wilson E. Speir, Crystal City, June 10, 1970; Speir to Richey, June 12, 1970, Company D files 1973, 1998/097-4, TSA.

24. Chris Bird, "Ranger's Encounter Fits in with Legend," *Dallas Morning News*, September 11, 1993; unidentified news clipping (probably San Antonio), ca. December 15, 1978; Fr. Michael Allen, O.M.I., to Wilson E. Speir, Edinburg, March 9, 1971; Pharr mayor R. S. Bowe to Speir, Pharr, July 29, 1971, MS 28, Capt. Jack O. Dean Collection, II-1/4–1/6, TRHF.

25. H. Joaquin Jackson and David Marion Wilkinson, *One Ranger: A Memoir* (Austin: University of Texas Press, 2005).

26. No DPS records have survived to record this critical election day. The story is related in fascinating detail by Jackson himself in *One Ranger*, 67–75, and by Gutiérrez in *Making of a Chicano Militant*, 190–93. Gutiérrez's account nicely complements Jackson's. Schockley, *Chicano Revolt in a Texas Town*, 202–3.

27. Gutiérrez, *Making of a Chicano Militant*, 190–91.

28. Zavala County judge Irl Taylor and three commissioners to Col. Wilson Speir, Crystal City, April 6, 1973; memo, Capt. John M. Wood to Senior Capt. Clint Peoples, "Incidents during Elections," San Antonio, September 24, 1973, Co. D Files 1973; memo, Capt. John M. Wood to Senior Capt. W. D. Wilson, "Incidents during April 1974," San Antonio, May 6, 1974, Co. D Files 1974, 1998/097-4, TSA.

29. Crystal city manager Esequiel Guzman to DPS Director Wilson E. Speir, Crystal City, July 9, 1975; Ranger H. Joaquin Jackson, Investigation Report, "Theft of Funds," August 25, 1975, DPS Case Files, TRS 10-22, "Crystal City Investigation, 1970–79," 1998/097-11, TSA.

30. Jackson, Investigation Reports, "Theft of Public Funds," November 21 and December 8, 1975, DPS Case Files, TRS 10-22, "Crystal City Investigation, 1970–79," 1998/097-11; memo, Co. D Sgt. H. R. Block to Senior Capt. W. D. Wilson, "Incidents during Month of September 1976," October 6, 1976, Co. D Files 1976, 1998/097-4, TSA.

31. Ranger H. Joaquin Jackson, Investigation Report, "Theft of Funds," August 25, 1975, DPS Case Files, TRS 10-22, "Crystal City Investigation, 1970–79," 1998/097-11; memo, Wood to Wilson, "Militant: José Angel Gutiérrez, Crystal City (County Judge)," May 13, 1975, Co. D Files 1975, 1998/097-4, TSA.

32. *San Antonio Express*, November 10, 1976; Jackson, Investigation Report, "Threats to Kill," November 22, 1976, DPS Case Files, TRS 10-22, "Crystal City Investigation, 1970–79," 1998/097-11, TSA.

33. Gutiérrez, *Making of Chicano Militant*, 192.

34. Woolley, "Raising 'La Raza.'"

Chapter 15

1. Stan Redding, "The Boss and the Heritage of the Force He Serves," *Houston Chronicle Texas Magazine*, February 9, 1969, 9. Again, no official DPS records of internal affairs have survived. Stan Redding wrote frequently about the Rangers, with clear credibility.

2. DPS, *50th Anniversary of the Department of Public Safety* (Austin: DPS, 1985), 14; James M. Day, *Captain Clint Peoples, Texas Ranger: Fifty Years a Lawman* (Waco: Texian Press, 1980), 154–55. A 1973 DPS organization chart is in James W. Robinson, *The DPS Story: History of the Development of the Department of Public Safety in Texas* (Austin: DPS, 1974), 47.

3. Series of four investigative reports in *Dallas Times-Herald*, July 6, 7, 8, and 9, 1969.

4. Sketch of Ray by Robert Nieman in *Texas Ranger Dispatch Magazine* 2 (Winter 2000), www.texasranger.org/dispatch/2/Ray.htm. See chap. 12 for Ray's role in the chase of Gene Paul Norris. His name really was Jim, but DPS bureaucracy insisted on more, so he gave his father's name.

5. Robert Draper, "Twilight of the Texas Rangers," *Texas Monthly* 22 (February 1994), 110.

6. Overtime crops up repeatedly in company files in 1998/097, TSA.

7. Memo, Chief CLE J. M. Ray to Col. Wilson E. Speir, "Investigative Assignment Re Donald 'Red' Barry," November 21, 1973, in a thick binder containing other documents, including a transcript of Ray's taped interview with the two producers in Hollywood, in DPS Case Files, TRS 10-22, 1998/097-11, "Clint Peoples Investigation"; Peoples to Speir, January 31, 1974, Wilson Correspondence, 1998/097-14, TSA.

8. Wilson to Ray, February 8, 1974, Wilson Correspondence, 1998/097-14, TSA. Kay Powers, "1 Career, 1 Ranger," *Dallas Morning News*, January 13, 1985.

9. Ed Gooding and Robert Nieman, *Ed Gooding: Soldier, Texas Ranger* (Longview, Texas: Ranger Publishing, 2001), 98.

10. DPS, *50th Anniversary*, 14.

11. Dick Stanley, "The New Texas Rangers, *Austin American-Statesman*, May 13, 1979.

12. Draper, "Twilight of the Texas Rangers," 110.

13. For Burks, see memo, Burks to Co. B Texas Rangers, "Ranger Service Performance Levels, Comparison Summaries and Company 'B' Performance Summaries," September 21, 1976; memo, Burks to Senior Capt. W. D. Wilson, "Article–McKinney Courier Gazette, Sunday May 16, 1976," May 20, 1976; memo, Burks to All Rangers Co. B, "Assignments of Responsibility," January 30, 1978; memo, Senior Capt. W. D. Wilson to Burks, "Duty Assignment of Sergeant Lester Robertson," February 13, 1978; memo, Co. B Sgt. James Wright to Personnel and Training, "Employment Termination Interview–Texas Ranger Frank Kemp #212, Paris, Texas," Co. B Files 1976, 1978, 1982, 1998/097-3, -8, TSA. Lewis Rigler to Capt. Robert Mitchell, Gainesville, May 10, 1988, MS 13, Mitchell Collection, I-2/11, TRHF.

14. Dick Stanley, "The New Texas Rangers."

15. DPS, *50th Anniversary*, 15. *Dallas Morning News*, January 26 and 28, 1981.

16. James B. Adams, interview by Robert Nieman, Waco, June 4, 2005, in e-mail, Nieman to Utley, June 8, 2005.

17. Transcript of Adams television interview with Cactus Pryor, March 13, 1980, in Adams Speeches, 1992/13-1, TSA.

18. E-mail, Nieman to Utley, June 8, 2005.

19. *Dallas Morning News*, January 28, 1981.

20. Memo, Dean to Col. James B. Adams, "Chronological Order of Incident Involving Local Federal Bureau of Investigation and Texas Ranger Captain Jack O. Dean," July 22, 1981, Co. D Files 1981, 1998/097-9, TSA.

21. Directives on MBO and Results Management are filed in Memos to Ranger Captains, 1977–81, 1981–83, 1983–85, 1985–87, 1998/097-1, TSA. Semiannual status reports from companies and CLE are filed in Ranger Status Reports, 1998/097-10, TSA.

22. Powers, "1 Career, 1 Ranger" Senior Capt. H. R. Bock to Chief CLE A. F. Hacker, "Semi-Annual Status Report," March 20, 1985, Ranger Status Reports, 1998/097-10, TSA.

Chapter 16

1. Company files from 1970 to 1994 contain these requests and investigation reports, 1998/097, TSA.

2. Memo, Capt. G. W. Burks to Senior Capt. Clint Peoples, "Investigation of the Fatal Wounding of Huron Ted Walters. . . ." November 1, 1971, 1998/097-13, Ted Walters; memo, Burks to Senior Capt. W. D. Wilson, "Company 'B' Status Report September 1, 1983, through February 29, 1984," March 5, 1984, Ranger Status Reports, 1998/097-10, TSA; Carl Freund, "Texas Ranger Kills Gangster," *Dallas Morning News*, October 15, 1971.

3. Glenn Elliott and Robert Nieman, *Glenn Elliott: A Ranger's Ranger* (Waco: Texian Press, 1999), chap. 9; *Dallas Morning News*, December 21, 1970; unidentified news clippings in MS 13, Capt. Robert K. Mitchell Collection, I-2/21, TRHF.

4. *Dallas Morning News*, January 12, 1971.

5. Elliott does not deal with this aftermath in his book. My account is based on Capt. Joe G. Murphy Jr., Criminal Intelligence, to Chief CLE A. F. Hacker, "Charles Mathis–Federal Investigation," May 17, 1979, recounting telephone conversation with an FBI agent in Dallas; affidavit of Ranger Stuart Dowell, May 18, 1979, recounting conversation with an FBI agent in Tyler (who was embarrassed) and assistant U.S. attorney Jeff Bynaham summarizing the charges that would be brought against Elliott, in TRS 10-43, 1998/097-11, Mathis Investigation, TSA; *Dallas Morning News*, October 21, 1979, and May 1, 1981; unidentified clipping, probably from a Tyler newspaper, May 2, 1981, in MS 13, Capt. Robert K. Mitchell Collection, I-2/21, TRHF. Glenn Elliott to Utley, July 20, 2005, responding to a series of questions framed by Utley, June 27, 2005.

6. Thomas Turner, "Home for the Rangers," *Texas Star*, July 11, 1971. I have also obtained details from TRHF director Byron Johnson and Archivist Christina Stopka.

7. *Dallas Morning News*, August 5, 1973; L. A. Wilke, "Texas Ranger: That Certain Kind of Man," *Texas Parade*, November 1973, 9.

8. William T. Harper, *Eleven Days in Hell: The 1974 Carrasco Prison Siege at Huntsville, Texas* (Denton: University of North Texas Press, 2004), 37–38. This is a well-researched and accurate history of the siege and is the major source for my account. DPS files contain news clippings but no official records except relating to Captain Rogers's investigation, following the incident, of how the inmates obtained arms. If he or Burks wrote a report about the standoff, they have not survived. DPS Case Files, 1998/097-2, Huntsville, TSA. Harper's book is based on firsthand sources and interviews with most participants. See also Ben H. Procter, *Just One Riot: Episodes of the Texas Rangers in the 20th Century* (Austin: Eakin Press, 1991), chap. 7, also based on interviews with participants.

9. In addition to O'Brien's contribution to Harper, *Eleven Days in Hell*, see King Waters, "Inside Carrasco's Shield: An Account," *Houston Chronicle*, August 25, 1974; undated clipping, "Chaplain Recalls Travail, Terror under Carrasco," *Austin American-Statesman*, taken from *San Antonio Light*. These detailed accounts are in DPS files cited in n8.

10. The story is told in detail by Sessions's assistant U.S. attorney, John E. Clark, in *The Fall of the Duke of Duval: A Prosecutor's Journal* (Austin: Eakin Press, 1996).

11. Ibid., chap. 1.

12. The details of the Ranger contributions are traced in the Company D files for 1975–78, 1998/097-4, TSA.

13. Robert Nieman, "20th Century Shining Star: Captain Jack Dean, United States Marshal," *Texas Ranger Dispatch Magazine* 15 (Winter 2004), www.texasranger.org/dispatch/12/Pages/Dean/htm.

14. Gary Cartwright, *Dirty Dealing: Drug Smuggling on the Mexican Border and the Assassination of a Federal Judge: An American Parable* (1984; repr., El Paso: Cinco Puntos Press, 1998).

15. Cartwright, *Dirty Dealing*, 220–26, deals with Harrelson's earlier escapades. The key document in Dean's role both before and after the Wood murder is memo, Senior Capt. W. D. Wilson to Col. James B. Adams, "Summary of Ranger Participation in Judge John Wood Murder Case," April 13, 1982, 1998/897-11, TRS 10-47, Judge Wood folder, TSA. Although ostensibly originating with Wilson, this memo was written and signed by Jack Dean. See also Nieman, "20th Century Shining Star."

16. Cartwright, *Dirty Dealing*, 219.

17. Gary Carwright's otherwise excellent history, *Dirty Dealing*, never once in 387 pages mentions the Texas Rangers. The emphasis is on the FBI, DEA, and other federal agencies that, in pursuing dirty-dealing drug traffickers, committed their own share of dirty dealing. In addition to the crucial memo of Captain Dean, April 13, 1982, cited above, 1998/097-11, TRS 10.47, Judge Wood file, TSA, contains a lengthy investigation report, June 4, 1979, and a shorter report dated June 7, 1979, by Ranger Adolfo Cuellar; memo, Commander Criminal Intellience W. A. Cowan Jr. to Chief CLE A. F. Hacker, "Federal Judge John Woods Murder Case," April 13, 1982; and San Antonio police records. For Woody Harrelson's effort to free his father see Denver *Rocky Mountain News*, June 27, 2000.

18. Memo, Cook to Capt. Grady C. Sessums, "Incident Involving Ronald Clayton Jones, Brother of Texas Senator Eugene Jones," May 30, 1979, 1998/097-11, TRS-10.46, folder Jones/Killer Bees, TSA. In a separate memo of June 7, ibid., Cook forwarded press clippings from Houston newspapers to Chief CLE Floyd Hacker.

Chapter 17

1. Assistant Attorney General Gerald C. Carruth to Senior Capt. W. D. Wilson, June 18, 1982; Ranger Rudolfo Rodriguez, Investigation Report, July 9, 1982, Co. D files 1982, 1998/097-9; unidentified newspaper clipping, ca. February 1983; memo, Senior Capt. W.D. Wilson to Chief CLE A. F. Hacker, "Request for Special Investigation by Duval County Grand Jury," July 6, 1983; memo, Sgt. George E. Powell, Co. D, to Wilson, same subject, July 1, 1983, Co. D files 1983, 1998/097-8; Co. D, Semi-Annual Status Report, September 1983–February 1984, Ranger Status Reports, 998/097-10, TSA. *San Antonio Express*, July 7, 1982.

2. Memo, Burks to Wilson, "Company B Status Report, March 1, 1984, through August 31, 1984," September 7, 1984, 1998/097-10, Ranger Status Reports, TSA.

3. Glenn Elliott and Robert Nieman, *Glenn Elliott: A Ranger's Ranger* (Waco: Texian Press, 1999), 215.

4. *Longview Morning Journal*, October 1 and 7, 1983; *Kilgore News Herald*, October 2 and 7, 1983, in MS 31, Captain James Wright Collection, III-2/4, TRHF; memo, Senior Capt. W. D. Wilson to Chief CLE A.F. Hacker, "Semi-Annual Status Report, 09-01-83 through 02-29-84," 1998/097, Ranger Status Reports, TSA.

5. *Dallas Morning News*, October 2, 1988.

6. Elliott and Nieman, *Glenn Elliott*, 216-17; *Dallas Morning News*, September 26, 1993, March 19 and November 16, 1995.

7. *Longview News-Journal*, October 28, 2005. I have also been aided by two written statements provided by Glenn Elliott on November 26 and December 4, 2005.

8. *Austin American-Statesman*, November 18, 2005.

9. Bob Prince, "The Meridian Hostage Crisis," *Texas Ranger Dispatch Magazine* 10 (Spring 2003), www.texasranger.org/dispatch/10/Pages/Prince.htm; memo, Co. F Capt. Robert K. Mitchell to Senior Capt. H. R. Block, "Status Report for Company F Texas Rangers March 1, 1985, through August 31, 1985," September 6, Ranger Status Reports, 1985, 1998/097-10, TSA.

10. Robert Nieman, "Captain Bob Mitchell," *Texas Ranger Dispatch Magazine* 15 (Winter 2004), www.texasranger.org/disptach/9/Mitchell.htm.

11. Howard (Slick) Alfred, interview by Robert Nieman, Athens, Texas, June 30, 2005. Made available by Robert Nieman.

12. *Dallas Morning News*, January 14, 1985.

13. Wadsworth tells the story of the night with explicit clarity in an e-mail to the author, August 22, 2005; Howard Alfred, interview by Robert Nieman; Bob Prince (then the Company F sergeant in Waco), interview by Robert Nieman, August 19, 2000. I am indebted to Nieman for the Prince and Alfred interviews.

14. These details are drawn from the Prince and Alfred interviews and aircraft observer Wadsworth's account.

15. Details of the gunfight are from the Alfred interview. The quotation is from the *Dallas Morning News*, January 14, 1985.

16. Johnny L. Waldrip, Report of Investigation, Denise Johnson, January 30, 1987, RS 10.17, Ranger Shooting, 1998/097-11, TSA.

17. Ibid.; detailed investigation reports by John Aycock and Johnny Waldrip and a DPS internal affairs report by Sgt. Kenneth L. Hailey, all filed with ibid., TSA.

18. In addition to sources already cited, see "In Memory: A Tribute to Texas Ranger Stan Guffey," *Texas DPSOA Monthly*, March 1987, 37-45. DPSOA stands for DPS Officers Association. On February 19, 1978, Ranger Bobby Doherty was killed in a drug raid in Denton. He was standing outside the building when a bullet from a suspected drug dealer punched through the wall and struck him. The guilt, conviction, and imprisonment of the killer were and remain controversial.

19. *Lubbock Avalanche-Journal*, October 17, 1983, quoting *Fort Worth Star-Telegram*.

20. *New York Times*, October 16, 1983. Much of my account of the Lucas chapter in Ranger history is drawn from Mike Cox, *The Confessions of Henry Lee Lucas* (New York: Pocket Books, 1991). This is an exceptional exercise in historical sleuthing and is readable besides.

21. Boutwell to Chief CLE Floyd Hacker, "Consideration of Seminar concerning Unsolved Homicides along I.H. 35," Georgetown, August 29, 1980, Co. F files 1980, 1998/097-6, TSA. Cox, *Confessions*, 121–24, tells of a telephone call that led to this memo and the symposium subsequently held.

22. Cox, *Confessions*, chap. 8.

23. Memo, Co. F Capt. Robert K. Mitchell to Senior Capt. W. D. Wlson, "Status Report for Company F Texas Rangers, September 1, 1983, through February 29, 1984," Waco, March 2, 1984, 1998/097-10, Ranger Status Reports; memo, Co. F Sgt. Bob Prince to Chief CLE A.F. Hacker, Report No. 12: Summary of Offenses Cleared by Suspect Henry Lee Lucas 3-02-84 through 3-14-84, Co. F files 1984, 1998/097-6, TSA.

24. Cox, *Confessions*, chap. 10.

25. Memo, Senior Capt. W. D. Wilson (by Assistant Supervisor H.R. Block) to Chief CLE A. F. Hacker, "Semi-Annual Status Report, 03-01-84 through 09-30-84," September 20, 1984, 1998/097-10, Ranger Status Reports; memo, Senior Capt. H. R. Block to All Ranger Captains, "Expenses Related to Henry Lee Lucas–Ottis Toole Investigations," February 11, 1985, Memos to Ranger Captains, 1998/097-1, TSA.

26. Hugh Aynesworth and Jim Henderson, "Henry Lee Lucas: Mass Murderer or Massive Hoax?" *Dallas Times-Herald*, April 14 and 15, 1995; *New York Times*, April 18, 1985; Cox, *Confessions*, chap. 11.

27. *Dallas Morning News*, January 31, May 7 and 8, 1986.

28. Cox, *Confessions*, chap. 12; *New York Times*, September 9, 1986; *Dallas Morning News*, October 4 and December 31, 1986.

29. Cox, *Confessions*, epilogue.

30. Bob Prince, interview by Robert Nieman, August 19, 2000, TRHF.

31. *Dallas Morning News*, June 7 and 25 and July 1, 1998, March 14, 2001.

32. *Dallas Morning News*, January 13, 1985; *Austin American-Statesman*, January 3, 1990.

33. Carlos Vidal Greth, "Today's Rangers: Modern Tradition," *Austin American-Statesman*, August 10, 1986.

Chapter 18

1. *Dallas Morning News*, May 25 and December 4, 1995; *Austin American-Statesman*, August 26, 1995.

2. Stuart A. Wright, ed., *Armageddon in Waco: Critical Perspectives on the Branch Davidian Conflict* (Chicago: University of Chicago Press, 1995); Dick J. Reavis, *The Ashes of Waco: An Investigation* (New York: Simon and Schuster, 1995; repr., Syracuse: Syracuse University Press, 1998).

3. Bob Prince, interview by Robert Nieman, August 19, 2000, TRHF; *Austin American-Statesman*, March 1, 1993.

4. Prince, Nieman interview.

5. David Byrnes, interview by Robert Nieman, January 7, 2006, provided by Nieman.

6. The process is well documented in investigative reports dated April and May 1993 in the Johnny Waldrip Collection, I-B-10/8, TRHF. Waldrip was one of the team leaders, and the reports were written by his team recorder, Sgt. Brian Taylor. Byrnes interview by Nieman. Three documents drawn from the DPS website are also instructive: memo, Sgt. George L. Turner to Senior Capt. Bruce Casteel, "Branch Davidian Evidence," June 30, 1999; memo, Sgt. Joey D. Gordon to Casteel, "Review of Evidence Related to the Branch Davidian Investigation," September 10, 1999; and Gordon to Casteel, "Branch Davidian Report #2," February 16, 2000, www.txdps.state.tx.us/director_staff/public_information/branch_davidian/to%20casteel%20090999.pdf.

7. Reavis, *Ashes of Waco*, chap. 29. I have also consulted newspaper reports on the progress of the trial.

8. Reavis, *Ashes of Waco*, chap. 29; *Austin American-Statesman*, February 27, March 1, June 17 and 18, 1994.

9. *Dallas Morning News*, July 13 and 28, August 5 and 10, September 4 and 8, 1999. A well-constructed account of the events leading to Judge Smith's decision is Peter J. Boyer, "Burned: As if the Justice Department Hadn't Made Enough Enemies over Waco," *New Yorker*, November 1, 1999: 62–68. Memo, Sgt. George L. Turner to Senior Capt. Bruce Casteel, "Branch Davidian Evidence," June 30, 1999; memo, Sgt. Joey D. Gordon to Casteel, "Review of Evidence Related to the Branch Davidian Investigation," September 10, 1999; Gordon

to Casteel, "Branch Davidian Report #2," February 16, 2000, www.txdps.state.tx.us/director_staff/public_information/branch_davidian/to%20casteel%20090999.pdf.

10. John C. Danforth, *Final Report to the Deputy Attorney General concerning the 1993 Confrontation at the Mt. Carmel Complex, Waco, Texas* (Washington, DC, November 8, 2000), www.apologeticsindex.org/b10a03.html.

11. Brynes, Nieman interview.

12. Memo, Col. James B. Adams to Gossett et al., "Attached Television Interview," May 1, 1980, 1992/13-1, Adams Speeches, TSA.

13. *Austin American-Statesman*, July 29 and September 27, 1988; Robert Draper, "Twilight of the Texas Rangers," *Texas Monthly* 22 (February 1994): 110. Draper recounts the experience of Michael Scott.

14. *Houston Chronicle*, June 23, 1993.

15. Quoted in Draper, "Twilight of the Texas Rangers," 110–11.

16. *Houston Chronicle*, June 23, 1993; Draper, "Twilight of the Texas Rangers," 112.

17. Draper, "Twilight of the Texas Rangers," 79–80; *Dallas Morning News*, May 24 and 25, 1995.

18. *Austin American-Statesman*, July 12, 1995.

19. Ibid.; Janet Wilson, "Rangers Show that Boys will Still be Boys," ibid.

20. *Dallas Morning News*, December 12, 1995, January 16 and 17, 1996, January 19, 2000.

21. *Austin American-Statesman*, February 9 and 19, 1996; *Dallas Morning News*, July 26, 1996.

22. *Austin American-Statesman*, August 26, 1998.

23. Ibid., August 8, 1998. Robert Nieman, "Senior Texas Ranger Captain, Retired, Bruce Casteel," *Texas Ranger Dispatch Magazine* 2 (Winter 2000), http://www.texasranger.org/dispatch/2/Casteel.html.

24. *Abilene Reporter-News*, July 10, 1996; Barry Caver, interview by Robert Nieman, June 27, 2004, in *Texas Ranger Dispatch Magazine* 16 (Winter 2004), www.texasranger.org/dispatch/15/pages/ROT_Standoff_Pt1.htm; Caver, unpublished MS, 2000, provided me by Captain Caver.

25. Caver, interview by Nieman. This is the principal source for what occurred inside the ring of state troopers who blocked off Fort Davis to entry. Also, DPS spokesman Mike Cox each day briefed the press, which each day by newspapers and television passed on as much as Caver wanted to make public. *Dallas Morning News*, April 28, 1997; *New York Times*, April 28, 1997; *Houston Chronicle*, April 28, 1997.

26. *Houston Chronicle*, April 28, 1997; *New York Times*, April 28, 1997.

27. *Dallas Morning News*, April 30, 1997; *Bryan Eagle*, April 30, 1997. CNN news releases (two), April 29, 1997. Both news releases may be found on the CNN website, www.cnn.com, by searching the archives for references to Richard McLaren and the date of the releases.

28. *Dallas Morning News*, May 1 and 2, 1997.

29. Caver, Nieman interview; *Dallas Morning News*, May 4, 1997.

30. Caver, Nieman interview.

31. *Dallas Morning News*, May 30, 1997.

32. Caver, Nieman interview; *Dallas Morning News*, May 5, 1997; CNN Release, May 6, 1997. May be found on the CNN website, www.cnn.com (see n. 27, above).

33. Caver, Nieman interview; *Dallas Morning News*, May 7, 1997.

34. *Dallas Morning News*, September 20, 1997.

35. AP dispatch in *Pecos Enterprise*, November 5, 1997 and April 9, 1998; *Dallas Morning News*, April 9, 1998; *New York Times*, April 15, 1998. See also for much

background, "Republic of Texas," April 26, 1998, Update, on the CNN website, www.cnn.com (see n. 27, above).

36. *Dallas Morning News*, May 12, 1997.

Chapter 19

1. Walter Prescott Webb, *The Texas Rangers: A Century of Frontier Defense* (Boston: Houghton Mifflin, 1935; repr., Austin: University of Texas Press, 1965), 478.

2. Ibid., 567.

3. *Dallas Morning News*, September 27, 1965.

4. Thomas Lee Charlton, "The Texas Department of Public Safety, 1935–1957," (master's thesis, University of Texas–Austin, 1961). Llerena Friend, "W. P. Webb's Texas Rangers," *SWHQ* 74 (January 1971): 295–322. A biography is Necah Stewart Furman, *Walter Prescott Webb: His Life and Impact* (Albuquerque: University of New Mexico Press, 1978).

5. E-mail, Dean to Utley, February 5, 2006.

6. H. Joaquin Jackson and David Marion Wilkinson, *One Ranger, a Memoir* (Austin: University of Texas Press, 2005), 251.

SOURCES

Akers, Monty. *Flames after Midnight: Murder, Vengeance, and the Desolation of a Texas Community*. Austin: University of Texas Press, 1999.

Aldrich, Roy W. Papers. CAH UTA.

Alexander, Charles C. *The Ku Klux Klan in Texas, 1920–1930*. Houston: Texas Gulf Coast Historical Association, 1962.

———. *The Ku Klux Klan in the Southwest*. Lexington: University of Kentucky Press, 1965.

Allred, James W. Texas Governors Papers. RG 301, TSA.

Amberson, Mary Margaret McAllen, James A. McAllen, and Margaret H. McAllen. *I Would Rather Sleep in Texas: A History of the Lower Rio Grande Valley and the People of the Santa Anita Land Grant*. Austin: TSHA, 2003.

Anders, Evan. *Boss Rule in South Texas: The Progressive Era*. Austin: University of Texas Press, 1982.

Barton, Thomas D. *State Ranger and Martial Law Activities of the National Guard of Texas, 1921 and 1922*. Austin: Von Boeckmann-Jones, 1923.

Bernstein, Patricia. *The First Waco Horror: The Lynching of Jesse Washington and the Rise of the NAACP*. College Station: Texas A&M Press, 2005.

Boyle, Robert D. "Chaos in the East Texas Oil Field, 1930–1935." *SWHQ* 69 (January 1966): 340–52.

Bridge, Joe H. Collection. MS 35, TRHF.

Bridge, Joe Jr. *Joe H. Bridge, Texas Ranger, 1936–1956*. N.p. 1988.

Brown, Norman D. *Hood, Bonnet, and Little Brown Jug: Texas Politics, 1921–1928*. College Station: Texas A&M Press, 1983.

Buenger, Walter L., and Robert A. Calvert, eds. *Texas through Time: Evolving Interpretations*. College Station: Texas A&M Press, 1991.

Burrough, Bryan. *Public Enemies: America's Greatest Crime Wave and the Birth of the FBI, 1933–34*. New York: Penguin, 2004.

———. Burton, Marvin. "The Johnny Holmes Murder Case." MS 26, Marvin Burton Collection, TRHF.

———. Interview of Roger Conger, May 1, 1956. MS 33, Oral History, Red Burton, TRHF.

———. "The Story of the Glen Rose Liquor War in 1923." MS 26, Marvin Burton Collection, TRHF.

Brynes, David. Interview by Robert Nieman. Kaufman, Texas, January 7, 2006. Files of Robert Nieman.

Carmichael, H. H. (as told to Westmoreland Gray). "We Rangers: Lawmen of the Frontier, 1937 Model." *Best Action Western Stories* (September 1937): 100–105.

Cartwright, Gary. *Dirty Dealing: Drug Smuggling on the Mexican Border and the Assassination of a Federal Judge: An American Parable.* 1984. Reprint, El Paso: Cinco Puntos Press, 1998.

Casey, Clifford B. *Soldiers, Ranchers and Miners in the Big Bend.* Washington, DC: GPO, 1969.

Caver, Barry. Interview by Robert Nieman, June 27, 2004. *Texas Ranger Dispatch Magazine* 16 (Winter 2004). Online at www.texasranger.org.

———. Untitled MS Narrative of Davis Mountains Standoff of 1997. 2000. Provided by Captain Caver.

Charlton, Thomas L. "The Texas Department of Public Safety, 1935–1957." Master's thesis, University of Texas–Austin, 1961.

Chatfield, W. H. *The Twin Cities of the Border.* New Orleans: E. P. Brandao, 1893. Reprint, Lower Rio Grande Valley Historical Society, 1959.

Clark, John E. *The Fall of the Duke of Duval: A Prosecutor's Journal.* Austin: Eakin Press, 1996.

Clendenen, Clarence C. *Blood on the Border: The United States Army and the Mexican Irregulars.* New York: Macmillan, 1969.

———. *The United States and Pancho Villa: A Study in Unconventional Diplomacy.* Ithaca, NY: Cornell University Press, 1961.

Coerver, Don M., and Linda B. Hall. *Revolution on the Rio Grande: Governor Colquitt of Texas and the Mexican Revolution, 1911–1915.* San Antonio: Trinity Border Research Institute, 1981.

———. *Texas and the Mexican Revolution: A Study in State and National Border Policy, 1910–1920.* San Antonio: Trinity University Press, 1984.

Colquitt, O. B. Texas Governors Papers, RG 301, TSA.

———. "The Texas Ranger as He Is." *Leslie's Illustrated Newspaper,* April 16, 1914.

Cox, Mike. *The Confessions of Henry Lee Lucas.* New York: Pocket Books, 1991.

———. *Silver Stars and Sixguns: The Texas Rangers.* Austin: DPS, 1987.

———. *Stand-off in Texas: "Just Call Me a Spokesman for DPS."* Austin: Eakin Press, 1999.

———. *Texas Ranger Tales: Stories that Need Telling.* Plano: Republic of Texas Press, 1997.

———. *Texas Ranger Tales II.* Plano: Republic of Texas Press, 1999.

———. *The Texas Rangers: Men of Valor and Action.* Austin: Eakin Press, 1991.

Crockett, Norman. "Crime on the Petroleum Frontier: Borger, Texas, in the Late 1920s." *Panhandle-Plains Historical Review* 64 (1991): 53–56.

Cumberland, Charles C. "Border Raids in the Lower Rio Grande Valley–1915." *SWHQ* 57 (January 1954): 285–311.

———. *Mexican Revolution: Genesis under Madero.* Austin: University of Texas Press, 1974.

———. "Mexican Revolutionary Movements from Texas, 1906–1912." *SWHQ* 52 (January 1949): 301–24.

Cunningham, Roger D. "Shaking the Iron Fist: The Mexican Punitive Expedition of 1919." *Army History* (Winter 1991): 1–16.

Danforth, John C. *Final Report to the Deputy Attorney General concerning the 1993 Confrontation at the Mt. Carmel Complex, Waco, Texas.* Washington, DC, November 8, 2000, www.apologeticsindex.org/b10a03.html.

Davenport, Harbert. Papers. CAH, UTA.

Davis, John L. *The Texas Rangers: Their First 150 Years.* San Antonio: University of Texas at San Antonio, Institute of Texan Cultures, 1975.

Day, James M. *Captain Clint Peoples, Texas Ranger: Fifty Years a Lawman.* Waco: Texian Press, 1980.

———. *One Man's Dream: Fort Fisher and the Texas Rangers Hall of Fame.* Waco: Texian Press, 1976.

Dean, Jack O. Collection. MS 28, TRHF.

De Leon, Arnoldo. *The Tejano Community, 1836–1900.* Albuquerque: University of New Mexico Press, 1982.

———. *They Called Them Greasers: Anglo Attitudes toward Mexicans in Texas, 1821–1900.* Austin: University of Texas Press, 1983.

Douglas, C. L. *The Gentlemen in White Hats: Dramatic Episodes in the History of the Texas Rangers.* Dallas: Southwest Press, 1934. Reprint, Austin: State House Press, 1992.

Draper, Robert. "Twilight of the Texas Rangers." *Texas Monthly* 22 (February 1994): 76–82, 107–18.

Dray, Philip. *At the Hands of Persons Unknown: The Lynching of Black America.* New York: Random House, 2002.

Durham, Kenneth R. "The Longview Race Riot of 1919." *East Texas Historical Journal* 18 (Fall 1980): 13–24.

Elliott, Glenn. Collection. MS 29, TRHF.

Elliott, Glenn, and Robert Nieman. *Glenn Elliott: A Ranger's Ranger.* Waco: Texian Press, 1999.

———. *Glenn Elliott: Still a Ranger's Ranger.* Longview, TX: Ranger Publishing, 2002.

Ferguson, James E. Texas Governors Papers. RG 301, TSA.

Ferguson, Miriam A. Texas Governors Papers. RG 301, TSA.

Fidler, Paul E. "A State Police Force for Texas." *Texas Municipalities* 22 (March 1935).

Frost, H. Gordon, and John H. Jenkins. *I'm Frank Hamer: The Life of a Texas Peace Officer.* Austin: Pemberton Press, 1968. Reprint, Austin: State House Press, 1993.

Furman, Necah Stewart. *Walter Prescott Webb: His Life and Impact.* Albuquerque: University of New Mexico Press, 1976.

Galveston Gambling. Papers and Records. MS 17, TRHF.

Gay, D. P. "The Amazing Bare-Faced Facts of the Norias Fight." MS in Harbert Davenport Papers, CAH, UTA.

Geer, James. Collection. MS 40, TRHF.

Gerlach, Allen. "Conditions along the Border–1915: The Plan de San Diego." *New Mexico Historical Review* 43 (July 1968): 194–212.

Gilliland, Maude T. *Horsebreakers of the Brush Country: A Story of the Texas Rangers and the Mexican Liquor Smugglers.* Privately published, Springman-King Co., 1968.

Ginzberg, Ralph. *One Hundred Years of Lynching.* Baltimore: Black Classic Press, 1988.

Gonzaullas, Manuel T. Collection. MS 4, TRHF.

Gooding, Edward. Collection. MS 33, TRHF.

Gooding, Edward, and Robert Nieman. *Ed Gooding: Soldier, Texas Ranger.* Longview, TX: Ranger Publishing, 2001.

Goodwyn, Frank. *Lone-Star Land: Twentieth-Century Texas in Perspective*. New York: Alfred A. Knopf, 1955.

Gould, Lewis L. *Progressives and Prohibitionists: Texas Democrats in the Wilson Era*. Austin: TSHA, 1992.

Graham, Don. *Kings of Texas: The 150-Year Saga of an American Ranching Empire*. New York: John Wiley & Sons, 2003.

Green, George Norris. *The Establishment in Texas Politics: The Primitive Years, 1938–1957*. Westport, CT: Greenwood Press, 1979.

Greene, A. C. *The Santa Claus Bank Robbery*. 1972. Reprint, Denton: University of North Texas Press, 1999.

Grieb, Kenneth J. *The United States and Huerta*. Lincoln: University of Nebraska Press, 1969.

Gutiérrez, José Angel. *The Making of a Chicano Militant: Lessons from Cristal*. Madison: University of Wisconsin Press, 1998.

Hall, Linda B., and Don M. Coerver. *Revolution on the Border: The United States and Mexico, 1910–1920*. Albuquerque: University of New Mexico Press, 1988.

Hamer, Frank. Collection. MS 3, TRHF.

Harper, William T. *Eleven Days in Hell: The 1974 Carrasco Prison Siege at Huntsville, Texas*. Denton: University of North Texas Press, 2004.

Harris, Charles H., III. "The Plan of San Diego and Mexican-United States War Crisis of 1916: A Reexamination." *Hispanic American Historical Review* 58 (1978): 381–408.

Harris, Charles H., III, and Louis R. Sadler. *The Texas Rangers and the Mexican Revolution: The Bloodiest Decade, 1910–1920*. Albuquerque: University of New Mexico Press, 2004.

Hartsfield, Loy William. "A Brief History of Breckenridge and the Stephens County Oil Fields." *West Texas Historical Association Year Book* 12 (July 1936): 100–123.

Hendrickson, Kenneth E., Jr. *The Chief Executives of Texas*. College Station: Texas A&M Press, 1995.

Hill, Kate Adele. *Lon C. Hill, 1862–1935: Lower Rio Grande Pioneer*. San Antonio: Naylor, 1935.

Hobby, William P. Texas Governors Papers. RG 301, TSA.

Horton, David M., and Ryan Kellus Turner. *Lone Star Justice: A Comprehensive Overview of the Texas Criminal Justice System*. Austin: Eakin Press, 1999.

House, Boyce. *Oil Boom: The Story of Spindletop, Burkburnett, Mexia, Smackover, Desdemona, and Ranger*. Caldwell, ID: Caxton Printers, 1941.

Jackson, H. Joaquin, and David Marion Wilkinson. *One Ranger: A Memoir*. Austin: University of Texas Press, 2005.

Jackson, Kenneth T. *The Ku Klux Klan in the City, 1915–30*. New York: Oxford University Press, 1967.

Johnson, Benjamin. *Revolution in Texas: How a Forgotten Rebellion and Its Bloody Suppression Turned Mexicans into Americans*. New Haven: Yale University Press, 2003.

Justice, Glenn. *Revolution on the Rio Grande: Mexican Raids and Army Pursuits, 1916–1919*. El Paso: Texas Western Press, 1992.

Keil, Robert. *Bosque Bonito: Violent Times along the Borderland during the Mexican Revolution*. Alpine: Center for Big Bend Studies, 2004.

Krenek, Harry. *The Power Vested: The Use of Martial Law and the National Guard in Texas Domestic Crisis . . . 1919–1932*. Austin: Presidial Press, 1980.

Ladino, Robyn Duff. *Desegregating Texas Schools: Eisenhower, Shivers, and the Crisis at Mansfield High*. Austin: University of Texas Press, 1996.

Leal, Ray Robert. "The 1966–67 South Texas Farm Workers Strike." PhD diss., Indiana University, 1983.

Lott, Virgil N. "The Rio Grande Valley." Virgil Lott Papers, CAH UTA.

Machado, Manual A., Jr., and James T. Judge. "Tempest in a Teapot: The Mexican-United States Intervention Crisis of 1919." *SWHQ* 74 (July 1970): 1–23.

Madsen, William. *Mexican Americans of South Texas.* 1964. Reprint, New York: Holt, Rinehart and Winston, 1964, 1973.

Malsch, Brownson. *"Lone Wolf" Gonzaullas, Texas Ranger.* 1980. Reprint, Norman: University of Oklahoma Press, 1998.

Martin, Jack. *Border Boss: Captain John R. Hughes, Texas Ranger.* San Antonio: Naylor, 1942.

Martínez, Ramiro. *They Call Me Ranger Ray: From the UT Tower Sniper to Corruption in South Texas.* New Braunfels, TX: Rio Bravo Publishing, 2005.

McClung, John B. "Texas Rangers along the Rio Grande, 1910–1919." PhD diss., Texas Christian University, 1981.

McKay, Seth S. *Texas Politics, 1906–1944.* Lubbock: Texas Tech Press, 1952.

McLynn, Frank. *Villa and Zapata: A History of the Mexican Revolution.* New York: Carroll & Graf, 2000.

Means, Joyce E. "Joe Sitter versus Chico Cano: What Really Happened." *West Texas Historical Association Year Book* 72 (1996): 86–104.

Meed, Douglas V. *Texas Ranger Johnny Klevenhagen.* Plano: Republic of Texas Press, 2000.

Meyer, Michael. *Mexican Rebel: Pascual Orozco and the Mexican Revolution, 1910–1915* Lincoln: University of Nebraska Press, 1967.

Mirandé, Alfredo. *Gringo Justice.* Notre Dame, IN: University of Notre Dame Press, 1987.

Mitchell, Robert K. Collection. MS 13, TRHF.

Montejano, David. *Anglos and Mexicans in the Making of Texas, 1836–1986.* Austin: University of Texas Press, 1987.

Moody, Daniel J., Jr. Texas Governors Papers. RG 301, TSA.

NARA. *Annual Report of the Headquarters, Big Bend District, 1917–18.* RG 165, Historical Section, Eighth Cavalry.

———. *Records of the Department of State Relating to Internal Affairs of Mexico, 1910–29.* Microfilm M274, reels 46–52.

———. Review of the Board of Review of the Yancey Court-Martial. RG 153, Judge Advocate General, CM #140113.

Neff, Pat M. *The Battles of Peace.* Fort Worth: Pioneer Publishing Co., 1925.

———. Texas Governors Papers. RG 301, TSA.

Newspapers. Various from throughout Texas. Many clippings and scrapbooks in Texas Ranger Hall of Fame and Museum Archives, many accessed on Internet archives, especially *Dallas Morning News, San Antonio Light,* and *Austin American-Statesman.*

Nieman, Robert. "Capt. Bob Crowder." *Texas Ranger Dispatch Magazine* 14 (Summer 2004). Online at www.texasranger.org.

———. "Capt. Johnny Klevenhagen." *Texas Ranger Dispatch Magazine* 10 (Spring 2003). Online at www.texasranger.org.

———. "Captain Bob Crowder and the Rusk State Hospital Riot." *Texas Ranger Dispatch Magazine* 3 (Spring 2001). Online at www.texasranger.org.

———. "Captain Bob Mitchell." *Texas Ranger Dispatch Magazine* 9 (Winter 2002). Online at www.texasranger.org.

———. "Jim Ray." *Texas Ranger Dispatch Magazine* 2 (Winter 2000). Online at www. texasranger.org.

———. "On the Trail of Bonnie & Clyde: Why Frank Hamer Wasn't Serving as a Texas Ranger." *Texas Ranger Dispatch Magazine* 13 (Spring 2004). Online at www.texasranger.org.

———. "Senior Texas Ranger Captain, Retired, Bruce Casteel." *Texas Ranger Dispatch Magazine* 2 (Winter 2000). Online at www.texasranger.org.

———. "20th Century Shining Star: Captain Jack Dean, United States Marshal." *Texas Ranger Dispatch Magazine* 12 (Winter 2003). Online at www.texasranger.org.

———. "20th Century Shining Star: Frank Hamer." *Texas Ranger Dispatch Magazine* 11 (Summer 2003). Online at www.texasranger.org.

Olien, Diana Davids, and Roger M. Olien. *Oil in Texas: The Gusher Age, 1895–1945.* Austin: University of Texas Press, 2002.

Olien, Roger M. *Oil Booms: Social Change in Five Texas Towns.* Lincoln: University of Nebraska Press, 1984.

Paredes, Américo. *"With His Pistol in His Hand": A Border Ballad and Its Hero.* Austin: University of Texas Press, 1958.

Parker, James. *The Old Army: Memories, 1872–1918.* Philadelphia: Dorrance & Co., 1929.

Pattie, James. "A. Y. Allee: The Man and the Legend." *Texas Parade,* July 1971.

Perez, Jesse. Memoirs. MS, CAH, UTA.

Phares, Louis. Collection. MS 84, TRHF.

Phillips, Edward Hake. "The Sherman Courthouse Riot of 1930." *East Texas Historical Journal* 25 (Fall 1987): 12–19.

Phillips, John Neal. *Running with Bonnie and Clyde: The Ten Fast Years of Ralph Fults.* Norman: University of Oklahoma Press, 1996.

Pierce, Frank C. *Texas' Last Frontier: A Brief History of the Lower Rio Grande.* Menache, WI: George Banta Publishing Co., 1917.

Prince, Bob. Interview by Robert Nieman, August 19, 2000. TRHF.

———. "The Meridian Hostage Crisis." *Texas Ranger Dispatch Magazine* 10 (Spring 2003). Online at www.texasranger.org.

Procter, Ben H. *Just One Riot: Episodes of Texas Rangers in the 20th Century.* Austin: Eakin Press, 1991.

———. "The Modern Texas Rangers: A Law Enforcement Dilemma in the Rio Grande Valley." In *Reflections of Western Historians,* ed. John A. Carroll. Tucson: University of Arizona Press, 1969. Also in *The Mexican Americans: An Awakening Minority,* ed. Manuel P. Servin. Beverly Hills: Glencoe Press, 1970.

Puckett, Linda Jay. *Cast a Long Shadow: A Casebook of the Law Enforcement Career of Texas Ranger Captain E. J. Banks.* Dallas: Ussery Printing, 1984.

Raper, Arthur F. *The Tragedy of Lynching.* Chapel Hill: University of North Carolina Press, 1933.

Reavis, Dick J. *The Ashes of Waco: An Investigation.* New York: Simon and Schuster, 1995. Reprint, Syracuse: Syracuse University Press, 1998.

Redding, Stan. "Abolish the Rangers." *Houston Chronicle Texas Magazine,* February 2, 1969.

———. "The Boss [Garrison] and the Heritage of the Force He Serves." *Houston Chronicle Texas Magazine,* February 9, 1969.

———. "A Man to Watch the Rugged Land [Allee]." *Houston Chronicle Texas Magazine,* February 9, 1969.

———. "Ranger Mystique." *Texas Magazine,* February 1969.

———. "Tall in the Saddle for 150 Years." *State Journal of Peace Officers,* May 1973.

———. "Top Gun of the Texas Rangers [Klevenhagen]." *True Detective Magazine,* February 1963.

———. "Trouble at Daingerfield." *Houston Chronicle Texas Magazine,* February 9, 1969.

———. "What is a Ranger?" *Houston Chronicle Texas Magazine,* February 9, 1969.

Ribb, Richard H. "José Tomás Canales and the Texas Rangers: Myth, Identity, and Power in South Texas, 1900–1920." PhD diss., University of Texas–Austin, 2001.

Rigler, Erick T. "A Descriptive Study of the Texas Ranger: Historical Overtones on Minority Attitudes." Master's thesis, Sam Houston State University, 1971.

Rigler, Lewis C., and Judyth Wagner Rigler. *In the Line of Duty: Reflections of a Texas Ranger Private.* 1984. Reprint, Denton: University of North Texas Press, 1995.

Robertson, Brian. *Wild Horse Desert: The Heritage of South Texas.* Edinburg, TX: New Santander Press, 1985.

Robinson, James W. *The DPS Story: History of the Department of Public Safety in Texas.* Austin: DPS, 1974.

Rocha, Rodolfo. "The Influence of the Mexican Revolution on the Mexico-Texas Border, 1910–1916." Ph.D. diss., Texas Tech University, 1981.

Rogers, M. D. "Kelly." Collection. MS 16, TRHF.

Rosenbaum, Robert J. *Mexicano Resistance in the Southwest: "The Sacred Right of Self-Preservation."* Austin: University of Texas Press, 1981.

Roth, Michael. "Bonnie and Clyde in Texas: The End of the Texas Outlaw Tradition." *East Texas Historical Journal* 35 (1997): 30–38.

———. "Courtesy, Service, Protection." In *Courtesy, Service, Protection: The Texas Department of Public Safety's Sixtieth Anniversary,* ed. Mike Cox et al. Dallas: Taylor Publishing Co., 1995.

Rundell, Walter, Jr. *Early Texas Oil: A Photographic History, 1866–1936.* College Station: Texas A&M Press, 1977.

Samora, Julian. *Gunpowder Justice: A Reassessment of the Texas Rangers.* Notre Dame, IN: University of Notre Dame Press, 1979.

Sandos, James A. "The Plan of San Diego: War and Diplomacy on the Texas Border." *Arizona and the West* 14 (Spring 1972): 5–24.

———. *Rebellion in the Borderlands: Anarchism and the Plan of San Diego, 1904–1923.* Norman: University of Oklahoma Press, 1992.

Schreiner, Charles, comp. *Pictorial History of the Texas Rangers: "The Special Breed of Men."* Mountain Home, TX: Y-O Press, 1969.

Schuster, Stephen W., IV. "The Modernization of the Texas Rangers: 1933–1936." *West Texas Historical Association Year Book* 43 (October 1967): 65–79.

———. "The Modernization of the Texas Rangers, 1930–1936." Master's thesis, Texas Christian University, 1965.

Shockley, John S. *Chicano Revolt in a Texas Town.* Notre Dame: University of Notre Dame Press, 1974.

Shoemaker, Kyle W. "How Mexia was Made a Clean City." *Owenwood Magazine* 1 (May 1922).

Simmons, Lee. *Assignment Huntsville: Memoirs of a Texas Prison Official.* Austin: University of Texas Press, 1957.

Sitton, Thad. *The Texas Sheriff: Lord of the County Line.* Norman: University of Oklahoma Press, 2000.

Smith, Bruce. *Police Systems in the United States.* New York: Harper and Row, 1960.

———. *State Police: Organization and Administration.* 1925. Reprint, Montclair, NJ: Patterson Smith, 1969.

Smithers, W. D. *Chronicles of the Big Bend: A Photographic Memoir of Life on the Border.* Austin: Madrona Press, 1976.

———. Papers. CAH, UTA.

———. "Ranching and Fighting Bandits." MS, ca. 1964, Smithers Papers. CAH, UTA.

———. "They Outstayed the Bandits." MS, ca. 1964, Smithers Papers. CAH, UTA.

Spellman, Paul N. *Captain John H. Rogers, Texas Ranger.* Denton: University of North Texas Press, 2003.

Stephens, Robert W. *Lone Wolf: The Story of Texas Ranger Captain M. T. Gonzaullas.* Dallas: Stephens, 1979.

———. *Texas Ranger Sketches.* Dallas, Privately published, 1972.

———. *Tribute to a Ranger: Captain Alfred Y. Allee, Company D, Texas Rangers.* Privately published, 1968.

Sterling, Ross. Texas Governors Papers. RG 301, TSA.

Sterling, William W. *Trails and Trials of a Texas Ranger.* Norman: University of Oklahoma Press, 1969.

Texas AG. Official Records. RG 401, TSA.

———. *Biennial Reports,* 1910–1935.

———. *Report of State Rangers and Martial Law Activities of the National Guard of Texas, 1921–22.* Austin: Von Boeckman-Jones, 1923.

———. "Rules and Regulations Governing the State Ranger Force, 1919." MS, CAH, UTA.

Texas DPS. Official Records, 1935–95. (Incomplete.) 1998.097, TSA.

———. *50th Anniversary of the Department of Public Safety.* Austin: DPS, 1985.

———. *Progress Report, 1942–44.*

———. *Texas Department of Public Safety, August 10, 1935, to December 1, 1936.* Report of the Public Safety Commission to Governor Allred.

———. *The Texas Ranger.* Austin: DPS, 1968.

———. *Twenty-five Year Review and Biennial Report, 1959–60.* DPS, January 1, 1961.

Texas Legislature. *General and Special Laws of the State of Texas,* 1910–2000.

———. The Joint Committee on Organization and Economy and Griffenhagen and Associates. *The Government of Texas.* Austin: Griffenhagen and Associates, 1933.

———. *Proceedings of the Joint Committee of the Senate and House in the Investigation of the Texas Ranger Force.* 1919. MS, TSA.

Texas Ranger Dispatch Magazine 1–18, 2000–06. Online at www.texasranger.org.

Texas Ranger Scrapbooks. CAH, UTA.

Texas Research League. *The Texas Department of Public Safety: Its Services and Organization.* Austin, 1957.

Texas Senate. *Report and Recommendation of the Senate Committee Investigating Crime.* 43rd Legislature, 1933–34.

Texas State Advisory Committee to the US Commission on Human Rights. *Civil Rights in Texas.* February 1970.

Texas State Historical Association. *The New Handbook of Texas.* 6 vols. Austin: TSHA, 1995.

Timmons, W. H. *El Paso: A Borderlands History.* El Paso: Texas Western Press, 1990.

Toland, John. *The Dillinger Days.* New York: Random House, 1963.

Thompson, Jerry. *A Wild and Vivid Land: An Illustrated History of the South Texas Border.* Austin: TSHA, 1997.

Trimble, Lee. Collection. MS 5, TRHF.

Tuttle, William. M., Jr. "Violence in a 'Heathen' Land: The Longview Race Riot of 1919." *Phylon* 33 (Winter 1972): 324–33.

Tyler, Ron C. *The Big Bend: A History of the Last Texas Frontier.* College Station: Texas A & M Press, 1996.

———. "The Little Punitive Expedition in the Big Bend." *SWHQ* 78 (January 1975): 271–91.

U.S. Commission on Civil Rights. *Hearings . . . San Antonio, December 9–14, 1968.* Washington: GPO, n.d.

———. *Mexican Americans and the Administration of Justice in the Southwest.* Washington: GPO, March 1970.

U.S. Congress. 62d Cong., 2d sess. House Ex. Doc. No. 1168, December 13, 1912. Claims growing out of insurrection in Mexico. Report of commission appointed by WD to investigate claims of U.S. citizens for damages suffered within U.S. territory as a result of Mexican insurrection. U.S. Serial 6382.

———. 66th Cong., 2d sess. Senate Ex. Doc. No. 285, 1920. Committee on Foreign Relations. Investigation of Mexican Affairs: Preliminary report and hearings pursuant to SR 106 relating to outrages on U.S. citizens. 2 vols. U.S. Serials 7665–7666.

Utley, Robert M. *Lone Star Justice: The First Century of the Texas Rangers.* New York: Oxford University Press, 2002.

Waldrip, Johnny. Collection. TRHF.

Ward, James R. "Establishing Law and Order in the Oil Fields: The 1924 Ranger Raids in Navarro County, Texas." *Texana* 8 (1970): 38–46.

———. "The Texas Rangers, 1919–1935: A Study in Law Enforcement." PhD diss., Texas Christian University, 1972.

Warnock, Roland A. (as told to Kirby F. Warnock). *A Texas Cowboy.* Dallas: Trans Pecos Productions, 1992.

Warren, Harry. "The Porvenir Massacre in Presidio County, Texas, on January 28, 1918." MS, Harry Warren Papers, Archives of the Big Bend, Sul Ross State University.

Webb, Walter Prescott. "Bank Robbers Slain: Texas Ranger Captain Takes No Chances on Escape of Two Desperadoes Taken in Crime." *State Trooper* 8 (November 1926): 7–8.

———. "Fight against the Texas Rangers: A Discussion of the Motives Involved in the Suit to Enjoin Continuance of the Force." *State Trooper* 6 (July 1925): 11–12, 18.

———. "Lawless Town Gets Ranger Justice: Cleanup of Law Breakers is Object Lesson of Need of Strong State Force." *State Trooper* 5 (April 1924): 13–14.

———. "Lone Ranger Gets Bandits: Texas Officer Secures Surrender of Gang Which Robbed Banks and Shot up Town." *State Trooper* 7 (March 1926): 9–10, 20.

———. "Oil Town Cleaned Up: Texas Rangers Summoned to Restore Order When Local Officials Could Not Enforce Law." *State Trooper* 8 (December 1926): 8.

———. Papers. CAH, UTA.

———. "Rangers Arrest Lawmakers: Texas Representatives Taken in Custody When One Accepts $1,000 from Opponent of Measure." *State Trooper* 8 (April 1927): 11–12.

———. "Rangers Reorganized: Governor of Texas Appoints Captains to Replace Men Appointed in Ferguson Regime." *State Trooper* 8 (July 1927): 13.

———. "Texas Ranger Case Important: Statement of Law Involved in Use of Force to Preserve State's Authority is Comprehensive." *State Trooper* 6 (August 1925): 13.

———. *The Texas Rangers: A Century of Frontier Defense.* Boston: Houghton Mifflin, 1935. Austin: University of Texas Press, 1965.

———. "Texas Rangers in Eclipse: Present State Administration Has Discredited Force by Policy of Interference with Its Duties." *State Trooper* 7 (January 1926): 13–14.

———. "The Texas Rangers in the Modern World, 1935–1960." MS, Webb Papers. CAH, UTA.

———. "Texas Rangers of Today: A Description of the Oldest Police Force in America." *State Trooper* 5 (March 1924): 5–6, 18.

———. "Texas Rangers Quell Trouble: Outbreaks of Lawlessness Require Treatment in Firm Fashion by Lone Star State Force." *State Trooper* 5 (August 1924): 13–14.

———. "Veteran Ranger Protects Border: Captain Wright Who Enforces the Law in the Big Bend Region is a Pupil of Famous Rangers." *State Trooper* 6 (September 1924): 13–14.

Webb, Walter Prescott, and M. F. Kennedy. "With the Texas Rangers." *State Trooper* 7 (October 1925): 11.

Wilke, L. A. "Texas Ranger: That Certain Kind of Man." *Texas Parade*, November 1973.

Wolters, Jacob F. *Martial Law and Its Administration.* Austin: Gammel Book Co., 1930.

Wright, James A. Collection. MS 31, TRHF.

Wright, Stuart A., ed. *Armageddon in Waco: Critical Perspectives on the Branch Davidian Conflict.* Chicago: University of Chicago Press, 1995.

Yockelson, Mitchell. "The United States Armed Forces and the Mexican Punitive Expedition." *Prologue: Quarterly of the National Archives and Records Administration* 29 (Fall 1997): 256–62 and (Winter 1997): 334–43.

INDEX